Music in Western Civilization

Volume B: The Baroque and Classical eras

Music in Western Civilization

Volume B: The Baroque and Classical Eras

Music in Western Civilization

Volume B: The Baroque and Classical Eras

Craig Wright
Yale University

Bryan Simms
University of Southern California

SCHIRMER
CENGAGE Learning

Australia • Brazil • Japan • Korea • Mexico • Singapore • Spain • United Kingdom • United States

SCHIRMER
CENGAGE Learning

Music in Western Civilization
Volume B: The Baroque and Classical Eras
Craig Wright
Bryan Simms

Publisher: Clark Baxter

Senior Development Editor: Sue Gleason

Senior Assistant Editor: Julie Yardley

Editorial Assistant: Emily Perkins

Executive Technology Project Manager: Matt Dorsey

Executive Marketing Manager: Diane Wenckebach

Marketing Assistant: Rachel Bairstow

Marketing Communications Manager: Patrick Rooney

Project Manager, Editorial Production: Trudy Brown

Creative Director: Rob Hugel

Executive Art Director: Maria Epes

Print Buyer: Karen Hunt

Permissions Editor: Sarah Harkrader

Production Service: Johnstone Associates

Text and Cover Designer: Diane Beasley

Photo Researcher: Roberta Broyer

Copy Editor: Judith Johnstone

Autographer: Ernie Mansfield

Cover Image: Carlo Saraceni (1585–1620), *Saint Cecilia*.
    Galleria Nazionale d'Arte Antica, Rome, Italy. Scala/Art
    Resource, NY.

Compositor: Thompson Type

Text and Cover Printer: Quebecor World/Dubuque

For product information and technology assistance, contact us at
Cengage Learning Customer & Sales Support,
1-800-354-9706
For permission to use material from this text or product, submit all requests online at **cengage.com/permissions**
Further permissions questions can be emailed to
permissionrequest@cengage.com

Student Edition
ISBN-13: 978-0-495-00868-2
ISBN-10: 0-495-00868-0

Wadsworth
10 Davis Drive
Belmont, CA 94002-3098
USA

Cengage Learning is a leading provider of customized learning solutions with office locations around the globe, including Singapore, the United Kingdom, Australia, Mexico, Brazil, and Japan. Locate your local office at: **international.cengage.com/region**

Cengage Learning products are represented in Canada by Nelson Education, Ltd.

For your course and learning solutions, visit **academic.cengage.com**

Purchase any of our products at your local college store or at our preferred online store **www.ichapters.com**

Printed in China by China Translation & Printing Services Limited
3 4 5 6 11 10 09

BRIEF CONTENTS

BAROQUE MUSIC

THE ENLIGHTENMENT AND THE CLASSICAL ERA

DETAILED CONTENTS

Part IV

Part V

THE ENLIGHTENMENT AND THE CLASSICAL ERA

PREFACE

The decision to write a new history of Western music must appear to others, as it occasionally still does to its authors, as an act of madness. Of course, we have taken up this challenge in order to create a book that will best serve our students and our own goals as teachers. But it seems appropriate at the outset to inform prospective readers—and even to remind ourselves—what these goals are and what specific things we think make this text better than other histories of Western music.

✺ THE "PLACE" OF MUSIC

Music is the expressive voice of a culture, and often that voice is clearest in one particular city, country, or region. For this reason, we have centered our discussion of music in the places where it took deepest root. For example, we link much of the presentation of medieval music to the city of Paris; Handel to London; Beethoven to Vienna; Richard Strauss to Berlin; jazz to Harlem. We have not attempted daring or esoteric connections. But by placing music in a culturally resonant setting, we can help our students to see and hear how the sociopolitical life of certain places not only gave rise to musical genres and styles but also broadened and shaped all of Western civilization. To accomplish our overarching goal, we made certain pedagogical decisions based on our many years of teaching music history.

✺ CONTENT AND ORGANIZATION

The most visible difference in the organization of this book is its arrangement of topics into 83 brief chronological chapters. The book includes everything we thought most important to cover, and its many brief chapters promote three main goals. First, the arrangement of chapters makes it easier for instructors to present the material to students in any order that best suits their courses. For example, we are accustomed to teaching the instrumental music of Bach before his vocal music. But instructors more comfortable leading with vocal music can easily do so by assigning Chapter 40 before Chapter 39. Second, as instructors all know, students do not invariably bring to their studies an unquenchable desire to read the assigned text material. We have found that assigning a smaller passage for every class session yields better results than long chapters. Third, short chapters allow time for supplementary or source readings, and thus promote a better-rounded treatment of the subject at hand.

To provide variety for the student while studying the basic materials and musical selections, we engage special topics in **Boxes.** These are always germane to the subject under discussion, and they give the student a momentary diversion on some relevant issue in the history of music. For example, students enjoy the quirky observations on sixteenth-century social dancing made by aging priest Thoinot Arbeau, so we have highlighted his *Orchésographie* in Chapter 22. Similarly, students are generally astonished to find that people were paid to attend opera performances in the nineteenth century and to applaud on cue, so a box in Chapter 62 explains the existence of the *claque*. Nine longer **Musical Interludes** appear between various chapters. These discussions—music printing in the Renaissance, the critical concept of romanticism, and the birth of rock, among others—deal with larger issues that characterize an entire musical and cultural age, and their greater length and placement between chapters reflect their added importance.

A comprehensive **Timeline** of composers interwoven with the important political, social, and artistic events of that era opens each of eight parts of the book. We intend each timeline to provide a visual synopsis of a major historical period and a cultural context for the many musical events that we will discuss in the chapters that follow.

At the root of any study of music history, of course, lies the music itself, and our 267 CD tracks represent the major genres, composers, and works in the history of Western music. The discussion in each chapter moves quickly from a geographical and cultural context to a close study of these works, which are placed in students' hands in the form of excellent recordings and scores. A **Listening Cue** in the text alerts the reader whenever the time is right to leave the text, pick up headphones and the Anthology, and grapple with the primary materials of music.

In our selection of music, we have emphasized the **coverage of women composers** by including works by Hildegard of Bingen, Beatriz de Dia, Barbara Strozzi, Elizabeth Jacquet de La Guerre, Clara Schumann, Alma Mahler, Lili Boulanger, Bessie Smith, Ruth Crawford Seeger, and Joan Tower. We are mindful that many important composers—male as well as female—have of necessity been omitted from our discussion to produce a text of reasonable size. We invite comments about our choices and have appended our e-mail addresses to the end of this preface for this and any other issues readers may wish to discuss with us. In rare instances, where we were unable to include a piece on the CD set, the Listening Cue directs the reader to the book's website or to the Internet.

MATERIAL TAILORED TO YOUR COURSE

Most schools offer music history for music majors in a sequence covering one, two, or three semesters. A few lucky colleagues have four or more semesters to cover this subject. We both teach at schools that devote three semesters to the history survey, and we are well aware of the problems that arise in adapting any one text to sequences of different durations. But the emerging web economy has taught us and our students that we must provide greater choices.

Accordingly, we offer the book, the Anthology, and the thirteen CDs that accompany the text in combinations that match a typical two- or three-semester course—march time or waltz time, as it were. The book is also available, of course, as a single-volume text, in hardcover for durability over the course of a year or more. Students rightly complain if they must buy a book and then are assigned only part of it. Our flexible configuration of print and audio material allows instructors to require students to buy only as much material as they will actually use. The ISBN and order information for these several print and audio options appear on the back cover of the text.

For teaching formats that we have not anticipated but may best fit your unique course syllabus, please write your local Cengage Learning sales representative to

craft a print medium customized to your course. For help contacting this person, use the Rep Locator on the Cengage Learning home page: www.cengage.com.

 ANCILLARIES

Several remarkable ancillaries accompany the text.

Anthology

Timothy Roden of Ohio Wesleyan University has joined us to create a splendid anthology of Scores. It contains all of the central works discussed in the text with the exception of a few jazz and modern pieces that lack scores. Tim has added informative introductory notes to each selection and supplied new translations for all works with texts in foreign languages. As mentioned earlier, the complete Anthology is available in two or three volumes.

Audio CDs and Web

Virtually every piece that we discuss in the text appears on one of thirteen audio CDs; recordings of a few works can be located on the book's website (academic .cengage.com/music). The recordings are of the highest quality; for example, much of the recorded medieval music comes from the prestigious Harmonia Mundi label. Recordings of hitherto unrecorded pieces have been specially commissioned from professional groups and performers, including The Washington Cornett and Sackbut Ensemble.

Workbook

Timothy Roden has also written a unique student workbook of analytical exercises and probing questions that will help students examine each piece of music in the Anthology and prepare for exams and quizzes. Nothing like it exists now, and by engaging the student, these exercises bring the music to life. The Workbook also includes an essay by Sterling Murray, "Writing a Research Paper on a Musical Subject," as well as a bibliography for students designed to help in the process of writing papers. The bibliography can also be found on the website (academic.cengage.com/music).

Instructor's Resource CD-ROM

An all-inclusive CD ROM contains ExamView computerized testing, as well as an electronic version of the Instructor's Manual/Test Bank. Also found here are PowerPoint presentations that include outlines for lectures, additional illustrations, musical examples in the text, audio clips, and other materials for use in the classroom.

 ACKNOWLEDGMENTS AND THANKS

A project this comprehensive and complex is naturally the work of many hands. We are grateful to colleagues who gave generously of their time, ideas, and good will to make this undertaking a success. Some read and critiqued large portions of the text, others answered specific questions, and still others graciously provided materials. We are sincerely grateful to all of the following for their help.

Jonathan Bellman, *University of Northern Colorado*

Jane Bernstein, *Tufts University*

Francisco Lorenzo Candelaria, *University of Texas, Austin*

Tim Carter, *University of North Carolina, Chapel Hill*

Cynthia J. Cyrus, *Blair School of Music, Vanderbilt University*

Jeffrey Dean, *The New Grove Dictionary of Music and Musicians*

Charles Dill, *University of Wisconsin, Madison*

Christine Smith Dorey, *Case Western Reserve University*

Lawrence Earp, *University of Wisconsin, Madison*

Robert Eisenstein, *University of Massachusetts and Mount Holyoke College*

Robert Galloway, *Houghton College*

David Grayson, *University of Minnesota*

James Grymes, *University of North Carolina, Charlotte*

Barbara Haggh-Huglo, *University of Maryland*

James Hepokoski, *Yale University*

Michael Holmes, *University of Maryland*

Derek Katz, *University of California, Santa Barbara*

Terry Klefstad, *Southwestern University*

Walter Kreyszig, *University of Saskatchewan*

James Ladewig, *University of Rhode Island*

Paul Laird, *University of Kansas*

Bruce Langford, *Citrus College*

Charles S. Larkowski, *Wright State University*

Lowell Lindgren, *Massachusetts Institute of Technology*

Dorothea Link, *University of Georgia*

Daniel Lipori, *Central Washington University*

Ralph Lorenz, *Kent State University*

Patrick Macey, *Eastman School of Music*

Thomas J. Mathiesen, *Indiana University*

Charles Edward McGuire, *Oberlin College Conservatory of Music*

Bryce Mecham, *Brigham Young University*

Donald C. Meyer, *Lake Forest College*

Sharon Mirchandani, *Westminster Choir College of Rider University*

Sterling Murray, *West Chester University*

Giulio Ongaro, *University of Southern California*

Leon Plantinga, *Yale University*

Keith Polk, *University of New Hampshire*

Hilary Poriss, *University of Cincinnati*

John Rice, *Rochester, Minnesota*

Anne Robertson, *University of Chicago*

Ellen Rosand, *Yale University*

David Rothenberg, *Colby College*

Ed Rutschman, *Western Washington University*

Christopher J. Smith, *Texas Tech University School of Music*

Tony C. Smith, *Northwestern State University of Louisiana*

Kerala Snyder, *Eastman School of Music*

Pamela Starr, *University of Nebraska*

Marica Tacconi, *Pennsylvania State University*

JoAnn Taricani, *University of Washington*

Susan Thompson, *Yale University*

Jess B. Tyre, *State University of New York at Potsdam*

Zachariah Victor, *Yale University*

Scott Warfield, *University of Central Florida*

Mary A. Wischusen, *Wayne State University*

Gretchen Wheelock, *Eastman School of Music*

Several colleagues who specifically asked to remain anonymous

Closer to home, we wish to thank our respective wives, Sherry Dominick and Charlotte E. Erwin, for reading and evaluating the text, for giving advice on many fronts, and, most of all, for their support and patience. Having ready access to the music libraries at Yale and the University of Southern California has been a special boon, and we are grateful to Kendall Crilly, Richard Boursy, Suzanne Lovejoy, and Eva Heater for help in acquiring materials, and to Karl Schrom and Richard Warren for advice with regard to recordings. Also offering invaluable assistance during the creation of new recordings were Richard Lalli and Paul Berry. At the end of the project we could not have done without the indefatigable labors of graduate students Pietro Moretti and Nathan Link in researching, editing, proofreading, and preparing materials for the instructor's CD; in the course of this project the students became the mentors.

Finally, the authors wish to thank the staff of Cengage Learning that has helped to produce this volume. First of all, the guiding light, from beginning to end, was our publisher and friend, Clark Baxter; in many ways, this book is his. Joining Clark in this enterprise were a number of exceptionally talented people including Trudy Brown, who coordinated with great finesse the production of every part of this massive undertaking. Judy Johnstone merged, with her accustomed skill and forbearance, countless print and electronic chapters, images, and autography into a book that Diane Beasley's design has made exceptionally attractive. Sharon Poore and Sue Gleason helped us develop the manuscript itself. Julie Yardley worked closely with us and with Tim Roden on the ancillaries, especially on the Anthology. Emily Perkins, Clark's remarkable assistant, kept an ocean of paper and electronic material moving in the right direction, and on schedule. Matt Dorsey oversaw the development of the book's website and the Instructor's Resource CD-ROM. Finally, a word of thanks to Diane Wenckebach, who brought boundless energy and commitment to the marketing of this text, and who, with Patrick Rooney, prepared its promotional material.

Craig Wright
(craig.wright@yale.edu)

Bryan Simms
(simms@usc.edu)

Music in Western Civilization

BAROQUE MUSIC

$\mathcal{M}$usic historians use the term "baroque" to describe the music, musical theater, and dance during the years 1600–1750. The composition of most art music in the Baroque period was sponsored by aristocratic courts—or by wealthy princes of the church. While France, Germany, England, and Spain were developing distinctive musical languages at this time, Italy had become the arbiter of musical tastes and practices for much of Europe. Italian musicians began to occupy positions at northern courts, and naturally they brought with them the genres that they had created in Italy during the seventeenth century: opera, oratorio, cantata, sonata, sinfonia, and concerto.

1500	1550	1600	1650

RENAISSANCE (–1600)   **BAROQUE (1600–1750)**

Giovanni Gabrieli (c1554–1612), first composer fully to exploit sonic opportunities of St. Mark's

Galileo Galilei (1564–1642)

● 1570s Florentine camerata, group of prominent Florentines, gathers

Salomone Rossi (c1570–c1630), violinist

Girolamo Frescobaldi (1583–1643), foremost organist in Rome and most influential organ composer in Europe during the first half of the 17th century

René Descartes (1596–1650), French philosopher

Denis Gaultier (1597?–1672) dominates lute

● 1598 Jacopo Peri creates first true opera, *Dafne*

● Early 1600s Baroque music first appears;

● 1600 Jacopo Peri writes *Euridice*, first

● 1600 Artusi-Monteverdi controversy, war of

● 1602 Giulio Caccini composes *Le nuove*

Giacomo Carissimi (1605–1674), remembered

● 1607 Claudio Monteverdi composes

● 1613 Claudo Monteverdi becomes

Johann Froberger (1616–1667),

Thirty Years' War (1618–1648)

Barbara Strozzi (1619–1677),

● 1621 Heinrich Schütz

Pope Urban VIII (1623–1644)

Louis XIV with Plans for Versailles

CORBIS

Palace of Versailles

CORBIS

Staats-und Universitätsbibliothek Hamburg

George Frideric Handel (1685–1759)

Part IV

Perhaps the single most important innovation for music during the Baroque era was the advent of opera, and of the dramatic style in general. The madrigal of the late Renaissance had sown the seeds of intense expression that would bear fruit in the form of seventeenth-century opera—and soon oratorio and cantata as well. By the end of the century, the system of dramatic expression that had been developed for dramatic vocal music was extended to instrumental music. Instruments, too, could sound out meaning without the benefit of text, and did so in new genres such as the sonata and the concerto. Thus, to chronicle the development of Baroque music is to see the growth, and ultimate dominance, of dramatic styles in sacred music as well as secular, and in instrumental music as well as vocal.

1650	1700	1750	1800

● 1653 Louis XIV appoints Giovanni Battista Lulli (1632–1687) *Compositeur de la musique instrumentale*

Johann Pachelbel (1653–1706), prolific composer writing hundreds of pieces, vocal and instrumental

● 1722 Rameau publishes *Treatise on Harmony*

to discuss literature, science, and arts

Arcangelo Corelli (1653–1717), violinist-composer of enormous influence in development of Baroque instrumental music

François Couperin (1668–1733), called "the Great," arguably the greatest of French Baroque instrumental composers

Georg Philipp Telemann (1681–1767), important composer and friend of Bach

1668 Dieterich Buxtehude (c1637–1707), greatest north German organ composer, becomes organist at church of St. Mary in Lübeck

playing in Parisian salons at mid-century

Frederick the Great of Prussia (1712–1786), musical enthusiast and skilled flautist

● 1669 Louis XIV establishes *Académie royale de musique* and starts to build Palace of Versailles

composers acknowledge new importance of bass and give it the name basso continuo

completely preserved opera

words over what was more important: music or text

musiche (The New Music) and writes opera *Euridice*

today for 14 surviving oratorios

early opera *Orfeo*

maestro di cappella at St. Mark's in Venice

German musician who establishes dance suite as primary genre of string keyboard music

1670 Heinrich Biber (1644–1704), violin virtuoso, enters employment at court of archbishop of Salzburg

daughter of Giulio Strozzi, publishes 8 volumes of vocal music

The Collection of William H. Scheide, Princeton, NJ

Johann Sebastian Bach (1685–1750)

appointed Kapellmeister at German court of Dresden

Antonio Vivaldi (1678–1741), violinist and composer important in development of concerto

Jean-Philippe Rameau (1683–1764), composer and theorist

Giuseppe Torelli (1658–1709), violinist, writes trumpet concertos for St. Petronio's basilica in Bologna

Chapter 29

Early Baroque Music

Music historians agree, with unusual unanimity, that Baroque music first appeared in the early seventeenth century in northern Italy, in cities such as Florence, Mantua, and Venice. Around 1600 the choral polyphony of the Renaissance gradually gave way to a new exuberant style of solo singing that musicians of the day called "the new music." Later, this new music was given a new name: Baroque.

Baroque is the term used generally to describe the art, architecture, and music of the period 1600–1750. It derives from the Portuguese word *barroco*, meaning a pearl of irregular shape then used in jewelry and fine decoration. Critics applied the term "Baroque" to indicate a rough, bold sound in music and excessive ornamentation in the visual arts. To the philosopher Jean-Jacques Rousseau (1712–1778), "A baroque music is that in which the harmony is confused, charged with modulations and dissonances, the melody is harsh and little natural, the intonation difficult, and the movement constrained." Thus originally the term "Baroque" had a pejorative meaning. It signified the extravagant, the excessive, even the bizarre. Only during the twentieth century, with a newfound appreciation of the painting of Peter Paul Rubens (1577–1640) and the music of Antonio Vivaldi (1678–1741) and J.S. Bach (1685–1750), among others, has the term "Baroque" come to assume a positive meaning in Western cultural history. Today we admire Baroque art for its drama, opulence, intense expression, and grandeur.

The period of Baroque art roughly corresponds with what political historians call the **Age of Absolutism.** The theory of absolutism held that a king enjoyed absolute power by reason of divine right. Rulers were said to govern with absolute authority so that citizens might live in a well-ordered society. The pope in Rome, the Holy Roman Emperor, the kings of France and Spain, and, to a lesser extent, the king of England were the most powerful absolute monarchs of the seventeenth century. Much Baroque art, architecture, and music came into being to reflect and extend their absolute power. In almost every way, the church and the aristocratic court remained the principal patrons of the arts, in Italy and elsewhere.

Most striking about many monuments of Baroque art, such as St. Peter's Square in Rome or the palace of Versailles outside of Paris, is their vast scale. The buildings and grounds are massive. St. Peter's Square, designed by Gian Lorenzo Bernini (1598–1680), is so enormous that it seems to swallow people, cars, and buses (Fig. 29-1). The palace of Versailles, built by French King Louis XIV (1638–1715), is not merely a building but was once an entire city under a single roof, designed to be home to several thousand court functionaries (see Part IV timeline).

The music composed for such vast expanses could also be grandiose. No longer was every part played by a single instrument, as had been the case generally during the Renaissance. By the end of the seventeenth century many parts were doubled so as to increase the volume of sound. The orchestra playing for the opera

※ FIGURE 29-1
St. Peter's Square, Rome, designed by Bernini in the mid seventeenth century. St. Peter's Basilica, the largest church in the world, is in the center; the smaller Sistine Chapel is to the right.

Archiv fur Kunst Und Geschichte, Berlin

and ballet at the court of King Louis XIV at Versailles sometimes numbered more than eighty instrumentalists, although
such an ensemble was exceptional. In Rome and elsewhere
composers wrote choral works for twenty-four, forty-eight, and
even fifty-three separate vocal parts. These vocal works were
generally intended for the great Baroque churches in Italy and
Austria, and this style of music for multiple choruses with instrumental accompaniment has come to be called the grand,
or colossal, Baroque.

Yet the art and architecture of the Baroque era is marked by
strong contrasts. Buildings of enormous scale, for example, are
usually adorned by much ornamental detail. Artists filled the
long lines and vast spaces of the palaces and churches with
abundant decoration. Monumental space created a vacuum,
and into this rushed the artist with intense, dramatic energy.
In creating his *Throne of St. Peter* for the interior of that basilica in Rome, the sculptor Gian Lorenzo Bernini filled the ex-
panse with twisting forms that energize the otherwise static
architecture (Fig. 29-2). Similarly, a Roman ceiling painting
entitled *Glorification of Pope Urban VIII* by Pietro da Cortona
(1596–1669) epitomizes the size and exuberance of the
Baroque art (Fig. 29-3). The architectural space is filled with
figures that writhe and clouds that swirl. The painting is monumental yet packed with countless energetic details.

This same approach to artistic expression is found in the
music of the Baroque era. Composers too created large-scale compositions and filled
them with energetic figures. In both vocal and instrumental music, strong chordal
blocks support highly ornamental melodic lines. The florid melodies add energy and

🌿 **FIGURE 29-2**

Bernini's *The Throne of St. Peter* within St. Peter's basilica. This is not the high altar of St. Peter's, merely a rear chapel, which sug-gests the enormous size of the basilica. Bernini responded to the architectural scale by filling the chapel with exuberant decoration.

🌿 **FIGURE 29-3**

Pietro da Cortona, *Glorification of Pope Urban VIII*. This ceiling fresco, executed in Rome in 1633–1639 for the family of the pope, is both energetic and monumental.

excitement to what would otherwise be a purely static harmonic background. Notice in the following excerpt from Giulio Caccini's aria *Ardi, cor mio* (*Burn, O my heart*) of 1602 how the energetic vocal line is supported by a solid bedrock of simple chords (Ex. 29-1).

EXAMPLE 29-1

CHARACTERISTICS OF EARLY BAROQUE MUSIC

Toward the end of the sixteenth century the madrigal was the most progressive genre of music in Europe. The more forward-looking of the madrigal composers—Gesualdo and Monteverdi among them—wrote experimental works that broke many of the established rules of counterpoint. They valued the text and its meaning above purely musical procedures. In 1600 Monteverdi was attacked in print by a conservative music theorist named Giovanni Maria Artusi and he responded in kind, thereby creating what has come to be called the **Artusi-Monteverdi controversy** (see also Chapter 28)—a war of words over what was more important, music or text. Monteverdi called his new text-driven approach the *seconda pratica* (second practice). This he distinguished from the more traditional *prima pratica*, the conservative, mainly church style that dutifully followed the traditional rules of linear counterpoint. Later, musicians would refer to the conservative church style as the *stile antico* (old or traditional style) and the newer *seconda pratica* as the *stile moderno* (modern style). Composers continued to write in both *antico* and *moderno* styles throughout the seventeenth century.

Monteverdi and his progressive colleagues believed that music had the power to move the soul, as had ancient Greek music. Their faith that the language of music could express many and varied emotions led to an aesthetic theory called the Doctrine of Affections. The **Doctrine of Affections** held that different musical moods could and should be used to influence the emotions, or affections, of the listeners. A musical setting should reinforce the intended "affection" of the text. As early as 1602 the composer Giulio Caccini, in his *Le nuove musiche* (*The New Music*), referred to "moving the affections of the soul." Later music theorists would advocate a unity of affections, holding that each piece of music should project only a single affection, be it anger, hate, sorrow, joy, or love (see Chapter 34). Indeed, Baroque music generally does not change quickly from one mood to another, as might a polyphonic madrigal in the Renaissance or a symphony from the later Classical period. The Baroque artist—whether painter, sculptor, or musician—created emotional units that were clearly defined, distinctly separate, and long-lasting.

Vocal Expression and Virtuosity

During the Renaissance, vocal music was mostly ensemble music—works for groups of vocalists, even if there were only one singer on a part. In the early Baroque, however, emphasis shifted from vocal ensemble to accompanied solo song. Vocal groups might be a useful way to convey the abstract religious thoughts of the multitudes but, to communicate raw human emotions, direct appeal by an individual soloist was now thought more effective. Solo madrigals, solo arias, and solo recitatives were all designated by a single word: **monody** (from Greek terms meaning "to sing alone"). The vogue of monody was simply a continuation of the attempts of poets, scholars, and musicians to emulate the music of ancient Greece by making the words intelligible and enhancing their effect. In Chapter 30 we shall discuss several types of monody (see Anthology, Nos. 79–81). For the moment it is enough to say that emphasis on the solo voice quickly led to a more flamboyant style of singing (see Ex. 29-1). Soon the vocal virtuoso would emerge, the star of the court theater and the operatic stage.

Harmonic Conception and the Basso Continuo

During the Renaissance the prevailing texture for music, vocal as well as instrumental, involved imitative counterpoint. In a Renaissance Mass, motet, or madrigal, for example, several equal parts spin out a web of polyphony, one line imitating another in turn. Early Baroque music has a fundamentally different orientation. Instead of having three, four, or five contrapuntal lines, composers now emphasized just the top and bottom parts, using the other voices to add chordal enrichment in the middle. If much of Renaissance music was created polyphonically and horizontally, working line by line, that of the early Baroque period is more homophonically conceived, its chords springing up vertically from the bass.

❋ FIGURE 29-4

A *Lady with Theorbo* (c1670) by John Michael Wright. The bass strings are at the top of the instrument and off the fingerboard. Each bass string plays just one note of a low, diatonic scale. The theorbo was often used to play the basso continuo in the seventeenth century.

In the early 1600s, composers acknowledged the new importance of the bass, and they gave it a new name: **basso continuo** in Italian (commonly called "thorough bass" in England). The basso continuo was a bass line that provided a never-ending foundation, or "continuous bass," for the melody above. Early in the Baroque, the basso continuo might be played by a single solo instrument such as the lute or the **theorbo**—a large lute-like instrument with a full octave of additional bass strings descending in a diatonic pattern such as F-E-D-C-B'-A' (Fig. 29-4). Gradually, a low melody instrument such as the *viola da gamba*, cello, or bassoon came to reinforce the bass line. Thus the basso continuo often consisted of an ensemble of two instruments; while one performer played the written bass line, another played a harmony above the bass on a chord-producing instrument—organ, harpsichord, lute, theorbo, or even guitar, for example. (For a clear example of the sound of the basso continuo, turn to the Anthology, No. 85.) The chord-playing instrument linked the melody on top to the bass below by improvising on the spot in a flexible, expressive way. But how did the player know what chords to improvise?

Columbus Museum of Art

The harmonies of the basso continuo were usually indicated by a notation called **figured bass**—a numerical shorthand placed with the bass line that tells the player which unwritten notes to fill in above the written bass note. Figured bass is similar in intent to the numerical code found in "fake books" used by modern jazz pianists that indicate which chords to play beneath the written melody. Today, music theory courses in conservatories and universities around the world still teach, and test, the capacity to realize (play chords above) a figured bass at sight (Ex. 29-2).

EXAMPLE 29-2

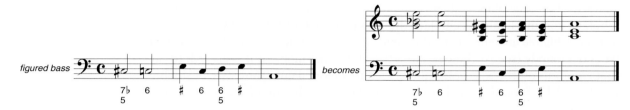

A musician who has mastered the ability to realize a figured bass has a solid understanding of chordal harmony. Indeed, in the early Baroque, chordal harmony was becoming increasingly important. More and more, composers were conceiving music as a series of chordal units, or chord progressions. In addition, they came to write these chord progressions within just the major and minor keys.

Major and Minor Tonalities

In the course of the seventeenth century, two scale patterns, major (the Ionian mode) and minor (the Aeolian mode), came to be employed to the virtual exclusion of all of the other church modes of the Renaissance and before. The old Dorian and Phrygian modes, for example, became less and less important. (For more on the increasing importance of major and minor tonalities, see Musical Interlude 5 following Chapter 36.) Of course, privileging just the major and minor modes meant that melodies were written mostly in just these two scales. But it affected harmony as well. Modal polyphony of the Renaissance had emphasized triads that were often only a second or a third apart; the new tonal polyphony of the Baroque, on the other hand, tended increasingly to construct chords upon notes of the scale that were a fourth or a fifth apart. Viewed from the perspective of harmony alone, the seventeenth century can be seen as a period in which modal harmony gradually gave way to tonal harmony. The difference between the two approaches can be seen by comparing two progressions centering on the home pitch E (Exs. 29-3a, 29-3b), the first by Renaissance composer Thomas Tallis and the second by Baroque composer Arcangelo Corelli.

EXAMPLE 29-3A   EXAMPLE 29-3B

Modal harmony (Tallis, 1567)

Tonal harmony (Corelli, c1690)

As harmonies were reduced to just the major and minor modes, the listener could more easily focus on the distinct properties of each. Composers could play the dark minor mode off against the bright major, or vice versa, to create the emotional effects and shadings of color so important in Baroque music in particular and Baroque art generally.

Instrumental Color and Musical Dynamics

The Baroque era is a crossroads in the progressive development of musical instruments. Some instruments of the Renaissance, such as the lute, theorbo, cornett, recorder, and *viola da gamba*, were peaking in popularity and would disappear with the Baroque era. Others, particularly the members of the violin family, including the violoncello (or cello), were relatively new and would grow in popularity during the Baroque period. In the early 1600s, however, all of these instruments were available and were called for by composers at various times. A variegated ensemble in which a theorbo, *viola da gamba*, cornett, sackbut, violin, recorder, transverse flute, bassoon, cello, and harpsichord played together was not uncommon. The early Baroque orchestra was not yet dominated by members of the violin family; instead it was remarkable for its diverse, colorful sounds.

Similarly, diversity of sound came to include the volume of sound. Certainly there were louds and softs in the music of the Middle Ages and Renaissance. Yet not until around 1600 did composers specify levels of volume in their music. At first they did so in a very simple way: they merely wrote *piano* or *forte* in the score. Generally, in Baroque instrumental music, dynamics do not change gradually within a section of a piece. Rather, a single dynamic range, whether loud or soft, holds fast until abruptly replaced by another. Setting loud against soft, winds against strings, soloist against chorus, major against minor—all these helped create the brilliant colors and strong contrasts that mark Baroque music.

Idiomatic Writing for Instruments and Voice

Finally, Baroque music welcomes for the first time truly idiomatic writing for both instruments and voice. In the Renaissance, melody was more or less all of one type. It was a direct, uncomplicated line that could be performed by either a voice or an instrument. Indeed, Renaissance publishers exploited the generic quality of melody, eagerly advertising their newest print as "suitable for both voices and instruments." Beginning about 1600, however, instrumental style began to diverge from vocal. Composers recognized that the violin, for example, can play a scale faster than the human voice can sing one. Thus they began to write idiomatic (well suited) music for particular instruments—rapid scales for the violin or repeating notes of a triad for brass instruments, for example. Vocal music, too, began to go its own way. Composers wrote vocal lines with starkly different levels of rhythmic activity and with trills and other ornaments that highlighted the acrobatic ability of the voice. Nowhere could this distinctly idiomatic vocal style be more clearly heard than in the newly emerging opera.

 SUMMARY

In Western cultural history the term "Baroque" identifies an artistic style that flourished during the years 1600–1750. Baroque art, architecture, and music are characterized by vivid colors, strong contrasts, and grand designs. Around 1600 the choral polyphony that had dominated the Renaissance gave way to an exuberant style of solo singing. If Renaissance music was mostly conceived contrapuntally and horizontally, line by line, that of the early Baroque period is organized more homophonically and vertically, chord by chord. Attention came to be focused almost entirely on an expressive melody supported by a strong bass. Tonality increasingly came to be limited to just the major and minor modes. Throughout the Baroque era, idiomatic writing created two distinctly different styles, one for instruments and another for voices.

KEY TERMS

Baroque
Age of Absolutism
Artusi-Monteverdi
  controversy

seconda pratica
Doctrine of Affections
monody
basso continuo

theorbo
figured bass

Chapter 30

The Birth of Opera:
Florence, Mantua, and Venice

Today opera is an enormously popular medium. While symphony orchestras struggle to stay in business, opera companies flourish, and demand for the best singers pushes ticket prices to the roof. Yet, oddly, opera emerged rather late in the history of Western art music, around 1600. By way of comparison, both China and Japan had had a flourishing tradition of opera since at least 1300. True, something approaching sung drama had existed in the West in the liturgical drama of the medieval church. But liturgical drama flowered only briefly around 1200 and then died, leaving no successor. The opera that we listen to today, and for which there are passionate devotees around the world, emerged in northern Italy about the year 1600.

Opera literally means "work." Musically speaking, the term was first employed in the Italian phrase *opera drammatica in musica* (a dramatic work, or play, set to music). In opera the lines of the actors and actresses are not merely spoken, but sung. At first this sounds like a very odd thing to do; human beings do not sing out their day-to-day conversations ("Please pass the peas as soon as possible," for example). But the fundamental premise of opera is that sung music can heighten the emotional intensity of a dramatic text. The text that conveys the story of the opera is called the **libretto,** and it is written in poetic verse. By combining music, poetry, drama, scenic design, and dance, opera can be the most powerful of all forms of art. Some consider it the supreme expression of the human spirit.

EARLY OPERA IN FLORENCE

Opera in the West first appeared at the court of the Medici princes in Florence, Italy, at the turn of the seventeenth century. In quick succession came *Dafne* (1598) by Jacopo Peri, *Euridice* (1600) again by Peri, and *Euridice* (1602) by Giulio Caccini. All three early operas set a libretto by the Florentine court poet Ottavio Rinuccini (1562–1621). The stories of Dafne and Apollo and of Euridice and Orpheus are based on ancient Greek myths. In fact, most early operas set a libretto drawn from mythology because the creators of opera were trying to recapture the spirit of ancient drama while carrying the listener to a magical world far from reality. The first operas of Peri and Caccini did not emerge out of thin air, however. Rather, they were the result of nearly twenty-five years of discussion and experimentation about the nature of ancient Greek music.

As early as the 1570s, a group of prominent Florentines had gathered in the home of Count Giovanni Bardi (1534–1612) to discuss the literature, science, and arts of the day. Later, one of Bardi's protégés dubbed this society the **Florentine camerata** ("club" or "circle"). Bardi was a soldier by profession, but an antiquarian by passion. Fellow camerata members included the translator and textual scholar Girolamo Mei (1519–1594) and the musician-scientist Vincenzo Galilei (c1528–1591). Galilei is important to history and music on several counts: he was the father of the famous astronomer Galileo Galilei (1564–1642); he was one of the earliest to advocate equal temperament as the most practical way of dealing with tuning in music; and he was one of the first to argue for a new style of solo singing, as stated in his *Dialogo della musica antica, et della moderna* (*Dialogue on Ancient and Modern Music*, 1581). Bardi, Mei, Galilei, and their colleagues shared a common purpose, to create a modern music that approximated the vocal declamation of ancient Greek tragedy. Though they lacked the actual music from ancient Greece, they knew that Greek drama had been sung, or at least declaimed in a musical manner. What the camerata advocated was a new type of vocal delivery called *stile rappresentativo*. **Stile rappresentativo** (dramatic style or theater style) was vocal expression somewhere between song and declaimed speech. The singer emphatically declaimed the text so that the pitches and rhythms of the voice matched exactly the rhythms, accents, and sentiments of the text. What began as an antiquarian study of Greek musical practices became a model for contemporary composition.

In 1589 the leaders of the camerata presented their new experimental style of singing to an aristocratic audience drawn to Florence for the wedding of the grand duke of Tuscany, Ferdinando de' Medici. The principal wedding entertainment was a play. Between each of the acts of the play, however, Bardi and his associates inserted a sung diversion, called an intermedio, a sung play within a play. Figure 30-1 shows Jacopo Peri (1561–1633) portraying the role of the mythological singer Arion in the fifth intermedio of 1589. Typical of such late Renaissance court entertainments, each intermedio was fully sung, yet each was an isolated dramatic scene; they did not form a unified sung drama.

Nine years later Jacopo Peri created the first true opera, *Dafne* (1598), a unified multi-scene drama entirely sung. Unfortunately, only fragments of *Dafne* have survived. The first completely preserved opera dates from two years later: Peri's setting of the story of Orpheus and Euridice, simply called *Euridice* (1600). The story of Orpheus and Euridice is important in the history of opera because numerous composers would set it to dramatic music over the next three centuries.

The **Orpheus legend** tells the tale of Orpheus (Orfeo in Italian), the son of Apollo, the Greek god of the sun and of music. (As mentioned, our word "music" comes from the muses who attend Apollo.) Orpheus, himself a demi-god, falls in love with the beautiful human Euridice. No sooner are they married than she is fatally bitten by a snake and carried off to Hades (the realm of the dead). Orpheus vows to descend into the Underworld and restore his beloved to earthly life. This he nearly accomplishes by exploiting his divine powers of musical persuasion, for Orpheus can make the trees sway, calm savage beasts, and even overcome the furies of Hades with the beauty of his expressive song.

✿ FIGURE 30-1
Composer-singer Jacopo Peri portraying the mythological poet-singer Arion in Florence in 1589.

In his preface to the published score of *Euridice*, Jacopo Peri explained his approach to setting a text "in the manner of the ancient Greeks and Romans":

> I recognized that in our [Italian] language certain words are uttered in such a way that they allow a harmony to be built on them, and that in the course of speech, one passes through many other words that are not stressed, until one eventually returns to another word capable of sustaining a new consonant harmony. Having in mind those affects and stresses that we use to create lamenting, rejoicing, and similar emotions, I set the bass moving at the same pace as human speech, now faster, now slower, according to the affections, and held it firm through dissonances and consonances until, running through the various notes, the voice of the singer arrived at a syllable stressed in ordinary speech that then allows a new harmony.[1]

Exactly the sort of music Peri describes can be heard at the climax of *Euridice*, when Orfeo, having descended into Hades to rescue Euridice, confronts the horrors of that region. In a vocal solo entitled "Funeste piagge" ("Deadly shores") the composer drives rapidly through lines of text, often with quickly repeating pitches. At strategic moments, however, usually at the ends of lines where rhyming words appear, he underscores the text through long notes. The bass moves more rapidly or slowly as the text requires. Along the way dissonance is treated freely—not prepared or resolved according to the traditional rules of counterpoint. The excerpt from "Funeste piagge" in Example 30-1 exemplifies both monody (the term used generally to describe accompanied solo song at the turn of the seventeenth century) as well as the more specific *stile rappresentativo* (the dramatic or theatrical style). The chords above the basso continuo have been realized by a modern editor following the indications of Peri's figured bass.

EXAMPLE 30-1

While with sad accents I lament with you my lost love; and you, oh, pitying my anguish…

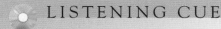

LISTENING CUE

JACOPO PERI
Euridice (1600)
"Funeste piagge"

CD 4/1
Anthology, No. 79

Jacopo Peri had a rival on the operatic stage in Florence: the composer, singer, and singing teacher Giulio Caccini (1551–1618). No sooner had Peri performed his *Euridice* (October 1600) than Caccini rushed into print with his own setting of the same libretto (January 1601). Caccini was intent on making sure his *Euridice* was seen to be as timely and as novel as Peri's. In the preface to his *Euridice*, Caccini was quick to point out that he too had set to music the fable of *Euridice* in the *stile rappresentivo* and he too had supported the recited parts with a basso continuo. He also announced that he would soon explain a new method for singing ornaments that he had invented.

The next year, Caccini made good on his promise by publishing **Le nuove musiche** (*The New Music*, 1602). Ironically, not all of *Le nuove musiche* was new music. It is, in fact, an anthology of solo madrigals and strophic solo songs gathered over time. Several of the madrigals, Caccini claims in his preface, had been greeted with "warm applause" when heard by the Florentine camerata as early as 1590. What is truly new about *Le nuove musiche* is Caccini's description of the vocal techniques that grace his monodies. Caccini was the first to describe early Baroque vocal ornaments and the first composer to write them directly in the score. The preface to *Le nuove musiche*, therefore, provides invaluable information on performance practices for modern performers seeking to re-create the true spirit of early Baroque vocal music. His instructions apply equally well to chamber singing and to early Baroque opera, because at that time both used the same techniques of singing.

Caccini has much to say about vocal execution, and his comments guide those singers who re-create Baroque opera today: Singers should inflect longer notes by means of slight crescendos and diminuendos, moments that he calls exclamations (*esclamazioni*); at that time musicians had no symbols to indicate crescendo and diminuendo. (Yet Caccini urges caution with the crescendo because the pitch may go sharp as the voice gets louder.) Singers are encouraged to fill in larger melodic intervals with running scales (*passaggi*). Singers may also vary the written rhythms to add lightness to the music. Most important, singers are urged to insert idiomatic vocal ornaments at cadences for emphasis, but to do so in moderation. To explain the principal two cadential ornaments, Caccini includes the following example (Ex. 30-2). His *trillo* is a repeating percussive effect placed on a single pitch, whereas his *gruppo* is the counterpart of our modern neighbor-note trill.

EXAMPLE 30-2

The monodies that follow the preface of *Le nuove musiche* exemplify Caccini's thoughts on vocal execution. The madrigal *Filli, mirando il cielo* (*Phyllis, admiring the heavens*), for example, is filled with well-placed vowels that offer opportunity for brief crescendos and diminuendos, and it ends with an elaborate *trillo* and *gruppo*. Indeed, the last line "What torment I shall have when my face turns sallow and my hair silver" is set three times with increasingly elaborate ornamentation. The principles of ornamentation set forth here apply not only to solo madrigals such as this but to all Florentine monodies including, as mentioned, those of early opera.

LISTENING CUE

GIULIO CACCINI
Le nuove musiche (1602)
Filli, mirando il cielo

CD 4/2
Anthology, No. 80

❋ EARLY OPERA IN MANTUA: MONTEVERDI'S *ORFEO*

"There is no lover of music who does not keep Orfeo's songs before him at all times."[2] This contemporary remark attests to the popularity of the newborn opera generally and to the legend of Orpheus in particular. Soon another important composer, Claudio Monteverdi, took up the legend of Orpheus and Euridice. Monteverdi, as we have seen (see Chapter 28), was a composer who wrote madrigals in the manner of the *seconda pratica*, the progressive style that flourished around 1600. During the early 1600s, Monteverdi was director of music at the northern Italian court of Mantua. He apparently got the idea of writing an opera on the Orpheus legend when he heard Peri's *Euridice* in Florence in the fall of 1600. By 1607 Monteverdi was ready to stage his own version of the tale, one built on a new libretto by Alessandro Striggio (1573–1630). Monteverdi's *Orfeo* is Mantua's answer to Florentine operas based on the same subject.

Monteverdi intended his Mantuan *Orfeo* to be a chamber opera heard by a small and elite audience. At the first performance on 24 February 1607 about two hundred aristocrats crowded into a standing-room-only chamber measuring just 30 × 40 feet. (The room, on the ground floor of the ducal palace in Mantua, survives today, but serves as a gift shop!) Monteverdi divides his *Orfeo* into five short acts that together last no more than ninety minutes.

Orfeo opens with a brief fanfare entitled "toccata." A **toccata** (literally a "touched thing") is an instrumental piece, for keyboard or other instruments, requiring the performer to touch the instrument with great technical dexterity. In other words, it is an instrumental showpiece. Here the full orchestra puts on the show. Monteverdi requires a remarkable variety of instruments that feature many distinctly different sounds, as is typical of early Baroque ensembles: strings including violins and viols, recorders, trumpets, trombones, cornetts, harpsichord, theorbo, harp, organ, and reed organ. At no time, however, do all the instruments sound together. In the opening toccata, for example, the trumpets lead the way, racing up and down the scale in brilliant fashion. In his printed score Monteverdi instructs that the toccata be sounded three times: presumably first to get the attention of the audience, then to announce the arrival of the patron, the duke of Mantua, and finally to signal that the action is about to begin.

LISTENING CUE

CLAUDIO MONTEVERDI
Orfeo (1607)
Toccata

CD 4/3
Anthology, No. 81a

Compared to earlier settings of the Orpheus legend, Monteverdi's *Orfeo* is a richer, more opulent score. The luxuriant sound is created partly by the large number and variety of instruments, and partly by the diverse kinds of music Monteverdi creates; his opera has a mix of choral songs, choral dances, instrumental dances, instrumental interludes, and, most important, solo singing of various kinds. The accompanied solo singing, the monody, is stylistically the most progressive music, and he saves it for the dramatic high points of the opera.

The first such moment of high drama comes midway through Act II, when Orfeo learns that his new bride Euridice has been killed by a snake and carried off to the Underworld. Two shepherds relate how the hero took the news. They do so in a style of monody that will soon be called *stile recitativo* ("recited style"). **Recitative** is musically heightened speech. When it is accompanied only by basso continuo, it is usually called **simple recitative** (*recitativo semplice* in Italian). Recitative in opera usually tells the audience what has happened. Because recitative attempts to mirror the natural stresses of oral delivery, it is often made up of rapidly repeating notes followed by one or two longer notes at the end of phrases, after which the reciter might pause to catch a breath. Thus the Second Shepherd relates the bitter news (Ex. 30-3).

EXAMPLE 30-3

At the bitter news the unfortunate one was turned to stone…

Orfeo now reacts to this thunderbolt. He tells us how he feels by using a more flexible, expressive style of monody that will soon be called "arioso." **Arioso style** is a manner of singing halfway between a recitative and a full-blown aria. It involves fewer repeating pitches and is more rhythmically elastic than a purely declamatory recitative, but is not as song-like and expansive as an aria. In Orfeo's arioso-style "Tu se' morta, mia vita" ("You are dead, my life"), Monteverdi uses expressive vocal intervals, changing rhythms of speech, and bitter harmonies to intensify the hero's grief (Ex. 30-4).

EXAMPLE 30-4

You are dead, my life, and I breathe,…

At the peak of his misery and rage, Orfeo vows to go where no human has ever tread: he will descend into Hades and rescue his bride. Here he confronts Caronte (Charon), the guardian of the Underworld. Now Orfeo must use all of his vocal skills to pacify the frightful guard (Fig. 30-2). His song, the central number in the opera, is the aria "Possente spirto" ("Powerful spirit"). An **aria,** Italian for "song" or "ayre," is more florid, more expansive, and more melodious than a recitative or arioso. It tends to have less rapid-fire delivery and more melismas (one vowel luxuriously spread out over many notes), as can be seen in Example 30-5. Occasionally, an aria is set for two or three singers, in which case the terms "duet" or "trio" are appropriate. Finally, an aria invariably sets a short poem made up of several stanzas. In fact, a closed strophic poem created by the librettist became a cue to the composer to create a lyrical aria. The text of "Possente spirto" has three strophes each with three eleven-syllable lines rhyming **aba.** Here is the first of these stanzas.

Possente spirto e formidabil nume,	**a**	Powerful spirit and formidable god
Senza cui far passaggio à l'altra riva	**b**	without whom no bodiless soul,
Alma da corpo sciolta in van presume.	**a**	onto the shore of Hades has trod.

EXAMPLE 30-5

The following two stanzas make use of the same melody and bass, somewhat varied each time. What results is a **strophic variation aria,** an aria in which the same melodic and harmonic plan appears, with slight variation, in each successive strophe. Composers of the early seventeenth century seized upon strophic variation form as a way of giving variety to the otherwise utterly repetitive strophic form.

Finally, an aria in a Baroque opera, unlike a recitative, is often accompanied by more than just the basso continuo, and, the later we go in the seventeenth century, the more this is true. Early in the Baroque, however, treble instruments accompanying the aria melody were rather rare, and Monteverdi was one of the first to experiment with this procedure. In his "Possente spirto" Orfeo's appeal to Caronte is accompanied at various times by organ, theorbo, violins, cornetts, and harps. With its expansive solo singing and rich accompaniment, the aria provides the musical high points of this and almost every opera.

❀ FIGURE 30-2

Monteverdi's aria "Possente spirto" with the vocal part in both an ornamented and an un-ornamented version. Why two versions? Perhaps Monteverdi needed to show the less experienced singer how to ornament this melody, leaving it to the more advanced singer to add ornaments to the simple, unadorned version at will. Notice that the printer is still making use of single-impression printing, a technique developed in Paris nearly a hundred years earlier (see Chapter 22). This accounts for the "wavy" lines on the staves.

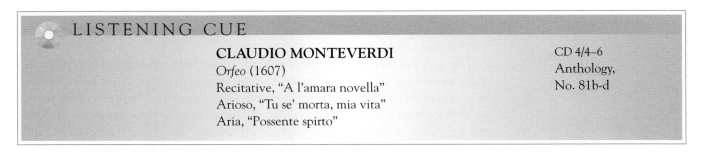

LISTENING CUE

CLAUDIO MONTEVERDI
Orfeo (1607)
Recitative, "A l'amara novella"
Arioso, "Tu se' morta, mia vita"
Aria, "Possente spirto"

CD 4/4–6
Anthology,
No. 81b-d

In truth, the terms just used to describe the expressive monody heard in Monteverdi's *Orfeo* were not coined in connection with this opera. The word "aria" was frequently employed to describe solo songs in strophic form in the late Renaissance, whereas the terms "recitative" and "arioso" did not become commonplace until the 1630s. Nevertheless, Monteverdi's use of different styles of monody is an important innovation. *Orfeo* is the first opera to differentiate styles of singing clearly so as to underscore different sorts of dramatic events. He shows that declamatory recitative can be used to deliver impersonal narration, whereas the more expansive aria is best saved for intense personal expression and rhetorical persuasion. As we shall see, the stylistic distinction between recitative and aria, and their different dramatic functions, will become even more pronounced in later Baroque opera.

EARLY OPERA IN VENICE

In 1613 Claudio Monteverdi quit his job as director of music in Mantua and moved to Venice. He had composed two path-breaking operas for the Mantuan court, *Orfeo* (1607) and *Arianna* (1608), but had received neither appreciation nor remuneration. "I have never in my life suffered greater humiliation of the spirit than when I had to go and beg the treasurer for what was mine," he said. Disgusted with Mantua, Monteverdi accepted the much coveted position of *maestro di cappella* (director of music) at St. Mark's Basilica in Venice (see Fig. 31-1), the most prestigious musical post in Italy. Naturally, his new job at this famous church required that he compose much religious music, and this he did for the next thirty years. In 1640, however, Monteverdi returned to the operatic stage, lured there by the sudden appearance of, not one but two, new opera houses in Venice.

When the citizens of Venice first embraced opera in 1637, they did so very differently than elsewhere in Italy. In Florence, Mantua, and Rome, opera was sponsored by aristocratic courts as a way to enhance the prestige of the prince. In Venice, on the other hand, opera became the enterprise of wealthy merchant families who saw it as a way to make money. To be commercially successful, however, an opera had to play night after night in a large theater. Thus the patrician families of Venice created theaters especially for opera. The audience was not a select group of two hundred aristocratic guests, but a fee-paying crowd of as many as 1,500 drawn from a cross section of society: merchants, soldiers, clerics, students, and the like. Soon several opera houses were competing head-to-head, much like Broadway theaters today. Between 1637 and 1678 Venetian audiences saw more than one hundred fifty operas in nine different theaters. To make the business of opera efficient (and to abide by the religious customs of the city), opera in Venice was confined to the carnival season (roughly from after Christmas to the beginning of Lent), when the population of Venice swelled to nearly 150,000. The leveling of social classes, in the streets and in the opera house, was facilitated by the fact that during carnival everyone wore masks. Opera was no longer the private preserve of an elite group. It had become a public spectacle.

The very public nature of opera in Venice soon led to changes. Star singers became more important as opera lovers became enamored with the special qualities of one or another of the leading voices of the day. Competition between opera houses in Venice inflated the salary of the singers, who soon were earning twice as much as the best composers. More and more, composer and librettist were forced to tailor the music to suit a leading singer's vocal range, capacity for ornamentation, and dramatic skills. In addition, stage machinery and elaborate sets created an air of the spectacular (Fig. 30-3). Angels flew across the sky and naval vessels did battle on the high seas of the stage. With its emphasis on glitzy sets and lavish costumes, Venetian opera had all the trappings of a modern-day mega musical.

By 1640 Claudio Monteverdi had reached the age of seventy-two and become the grand old man of Venetian music. Yet, that year, having apparently finished no new operas in more than three decades, he returned to the stage, first with *Il ritorno* d'Ulisse in patria (*The Return of Ulysses*), followed by *Le nozze d'Enea* (*The Marriage of Aeneas*, 1641) and *L'incoronazione di Poppea* (*The Coronation of Poppea*, 1642). *Poppea*, as this last opera is known, would be the final composition of Monteverdi's long and distinguished career.

Many believe *Poppea* to be the greatest opera of the seventeenth century. Certainly, it is a very different sort of opera from those that preceded it. The subject matter is not drawn from Greek mythology but Roman history. It celebrates, not the virtues of the ruling class, but their vices. The somewhat sensational plot goes as follows: The Roman emperor Nero lusts for the beautiful Poppea, a lady of the court; to achieve his desires, he sentences to death his wise but prudish counselor Seneca, banishes his own wife Ottavia, and places the ambitious Poppea triumphantly on the throne of all Rome.

In many ways, the realistic dramaturgy of Monteverdi's opera resembles that of his older contemporary, William Shakespeare. Sovereigns share the stage with servants; high tragedy alternates with low comedy; and wise advice goes unheeded by passionate young lovers. But unlike the works of Shakespeare, where ill deeds are condemned if not punished, here vice triumphs over virtue. Poppea is crowned empress and revels in her triumph in a final love duet with Nero. In this duet "Pur ti miro" ("I adore you") the guilty lovers are left on stage to sing a seemingly endless chain of voluptuous dissonance-to-consonance progressions. This ravishing conclusion encapsulates the passionate, sensuous nature of their love and the entire opera as well. Above all, it demonstrates just how far opera had progressed since Monteverdi left Mantua. The orchestral writing is luxuriant and the musical numbers are distinctively different so as to highlight the special qualities of the principal characters. Most important, a clear stylistic distinction exists between recitative and aria—the one syllabic and declamatory, the other florid, even rhapsodic.

❧ FIGURE 30-3
Ships sail on the high seas as gods descend from the heavens in Giacomo Torelli's stage set for the opera *Bellerofonte* (Venice, 1642).

LISTENING CUE

CLAUDIO MONTEVERDI? (see Box)
L'incoronazione di Poppea (1642)
Duet, "Pur ti miro"

CD 4/7
Anthology, No. 82

Venetian opera did not end with the death of Claudio Monteverdi in 1643 but lived on in the hands of his pupil Francesco Cavalli (1602–1676) and follower Antonio Cesti (1623–1669). Cavalli composed thirty-three operas, the best known of which was the often-performed *Giasone* (1649), which deals the myth of Jason and the Argonauts. Of the twelve or so operas attributed to Cesti, certainly the most

Did Monteverdi Write the Finale? Does It Matter?

Today, when a composer finishes an opera the creative process usually ends and the score becomes the blueprint for the performance. That was true for the earliest court operas from Florence and Mantua as well. But beginning with public opera in seventeenth-century Venice, composers, librettists, and impresarios (producers) started to tinker with the score, making additions and cuts, right up to the premier and even after. Requirements of the particular theater, the cast, and the tastes of the audience had to be met. As with new Broadway shows today, a mid-century Venetian opera was not so much a finite work of art as a continuing work in progress.

There is reason to believe that the final duet, "Pur ti miro" ("I adore you"), may have been added later to Monteverdi's *Poppea*, and perhaps was not composed by Monteverdi at all. The text of the duet does not appear in the separately published libretto and it can be argued that the musical style differs slightly from Monteverdi's norm. Could the duet have been the work of Monteverdi's pupil Francesco Cavalli, whose hand can be seen elsewhere altering Monteverdi's score, or perhaps that of an admirer, Benedetto Ferrari, who wrote the text of the duet (and possibly the music)? Conversely, did Monteverdi himself write "Pur ti miro" to Ferrari's text and append it to his own score in order to make the finale of *Poppea* even more glamorous?

This issue of authenticity of "Pur ti miro" leads us to ask: Does it matter who creates a work of art? Would the *Mona Lisa* be any less beautiful were it painted, not by Leonardo da Vinci, but by someone else named Leonardo? Authorship should not matter, of course, unless we are more concerned with the life of the composer than the created work, more concerned with biography than art. Whether by Monteverdi or someone in his circle, "Pur ti miro" is an exquisite aria (duet), one perfectly exemplifying mid-century Venetian opera.

spectacular was *Il pomo d'oro* (*The Golden Apple*); in 1668 it received a lavish production with twenty-four different stage sets at the court of the Holy Roman Emperor in Vienna. Generally speaking, the operas of Cavalli and Cesti contain fewer choruses and instrumental interludes and more arias for the star singers. In addition, they distinguished more clearly between the recitative and the aria. Arias became not only more numerous but longer. These trends—more emphasis on solo singing in opera, more and longer arias, and more vocal display—would accelerate during the second half of the seventeenth century. Singers were wresting control of opera away from the composer.

SUMMARY

Nowhere was the new Baroque style more clearly evident than in a new genre of music that emerged around 1600: opera. Fully sung dramatic works were at first dominated by a style of monody called *stile rappresentativo*. Gradually, a distinction emerged between the declamatory recitative used for narration, and the more florid, melodious aria intended for personal expression. Florence, Italy, was the home of early opera, but the genre soon spread to Mantua, Rome, Naples, and Venice, and then north of the Alps. What began as a small-scale courtly experiment in Florence within fifty years had become a large-scale public spectacle. The opening of public theaters for opera in Venice in the 1630s accelerated the growing tendency to turn the operatic spotlight entirely upon the aria and the star singers. By 1650 the framework for Baroque opera was fully in place involving: (1) a multi-act, fully sung drama setting either a mythological or historical subject, and (2) a clear distinction between recitative and aria. Already by mid-century the balance of power within the opera theater was beginning to shift, with less importance placed on the composer and more on the star singers.

KEY TERMS

opera	Orpheus legend	simple recitative
libretto	*Le nuove musiche*	arioso style
Florentine camerata	toccata	aria
stile rappresentativo	recitative	strophic variation aria

Chapter

31

The Concerted Style in Venice and Dresden

Venetia, Venetia, chi non ti vede non ti pretia! This sixteenth-century proverb can roughly be translated as: To appreciate Venice, you have to see it! The proverb is still true today. Venice remains a fantasyland of maze-like walkways and exotic buildings, all perched precariously above the waters of a lagoon. Venice was formerly a republic directed by a Doge (duke or chief magistrate) and an oligarchy of leading families. By 1630 the city had a population of 102,000 and was already a mecca for tourists and spies. Visitors came in search of the exotic, the foreign (the city enjoyed a thriving trade with the Near East), and the forbidden (prostitution and gambling flourished). They also came for the music. From the late 1630s onward, opera held sway at several opera houses during carnival season (see Chapter 30). By mid-century, 144 organs could be found in 121 different churches. Religious music in churches, civic music in processions of the Doge, and, later, public concerts at orphanages for females could be heard year-round.

The focus of civic and spiritual life in Venice, then and now, was the **basilica of St. Mark,** where the bones of the Evangelist Mark were believed to be buried. Because St. Mark's served as the chapel of the Doge, the political leader, it functioned as the goal of processions on occasions of state as well as religious festivals. St. Mark's has an architectural plan unique among the major churches of the West. It is built in the form of an equal-sided Greek cross, likely because in its early history Venice had strong ties to the Byzantine Empire in the East.

Beginning in the mid sixteenth century, Venetian musicians exploited the unusual architectural plan of St. Mark's by composing **cori spezzati**—literally "broken choirs," music for two, three, or four choirs placed in different parts of a building. At first these separate ensembles at St. Mark's were situated in the two choir lofts to the left and right of the main aisle (Fig. 31-1). Later, on days of special ceremonial importance, they were also stationed in other elevated galleries that adjoined the central dome. By positioning musicians in groups at points around the central axis of the church, the authorities of St. Mark's created something akin to multiphonic

🌿 FIGURE 31-1

A view of singers in a gallery at St. Mark's Basilica drawn by Canaletto in the eighteenth century. A matching gallery for musicians was at the opposite side of the church.

Bridgeman Art Library

surround sound for special, festive motets. Into these musicians' galleries crowded not only singers, but instrumentalists as well.

Seventeenth-century Venice was at the forefront of technology. The city was the European center for printing generally, and for music printing in particular, as well as for shipbuilding, glass production, and the fabrication of musical instruments. Recorders, shawms, cornetts, sackbuts, viols and violins, harpsichords, and clavichords were all produced in Venice for use there or for export to other cities in Italy and north of the Alps. The tradition of polychoral religious music at St. Mark's joined happily with the civic interest in musical instruments to foster a new style of music, the concerted style.

Stile concertato is Italian for "concerted style." It is a term broadly used to identify Baroque music marked by grand scale and strong contrast, either between voices and instruments, between separate instrumental ensembles, between separate choral groups, or even between soloist and choir. Our term "concerto" derives from the same word and has the same connotation, "to act together," perhaps within the spirit of friendly competition. The first publication that employed the word "concerto" was printed in Venice in 1587: *Concerti . . . continenti musica di chiesa* (*Concertos . . . containing church music*). The church music contained herein was the creation of two organists and composers at St. Mark's, Andrea Gabrieli (1533–1585) and his nephew Giovanni. A clear example of the concerted style can be seen in Example 31-1, the beginning of a polychoral *Gloria* by Giovanni Gabrieli. Here simple chordal units create an echo-like effect. Generally speaking, the composers at St. Mark's and other large Baroque churches avoided complex counterpoint and quick harmonic changes in favor of short units of homophonic declamation in which the text is clearly audible. Textual clarity is particularly important in a large, stone building such as St. Mark's which, then and now, has "muddy" acoustics.

EXAMPLE 31-1

And peace on earth…

GIOVANNI GABRIELI AND THE CONCERTED MOTET

Giovanni Gabrieli (c1554–1612) was among the first composers fully to exploit the sonic opportunities afforded by the architecture of St. Mark's. Gabrieli had studied with Lassus in Munich and knew well the tradition of the expressive Latin motet. Yet, as a native of Venice, he was intimately familiar with the Doge's windband of cornetts and trombones, as well as the newly emerging violin. In his *Sacrae symphoniae* (*Sacred Symphonies*, 1597), Gabrieli became the first composer in the history of music to indicate dynamic levels in a musical score. Specifically, his *Sonata pian e forte* requires the instruments to play soft and loud at various times; one four-voice choir of cornett and trombones alternates with another of violin and trombones in short bursts of louds and softs. Gabrieli was also one of the first composers to use the term "sonata" (for more on the sonata, see Chapter 33). One sonata by Gabrieli, published posthumously in 1615, is scored for twenty-two separate instrumental parts (mostly violins, cornetts, and trombones), plus basso continuo. For the early seventeenth century, this was a large-scale orchestra.

Giovanni Gabrieli was also the first composer to write idiomatically for particular instruments and specify the instruments in the score. In his motet *In ecclesiis* (*In the Churches*), which appeared in the second volume of *Sacred Symphonies* (1615), he explicitly stipulates the makeup of three separate ensembles: choir 1, an instrumental sextet requiring violin, three cornetts, and two trombones; choir 2, a group of four solo voices (soprano, alto, tenor, and bass); and choir 3, a four-voice chorus covering the same parts. To this is added a basso continuo played by the organ and perhaps a bassoon. Because the concertato style is evident everywhere in the motet *In eclesiis*, we call it a **concerted motet.** Gabrieli assigned the soloists (choir 2) difficult parts, often with long melismas. To the chorus (choir 3) he gives a completely different kind of music: merely a chordal refrain on the word "Alleluia," a sign of collective rejoicing. The instruments (choir 1) have their own timbre, one distinct from the voices. Sometimes they play entirely by themselves, while at others they merely double the vocal parts; sometimes the instruments insert their own lines independent of the voices. When this occurs, a highly complex texture results with fourteen independent musical strands. *In ecclesiis* is a concerted motet full of luxuriant sounds designed to make more splendid one of the grand occasions of state that culminated beneath the domes of St. Mark's.

LISTENING CUE

GIOVANNI GABRIELI
In ecclesiis (c1612)

CD 4/8
Anthology, No. 83

CLAUDIO MONTEVERDI AND THE CONCERTED MADRIGAL

We have met Monteverdi twice before, first as a creator of a new-style madrigal at the end of the Renaissance (see Chapter 28), and then as the main progenitor of a new musical genre, opera (see Chapter 30). To this might be added the fact that in 1610 he composed a spectacular *Vespers* that brought the new dramatic style into the church. Herein lies the important point: Claudio Monteverdi, more than any other composer, set the standard for early Baroque music. First in Mantua and then in Venice, he led the avant-garde toward the creation of new musical genres and styles.

Monteverdi moved to Venice in 1613 to succeed Giovanni Gabrieli as the principal composer of the basilica of St. Mark. His new job required him to compose religious works and to oversee the performance of music generally in the church. After three years his superiors were pleased with Monteverdi's work. They extended his contract for ten years into the future at an annual salary of 400 ducats (he earned another 200 from freelance work fulfilling commissions from other Venetian churches). The extension was offered, so the contract stipulated, in order to assure that Monteverdi "live and die in the service [of this church]." And this is precisely what happened. Monteverdi served as *maestro di cappella* at St. Mark's until his death in 1643 at the age of seventy-six.

Sadly, most of the music Claudio Monteverdi composed for St. Mark's has been lost. It existed only in manuscript copies. By contrast, Monteverdi's secular music, intended for the large domestic market, was published and thus survives mostly intact. In all, Monteverdi wrote nine books of madrigals; the first five date from his years in Mantua, and the last four from his time in Venice. In the earlier madrigals, five voices sing continually with a uniform texture from beginning to end (see *Cruda Amarilli,* Chapter 28). In the later Venetian madrigals, however, instruments appear, and textures and timbres are strongly contrasting; all are characteristics of the **concerted madrigal.**

The concerted madrigal appears most prominently in Monteverdi's eighth book (1638). He entitled the collection *Madrigali guerrieri, et amorosi* (*Madrigals of War and Love*). Indeed, most of the pieces are about love and battles of the heart. In his preface Monteverdi says:

> I have come to realize that the principal passions or affections of our mind are three: anger, moderation, and humility; so the best philosophers declare. The very nature of our voice suggests this by having a high, low, and middle range. The art of music also points clearly to these three emotions in its terms "agitated," "soft," and "moderate" [*concitato, molle,* and *temperato*]. In all the works of earlier composers I have found examples of the "soft" and the "moderate," but never of the "agitated," a type of music nevertheless described by Plato in the third book of his *Republic* in these words: "Create a harmony that would fittingly imitate the words and accents of a brave man who is engaged in warfare."[1]

In other words, Monteverdi intends to create a new style of music, **stile concitato** (the agitated style), one particularly suited to warlike music. In truth, there had been martial music earlier during the Renaissance, but Monteverdi's agitated warlike music is more direct and insistent. To create it, he tells us, he simply took whole notes and divided them into machine gun–like short notes—sixteenth notes all firing on the same pitch.

The madrigal *Hor che 'l ciel e la terra* (*Now that the heavens and earth*) from the eighth book shows clearly how Monteverdi incorporates *stile concitato* to create bellicose sounds. It is scored for six voices, two violins, and basso continuo. The text is by the venerable Francesco Petrarch (see Chapters 13 and 14), a favorite poet of madrigal composers. It speaks of a quiet night, when the heavens, the earth, and the sea are calm; yet the lover battles the pains of unrequited love. He is both lover and warrior, supple yet violent. At the words "War is my state, full of rage and pain" (Ex. 31-2), Monteverdi unleashes a barrage of notes in *stile concitato,* continually repeating the word "guerra" (war).

EXAMPLE 31-2

War, war, war is my state…

Monteverdi's *Hor che 'l ciel e la terra* is both old and new. By 1638 the madrigal as a genre was then a hundred years old and at the end of its history. Monteverdi's attempt to capture a particular emotion (agitation) following the dictates of Plato is the last gasp of the Renaissance humanists who sought to re-create the affective powers of ancient Greek music. On the other hand, there is much here in the modern Baroque style. In this Baroque concerted madrigal, a basso continuo supports the voices, and here there are two violins as well. Not only do the violins accompany the voices, they also play independently from time to time. Most important, there is strong textural contrast as is typical of the concerted madrigal. All six voices begin and end in chordal harmony. Along the way we hear a duo alternate with interjections from the full chorus, as well as a four-voice chorus set in opposition to a six-voice one. Most striking is the moment when the two violins take charge in *stile concitato* on the word "guerra" ("war"). In this late madrigal by Monteverdi, the coolly uniform texture of the Renaissance gives way to the opulent sonic variety of the Baroque.

LISTENING CUE

CLAUDIO MONTEVERDI
Hor che 'l ciel e la terra (1638)

CD 4/9
Anthology, No. 84

❀ BARBARA STROZZI AND THE EARLY BAROQUE CANTATA

The life of Barbara Strozzi (1619-1677) shows yet another aspect of the colorful world of seventeenth-century Venice: the cultured literary salon where chamber music flourished. Barbara Strozzi (Fig. 31-2) was the illegitimate daughter of Giulio Strozzi, a merchant, diplomat and noted poet who provided texts for Monteverdi, among others. Barbara studied music with opera composer Francesco Cavalli (see Chapter 30) and began to compose herself. In 1637 her father Giulio founded a literary society called the Accademia degli Unisoni (Academy of the Like-Minded) to showcase his daughter's musical skills. Intellectual academies for males only (as was the custom at this time) were popular in Italy because they offered a place to debate the social, moral, and artistic issues of the day. The minutes of the Academy of the Like-Minded show that Barbara sang at their meetings as well as suggested topics that the members of the club might debate. In all, she published eight volumes of vocal music, mostly solo madrigals, arias, and cantatas with basso continuo.

Whereas opera was the dominant form of theatrical music of the Baroque era, the cantata became the primary genre of vocal chamber music. The word **cantata** literally means "something sung," as opposed to the sonata, "something sounded" or played on an instrument. Because it was usually performed before a select group of listeners in a private residence, this genre is called the **chamber cantata** (see also Chapter 32). In the seventeenth century the Italian cantata was usually a piece of accompanied solo vocal music that most often dealt with a secular topic: tales of unrequited love, stories from ancient history and mythology, or discussions of the pressing moral issues of the day. (Later, Bach and his fellow German composers would transform the cantata into a religious work for the church; see Chapter 40.) The cantata grew out of, and ultimately replaced, the monodic madrigal of the early seventeenth century. A solo madrigal will typically last three to four minutes, but a cantata by Barbara Strozzi or one of her contemporaries usually runs eight to twelve minutes or even more. The greater length of the cantata is caused by its sectional design, one in which singing in aria, recitative, and arioso style can come in any order. A single work could thus encompass more moods, or points of view. Aria, recitative, and arioso style yield to one another almost imperceptibly. In fact, a flexible mixture of the three styles typifies the cantata of 1620 to 1680. To hold the various sections together—to bring unity to the cantata—composers of the mid seventeenth century often employed a repeating bass line, or *basso ostinato*.

In Italian "*ostinato*" is the word for someone or something obstinate, stubborn, or even pigheaded. Thus a **basso ostinato** is a bass line that insistently repeats, note for note. Seventeenth-century musicians favored short patterns that had fanciful-sounding names such as *passamezzo antico*, *folia*, *passacaglia*, and *ciaconna*. Above these popular bass lines composers wrote vocal and instrumental variations (much like composers do today above the blues pattern). The beloved English ballad *Greensleeves* is built above a repeating *passamezzo antico*, and from the pen of Corelli we have a well-known violin piece above a repeating *folia* bass.

FIGURE 31-2

A portrait of Barbara Strozzi painted in the 1630s by Bernardo Strozzi, perhaps a relative.

EXAMPLE 31-3

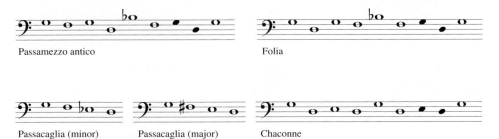

Passamezzo antico

Folia

Passacaglia (minor)   Passacaglia (major)   Chaconne

The *ciaconna* (called *chaconne* in French) and *passacaglia,* both of Spanish origin, originally were separate and distinct bass melodies. But during the seventeenth century the distinction between them began to blur. The two terms came to be used indiscriminately to indicate almost any repeating bass pattern of short duration.

Just how a *basso ostinato* might provide a unifying structure within a lengthy cantata can be seen in Barbara Strozzi's *L'Amante Segreto: Voglio morire* (*The Secret Lover: I wish to die*) from her collection *Cantate, ariette e duetti* of 1651. Here a four-note descending *passacaglia* bass regulates the flow of most of the piece. Such descending tetrachordal figures, almost always in triple meter, are common in the Baroque period. Most often they are associated with pain, tears, and lamentation. Accordingly, such a tetrachordal *ostinato* is called a **lament bass.** (We will encounter it again in Dido's Lament by Purcell and in the "Crucifixus" of the B-Minor Mass by Bach.) Here the "Secret Lover" cannot reveal his feelings to his beloved, and wishes to die. An aria-like vocal line spins out the lover's despair above the repeating bass in the basso continuo (Ex. 31-4a). Yet periodically, the aria and supporting *ostinato* stop and a passage of declamatory recitative appears so as to move the "plot" along (Ex 31-4b). This is typical of the early Baroque cantata by Strozzi and her contemporaries: triple-meter arias alternate with duple-meter recitatives. Thus in a cantata, *stile concertato* is effected not so much by alternating units of contrasting timbres, but rather by changing to distinctly different vocal styles. What Barbara Strozzi has created is a variegated showpiece for soprano voice.

EXAMPLE 31-4A

I wish to die...

EXAMPLE 31-4B

As if she wished to say "Reveal, reveal your pain,"...

LISTENING CUE

BARBARA STROZZI   CD 4/10
L'Amante Segreto: Voglio morire (1651)   Anthology, No. 85

THE CONCERTED STYLE MOVES NORTH: HEINRICH SCHÜTZ IN DRESDEN

Venice is only 225 miles from Munich, Germany, about the same distance it is from Rome. Indeed, as the northern-most large Italian city, Venice had frequent commerce—musical and otherwise—with the German and Austrian cities to the north.

Most important among these were Munich, Dresden, and Vienna. Monteverdi dedicated his eighth book of madrigals to the Holy Roman Emperor in Vienna, as did Barbara Strozzi her *Cantate* of 1651. Musicians from Italy went north to study, and vice versa. Both Andrea and Giovanni Gabrieli had gone to Munich to sit at the feet of Lassus in the 1560s and 1570s. Yet in the next generation, the most promising German composer, Heinrich Schütz, came to Venice to study, first with Gabrieli and again later with Monteverdi. When he returned to the court of Dresden, Germany, in 1629, Schütz carried with him seven cornetts of various sizes and numerous collections of Italian music. Paintings, too, flowed north from Italy. Today one of the finest holdings of Italian art of the Renaissance and Baroque is in the former court collection in Dresden, including the famous portrait of Barbara Strozzi (see Fig. 31-2). Similarly, the equally renowned portrait of Monteverdi (see Fig. 28-2) found a home in Innsbruck, Austria. Paintings, instruments, music, musicians, and musical styles—the concerted style in particular—moved from Italy to German-speaking lands during the first half of the seventeenth century.

Heinrich Schütz (1585–1672) was among the first of a long line of seventeenth- and eighteenth-century composers who made their way to Italy to learn the Italian style (Handel and Mozart would follow). Schütz, who came from the area of central Germany not far from Dresden, had shown musical talent as a youth. Consequently, a patron sent him to study with the renowned master Gabrieli in Venice. As Schütz later recounted:

> Since at that time a very famous if elderly musician and composer [Giovanni Gabrieli] was still alive in Italy, I was not to miss the opportunity of hearing him and gaining some knowledge from him. And the aforementioned Princely Highness ordered that a yearly stipend of 200 thalers be presented to me for the journey. Then (being a young man, and eager to see the world besides) I quite willingly accepted the recommendation with submissive gratitude, whereupon I set out for Venice in the year 1609, against my parents' wishes [they intended a career in law for young Schütz].[2]

After two years of tuition with Gabrieli, Schütz published the fruits of his study (a book of madrigals in Italian) and then returned to Germany.

In 1615 Schütz joined the chapel of the Elector[†] of Saxony in Dresden, then the largest musical institution in the largest city in Germany. By 1621 he had been appointed **Kapellmeister**—chief of music at court, the German equivalent of *maestro di cappella* (chapel master) in Italy. The job required that he supervise the selection and performance of the singers and instrumentalists, and oversee the education and musical preparation of the choirboys. Schütz also began to publish sacred music for the court, but his professional activities were severely hindered by the wars of religion that swirled around Saxony, specifically the Thirty Years' War.

The **Thirty Years' War** (1618–1648) was one of the great conflicts in the history of early-modern Europe. It consisted of a series of declared and undeclared wars fought essentially between the Protestants and the Catholics over political control—and religious dominance—in central Europe. On one side were the Protestants, led by the northern German princes and the king of Sweden. Arrayed against them were the Catholic forces of southern Germany and Austria, led by the Holy Roman Emperor. Hostility quickly grew into a "world war," or at least "pan-European war," as France and Denmark joined the Protestants and Spain aided the Catholic Emperor. Saxony, with Dresden as its capital, was politically and geographically caught in the

---

[†]In German history, an elector was one of nine powerful princes with the right to vote in the election to choose the Holy Roman Emperor.

middle. Musical institutions at Dresden and elsewhere in Germany were devastated. Schütz himself began to write for smaller musical forces, fearing there were no German ensembles left capable of performing fully concerted scores for voices and instruments. Even as Kapellmeister, his own salary often went unpaid.

Schütz's publications reflect these troubled times. Two early collections of polychoral motets, *Psalmen Davids* (1619) and *Symphoniae sacrae* Part I (1629), are large-scale works. But his *Kleine geistliche Konzerte* (*Little Sacred Concertos*; 1639 and 1641), written during the middle of the Thirty Years' War, suggests that only reduced forces were now available. Around the end of the war, however, Schütz was hopeful enough to publish large-scale works, specifically his *Symphoniae sacrae* Parts II and III (1647 and 1650). Schütz composed vocal music almost exclusively, most of it setting German texts. His religious music is most often not in the Latin of the Roman Catholic Church but in the German of the Protestant Church—Dresden and its court adhered to the Lutheran doctrine. Schütz was also the first composer to write an opera in German, specifically his *Dafne* (now lost) of 1627. In 1629 Schütz undertook a second trip to Venice, this time to study with Monteverdi, the master of the opulent Venetian style in general and early opera in particular. There, to quote his own words, Schütz learned "fresh devices" used by the newest Venetian composers "to tickle the ears of today."

Schütz's knowledge of the dramatic conventions of opera and the Venetian concerted motet can be seen in his *Saul, Saul, was verfolgst du mich?* (*Saul, Saul, Why doest thou persecute me?*). Published in 1650 as part of the *Symphoniae sacrae* Part III, Schütz's motet sets five short lines from the New Testament book of Acts (26:14–18). Here the Bible recounts how Christian-persecutor Paul, addressed by the Hebrew name Saul, was confronted on his way to Damascus, Syria; a blast of divine light knocks him dumb. The voice of Jesus asks:

> Saul, Saul, why doest thou persecute me? It is hard for thee to kick against the pricks . . . [go preach to] the Gentiles, unto whom now I send thee, to open their eyes, and to turn them from darkness to light, and from the power of Satan unto God.

Saul converts to Christianity, adopts the Christian name Paul, and goes on to write the New Testament epistles (letters) attributed to him. Painters of the early Baroque, among them Caravaggio (Fig. 31-3), were fond of depicting this scene with strong contrasts of light and dark to emphasize this dramatic moment of divine illumination.

Dramatic contrast also lies at the heart of Schütz's motet. A choir of six soloists is set against two four-voice choruses. Two violins and a basso continuo of organ and double bass are the only instruments specified, though others such as cornetts and trombones could double the two choruses if they were available. Throughout the score, the texture switches quickly among passages in *cori spezzati*, monody, and six-voice concerted madrigal style. Equally important, Schütz employs dynamic markings of *forte*, *piano*, *mezzopiano*, and *pianissimo*. As we have seen, his teacher in Venice, Giovanni Gabrieli, was the first to

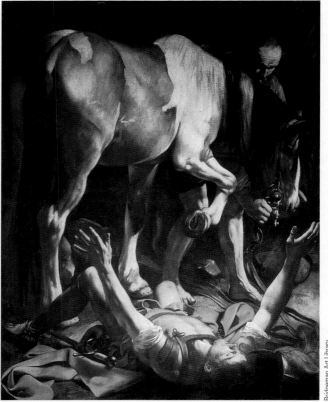

🌿 FIGURE 31-3

Caravaggio, *Conversion of Saint Paul*, 1601. Caravaggio's depiction of Saul's transformation on the road to Damascus uses stark contrast between light and dark to suggest a ray of divine revelation coming from above. This sort of dramatic juxtaposition is typical of both Baroque art and music.

include dynamic markings in a musical score. At the very end of *Saul*, Schütz removes the double choruses and asks the soloists to conclude by singing in succession *forte*, *mezzopiano*, and finally *pianissimo*. Clearly, his intent was to end the motet with a *diminuendo*, even though in 1650 there was no musical term or sign for this effect. Thus not only by alternating vocal and instrumental forces but also by the use of different dynamic levels does Schütz masterfully re-create the dramatic conversion of Saul/Paul on the road to Damascus.

LISTENING CUE

HEINRICH SCHÜTZ
Symphoniae sacrae (1650)
Saul, Saul, was verfolgst du mich?

CD 4/11
Anthology, No. 86

SUMMARY

In the early Baroque a new musical style developed, *stile concertato*. The concerted style employed distinctly separate units of voices and instruments to create vivid contrasts. Composers applied the concerted style to several different genres of music, most notably to the motet and madrigal. The solo chamber cantata also developed at this time, but here the concerted style was less pronounced because no chorus was involved. St. Mark's Basilica was the epicenter of musical life in Venice. The polychoral concerted motets of Gabrieli and Monteverdi exploited the particular acoustics of the church. The concerted madrigal and cantata, however, were intended for homes of the well-to-do and the literary academies that enlivened Venetian life.

By 1650 the musical tide had fully turned around. During the Renaissance, northern composers such as Dufay and Josquin brought the newest styles of learned art music to Italy; during the Baroque, however, Italian musicians became the leaders, and they carried the Italian style northward across the Alps. Thus the progressive Venetian concerted style of Gabrieli and Monteverdi made its way to Germany, specifically to the important court centers in Dresden and Vienna. The culmination of the concerted style north of the Alps can be found in the dramatic polychoral works of Heinrich Schütz, Kapellmeister to the Elector at Dresden.

KEY TERMS

basilica of St. Mark	*stile concitato*	*passacaglia*
cori spezzati	cantata	lament bass
stile concertato	chamber cantata	Kapellmeister
concerted motet	*basso ostinato*	Thirty Years' War
concerted madrigal	*ciaconna* (*chaconne*)	

Religious Music in Baroque Rome

Rome is a city of churches. It is also the home of the largest single organized church in the world, the Roman Catholic Church, which numbers approximately 700 million adherents. So important is the Catholic Church to Rome that it occupies its own nation-state, the Vatican, in the middle of the city. Here resides the pope as well as the numerous cardinals and other officials who direct the affairs of the Church. Within the Vatican are the Sistine Chapel, an interior sanctuary serving the pope, as well as the larger and more public St. Peter's Basilica. St. Peter's, by far the largest church in the world, provides a gathering place for thousands of the faithful during moments of extraordinary religious display. As is true for most of the largest churches in Rome, St. Peter's was completed during the Baroque era. By 1650 the city already possessed no fewer than 250 churches—basilicas such as St. Peter's, parish churches, chapels, and oratories, as well as numerous monasteries and convents.

Naturally, this concentration of religious institutions led to an emphasis on religious art and music. As nowhere else, art and music in Baroque Rome was overwhelmingly sacred, and the men who sponsored it were predominantly high-ranking church officials, specifically the pope and his attending cardinals. In truth, the papacy was very much a family affair. During the first half of the seventeenth century, for example, cultural life in Rome was dominated by Pope Urban VIII (1623–1644) and his three nephews. Urban appointed two of these nephews cardinals—hence the term "nepotism," from the Italian "*nipote*" for "nephew." This unique situation—family sponsorship of almost all high culture in the name of the Church—led to styles of sacred music particular to Rome as well as to one new musical genre, the sacred oratorio.

Art and music in seventeenth-century Rome expressed the spirit of the **Counter-Reformation,** the Church's aggressive response to the Protestant Reformation (for the Counter-Reformation in the Renaissance, see Chapter 25). The Catholic reformers purified the sanctuary by banning secular tunes and painting over nudity in religious art, and they limited corruption by curtailing the sale of indulgences (payment of money for remission of sin). Yet the Counter-Reformation Church also clung to the traditional Catholic practices: the centralization of power in Rome, celibacy for the clergy, a limited role for women, the veneration of images, and the continued support of monasteries and convents. The newly strict Church also strengthened the Inquisition (a Church court with the power of imprisonment) and imposed censorship by means of the Index of Prohibited Books. To foster the teachings of the Church, the popes promoted the work of a relatively new religious order, the **Jesuits.** Jesuit priests established colleges to impart a sense of a true Catholic life by means of education. Today, the Jesuit rule is still the principal sponsor of Catholic universities in the United States and around the world.

By the 1620s the Catholic Church had achieved something of a victory. Territory north of the Alps was no longer being lost to the Protestants, and some regions had even been reclaimed for the Church of Rome. A mood of triumph and celebration came over the Eternal City. Colleges and large churches sprang up everywhere. Into a few large churches on the high feast days went groups of musicians, sometimes as many as a hundred and fifty of them. Taking the largest view, music in Baroque Rome can be seen as belonging to one of three distinctly different types:

(1) a conservative style of vocal polyphony called *stile antico* (the old or traditional style) sung by the papal chapel; (2) a newer style of concerted music intended for a few vast churches and called "the colossal Baroque"; and (3) a highly progressive style in which the innovations of opera (aria and recitative) were manifest in sacred operas, oratorios, and cantatas.

❀ THE *CAPPELLA PONTIFICIA SISTINA* AND THE *STILE ANTICO*

During the seventeenth century, the pope's (pontiff's) private vocal ensemble came to be called the **cappella pontificia sistina** (papal Sistine Chapel). As the last name suggests, the home of this group was the Sistine Chapel, which had been constructed during the late fifteenth century (see Chapter 25). In 1625 there were thirty-four singers on the chapel's roster, and thus in principle about eight singers for each vocal part. All singers were male clerics, with the soprano and alto parts allocated about equally to both castrati and falsettists. Yet, despite these impressive numbers, rarely did the entire group perform at once. The long hours needed each day to sing through the lengthy cycle of the Mass and offices required that the singers perform in shifts, usually with no more than one on a particular vocal part.

The *cappella pontificia sistina* employed a distinctive mode of performance and a unique musical repertory. All music was vocal music sung *a cappella* (no instruments, not even the organ, participated). The core of the chapel's music was a conservative repertory centering on the compositions of Palestrina and others engaged at the Sistine Chapel during the Renaissance and early Baroque. This conservative style, at first called the *prima pratica*, emphasized imitative counterpoint and followed strict rules of sixteenth-century part writing. More recent composers of the chapel—among them Tomás Luis de Victoria (1548–1611), Felice Anerio (c1560–1614), Stefano Landi (1587–1639), and Gregorio Allegri (1582–1652)—perpetuated this traditional style well into the seventeenth century. Because the *prima practica* increasingly looked backward rather than forward, the conservative music emanating from the papal chapel came to be dubbed the **stile antico** (old or traditional style).

By far the most famous example of *stile antico* music written for the papal chapel is the *Miserere*, composed by Gregorio Allegri in 1638. In truth, were it not for his *Miserere*, Allegri would be virtually unknown today. But this one piece, a setting of Psalm 50 (*Miserere mei, Deus; Have mercy upon me, O Lord*), captivated the imagination of listeners for two hundred and fifty years, including the likes of Goethe, Mozart, Mendelssohn, Ralph Waldo Emerson, and Samuel F. B. Morse (the inventor of Morse Code). Allegri's *Miserere* owed its appeal to the unusual atmosphere in which it was performed in the Sistine Chapel. The Penitential Psalm *Miserere* was the musical high point of each of the three most solemn days of Holy Week: Maundy Thursday, Good Friday, and Holy Saturday. The morning offices of these three days were (and are still) called the **Tenebrae service** (Latin for "darkness"), because the service was sung in almost total darkness. To represent the blackness of the world in which the light of Christ had been extinguished, the candles around the chapel were blown out one by one, leaving the pope and his cardinals prostrate on the floor as the voices of the *cappella pontificia* resounded from on high. The effect of the *a cappella* singing of the castrati and falsettists, as reported by countless visitors, was an eerie, ghostly sound like no other.

Despite its fame, Allegri's composition is a rather simple piece that represents a type of music called **falsobordone.** *Falsobordone* originated in Spain and Italy around 1480. Like its earlier cousin *fauxbourdon* (see Chapter 16), *falsobordone* was at first an improvisatory technique used by church singers. In early *falsobordone,* three voices chanted along with the psalm tone to produce four-voice, root-position chords (Ex. 32-1), an easy way of making simple chant sound more splendid. By the seventeenth century, however, both the psalm tone and improvisation had been largely abandoned, resulting in a newly composed piece for four or even five voices, as can be seen in the opening of Allegri's *Miserere* (Ex. 32-2). The voices chanted in simple psalm-tone style employing root-position chords with slightly ornamented cadences.

EXAMPLE 32-1

The Lord said to my Lord, "Sit on my right [hand]."

EXAMPLE 32-2

Have mercy upon me, O Lord, according to thy great [mercy].

Ironically, the thing that made Allegri's *Miserere* famous was not included in his score: vocal ornamentation. To Allegri's simple *falsobordone* foundation, soloists added unwritten, but carefully calculated counterpoint. As the generations went by, the nature of the ornamentation changed, as did, in fact, Allegri's written score. Nevertheless, visitors to the Sistine Chapel—from musicians such as Mozart, Mendelssohn, and Liszt to writers like Goethe, Shelly, and Dickens—came to marvel at Allegri's *stile antico* music and the eerie beauty of the Tenebrae service.

Mozart Pirates Allegri's *Miserere*

The *cappella pontificia sistina* was a closed men's club. It was a private all-male singing group, controlled by the pope, which elected its own members and selected its own musical repertory. In general, the papal chapel sang only Gregorian chant approved by the pope or polyphony composed by its own members, past or present. After 1638 Allegri's *Miserere* became a popular favorite with the faithful throngs who crowded into the back of the Sistine Chapel to witness the Tenebrae service annually just before Easter. But Allegri's motet was never published or even copied outside the chapel itself. Successive popes banned its reproduction on pain of excommunication. By the eighteenth century, however, pirated editions had begun to leak out. One of those who secretly copied the *Miserere* was the 14-year-old Wolfgang Amadeus Mozart.

How much music can you retain on first hearing: three seconds, seven seconds, ten seconds? It all depends on the capacity of your musical ear and your ability to process and retain musical patterns—on your innate musical talent. Needless to say, Mozart possessed extraordinary talent and he was able to write down by memory the essentials of all of Allegri's *Miserere* during just one performance. Mozart and his father, Leopold, were in Rome in April 1770 and, like many tourists, went to the Sistine Chapel to observe the famous Tenebrae service culminating with Allegri's *Miserere*. But let Mozart's father tell the story:

> You have often heard of the famous *Miserere* in Rome, which is so greatly prized that the performers in the

chapel are forbidden on pain of excommunication to take away a single part of it, to copy it or to give it to anyone. But we have it already! Wolfgang has written it down and we would have sent it to Salzburg in this letter, if it were not necessary for us to be there to perform it. But the manner of performance [the ornamentation] contributes more to its effect than the composition itself. So we shall bring it home with us. Moreover, because it is one of the secrets of Rome, we do no wish to let it fall into other hands, lest we incur, directly or indirectly, the punishment of the Church.[1]

Mozart's sister adds that Wolfgang returned to the Sistine Chapel two days later, hiding his pirated copy in his hat, and made a few corrections to his score.

In truth, remarkable as Mozart's accomplishment was, it may not be quite as astonishing as it first appears. Although Allegri's setting of Psalm 50 can take eight to twelve minutes to perform, depending upon the tempo, it consists of fewer than thirty bars of original music: a five-part *falsobordone* section alternates with a four-voice *falsobordone* section, and between each of these come verses of monophonic chant (see Anthology, No. 87). The amount of original polyphonic music to be copied, in either five or four parts, runs about one minute and thirty seconds. In addition, because the *falsobordone* sections repeat in successive verses, Mozart had a chance to hear each polyphonic section five times. How much of the improvised ornamentation he tried to capture is anyone's guess.

LISTENING CUE

GREGORIO ALLEGRI
Miserere mei, Deus (1638)

CD 4/12
Anthology, No. 87

ST. PETER'S BASILICA AND THE COLOSSAL BAROQUE

A **basilica** is a special, grand church that happens not to be a cathedral (not the seat of a bishop). St. Peter's Basilica is special, of course, because on this site, directly below the high altar, are believed to be the bones of Peter, the Apostle, to whom Christ gave the authority to build the Church. Emperor Constantine had constructed a sanctuary on this site around 324 C.E., and a new, more magnificent building was begun in the sixteenth century. The central dome of the new St. Peter's, designed by Michelangelo, was completed in 1586; the nave and the great façade went up during the early decades of the seventeenth century. At the height of activity in 1611, more than eight hundred men worked at the site, sometimes at night by torchlight. Pope Urban VIII consecrated the structure in 1626, exactly one hundred years after the first cornerstone had been set. This was a triumphant moment for the Church. St. Peter's symbolized a newfound optimism of the clergy and people of Rome. The Counter-Reformation had purified the Church, and now its splendor could be revealed for all the world to see. St. Peter's was simply the largest visible symbol of this triumphant moment in Roman Church history.

Given its great size and acoustical resonance, it is in no way surprising that the music heard in St. Peter's was very different from that at the smaller Sistine Chapel. Indeed, the vast scale of the basilica invited composers to exploit size to achieve sonic magnificence. Accordingly, the musicians of St. Peter's, who formed an ensemble separate and independent from the singers of the Sistine Chapel, turned to large-scale compositions in the concerted style. Composers at St. Peter's—Paolo Agostini (c1583–1629), Virgilio Mazzocchi (1597–1646), and Orazio Benevoli (1605–1672), for example—wrote Masses and motets for as many as twelve choirs of voices and instruments. We have come to call this idiom of large-scale multiple-choir music for voices and instruments the **colossal Baroque.** Colossal Baroque church style usually involves four or more choirs, both answering each other and sometimes singing together in impressive tutti passages. Echoing units of choral sound provide the fundamental building blocks, and from these one or more solo voices occasionally emerge. This is concerted music, but concerted music on the largest possible dimension. For example, in 1639 musicians from St. Peter's and other choirs around Rome performed a work by Virgilio Mazzocchi, in honor of the patron saint. A contemporary reported that the piece was executed by "twelve or sixteen choirs"—apparently there were so many that it was impossible to count them all with confidence. Moreover, "an echo choir was placed at the top of the dome [and] in the space of that vast temple it was wonderfully effective." Obviously, Mazzocchi wished to achieve a heavenly effect by having at least one choir echo down from the top of Michelangelo's gigantic dome (Fig. 32-1). For this performance musicians stood on the floor, in the galleries above the floor, and on high in the cupola (dome). Instruments, specifically violins, cornetts, and trumpets, are reported in the dome as early as 1637. On these days honoring the patron saint, St. Peter, the church itself served as a giant resonator for both voices and instruments.

Unfortunately, little of the music in the style of the colossal Baroque survives. These were large pieces designed for specific events and usable within only a few specific churches. None of the large scores was ever published, and only a few manuscript copies are preserved. To get a sense of the sound of the colossal Baroque, therefore, we must turn to a Mass composed for the Catholic cathedral of Salzburg, Austria, where the colossal style had spread. This anonymous Mass, called simply the *Missa Salisburgensis* (*Salzburg Mass*), was first attributed to the Roman composer Orazio Benevoli of St. Peter's, and more recently to the German Heinrich Biber. Most likely, the Mass was composed in 1682 to celebrate the eleven-hundredth anniversary of the founding of the diocese of Salzburg. Despite

🌿 FIGURE 32-1

Interior of the dome of St. Peter's Basilica. This grand church, the largest in Christendom, was dedicated in 1626.

its likely Austrian origin, however, the *Missa Salisburgensis* arises from the spirit of the Roman colossal Baroque, because during the seventeenth century both the Roman musical style and musicians trained in Rome held sway at this Austrian church. A glance at the gigantic score (Anthology, No. 88) will show that the composer wrote for seven separate musical ensembles and a total of fifty-three independent parts. The choirs were placed around the church, with two trumpet groups somewhat removed from the singers.

To avoid creating a sonic muddle with so many different parts, the composer of the *Missa Salisburgensis* employed only a few basic chords and changed them only very slowly. Because large Baroque churches generally had a long **reverberation time** (the time it took the sound to die out), composers of the colossal Baroque style in particular avoided quick harmonic changes. Otherwise, the simultaneous reverberation of two different chords would yield a dissonance. Of necessity, then, the harmony of the *Missa Salisburgensis* is conservative and the counterpoint very basic. The sound, however, is simply magnificent.

LISTENING CUE

UNKNOWN
Kyrie of the *Missa Salisburgensis* (1682?)

CD 4/13
Anthology, No. 88

ORGAN MUSIC BY GIROLAMO FRESCOBALDI

Except at the Sistine Chapel, instruments usually accompanied choral singing in the larger Baroque churches. The primary church instrument was the organ, which sounded both by itself and with the singers, providing a basso continuo and helping to keep the voices on pitch. Owing to the city's intense religious activity, Rome had more church organs than any European city; at least two hundred organs had been installed by 1640, and individual organists owned numerous portative organs that they transported from church to church as needed.

The foremost organist in Rome during the first half of the seventeenth century was Girolamo Frescobaldi (1583–1643; Fig. 32-2). By the end of his life Frescobaldi was universally recognized as the greatest organ composer, not just in Italy but in all of Europe. Frescobaldi was born in Ferrara, but by as early as 1601 had moved to Rome. Here he remained, with few absences, for more than forty years. Like many organists today, Frescobaldi was employed at more than one church, and he combined an active career as a teacher with his work as a composer and performer. He also received income for being "musician in residence" to a succession of wealthy clerical patrons, notably Cardinal Francesco Barberini, nephew of Pope Urban VIII. Yet Frescobaldi's principal post, from 1608 until his death in 1643, was organist at St. Peter's Basilica.

As organist at St. Peter's, Frescobaldi performed at the massive displays of concerted polychoral music that marked the feasts honoring St. Peter. He also participated in the more usual music-making at the basilica, playing organ at Sunday and feast-day Masses. For these services, Frescobaldi would have regularly improvised music, such as toccatas, ricercars, and canzonas, to introduce or

 FIGURE 32-2

An engraving showing the likeness of Girolamo Frescobaldi. The inscription reads, "Girolamo Frescobaldi of Ferrara, organist of the basilica of St. Peter in the Vatican, thirty-six years of age."

Bridgeman Art Library

replace the choral singing during Mass. The organist might also alternate with the choir, playing a solo in place of the choral chant or polyphony. When the organ played alternate verses of the *Kyrie* or *Gloria,* for example, the result (see Chapter 24) was a performance using **alternatim technique.**

In 1635 Frescobaldi published a collection of Mass music to serve St. Peter's and other churches, his ***Fiori musicali*** (*Musical Flowers*). It includes organ music for Mass for most of the Sundays and feast days of the church year. Each Mass begins with an organ prelude, and is followed by an *alternatim* setting of the *Kyrie.* Then come other organ solos, in which the instrument replaces the choir in the Proper of the Mass. A Mass in which an organ alternates with, or entirely replaces, the choir is simply called an **organ Mass.** The heyday of the organ Mass was the seventeenth century, and Frescobaldi was its principal exponent.

For an example of an organ Mass from Frescobaldi's *Fiori musicali*, let us turn to the opening piece, the *Toccata avanti la Messa* (*Toccata before the Mass*). A **toccata,** as we have seen (see Chapter 30), is an instrumental work designed to show off the creative spirit of the composer as well as the technical skill of the performer. Although the term sometimes applies to pieces for other instruments, "toccata" most often signifies a freeform keyboard piece in which a "touching" of the keyboard is needed to demonstrate digital dexterity. The opening toccata of this particular organ Mass is shorter than most, being compressed into just thirteen measures (Ex. 32-3). Frescobaldi extended his keyboard figuration into the middle and lower ranges of the instrument, a far different practice from Renaissance keyboard music, in which the figuration is confined mostly to the highest register. Notice the two G sharps in this toccata (mm. 4 and 5) that pull toward the note (A) a fifth away from the home pitch (D); this is clear evidence of a growing awareness of what we today call functional tonality and secondary dominant chords.

EXAMPLE 32-3

A *Kyrie* using *alternatim* technique comes next, and here the organ plays the first verse and the choir chants the next, continuing thus through all nine verses of the *Kyrie*. Each independent organ section in an *alternatim* organ Mass is called an **organ verset,** a short piece that replaces a liturgical item otherwise sung by the choir. The organ versets in this *Kyrie* make use of *cantus firmus* technique; here (Ex. 32-4) the ancient *Kyrie* chant sounds in long notes, not in the tenor, but in the highest line.

EXAMPLE 32-4

Whereas the organ versets of the *Kyrie* employ an old technique from the Renaissance, the following organ ricercar is radically new. In this organ Mass, the ricercar replaces the Offertory usually sung by the choir. A **ricercar,** as we have seen (see Chapter 23), is an instrumental piece, usually for lute or keyboard, that is similar in style to the sixteenth-century imitative motet. Frescobaldi's newer ricercar, however, is very different from its sixteenth-century forebear. To begin with, it is monothematic. The composer has fashioned a single distinct subject and a countersubject (an important counterpoint to the subject; see Ex. 32-5, bar 3). Moreover, when the second voice imitates the subject at the interval of a fifth above, it changes the subject so as to keep the music in the home tonality, thus producing a **tonal answer** (Ex. 32-5, bar 3). Finally, the second section of the ricercar presents a new countersubject, which appears both in a normal and an inverted form. In every measure of this ricercar either the subject or a countersubject can be heard—a remarkably dense web of counterpoint. Developing a contrapuntal piece from a single subject and its countersubjects points directly toward the German fugue of the eighteenth century. In fact, J. S. Bach knew Frescobaldi's *Fiori musicali* well, for he obtained a manuscript copy as early as 1714 and kept it with him to the end of his life.

EXAMPLE 32-5

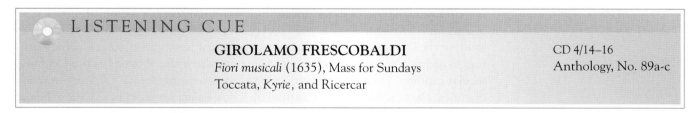

LISTENING CUE

GIROLAMO FRESCOBALDI
Fiori musicali (1635), Mass for Sundays
Toccata, *Kyrie,* and Ricercar

CD 4/14–16
Anthology, No. 89a-c

✽ SACRED OPERA AND ORATORIO: GIACOMO CARISSIMI'S *JEPHTE*

Rome was predominantly a city of religious music, but not exclusively. During the early seventeenth century, opera spread from its home in Florence to Mantua, Venice, Naples, and Rome. Traditional secular operas using plots drawn from classical mythology, such as Stefano Landi's *La morte d'Orfeo* (*The Death of Orpheus*, 1619), saw the light of day in Rome. Even comic opera had a hearing, as evidenced by *Chi soffre speri* (*Who suffers may hope*, 1637), an opera by Virgilio Mazzocchi and Marco Marazzoli based on a story by Boccaccio.

But opera in Rome was not like opera in other cities. First of all, Rome produced a far higher percentage of sacred, or Christian, operas. As early as 1600, Emilio de' Cavalieri's sacred music drama *Rappresentatione di Anima, et di Corpo* (*Representation of Soul and Body*) was performed in a Roman church. In 1631 Stefano Landi set to music a libretto treating the life of St. Alexis (*Il Sant'Alessio*); in subsequent years it was performed spectacularly at the palace of Cardinal Francesco Barberini in a huge hall seating three thousand spectators. Typical of Christian opera, the libretto for *Il Sant'Alessio* was written by a priest, Giulio Rospigliosi (1600–1669), who went on to become Pope Clement IX (1667–1669). In a way unique to Rome, most opera, secular or sacred, was sponsored by clergymen—usually not by the pope himself, but by his cardinals in their lavish palaces. Also peculiar to Rome was the absence of female singers; women were not allowed to appear on stage in Rome or in papally controlled lands (though they could do so in "extraterritorial" foreign embassies!). Thus, Roman opera usually made use of castrati and boys for the highest parts. Finally, religious scruples here as elsewhere dictated that opera, as with spoken drama, be heard during the festive season of carnival, but not during the solemn time of Lent.

To satisfy the Roman desire for dramatic music during Lent, patrons and musicians developed a new musical genre: **oratorio.** Conforming to the solemn tone of Lent, oratorio put away lavish sets, costumes, and choreography. The dramatic text, either in Italian or Latin, usually elaborated upon a story found in the Old Testament, one recounting a tale of sacrifice and self-denial concordant with the spirit of Lent. Oratorio differs from opera because the singers are not in costume and do not fully act out their dramatic roles. A narrator simply reports what happens. Nevertheless, the fundamental musical processes of opera—recitative, aria, and chorus—also animate oratorio. Choruses (even if sung by only one on a part) loom larger in oratorio than in opera, for the chorus often carries a moral message delivered by the people to the people.

As the Italian term "oratorio" suggests, an oratorio was performed in an **oratory,** a prayer hall set aside just for praying, preaching, and devotional singing. Each oratory in Rome was supported by a **confraternity,** a fraternal order emphasizing religious devotion and charity. The most prestigious Roman confraternity was that of the Most Holy Crucifix, a brotherhood of educated noblemen. Every Friday during Lent its members gathered in their oratory in the center of Rome to hear one or more oratorios, works often composed by Giacomo Carissimi.

Giacomo Carissimi (1605–1674) served for more than forty years as director of music at the German College in Rome, an important Jesuit institution of higher learning. In addition to Masses and motets, Carissimi also wrote about a hundred and fifty secular cantatas. He is remembered today, however, mainly for his fourteen surviving oratorios. Most are based on stories from the Old Testament recounting deeds of heroic characters such as David killing Goliath or Jonah escaping from the belly of the whale. Rather than simply quote verbatim from scripture, the text of an oratorio embroiders upon the story; a more elaborate text allowed for a more vivid musical setting.

Just how Carissimi might bring a biblical story to life can best be judged in his oratorio *Jephte* (c1648), which embellishes upon events in the Old Testament book of Judges 11. There are three principal characters, the *Historicus* (narrator), Jephte, and his nameless daughter, as well as a chorus representing the people of Israel. Jephte is the leader of the Israelites, about to do battle against the Ammonites. He promises

God that if victory be granted, he will sacrifice upon his return the first living creature to greet him. This welcomer proves to be his own daughter. Dutifully, the daughter retreats to the mountains to lament her fate and bravely commends her soul to God. Her willingness to sacrifice was meant to inspire every good Christian during Lent.

In mid seventeenth-century oratorio, just as in early opera, the distinction between vocal styles is not always clearly drawn. Generally speaking, simple recitative is used to report events, and arioso style (more expressive recitative) appears for moments of greater intensity, while the aria projects poetic texts of special beauty or feeling. This is true of the climax of *Jephte*, where the daughter's lamentation ("Plorate, colles") is in four sections, each beginning syllabically like a recitative, but ending with a long melisma, as might an aria. Also typical of an aria, the text is often repeated for rhetorical emphasis. At first the daughter repeats her own words, then voices from the chorus provide a mountain echo. The daughter's lamentation is followed by a choral treatment of the same subject ("Plorate, filii Israel"), one of the most beautiful choruses ever written. At the beginning the basses descend in a repeating tetrachord, or lament bass, the musical symbol of despair and suffering. Toward the end, however, they rise by step while the upper voices fall down in a chain of mournful suspensions (Ex. 32-6). Such beauty is timeless, and nearly a century later Handel "borrowed" Carissimi's music and made it serve in his own oratorio *Samson* (1743); the Latin words "Plorate, filii Israel" ("Weep, children of Israel") were simply changed to the English "Hear, Jacob's God."

EXAMPLE 32-6

★ = suspension

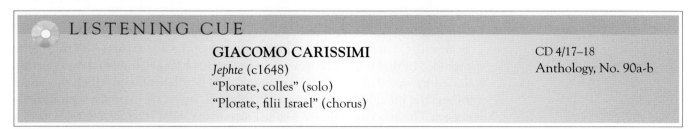

LISTENING CUE

GIACOMO CARISSIMI
Jephte (c1648)
"Plorate, colles" (solo)
"Plorate, filii Israel" (chorus)

CD 4/17–18
Anthology, No. 90a-b

❀ THE CHAMBER CANTATA: A CHRISTMAS CANTATA BY ALESSANDRO SCARLATTI

Late seventeenth-century Rome saw the culmination of the chamber cantata, a genre that had originated in northern Italy and is exemplified in the works of Barbara Strozzi (see Chapter 31). As the name suggests, a **chamber cantata** was performed for a select audience in a private residence. By the end of the century it consisted of a succession of movements for solo voice and accompaniment that alternated between rapid declamation (recitative) and florid song (aria). Most cantatas were in Italian and spoke of love, though some revisited events in Roman history and a few embraced sacred subjects. Compared to an opera or an oratorio, a chamber cantata usually required only a single voice, was accompanied only by basso continuo and a few strings at most, and incorporated only a small number of recitatives and arias. Thus, while an opera or oratorio might extend well beyond an hour, the briefer chamber cantata usually lasted no more than fifteen minutes. Owing to its brevity and concentration, it was customary for a cantata to be repeated several times to allow the audience to savor the poetry and the music. At the end of the seventeenth century no composer in Rome was more celebrated as a creator of chamber cantatas than Alessandro Scarlatti.

Alessandro Scarlatti (1660–1725) belonged to a large family of musicians and was himself the father of the famous keyboard composer Domenico Scarlatti (see Chapter 43). It is not entirely certain with whom Scarlatti studied, but by 1680 he had been appointed composer-in-residence to exiled Queen Christina of Sweden, an important Roman patroness. After her death in 1689, Scarlatti eventually assumed a similar role at the court of Cardinal Pietro Ottoboni, great-nephew of Pope Alexander VIII. With their support, Scarlatti progressed to become the leading composer of opera in Rome, and later in Naples.

Patrons such as Queen Christina and Cardinal Ottoboni sponsored not only operas and oratorios but also chamber cantatas. Cardinal Ottoboni had responsibility for arranging to have Christmas cantatas performed annually on Christmas Eve in the papal apartments at the Vatican. Here, between the celebration of Christmas Vespers and the midnight Mass, the pope and perhaps twenty-five guests enjoyed spiritual refreshment in the form of a Christmas cantata and then moved on to an abundant meal.

We do not know precisely when, where, or for whom Alessandro Scarlatti composed his beautiful Christmas cantata *Oh di Betlemme* (*O Bethlehem*), but surely it was written around 1700 for one of the patrician houses in Rome. In the surviving manuscripts the cantata is identified simply as a *Cantata pastorale. . . . per la Natale* ("Pastoral cantata . . . for the Nativity"). In this work, as in many of his more than six hundred cantatas, Scarlatti developed a new structure for the aria.

In the 1690s Alessandro Scarlatti established the *da capo* **aria,** a formal arrangement that would come to enjoy enormous popularity. The text of the aria, usually consisting of just a single stanza, was assigned to two contrasting musical sections, and at the end of the second the first would return exactly, thus producing **ABA** form. The reprise of **A,** of course, was not written out, but simply signaled by the inscription "*da capo*" (take it from the top or, literally, "from the head").

Scarlatti's *Oh di Betlemme* makes exclusive use of the *da capo* aria—all three arias are molded in that form. The cantata begins with a brief instrumental introduction followed by a recitative, "Oh di Betlemme" ("O Bethlehem"), in which the singer contrasts the humble former status of Bethlehem, site of the nativity, with its present glory. The aria that follows, "Dal bel seno d'una stella" ("From a fair bosom of a star"), sets only four lines of text; the first two evoke the image of the sun (and Son), while the third and fourth refer to the Virgin Mary. To form the *da capo* structure, Scarlatti simply allocates his music to the text in pairs of lines, as shown below. He then emphasizes the distinction between **A** and **B** in two ways: he shifts tonalities from D major to B minor (the relative minor), and he assigns an instrumental ritornello to section **A,** but not **B.** As the term suggests, an instrumental **ritornello** (refrain) is a distinctive musical phrase that comes at the beginning of the aria and returns frequently thereafter. Here, in the charming aria "Dal bel seno d'una stella," the instrumental ritornello, played by a solo violin, establishes a dialogue with the voice. Thus, in *Oh di Betlemme,* Alessandro Scarlatti shows clearly why he is important to the history of the Italian cantata and to vocal music generally: he established the form and style of the chamber cantata, which would remain the norm for this genre in the first half of the eighteenth century; and he crafted a particular musical form, the *da capo* aria, that would continue to be favored by composers of operas, oratorios, and cantatas to the very end of the Baroque era.

Dal bel seno d'una stella	**A**	From a fair bosom of a star
Spunta a noi l'eterno sole.		Rises for us an eternal sun.
Da una pura verginella	**B**	From a pure maiden
Nacque già l'eterna prole.		is born an eternal son.
Dal bel seno d'una stella	**A**	From a fair bosom of a star
Spunta a noi l'eterno sole.		Rises for us an eternal sun.

LISTENING CUE

ALESSANDRO SCARLATTI
Cantata *Oh di Betlemme* (c1700?)
Recitative, "Oh di Betlemme"
Aria, "Dal bel seno d'una stella"

CD 4/19–20
Anthology, No. 91a-b

SUMMARY

More than any European city, Rome was and is dominated by the Roman Catholic Church, and this simple fact accounts for the preeminence of religious music there. During the seventeenth century, at the end of the Counter-Reformation, the fortunes of the Church reached a high point, as symbolized by the completion of St. Peter's Basilica, consecrated in 1626. Generally, the size and function of the church determined the nature of the music to be performed. Three musical styles predominated: (1) a dignified, conservative style of vocal polyphony called *stile antico* (old or traditional style) sung by the papal chapel in the Sistine Chapel; (2) a harmonically conservative style of concerted polychoral music called the colossal Baroque that was intended for a few vast spaces such as St. Peter's Basilica; and (3) a highly progressive style in which the innovations of opera (aria and recitative) were manifest in sacred operas, oratorios, and cantatas, many of which were performed in private residences of aristocratic churchmen. Organ music, most notably that of Girolamo Frescobaldi, also grew in importance at this time as a way of providing sonic variety for what otherwise was a religious service of exclusively vocal music.

Opera was known in early seventeenth-century Rome, but Roman opera usually emphasized moral and especially Christian themes. The religious orientation of

Rome also contributed to the creation of oratorio, a new musical genre. Although oratorio made use of the same conventions as opera (recitative, aria, and chorus), its message was spiritual and its plot usually drawn from dramatic events of the Old Testament, as is the case of the oratorios of Giacomo Carissimi. The chamber cantata, too, involved neither costumes nor histrionics. A lone singer sang a succession of recitatives and arias, accompanied by a basso continuo and a few strings at most. Alessandro Scarlatti solidified the general form and style of the Italian cantata, as well as popularized *da capo* form, a structure that would become the norm for the late Baroque aria in cantata, oratorio, and opera alike.

KEY TERMS

Counter-Reformation	reverberation time	tonal answer
Jesuits	*alternatim* technique	oratorio
cappella pontificia sistina	*Fiori musicali*	oratory
stile antico	organ Mass	confraternity
Tenebrae service	toccata	chamber cantata
falsobordone	organ verset	*da capo* aria
colossal Baroque	ricercar	ritornello

Chapter 33

Instrumental Music in Italy

Instrumental music came into its own in the Baroque era. During the sixteenth century (late Renaissance) composers had written much instrumental music, and a variety of colorful instruments played it (see Chapter 23). Yet, not until the seventeenth century (early Baroque) did composers write for instruments in a truly idiomatic way, in a way that matched particular musical figures with the strengths of each separate instrument. Not until then was instrumental music printed in abundance. Indeed, during the seventeenth century, publishers began to issue as much instrumental music as vocal music, and by the eighteenth century, publishers' catalogues show a preponderance of instrumental music for sale. New instruments, new styles of playing, and new genres of pieces, including the sonata and concerto, all sprang forth during the seventeenth century.

The place of origin of these innovations was northern Italy (Map 33-1). Northern Italy saw the rise of the violin—the Baroque instrument *par excellence*. The first great violinmakers were all northern Italians and so, too, were most of the composers who satisfied the rapidly growing demand for music for this instrument. From northern Italy the violin and its music spread to the rest of Italy, and eventually to the rest of Europe as well.

THE VIOLIN FAMILY

As we have seen (see Chapter 23), the violin originated in the sixteenth century as a "low-class" instrument used for playing

MAP 33-1

Northern Italy in the seventeenth century.

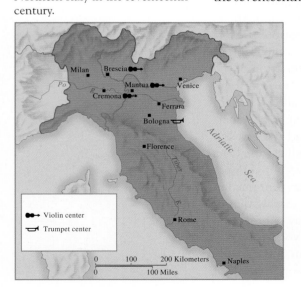

dance music in inns and taverns. Appearing first in such northern Italian towns as Cremona and Brescia, the violin quickly spread to larger northern cities like Mantua and Venice, and eventually south to Rome and Naples. **Cremona** is crucial to the development of the violin. Claudio Monteverdi, the first great composer to write consistently for the violin, was a native of the city. Here, too, were born and lived many of the great violin-makers, including Antonio, Girolamo and Nicolò Amati, and Pietro and Giuseppe Guarneri, as well as **Antonio Stradivari** (c1644–1737). Today instruments by these exceptional Cremonese artisans are so highly prized that they fetch millions of dollars at auction houses in London and New York.

All members of the violin family have four strings and are tuned in fifths, the violin g-d'-a'-e". Violas and cellos are simply larger-sized violins. The cello developed from an early bass violin called the *violone* (large bass violin) tuned B♭', F, c, g. After 1650 a somewhat smaller instrument, tuned C, G, d, a, became popular, so the diminutive expression "cello" was appended to *violone* creating "violoncello," or "small large bass violin," which we now abbreviate as "cello."

The double bass emerged only at the end of the seventeenth century. Its ancestor was not the violin, but the viol, and it retains to the present day two viol-like characteristics: it is tuned in fourths (rather than fifths, as with the violin, viola, and cello); and it is often played with an "underhand" viol bowing, not "overhand" as used for violin, viola, and cello. Then, as now, the double bass sounded an octave below written pitch, and usually doubled the cello an octave lower. By the end of the seventeenth century, the violin, viola, cello, and often the more distantly related double bass, had come to form the nucleus of the Baroque orchestra.

FORMATION OF THE BAROQUE ORCHESTRA

The symphony orchestra as we know it today had its origins in Italy during the seventeenth century. At its beginning, the early Baroque orchestra was something of a "mixed bag" of instruments. The ensemble accompanying Monteverdi's *Orfeo* (1607), for example, consisted of violins and viols, recorders, trumpets, cornetts, sackbuts (trombones), harpsichord, theorbo, harps, organ with metal pipes, and organ with reed pipes. It was an ensemble of soloists; players did not normally double on the same instrumental part. The sound was diverse and colorful, but not especially powerful.

After the mid seventeenth century, however, several instruments important in the Renaissance—viol, cornett, sackbut (trombone), shawm, and theorbo—began to lose favor.[†] In their place stepped forward the instruments of the violin family to form a core ensemble, and to this group other instruments were gradually added. As the seventeenth century progressed, composers came to specify oboes, bassoons, flutes, trumpets, and, last, horns along with the strings. A single harpsichord (or organ in church) gradually replaced the theorbo and other plucked string instruments as the provider of a chordal support in the basso continuo. By the end of the century more than one player—two, three or even four—might sometimes execute one and the same string part. Yet, even with some parts doubled, what resulted was

---

[†]The large *viola da gamba* remained popular into the eighteenth century as a bass instrument in ensembles and as a solo instrument. The shawm evolved into the modern oboe. The sackbut, generally called the trombone during the Baroque era and thereafter, continued to be heard in church music and provide special effects in the opera theater. It was not added to the symphony orchestra, however, until the time of Beethoven.

The Violin Then and Now

What makes a great violin? They all look remarkably similar, with a common shape and common features, characteristics that were established in the sixteenth century. But the type and place of origin of the wood chosen for the front (usually spruce) and the back (usually maple), the way the wood is cured and then carved, the way the pieces are assembled, the type of final varnish applied— these are just a few of the features that separate a superb instrument from a mediocre one. Antonio Stradivari was among the greatest of the Cremonese violinmakers. Some six hundred fifty Stradivari instruments survive today: violins, violas, cellos, and even guitars. Today professional virtuosos such as Joshua Bell or Midori are willing to pay millions of dollars for the magnificent sound of a Stradivari.

In truth, the Stradivari violin sold today in New York or London is not precisely the one Stradivari made; all Stradivari violins have been rebuilt and significantly modified over the centuries. The size and general shape of the Baroque and modern instruments are the same, but the Baroque violin had a shorter fingerboard, and thus could not play pitches as high as can the modern instrument (Fig. 33-1). The bridge was lower, in part because there was less tension placed on the strings. Strings were made of animal gut (often cat intestine) sometimes spun around with a thin thread of brass or silver wire for added resonance. The Baroque violin bow had a narrower band of horsehair and was under less tension than its modern counterpart. Finally, there was no chin rest in the seventeenth century, and the violin was often played off the shoulder rather than under the chin (Fig. 33-2). With gut strings and less tension on both instrument and bow, the Baroque violin had a light, clean sound, not nearly as loud and rich as that produced by the modern violin. The Baroque violin was prized because it could play rapidly and could clearly articulate the lively rhythmic patterns of the new Baroque style.

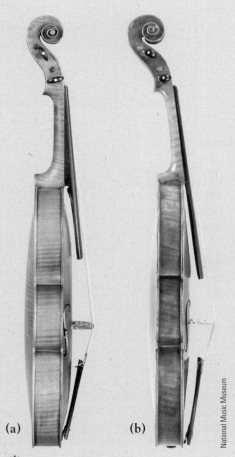

National Music Museum

(a)   (b)

❀ FIGURE 33-1
Baroque violin (a) compared to modern one (b), side view.

Elvehjem Museum of Art

❀ FIGURE 33-2
Young Man Playing a Violin, attributed to Pietro Paolini, c1620. Note that the instrument is played off the shoulder rather than under the chin.

a modest-size orchestra with no more than twenty-five players. By way of example: eighteen instrumentalists were on the payroll at the basilica of St. Mark in Venice in 1643; twelve were employed at the basilica of St. Petronio in Bologna about 1680. By contrast, King Louis XIV (r. 1643–1715) sometimes augmented his core of twenty-four string players to more than eighty for performances of court ballet and opera at Versailles, and Cardinal Ottoboni once employed an orchestra of a hundred to play for a sacred opera in Rome. These large orchestras, however, were very much the exception rather than the rule.

In sum, during the seventeenth century the instrumental ensemble gradually coalesced around the instruments of the violin family (violin, viola, and cello) with a low string instrument such as the double bass sometimes added. After mid-century, oboes and bassoons might also double the strings, and a trumpet sound forth for extra brilliance. Beneath them all was the basso continuo held together by a harpsichord or, in church, by an organ.

CHURCH AND CHAMBER MUSIC

Today we distinguish between orchestral music (music with more than one on a part played before a large audience) and chamber music (music with just one on a part played before a small audience). In the Baroque era, the line separating orchestral and chamber music was not as clearly drawn. Most instrumental ensemble music, regardless of the place of performance and size of the audience, was played by just one performer on each part. Similarly, the same sonata or sinfonia might be performed in a church accommodating several thousand or a salon seating only a handful of listeners.

In an age in which there were no public concert halls and few public opera houses, church and chamber were the only two venues for ensemble music. Indeed, in the second half of the seventeenth century, composers gradually began to identify music as **da chiesa** (of the church) and as **da camera** (of the chamber). Thus were born the *sonata da chiesa* and the *sonata da camera*. The chamber sonata was usually made up of a series of dance-like movements, each of which had the name and character of a particular dance such as allemande, courante, and gigue. The church sonata included fewer pieces with dance rhythms, and the titles of the movements were simply tempo markings such as *grave, adagio, allegro,* or *presto*; it was thought inappropriate to have the movements of a piece destined for the church associated with secular dances.

SALOMONE ROSSI AND THE EARLY BAROQUE SONATA

A **sonata** (something to be sounded) is a piece for a single instrument or small instrumental ensemble. The term was first used in Venice around 1600 to indicate a composition intended specifically to be played or sounded, as opposed to one that was to be sung (a cantata). At first a sonata might be written for four, five, or as many as twenty-two, instrumental parts. It consisted of a single movement, which often had distinct sections with different tempos and moods. Thus around 1600 there was little difference between an early-Baroque sonata and a late-Renaissance canzona. In the course of the seventeenth century, however, the sonata took on its own distinctive features and the canzona gradually disappeared. In brief, the sonata experienced a gradual reduction of the number of parts, leaving just the solo sonata and trio sonata (see below); simultaneously, it expanded from a single movement, with separate sections, to multiple movements. Two important figures in this development were Salomone Rossi and Arcangelo Corelli.

To learn that violinist Salomone Rossi (c1570–c1630) was a native of Mantua is not surprising; northern Italian cities such as Cremona, Brescia, and Mantua were among the first to embrace the newly popular violin. More remarkable is the fact that Rossi was a Jew who flourished within the Christian court of Duke Vincenzo Gonzaga at Mantua. Duke Vincenzo showed the esteem in which he held Rossi by exempting him from wearing the identifying yellow star, a requirement of most other Jews in Italy at this time. Not only did Rossi compose instrumental music for the Mantuan court, he also created *Hashirim asher lish'lomo* (*The Songs of Solomon*, 1622), the first print to set Hebrew texts to music. The intent of this collection of thirty-three polyphonic settings of Hebrew psalms and hymns was to provide music for the synagogues thriving within the strictly defined Jewish zones (ghettos) in northern Italian cities such as Ferrara, Mantua, and Venice. Nevertheless, it is not for his vocal music for the synagogue, but rather for his contribution to the instrumental sonata, particularly the trio sonata, that Rossi is today considered most influential.

Salomone Rossi published four collections of instrumental ensemble music in the early decades of the seventeenth century. In these he moves away from the instrumental canzona of the late Renaissance (see Chapter 23) with its four-voice imitative texture. Instead, Rossi prefers a top-bottom texture with a duet for two violins on top and a basso continuo below. He clearly was influenced by the lyrical vocal monody and duets that he heard in the operas and concerted motets of his colleague at Mantua, Claudio Monteverdi. Indeed, a flamboyant vocal style for one or two high instruments dominates Rossi's sonatas. Yet Rossi goes beyond this vocally inspired manner, adding dashing turns, quick repeated notes, and rapid runs to exploit the idiomatic capabilities of the violin; such figures can be played faster and cleaner on the violin than they can be sung. Supporting the acrobatic upper parts is a rock-solid basso continuo that clearly sets out the direction of the harmonies.

Typical of Rossi's early Baroque sonatas is his *Sonata sopra l'aria di Ruggiero* (*Sonata on the song Ruggiero*). *Ruggiero* was a popular tune of the late Renaissance that continued to fascinate learned composers well into the seventeenth century. It possessed not only a melody but also a distinctive bass pattern. In fact, it was one of several bass patterns of the early seventeenth century that often served as a *basso ostinato*, a bass line repeating over and over, above which the composer built a set of variations (see Ex. 31-3). Rossi's *Sonata sopra l'aria di Ruggiero* consists of eight variations upon the *Ruggiero* bass (Ex. 33-1), the last of which is repeated at a faster tempo. Most of Rossi's variations involve a rapid interplay between the two upper violins. At times, the growing competition between them leads to virtuosic display. However, at strategic points (the beginning, and beginnings of variations four and seven), Rossi inserts passages of longer note values that have the effect of creating a much slower tempo. This alternation of slow/fast/slow/fast became a hallmark of the sonata. Here the alternation occurs within a single substantive movement. By the late seventeenth century the sections with differing tempos and moods would be separated and made to stand as independent movements, some of substantial duration, others very brief. Rossi and contemporaries such as Dario Castello and Biagio Marini intuited that the future of the sonata would rest in a multi-movement format.

EXAMPLE 33-1

LISTENING CUE

SALOMONE ROSSI
Sonata sopra l'aria di Ruggiero (1623)

CD 4/21
Anthology, No. 92

ARCANGELO CORELLI: SOLO SONATA AND TRIO SONATA

From the northern centers of Cremona and Mantua, the violin, and music for it, spread south to the rest of Italy. One important conduit was the composer Maurizio Cazzati (1616–1678), who carried the northern idioms from Mantua to Bologna. Bologna, on the main road south to Rome, soon became a center for the composition and performance of instrumental music. Opportunity for employment at the gigantic basilica of St. Petronio provided a special lure. Among the violinists attracted there was Arcangelo Corelli (1653–1713). Corelli learned his craft in Bologna, but by about the age of twenty had moved farther south to Rome. In Rome he became the darling of the aristocratic salon, admired for the rigor and precision of his playing.

Rome in the late seventeenth century was a city of about 150,000 people, and many contradictions. The Holy City had more than two hundred temples of worship, yet houses were crowded together, sanitary conditions appalling, and crime rampant. Virtually everyone of any means carried a sword, pistol, or dagger. Nonetheless, art and music flourished under the sponsorship of patrons with strong religious convictions. Corelli's first patron was Christina, exiled queen of Sweden, who in 1654 had renounced the Protestant religion and her throne, and moved to Rome to embrace Catholicism. To her Corelli dedicated his first publication, Opus 1 (1681), a set of twelve trio sonatas. Another important patron was young Pietro Ottoboni (1667–1740), who had been elevated to the rank of cardinal by his uncle, Pope Alexander VIII (more nepotism, as discussed in Chapter 32). Ottoboni collected paintings and musical instruments, and maintained an orchestra in his splendid Palazzo della Cancelleria in the center of Rome. In 1690 he engaged Corelli to serve as its *maestro di concerto* (concert master).

Corelli was the first composer in the history of music to make his reputation exclusively as an instrumental composer. He did not compose a great deal, but almost all of what he wrote was instrumental, not vocal, music. Corelli published four sets of trio sonatas, two *sonate da chiesa* (Opus 1 and Opus 3) and two *sonate da camera* (Opus 2 and Opus 4); a set of twelve solo sonatas for violin (Opus 5); and a collection of twelve ensemble concertos (Opus 6). Both of the latter publications contain examples of *da chiesa* as well as *da camera* format. Corelli was also the first composer to achieve international fame primarily from musical publications, because whatever was printed first in Italy under his name was quickly pirated by printers in Amsterdam and London. His solo sonatas in particular became enormously popular; forty-two editions of Opus 5 appeared before 1800, including arrangements for other instruments such as recorder. Appearing in Corelli's violin sonatas are modern bowing practices and frequent use of **multiple stops,** playing two or more notes simultaneously as chords. Corelli set the standard for composers throughout Europe at the turn of the eighteenth century, and his style was often imitated.

To be sure, the sonata was at the heart of Corelli's creative activity, and in his hands this genre became standardized both with regard to instrumentation and form. Earlier sonatas had been written for ensembles of various sizes, from one to as many as twenty-two instrumental players. With Corelli, however, the norm took two types: the solo sonata and the trio sonata. These two instrumental combinations became standard for composers until the end of the Baroque era around 1750. The **solo sonata** comprised a line for a single melody instrument (usually a violin) and basso continuo, while the **trio sonata** had two treble instruments (usually two violins) and continuo. (Because the basso continuo often required two instruments—one playing chords and the other the bass line—the solo sonata actually involved three players, and the trio sonata four.)

Form, too, now coalesced into a stereotypical pattern. Sonatas, whether solo or trio, usually consisted of a succession of four movements alternating slow/fast/slow/fast. All movements were in the same key (or relative major or minor). Sonatas intended for church (*da chiesa*) had movements simply labeled with a tempo marking such as *allegro* or *adagio*; sonatas for the private chamber (*da camera*) usually had not only a tempo indicator but also a title of a dance such as allemande or gigue. These were not real dances, but stylized pieces intending to conjure up in the mind of the listener a sonic image of the dance in question.

Corelli also standardized form within movements through a new emphasis on tonality. He developed a strategy of dividing the music of a movement into two balanced sections and repeating each. The first begins in the tonic key and ends on a dominant chord; the second begins on that dominant and works its way back to the tonic. In this process Corelli helped create what is now known as **binary form,** a structure consisting of two complementary parts, the first moving to a closely related key and the second beginning in that new key but soon returning the music to the tonic. In other words, it uses tonality to clarify form. Binary form became the standard form for single movements in sonatas and dance suites throughout the Baroque era.

In Corelli's music, tonality not only regulates the larger formal plan but also directs the smaller, more localized, harmonic event. Corelli's harmonies sound modern to our ears because they are often composed of triads, the roots of which are a fifth apart. Corelli also modulates, using melodic sequence, around the circle of fifths. One chord moves to the next in a purposeful, well-directed fashion, in a chord progression. The feeling of chords pulling one to another is often created by the use of chromatic inflection. The dominant chord has a leading tone that pulls to the tonic and a secondary chord often has a chromatic inflection (usually a sharp) that leads by half-step to the dominant pitch (see Ex. 33-3). What we hear in Corelli is a strong sense of functional tonality as we know it—the kind of harmonic movement still studied in music theory classes today.

In 1694 Corelli published his Opus 4, a set of *sonate da camera* dedicated to his art-loving patron, Cardinal Ottoboni. All twelve sonatas are trio sonatas scored for two violins and basso continuo (here, cello and harpsichord). In addition, all twelve sonatas proceed in a sequence of movements with alternating tempos: slow/fast/slow/fast. Sonata No. 1 in C Major opens with a slow *Preludio* (*Prelude*), which gives the players a chance to warm up while it sets the general mood of the sonata. Movement two is entitled *Corrente* (from the Italian *correre*, "to run") and proceeds in a fast triple meter. The fourth and final movement is also brisk and carries the title *Allemanda* (literally, "the German dance"). In the *Allemanda* the bass moves consistently in eighth notes, often up or down the scale (Ex. 33-2). A bass moving in a steady pace in this fashion is called a **walking bass.** Here, however, the fast tempo transforms it into something akin to a running or sprinting bass.

EXAMPLE 33-2

Between the fast *Corrente* and the brisk concluding *Allemanda*, Corelli places a slow *Adagio* in A minor, the relative minor key. Notice how, toward the end, a steadily rising bass line moves by half-step chromatic inflection to the tonic (Ex. 33-3). Combining the steady motion of a walking bass with chromatic inflections that pull to neighboring chords, or to those a fifth away, is just one way in which Corelli lends to his music a newfound sense of tonal direction.

EXAMPLE 33-3

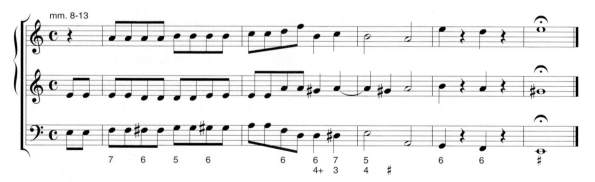

In sum, Corelli is important in the history of music for developing modern violin techniques such as multiple stops, for standardizing the Baroque sonata as either a solo sonata or trio sonata, for popularizing binary form, for impressing a four-movement format on the whole, and for creating a purposeful harmonic language, one that other composers throughout Europe would soon eagerly adopt. Today, Corelli remains the only instrumental composer to be buried in Rome's famous Pantheon, a hall of fame for Italy's most illustrious artists and statesmen.

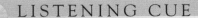

LISTENING CUE

ARCANGELO CORELLI
Opus 4, No. 1 (1694)
Preludio, Corrente, Adagio, Allemanda

CD 4/22–25
Anthology, No. 93a–d

TRUMPET MUSIC BY GIUSEPPE TORELLI: THE BEGINNINGS OF THE SOLO CONCERTO

The violin and members of the violin family were not the only instruments to thrive in seventeenth-century Italy. The harpsichord, which had been around since the fifteenth century, became the workhorse of the Baroque ensemble, holding together the basso continuo. And melody instruments, such as the oboe, flute, and trumpet, saw a body of solo music created especially for them. For the trumpet in particular, the period of the seventeenth and early eighteenth centuries was a glorious moment. The trumpet, of course, had existed in Europe since Roman antiquity (see Chapter 2). But it flourished during the seventeenth century, perhaps because of the growing interest in brilliant instrumental sounds during the Baroque era. Trumpet makers in London, England, and Nuremberg, Germany, produced large numbers of quality instruments; and composers such as Henry Purcell in London and Giuseppe Torelli in Bologna created pieces that exploited its brilliant upper register as well as the advanced playing techniques of virtuoso performers.

During the seventeenth century the most important center for trumpet music was Bologna, Italy. The city had a long history of interest in civic music played by municipal trumpeters, one that extended back into the Middle Ages. Increasingly, trumpet music, and music generally in Bologna, was concentrated in the gigantic basilica of St. Petronio, a church far larger than either the Sistine Chapel in Rome or the basilica of St. Mark in Venice. Music at St. Petronio's entered a golden era with the appointment of Maurizio Cazzati as *maestro di cappella* in 1657. Cazzati, inspired by the skill of several trumpeters in Bologna, published the first sonatas for solo trumpet in 1665. By the early eighteenth century, the music library at St. Petronio's comprised hundreds of instrumental works by Cazzati and other composers, including some eighty-three pieces for trumpet. Foremost among the composers of trumpet music in this collection was Giuseppe Torelli. Indeed, judging from the number of pieces surviving under his name in Bologna and elsewhere (approximately forty-five), Torelli was the preeminent composer of trumpet music of the entire Baroque era.

Giuseppe Torelli (1658–1709) was born in Verona, near Venice, but moved to Bologna and a position at St. Petronio's in 1684. He remained in Bologna, except for a brief sojourn in Berlin and Vienna around 1700, for the remainder of his life. Ironically, Torelli was himself a violinist, not a trumpeter. He published two early sets of trio sonatas for strings (1686) as well as two somewhat-later sets of string concertos (1692 and 1698). The concertos of 1692 are important because they are among the first to specify that the orchestral string parts are to be multiplied—as many as three or four players are to reinforce each orchestra line. Yet, following in the footsteps of Cazzati, Torelli also chose to write for the virtuoso trumpeters of Bologna, who filled St. Petronio's with brilliant sound on the high feast days of the church year.

Between 1684 and his death in 1709, Torelli wrote nearly four dozen trumpet pieces for St. Petronio's. Most were performed as a prelude to the Mass or as a substitute for the Mass Offertory on the feast of St. Petronio (4 October), the patron saint of Bologna. Some of these pieces Torelli called sonatas, others sinfonias, and still others concertos. Some he wrote in the slow/fast/slow/fast movement format typi-cal of a sonata, and others in the fast/slow/fast arrangement that was coming to be common for the sinfonia. By 1700 the term **sinfonia** was used to designate a three-movement instrumental overture, one that might preface an opera or a Mass. In truth, Torelli employed the terms "sonata," "sinfonia," and "concerto" without distinction; there is no difference in form or musical process from one genre to the next. Indeed, this indiscriminate use of the terms is a hallmark of Italian instrumen-tal music around 1700.

Consequently, Torelli's Sinfonia in D Major for trumpet should be heard as a three-movement sinfonia, but one possessing early signs of the solo concerto (on the concerto, see below under Antonio Vivaldi). It opens with an orchestral pre-sentation of a theme that will return repeatedly in the first movement (Ex. 33-4). When the trumpet enters, it emphasizes a rising fourth motive (Ex. 33-5), and it alone plays lengthy trills. Thus a distinction is made between the music assigned the soloist and that given the orchestra. Moreover, the trumpet's rising fourth mo-tive is clearly drawn from the opening theme played by the orchestra. These two procedures—differentiating the music of the soloist from that of the orchestra, and having the soloist expand upon material derived from a recurring orchestral theme (ritornello)—are hallmarks of the emerging Baroque concerto. They will become especially prominent in the mature concertos of Antonio Vivaldi.

EXAMPLE 33-4

EXAMPLE 33-5

By contrast, the trumpet is entirely silent during the slow second movement. Here, Torelli writes a short, simple succession of chords and ends with a half-cadence that leads directly into the finale. Above most of these chords Torelli has placed a small dash, the sign for *spiccato*. **Spiccato** (Italian for "sharp") requires the performers to play in a detached fashion, but not quite as short as *staccato*. Compared to nor-mal playing, *spiccato* produces less resonance but greater clarity, a desirable feature in a large, resonant church such as St. Petronio's, where the reverberation time is an astonishing twelve seconds.

Finally, there is a distinction here as to what the violin can play and what the trumpet cannot. In measures 20–24, the violin leads a modulation that touches on chords moving around the circle of fifths: B-E-A-D. This is effected by means of chromatic notes, some of which, such as g#', c#", and d#", are not easily available on

National Music Museum

✻ FIGURE 33-3

Two trumpets by Johann
Wilhelm Hass, Nuremberg,
c1690–1700. Trumpets like
these were frequently purchased
by Italian trumpeters.

a trumpet pitched in D. Thus this modulatory passage is assigned to the strings but
not the trumpet. The Baroque trumpet could play *in* keys such as tonic and dominant, but it could not easily move *through* different keys.

Recall that the trumpet during the seventeenth century is a natural instrument
without keys or valves (Fig. 33-3). The notes it can produce are those of the harmonic series. Most trumpets around 1700 were pitched with a fundamental that
sounded low D, and therefore most compositions for them in the Baroque are in the
key of D major. Example 33-6 shows the notes of the harmonic series, and thus the
pitches available to a natural trumpet pitched in D. Notice that the notes g♯', c♯",
and d♯", among others, are not present in this series. In addition, some of the harmonics (7, 11, 13, and 14) are not in tune and only approximate the black notes
written in the example. A skilled performer, however, could blow more or less hard
to produce a sharp or flat inflection (B♮ or C for harmonic 7, for example). As the
trumpet entered the highest harmonics, a fully chromatic scale resulted. Only in
this highest register could the trumpet play conjunct melodies and not merely jump
around in fourths and fifths. Playing in this high register, called the **clarino register,**
was a special technique of Baroque trumpeters. By 1760, however, this brilliant
upper-register playing had became something of a lost art. The trumpet parts written by Baroque composers Torelli, Purcell, and Bach are much more difficult than
those composed by Classical masters Haydn, Mozart, and Beethoven.

EXAMPLE 33-6

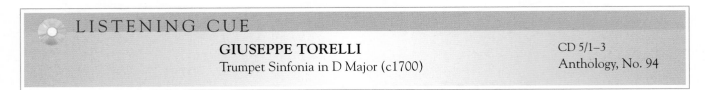

LISTENING CUE

| **GIUSEPPE TORELLI** | CD 5/1–3 |
| Trumpet Sinfonia in D Major (c1700) | Anthology, No. 94 |

✿ ANTONIO VIVALDI:
SOLO CONCERTO AND CONCERTO GROSSO

The seventeenth century witnessed the advent of several new musical genres, among
them opera, oratorio, cantata, sonata, and concerto. In the early seventeenth century, the term "concerto" appeared in many contexts and meant many things. Generally, it connoted a composition that involved opulent, contrasting sound created
by diverse musical forces, whether instrumental or vocal. In this sense it was closely
related to the early Baroque term *concertato*, music marked by strong contrasts (see
Chapter 31). Only during the last two decades of the seventeenth century did the
word **concerto** come to denote a purely instrumental piece for ensemble in which
one or more soloists both complemented and competed with an orchestra.

The most prolific composer of Baroque concertos was Antonio Vivaldi. In fact,
Vivaldi has left us nearly five hundred concertos. Roughly three hundred fifty of

these are for one solo instrument or another, and thus they belong to the category **solo concerto.** Of the solo concertos most (some two hundred thirty) are for violin, but some are for bassoon, cello, oboe, flute, recorder, and even mandolin. Vivaldi himself was a virtuoso violinist. He was one of the first to showcase his skill as a soloist at the end of a movement of a concerto. In 1715 a visitor from Germany to Venice heard the master play such an improvised conclusion.

> Towards the end Vivaldi played a solo accompaniment—splendid—to which he appended a cadenza which really frightened me, for such playing has never been nor can be: he brought his fingers up to only a straw's distance from the bridge, leaving no room for the bow—and that on all four strings with imitations and incredible speed. With this he astounded everyone, but I cannot say that it pleased me, for it was not so pleasant to listen to as it was skillfully executed.[1]

Thus the instrumental **cadenza**—a technically demanding, rhapsodic, improvisatory passage near the end of a movement—entered the concerto in the early eighteenth century in the music of Vivaldi and other contemporary Italian composers.

Antonio Vivaldi (1678–1741) was a native of Venice and became an important figure in that city's long and distinguished musical history (see Chapter 31). His father was a barber and part-time violinist on the payroll of the basilica of St. Mark, the principal church of the city. The young Vivaldi's proximity to St. Mark's naturally brought him into contact with the clergy. Although a violin virtuoso at an early age, he entered Holy Orders and gained the priesthood in 1703. Yet Vivaldi's life was by no means confined to the realm of the spirit. He concertized on the violin throughout Europe; he wrote and produced nearly fifty operas, which brought him a great deal of money; and for fifteen years he lived with an Italian opera soprano. The worldly pursuits of *il prete rosso* (the red-haired priest) eventually provoked the wrath of the Church of Rome, and in 1737 Vivaldi was forbidden to practice his musical artistry in certain papally controlled lands. This ban seems to have affected his income as well as his creativity. He died poor and obscure in 1741 in Vienna, where he had moved in a futile effort to resuscitate his career.

Despite his frequent travels, Vivaldi's career was centered in Venice. From 1703 until 1740 he served variously as a violinist, music teacher, and composer-in-residence at the *Ospedale della Pietà* (Hospice of Mercy). The Hospice of Mercy was a combination orphanage, convent, and music conservatory providing for the care and education of young women. It was one of four such charitable institutions in Venice that accepted abandoned, mostly illegitimate, girls, who, as several reports state, "otherwise would have been thrown in the canals." All girls received religious training and some instruction in domestic crafts (cooking, embroidery, lace-making, and the like). The more musically talented were given lessons on instruments and required to practice as much as four hours a day. Each Sunday afternoon the all-female orchestra offered public performances for tourists and well-to-do Venetians alike. The girls appeared in the chapel of the orphanage standing on high in a special gallery, a musicians' loft, and played to the outside world through a grill (Fig. 33-4). The report of a French diplomat in 1739 is typical of the impression they made.

> These girls are brought up at the expense of the state and trained solely to excel in music. Moreover, they sing like angels and play the violin, the flute, the organ, the oboe, the cello, and the bassoon; in short, there is no instrument, however unwieldy, that can frighten them. They are cloistered like nuns. It is they alone who perform, and about forty girls take part in each concert. I vow

FIGURE 33-4
Women musicians perform behind a grill at an eighteenth-century Venetian orphanage.

to you that there is nothing so diverting as the sight of a young and pretty nun in a white habit, with a bunch of pomegranate blossoms over her ear, conducting the orchestra and beating time with all the grace and precision imaginable.[2]

Vivaldi composed many of his concertos specifically for his female pupils at the Hospice of Mercy in order that they might develop and demonstrate their musical skills. Some of these concertos he published, but most he left in manuscript copies at the time of his death. Among the works Vivaldi published are a set of twelve concerti grossi, comprising Opus 3, entitled *L'estro armonico* (*Harmonic Whim*, 1711) and a group of twelve solo concertos, comprising Opus 8, called *Il cimento dell'armonia e dell'inventione* (*The Contest between Harmony and Invention*, 1725). The first four concertos of this latter set are the famous **The Four Seasons.** In these, Vivaldi writes some of the earliest program music, for the composer inserts a poem about each season into the first violinist's part and then fashions music to match the poetic images (singing birds, a gathering storm, a babbling brook, and so on). Today Vivaldi's *The Four Seasons* concertos are perhaps the most popular of all Baroque compositions—standard background music in restaurants and coffee houses, as well as films and TV commercials.

Less popular today, but more influential in Vivaldi's day, are the concertos contained in the *L'estro armonico.* This collection, which greatly influenced the leading composers of the day, has been called "the single most important collection of instrumental music to appear during the whole of the eighteenth century."[3] Most of the twelve concertos are of the concerto grosso type. In a **concerto grosso** a larger body of performers, namely the full orchestra, contrasts with a smaller group of soloists. The larger ensemble is sometimes called the concerto grosso ("large concerto"), but more commonly identified as the *ripieno* (Italian for "full"). The smaller group of two, three, or four soloists is called the *concertino* ("little concerto"). In the Baroque era these soloists were not expensive stars brought from afar, but the regular first-chair players of the orchestra. When they were not serving as soloists, these leaders simply melted back into the ripieno to play the orchestral parts.

As with the solo concerto, the Baroque concerto grosso is in three movements, fast/slow/fast. The serious first movement is usually composed in a carefully worked-out structure called **ritornello form.** The Italian word **ritornello,** as we have seen (see Chapter 32), simply means "return" or "refrain." Vivaldi employs ritornello form in both his solo concerto and concerto grosso. A piece in ritornello form begins with a distinct main theme, the ritornello, which returns again and again, invariably played by the *ripieno.* Between statements of the ritornello, the *concertino* (or soloist in a solo concerto) comes forward to expand and elaborate upon musical ideas contained or suggested within the ritornello. The *concertino* also provokes modulations to more distant keys. In general, the *ripieno* provides tonal stability, while it is up to the *concertino* to push the piece farther afield tonally. The tension between these two different sound masses and between the tonal zones of the two groups is what gives the concerto grosso its exciting, dynamic quality.

A classic example of a concerto grosso is the eighth within Vivaldi's *L'estro armonico* (Opus 3, No. 8, in A Minor). No less a person than the young J.S. Bach transcribed it for organ so as to study and absorb Vivaldi's style. The opening movement is in ritornello form. Here the ritornello is comprised of four distinct parts. Part 1 (Ex. 33-7a) begins with three strong chords followed by a descending scale played in unison by the strings (unison string writing is a favorite device of Vivaldi). Part 2 (Ex. 33-7b) presents a repeated figure that soon gives way to a descending melodic sequence (frequent use of melodic sequence is another hallmark of

Vivaldi's style). Part 3 (Ex. 33-7c) is marked by a gesture idiomatic to the violin (rocking back and forth with slurred down bows); while Part 4 (Ex. 33-7d) inserts a striking chord (B♭ chord in A minor) as the violins saw away. All four sections are energized by small repeating rhythmic cells, thereby creating the motor-like rhythms that typically propel Vivaldi's music forward. Now the *concertino* (here two violins and cello) takes over from the *ripieno,* and it interjects an insistent, repeated figure borrowed from Part 1 of the ritornello. Thereafter the movement unfolds as a succession of increasingly ornate elaborations of bits of the ritornello played by the *concertino* and returns of one or more sections of the ritornello performed by the *ripieno* (see below). The *concertino* sounds daring and adventuresome; the *ripieno* solid and secure. The interplay between the two goes to the very heart of the concerto, a spirited give-and-take between opposing musical forces.

EXAMPLES 33-7 A–D

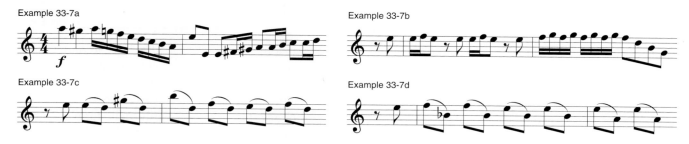

Example 33-7a

Example 33-7b

Example 33-7c

Example 33-7d

Formal diagram of Vivaldi, Opus 3, No. 8, 1st movement

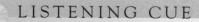

Ritornello part:	1–4		4		2		1		3		1		2+4		4
R (*ripieno*) or c (*concertino*):	R	c	R	c	R	c	R	c	R	c	R	c	R	c	R
Key:	a			a	C			d		a		a		a		a

 LISTENING CUE

ANTONIO VIVALDI
Opus 3, *L'estro armonico* (1711)
Concerto Grosso, No. 8, First movement

CD 5/4
Anthology, No. 95

 SUMMARY

During the seventeenth century, instrumental music became just as important as vocal music, judging from the amount of music published. For the first time in the history of music, composers began to write idiomatically for instruments. By mid-century the sonata had become the dominant genre of instrumental music, though by the end of the century another new genre, the concerto, began to compete for pride of place. At first the sonata was a single-movement composition with sections having different tempos and moods. Similarly, the early sonata might involve as many as twenty-two individual parts. The sonatas of Salomone Rossi, while still embodying a single movement, reduce the instruments to just two high parts and a basso continuo. Arcangelo Corelli standardized the Baroque sonata as either a solo sonata or a trio sonata, and as either *da chiesa* or *da camera*. He impressed a four-movement format on each sonata and binary form on each movement within each sonata. Corelli also created a purposeful harmonic language by using chromatic inflections, secondary dominant chords, and abundant melodic sequences. Giuseppe Torelli wrote trumpet sonatas, sinfonias, and concertos in which can be seen the beginnings of the solo concerto: a separation of material assigned to soloist and opposing orchestra. Antonio Vivaldi popularized both the solo concerto, as exemplified by *The Four Seasons*, and the concerto grosso. In both genres Vivaldi often employs ritornello form to set up a dialogue involving theme and key between the full orchestra (*ripieno*) and a single soloist, or a group of soloists (*concertino*).

KEY TERMS

Cremona	binary form	*The Four Seasons*
Antonio Stradivari	walking bass	concerto grosso
da chiesa	sinfonia	*ripieno*
da camera	*spiccato*	*concertino*
sonata	clarino register	ritornello form
multiple stops	concerto	*ritornello*
solo sonata	solo concerto	
trio sonata	cadenza	

Chapter 34

Instrumental Music in Germany and Austria

Italy was the fountainhead of Western art music during the seventeenth century. Almost all of the new musical genres of the Baroque era—opera, concerted motet, oratorio, cantata, sonata, sinfonia, and concerto—originated there. So dominant was Italy during this period that the terminology the Italians developed for music soon spread to other countries, and it remains fundamentally the one we use today. Terms for dynamics (such as *piano, forte, fortissimo*), for tempo (*allegro, adagio,* and *moderato*), for processes (*ostinato, obbligato, staccato,* and *spiccato*), and even for instruments (violin, viola, cello) were popularized in Italy during the seventeenth century. But other nations had their own distinctive musical styles and practices. In German-speaking lands (mainly modern Germany and Austria; Map 34-1), intensely contrapuntal pieces and those built upon a sacred melody (either Catholic or Protestant) were especially favored. As we have seen, German musicians journeyed to Italy to study the latest Italian musical styles and, similarly, Italian musicians were much prized at German and Austrian courts. With such comings and goings on the Continent, musical styles (Italian, German, French, and Spanish) inevitably became intertwined, and we are sometimes at pains to know exactly which musical characteristics originated where. Some German-speaking composers restricted themselves

✻ MAP 34-1
Northern Europe in the
seventeenth century.

to a distinctly Germanic style. Others were proficient at adopting or adapting several national idioms. One such cosmopolitan master was Johann Froberger.

❀ JOHANN FROBERGER AND THE BAROQUE DANCE SUITE

Who was Johann Froberger (1616–1667) and why should we care? Froberger was a German musician who worked mainly in Austria, spent years studying in Italy, and traveled extensively as a virtuoso performer in France and England. He is important to the history of music because he established the dance suite as an important genre of music for string keyboard instruments (harpsichord and clavichord). Handel and Bach later composed keyboard suites building on Froberger's model; young Bach in particular copied keyboard pieces by Froberger to learn his craft, and held him in high esteem throughout his life. Dance suites for keyboard and instrumental ensembles proliferated during the Baroque era and then disappeared after 1750, only to enjoy a renaissance during the twentieth century in the hands of Debussy, Strauss, Respighi, Schoenberg, Stravinsky, and others.

Johann Froberger was born in Stuttgart, Germany, the son of a court musician. In 1634 he moved to the Austrian capital of Vienna and three years later was appointed organist to the imperial court. That same year, Froberger received a stipend from the emperor, which allowed him to study for several years in Rome with the renowned keyboardist and composer Girolamo Frescobaldi (see Chapter 32). Froberger was again given leave from the imperial court in 1651–1652, when he visited London and Paris, meeting and absorbing the musical styles of the leading Parisian composers in particular. He returned to imperial service in Vienna in 1653, but was released in 1657 when a new emperor came to the throne. He ended his days as artist-in-residence for the aristocratic family that his father had once served in Stuttgart.

Froberger composed almost exclusively keyboard music. Those compositions belonging to the Italian tradition (canzonas, toccatas, and ricercars, for example) he intended mainly for organ, while those showing French influence (mostly the dance suites) were designed for harpsichord or clavichord. In Paris, Froberger had come under the sway of the French school of lutenists centering around Denis Gaultier (see Chapter 36), and he transferred their style to the harpsichord. The French, of course, had enjoyed a long history of composed dance music, and by the seventeenth century their earlier dance pair of pavane and galliard (see Chapter 22) had been greatly expanded. Sometimes as many as a dozen dances were organized by key into a group, and it was left to the performer to pick and choose a set to create the desired mood. Our English word "suite" simply means a succession of pieces coming in an order pleasing to performer and audience. The audience listened but did not dance. These were stylized dances in which the composer aimed to capture in music the spirit of the dance in question. As one musician of the day commented, they are written "for the refreshment of the ear alone."[1]

Johann Froberger crystallized the dance suite by creating some thirty suites that usually had the same four dances: allemande, courante, sarabande, and gigue.[2] Subsequent composers such as Handel and Bach would add one or more other dances, but these four dances henceforth remained the backbone of the suite. A **dance suite** can therefore be defined as an ordered set of dances (often on the sequence of allemande, courante, sarabande, and gigue) for solo instrument or ensemble, all written in the same key and intended to be performed in a single sitting.

Below are listed the main traits of these four core dances as well as those of other dances sometimes inserted into the suite as fashion or fancy demanded:

- **Allemande.** The name suggests the place of origin of this dance ("allemande" is French for "German"); a stately dance in $\frac{4}{4}$ meter at a moderate tempo with an upbeat and gracefully interweaving lines that create an improvisatory-like style
- **Courante.** A lively dance ("courante" is French for "running") characterized by intentional metrical ambiguity created by means of hemiola—measures of two beats with triple subdivision $\frac{6}{4}$ interplay with those of three beats with duple subdivision $\frac{3}{2}$
- **Sarabande.** A slow, stately dance in $\frac{3}{4}$ with a strong accent on the second beat
- **Gigue.** A fast dance in $\frac{6}{8}$ or $\frac{12}{8}$ with a constant eighth-note pulse that produces a galloping sound; the gigue is sometimes lightly imitative and often used to conclude a suite
- **Minuet.** An elegant dance of French origin in triple meter and performed at a moderate tempo; the only Baroque dance to remain popular in the Classical period
- **Bourrée.** A fast dance in $\frac{4}{4}$ (or in cut time) with a quarter-note upbeat that usually follows a slower dance in $\frac{3}{4}$ such as the sarabande
- **Gavotte.** Another dance of French origin marked by a moderate tempo, duple meter, and four-bar phrases
- **Hornpipe.** An energetic dance of English origin, derived from the country jig, in either $\frac{3}{2}$ or $\frac{2}{4}$

Froberger's Suite No. 6 in C Major is typical of his thirty keyboard suites. It also demonstrates a unique peculiarity of his music: Froberger had a penchant for composing a highly expressive lament as a response to personal or national tragedy. When he witnessed a well-known French lutenist take a fatal tumble down a flight of stairs, he composed a lament in honor of the fallen musician; and when he had been robbed by pirates on his way from Paris to London in 1652 he composed a "plaint" (musical complaint). Sometimes Froberger's laments were independent, free-standing pieces, as is true for the one he composed on the death of Emperor Ferdinand III in 1657. In other instances, Froberger placed the descriptive piece at the opening of a suite, where it serves as an allemande. In Suite No. 6 in C Major, the allemande is entitled *Lamento sopra la dolorosa perdita della Real Maestà di Ferdi-*

FIGURE 34-1
Autograph keyboard score from the end of the opening *Lamento* (*Allemande*) of Johann Froberger's Suite No. 6 in C Major. These final two staves conclude with a three-octave C-major scale ascending to heaven. (Turn sideways to better see the faces of the angels.)

Österreichische Nationalbibliothek

nando IV Rè de Romani (*Lament on the occasion of the sad loss of his Royal Majesty Ferdinando IV, King of the Romans*). The son and heir of Froberger's employer, Ferdinand IV, died unexpectedly in 1654. Froberger's lament is full of painful dissonance and ends with a run up the C major scale, a graphic depiction of the hoped-for ascent of the young man's soul. Indeed, Froberger's autograph manuscript, preserved today in Vienna (Fig. 34-1), shows the soul-bearing scale being welcomed by the light of three heavenly angels. The remaining dances of the suite are all in the same mood, key, and form as the opening *Lamento* (*Allemande*).

LISTENING CUE

JOHANN FROBERGER
Suite No. 6 in C Major (1654)
Lamento (*Allemande*), *Courante, Sarabande, Gigue*

CD 5/5–8
Anthology, No. 96a-d

BIBER AND KUHNAU: THE PROGRAMMATIC SONATA

Johann Froberger wrote mainly suites for solo keyboard, while Heinrich Biber, a contemporary virtuoso violinist, composed mainly sonatas for violin and basso continuo. In the late seventeenth century, the suite and the sonata had much in common. Both were multi-movement instrumental works with the movements generally in one key, and both were comprised of a succession of dances (the suite always, the sonata often). Moreover, both suite and sonata began to display programmatic influence. In **program music** some external influence or non-musical event affects the general spirit and the specific details of an instrumental composition. We have just seen how the expected upward spiritual journey of King Ferdinand IV received musical depiction at the end of the opening movement of Froberger's Suite No. 6.

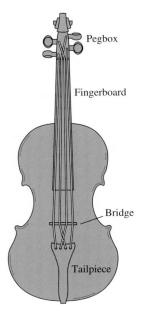

Bayerische StaatsBibliothek, München

Pegbox

Fingerboard

Bridge

Tailpiece

❀ FIGURE 34-2

Twice-crossed strings on the violin suggests the theme of Christ's resurrection. This arrangement is one possible way to effect the *scordatura* required for Biber's sonata for the resurrection.

❀ FIGURE 34-3

The image of the resurrection accompanying Biber's sonata of that name. In the autograph manuscript of Biber's "Mystery" Sonatas, each sonata is prefaced by an engraving that suggests the spiritual meaning of the music to follow. The rather dramatic ascent of Christ from the sepulcher may explain the agitated music with which this sonata opens.

So too in Heinrich Biber's "Mystery" Sonatas, things outside of music shape (provide a program for) a lengthy musical creation.

Heinrich Biber (1644–1704) was a Bohemian-born virtuoso violinist. In 1670 he entered employment at the court of the archbishop of Salzburg in northern Austria (where Mozart and his father would serve some hundred years later), and in 1684 he became Kapellmeister (a coveted position neither Mozart attained). Salzburg was a German-speaking city, but, like most of those in Austria and southern Germany, it sat squarely within the spiritual realm of the Roman Catholic Church. Thus Italian music, and especially Roman-style church music, was very much in favor here. Biber wrote *a cappella* Masses in *stile antico* as well as more flamboyant, large-scale *stile concertato* Masses. He is probably the author of the colossal, fifty-three part *Missa Salisburgensis (Mass of Salzburg;* c1682), once ascribed to the Roman master Orazio Benevoli (see Chapter 32).

Despite his skill as a composer of sacred music, Biber is best known today for his instrumental pieces, specifically his programmatic "Mystery" Sonatas composed for Salzburg about 1674. The **"Mystery" Sonatas,** also known as the **"Rosary" Sonatas,** are a set of fifteen sonatas for solo violin and continuo that project through music the sacred devotion of the rosary (votive prayers coming in fifteen groups). During the recitation of each of these groups, the faithful Catholic meditates upon one of fifteen events associated with the life of Christ or the Virgin Mary, keeping count of the prayers by means of rosary beads. Thus the program for the fifteen "Mystery" Sonatas follows a sequence of fifteen miraculous, or mysterious, events in the lives of Christ and Mary: the annunciation, visitation, nativity, crucifixion, resurrection, and ascension, for example. The violinist projects each mystery by means of a solo sonata with one to four movements.

Yet there is another "mystery" in the "Mystery" Sonatas, and that has to do with the tuning of the violin. Biber instructs that the violinist must tune the instrument a different way for each of the fifteen sonatas. The first sonata requires the standard violin tuning with the strings in fifths (g-d'-a'-e"). Subsequent sonatas instruct that the strings must be set at an interval of a third or a fourth, or even an octave, apart. Tuning a string instrument to something other than standard tuning is called *scordatura* (from an Italian word literally meaning "mistuning"). The purpose of *scordatura* is to make certain passages easier to play, to produce special effects, and to make the instrument sound more brilliant by emphasizing the resonance of particular strings. Biber's "Mystery" Sonatas provide the most extensive use of *scordatura* in the entire repertory of Western music.

Exactly how *scordatura* works, and how it helps project the meaning of Biber's "Mystery" Sonatas, can be seen in Sonata No. 11, *The Resurrection.* Here the violinist must tune the strings to g-g'-d'-d". This may be accomplished one of two ways: (1) by simply switching the two inner strings and tuning them in octaves with the adjacent outer string; or (2) by tuning them g-d'-g'-d" but twice crossing the inner two strings thereby producing g-g'-d'-d" (Fig. 34-2). This crossing of the instrument adds a visible sign of the resurrection (see the cross on Christ's standard in Fig. 34-3).

No violinist could have learned to play these *scordature* in the "Mystery" Sonatas without great labor. To simplify things, Biber writes out his music as if the violinist has the standard tuning in mind (g-d'-a'-e"). This creates an apparently nonsensical collection of notes on the page (top line in Ex. 34-1), but, owing to the *scordatura,* the written notes are mysteriously transformed into pitches that will sound harmonious with those of the basso continuo (second line in Ex. 34-1).

EXAMPLE 34-1

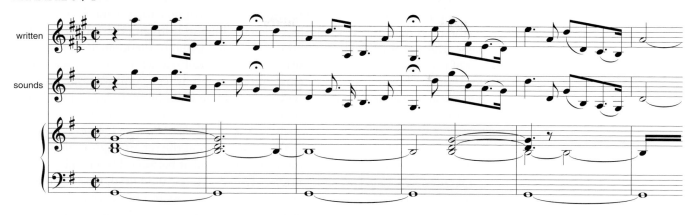

A *scordatura* emphasizing G's and D's, as in Sonata No. 11, naturally works well in the key of G, for here the G-string and D-string are open strings (not stopped), and the tonic and dominant chords sound especially resonant. Sonata No. 11, in fact, is written almost entirely in G major. Notice also that Biber is fond of writing multiple stops to create his virtuosic violin style. This adds to the resonant sound, but it also gives the impression of two, or sometimes three, independent lines working together; polyphony, even when projected on a melodic instrument like the violin, is very much a hallmark of German Baroque music.

Finally, consider the core of this sonata—the stately second movement. Here Biber has constructed a lengthy chaconne upon a popular Latin hymn *Surrexit Christus hodie* (*Christ has risen today*). The hymn first appears in the basso continuo as a chaconne bass, and upon it Biber then constructs a set of variations for the violin. By means of this hymn the "program" of the sonata is communicated to the faithful. Lest the listener miss the point, the movement concludes with the violin playing the hymn in octave double-stops and the continuo an additional octave below (Ex. 34-2)—an emphatic affirmation of the mystery of Christ's resurrection.

EXAMPLE 34-2

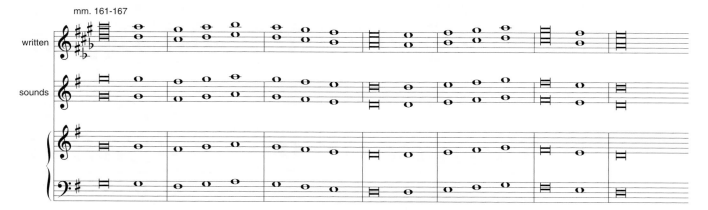

mm. 161-167

LISTENING CUE

HEINRICH BIBER

"Mystery" Sonatas (c1674)

The Resurrection, Movements 1–2

CD 5/9–10

Anthology, No. 97a-b

Heinrich Biber, working at the Catholic court of the archbishop of Salzburg, Austria, was not the only composer to embrace the programmatic sonata. To the north, in the Protestant town of Leipzig, Germany, Johann Kuhnau (1660–1722) did the same. Kuhnau was the cantor of the St. Thomas Church, the immediate predecessor of the great Bach in that position in Leipzig. Kuhnau wrote sacred vocal music for the St. Thomas Church (almost all of it unpublished), and two collections of sonatas and two sets of suites for keyboard (all four published). Today Kuhnau's reputation rests almost exclusively on his last published work for keyboard, a set of six sonatas entitled *Musicalische Vorstellung einiger biblischer Historien* (*Musical Representation of a few Biblical Histories*; 1700). Each sonata in the set attempts to illustrate a particular event from the Old Testament: the combat between David and Goliath, Saul cured by David through music, and Jacob's death and burial, for example. To guide the listener, Kuhnau adds a synopsis of each story in phrases of Italian. Thus the first sonata is entitled *Il combattimento trà David e Goliath* (*The Battle between David and Goliath*) and opens with the phrase "Le bravate di Goliath." The dramatic events within the story are depicted musically by a series of self-contained movements, each having a sound distinctly appropriate to the narrative. Example 34-3 suggests the way in which Kuhnau's explicitly pictorial music works.

EXAMPLE 34-3A

The bravado of Goliath [pompous, dotted rhythms]

EXAMPLE 34-3B

The quavering of the Israelites in the face of the giant and their prayer made to God. [trembling chords that fall down and to which is soon added the chorale tune *Out of the Deep I Cry to Thee*]

EXAMPLE 34-3C

The courage of David and his eagerness to prevail over the pride of his terrifying enemy through his confidence found with the help of God. [David steadfastly remains in the key of C major]

The Doctrine of Affections

In the winter of 1645–1646 the French philosopher René Descartes (1596–1650) published an essay entitled *Les Passions de l'âme* (*Passions of the Soul*), in which he sought to classify and explain the full spectrum of human emotions. With each description of an emotion came a physiological diagnosis, as here in the case of sadness:

The definition of Sadness. Sadness is a disagreeable languor in which consists the discomfort and unrest which the soul receives from evil. . . .

The movement of the blood and spirits in Sadness. In sadness, the openings of the heart are much contracted by the small nerve which surrounds them, and the blood of the veins is in nowise agitated, which brings it to pass that very little of it goes toward the heart and yet the passages by which the juice of the food flows from the stomach and the intestines towards the liver remain open, which causes the appetite not to diminish at all, excepting when hatred, which is often united to sadness, closes them.[3]

Obviously, Descartes's understanding of the workings of the mind and body was somewhat different from our own. But his views greatly influenced intellectuals generally and music theorists in particular, both French and German. One such theorist was Johann Mattheson (1681–1764) of Hamburg, Germany, who codified a theory of *Affektenlehre*, or what came to be called the Doctrine of Affections. The **Doctrine of Affections** embodies the Baroque belief that emotions are objective phenomena that can be represented by analogous tones and rhythms. As Mattheson explains in his *Der vollkommene Capellmeister* (*The Complete Music Director*; 1739):

Those who are learned in the natural sciences [i.e. Descartes] know how our emotions function physically, as it were. It would be advantageous to the composer to have a little knowledge of this subject. Since, for example, joy is an *expansion* of our vital spirits, it follows sensibly and naturally that this affect is best expressed by large and expanded intervals. Sadness, on the other hand, is a *contraction* of those same subtle parts of our bodies. It is, therefore, easy to see that the narrowest intervals are the most suitable. Love is a *diffusion* of the spirits. Thus, to express this passion in composing, it is best to use intervals of that nature. Hope is an *elevation* of the spirit; despair, on the other hand, a *casting down* of the same. These are subjects that can well be represented by sound, especially when other circumstances (tempo in particular) contribute their share. In such a manner one can form a concrete picture of all the emotions and try to compose accordingly.[4]

Of course, composers had long been writing music that gave expression to the emotions, in the text painting of the Renaissance madrigal and in the laments and revenge arias of Baroque opera and cantata, for example. Eighteenth-century musician Mattheson is simply providing a theory, or doctrine, for this phenomenon of the "affects" of music well after the fact. This posterior description demonstrates a maxim in music history: theory follows practice. The important point, however, is that when overt musical depiction entered the seventeenth-century sonata, it proved that music without text (instrumental music) could sway the emotions just as much as music with text. Instrumental music had taken on the same emotive power as vocal music.

EXAMPLE 34-3D

And so it goes. This music is overtly descriptive, indeed onomatopoeic, because it sounds out its own meaning. One French composer even went so far as to set in musical tones the gruesome stages of a Baroque kidney-stone operation (without anesthesia)! To our modern ears, program music of this sort is almost comical, like melodramatic silent film scores or even cartoon music. But around 1700 the insertion of such intensely emotional music into the sonata had a profound result. The programmatic sonatas of Biber and Kuhnau deepened the emotional content of the genre, making the sonata far richer and more satisfying than a series of merely pleasing dance pieces. Instrumental music was appropriating the sort of expressive, and sometimes extravagant, gestures that had been the exclusive preserve of vocal music. Gravity and intensity of expression were the legacy the sonata composers of the Baroque bequeathed to those of succeeding generations, specifically to C.P.E. Bach, Haydn, and Mozart.

DIETERICH BUXTEHUDE AND THE NORTH GERMAN ORGAN TRADITION

The pipe organ is known as the king of instruments, in part because in medieval times it was the only instrument sanctioned within the walls of the church. In truth, organs in churches did not become widespread until the fourteenth century, but thereafter most large institutions in the West had at least one, and often two, instruments to support religious music-making. Building an organ requires precise woodworking skills and a knowledge of metallurgy, physics, and acoustics—all attributes German artisans have traditionally possessed. During the years 1650–1750, north Germany produced some of the most remarkable organs ever fabricated. By the early eighteenth century, large organs with three or four manuals (keyboards) and thousands of pipes had been installed in north German port cities such as Hamburg and Lübeck.

At this time, the commercial cities around the Baltic and North Seas (see Map 34-1) formed a distinct region with regard to politics, culture, and music. Here emerged a particular style of organ composition and performance, one beginning with Jan Sweelinck (1562–1621) in Amsterdam and extending to Jan Reincken (1643?–1722) in Hamburg and to Dieterich Buxtehude (c1637–1707) in Lübeck. The practices of the north German organists greatly influenced J. S. Bach, who heard and played for Reincken and studied with Buxtehude.

Dieterich Buxtehude was the greatest of the north German organ composers. He was born in Denmark, but by 1668 had become organist at the church of St. Mary in Lübeck, Germany, where he remained until his death. (Both Bach and Handel apparently had the opportunity to succeed Buxtehude in this post, but both declined because local custom required the new incumbent to marry his predecessor's daughter!) At the time of Buxtehude's arrival, Lübeck was an important shipping center of nearly 30,000 people, a free city loosely linked to the Holy Roman Empire. At Lübeck's center stood its largest church, St. Mary's, which was Lutheran, like all churches in the city; by 1670 the city fathers had expelled most Catholics, Calvinists, and Jews. St. Mary's had two organs, one near the high altar at the east end of the church for votive services and funerals, and the other a gigantic all-purpose instrument at the west end. A guidebook to the church of 1697 says the following about the organs and music at St. Mary's:

> On the west side, between the two pillars under the towers, one can see the large and magnificent organ, which, like the small organ, is now presided over by the world-famous organist and composer Dieterich Buxtehude. Of particular note is the great Abend-Music, consisting of pleasant vocal and instrumental music, presented yearly on five Sundays between St. Martin's and Christmas, following the Sunday vesper sermon, from 4 to 5 o'clock, by the aforementioned organist as director, in an artistic and praiseworthy manner. This happens nowhere else.[5]

The **Abendmusik** proudly advertised in the guidebook was an hour-long concert of sacred music with arias and recitatives—something akin to a sacred opera or oratorio. A single religious theme unfolded in music over the course of five late-afternoon performances on the Sundays immediately before and during Advent (prior to Christmas). Large crowds flocked to the *Abendmusik* at St. Mary's Church. A report from an early eighteenth-century observer suggests, however, that the populace may have been attracted by things other than great music and the opportunity for spiritual enlightenment.

> The composer [Buxtehude] has never failed also to give an artistic and beautiful setting. However, . . . it is also a great inconvenience that the *Abendmusiken* are held at such an unfriendly and bleak time of the year, namely in the middle of the winter, so that after one has already spent three hours in the cold [for Vespers and the Vespers sermon] one must freeze for a fourth hour as well [for the *Abendmusik*]. The atrocious noise of the mischievous young people and the unruly running and romping about behind the choir take away all the enjoyment that the music might have given, to say nothing of the sins and wickedness that takes place under cover of darkness and poor light.[6]

Such a report reminds us of the limited opportunities for fun and recreation during the long, bleak winters of northern Europe before electricity and central heating. Communal religion, enhanced by voices, instruments, and the organ, was then the chief form of public entertainment. So popular did the *Abendmusik* become at St. Mary's that a special police guard was hired to help maintain order. Among those auditors attracted to these Sunday concerts at St. Mary's was young J.S. Bach, who in 1705 walked some 280 miles to hear them (see also Chapter 39) and who later modeled his own six-part Christmas Oratorio on Lübeck's *Abendmusik*.

Sadly, most of the music Buxtehude composed for the *Abendmusik* has been lost, though the many cantatas surviving under his name are sufficient to give us a sense of his sacred music. Similarly, although Buxtehude composed hundreds of organ pieces (toccatas, preludes, fugues, and chorale settings), fewer than eighty works have escaped the ravages of time. To get an idea of the type of organ piece he wrote in Lübeck, we turn to Buxtehude's *Wie schön leuchtet der Morgenstern* (*How Brightly Shines the Morning Star*), built on a chorale of that name. Recall that a chorale is a monophonic spiritual melody or religious folksong of the Lutheran church—what many Christian denominations today would simply call a hymn (see Chapter 24). The chorale *Wie schön leuchtet der Morgenstern* was one of two melodies composed, or at least adapted, by Lutheran pastor Philipp Nicolai in 1599 (the other is discussed in Chapter 40). Here the shining light of the Lord is equated with the bright star leading to the Christ child, and so this chorale was often heard at Advent and during the *Abendmusik* in Lübeck. The entire chorale is given as Example 34-4.

EXAMPLE 34-4

How brightly shines the Morning Star, With mercy beaming from afar; The host of heav'n rejoices;
O Righteous Branch, O Jesse's Rod! Thou Son of Man and Son of God! We, too, will lift our voices;
Jesus, Jesus! Holy, holy, yet most lowly, Draw thou near to us; Great Emmanuel, come and hear us.

North German organists made a specialty of projecting the Lutheran chorale on their large and colorful instruments. Buxtehude's forty-seven chorale settings constitute the main part of his organ music. Building on the chorale *Wie schön leuchtet der Morgenstern*, Buxtehude creates a **chorale fantasia,** a lengthy composition for organ that takes a chorale tune as a point of departure but increasingly gives free rein to the composer's imagination. In this case, the chorale is first placed in long notes in the bass with two-voice counterpoint set against it (Ex. 34-5a). Then the tune appears a second time, in the treble with the counterpoint coming below. Because the organ can create very different sorts of sonic colors and assign them to separate musical lines on separate keyboards, the chorale tune can be made to stand out distinctively no matter where in the texture it appears. For that reason, chorale settings are more effective on organ than on harpsichord or clavichord. But, as Buxtehude's piece progresses, his creative fancy more and more obscures the tune. Example 34-5b demonstrates how the composer transforms the opening of the chorale into an energetic fugue subject. Example 34-5c shows how he turns the descending scale at the end of the tune into a concluding theme in first three- and then four-voice counterpoint. This is an impressive composition! Remarkably, north German organists such as Buxtehude were expected to improvise such chorale fantasias on the spot as part of every audition. Without this skill, they could not get a job.

EXAMPLE 34-5A

EXAMPLE 34-5B

EXAMPLE 34-5C

LISTENING CUE

DIETERICH BUXTEHUDE
Wie schön leuchtet der Morgenstern (c1690)

CD 5/11
Anthology, No. 98

JOHANN PACHELBEL AND THE SOUTH GERMAN TRADITION

Who has not heard Pachelbel's Canon? Although he is popularly known today only through this one composition, Johann Pachelbel (1653–1706) was a prolific composer who wrote hundreds of pieces, vocal as well as instrumental. Pachelbel was born in Nuremberg, in southern Germany, studied in the Catholic church tradition in Vienna, worked in the central German Lutheran town of Eisenach (where he befriended the Bach family), and ended his days at the Lutheran church of St. Sebaldus back in Nuremberg (see Map 34–1). Pachelbel himself was keenly aware that he had been trained in the south German and Austrian tradition, not that of the north. What exactly differentiated the north and south German styles?

To contrast the two, compare the beginning of Buxtehude's setting of *Wie schön leuchtet der Morgenstern* (see Ex. 34-5) with that of Pachelbel (Ex. 34-6). First, however, keep in mind that Buxtehude's is a chorale fantasia (with the tune in G), while Pachelbel's is a chorale prelude (with the tune in F), and that north and south German composers wrote both types of pieces. A **chorale prelude** is a work for organ that sets a Lutheran chorale tune, surrounding it with counterpoint and florid embellishment. It is called a "prelude" because the organist played it immediately before the congregation sang the chorale in the Sunday service. (For more on the German chorale prelude, see Chapter 39.) Different from the lengthy chorale fantasia, the chorale prelude sounds the tune just once, enough to remind the faithful of the melody they are about to sing. A typical chorale fantasia takes six or seven minutes to perform, while the average chorale prelude lasts only half that time. So, what is the stylistic difference between the two German traditions? The southern style is a bit more tuneful. Pachelbel's counterpoint flows gently along, whereas Buxtehude's denser counterpoint is marked by a high degree of virtuosic and improvisatory-like gestures. In Pachelbel's chorale prelude, melody and counterpoint are joined in equal measure. It is primarily this greater fondness of lyricism that sets apart the south German tradition from the more rigid north German one.

EXAMPLE 34-6

LISTENING CUE

JOHANN PACHELBEL
Wie schön leuchtet der Morgenstern (c1690)

CD 5/12
Anthology, No. 99

This same mixture of counterpoint and pleasing melody marks Pachelbel's most famous work, his Canon in D Major (c1690). The Canon is part of a brief instrumental suite consisting of just a canon and a concluding gigue. The canonic process unfolds in three violin parts, one imitating another at the temporal interval of two measures. Below the canon, a basso continuo sets forth a relentless two-bar *basso ostinato,* which appears twenty-eight times. As the *ostinato* churns away beneath, the canon above gathers rhythmic energy and ascends to ever-higher peaks (Ex. 34-7). Though a musical commonplace for us today, Pachelbel's Canon amply demonstrates that in this south German music rigorous counterpoint (a three-voice canon) can generate soaring lyricism.

EXAMPLE 34-7

 LISTENING CUE

JOHANN PACHELBEL   Book Companion Website (http://schirmer.wadsworth.com/wright_1e)
Canon in D Major (c1690)   Anthology, No. 100

SUMMARY

Composers in Germany and Austria were important in the development of seventeenth-century instrumental music. Johann Froberger established the dance suite as the primary genre of music for string keyboard instruments (harpsichord and clavichord). Through programmatic works such as his "Mystery" Sonatas for violin, Heinrich Biber added greater gravity and breadth of expression to the sonata. Here we see an early demonstration that purely instrumental pieces could project the same sort of deep emotional expression as did the texted vocal music of the Baroque period.

Historically, the Germans and the French have excelled in organ-making, the German skill in crafting precision instruments of all sorts proving a special advantage in this regard. The organ's multiple keyboards and separate groups of pipes not only encouraged the creation of multiple musical lines but also made it possible to project a religious melody (chorale tune or chant) with distinct clarity. The north German organ tradition, exemplified by the chorale fantasia of Dieterich Buxtehude, is thus marked by intense counterpoint, the use of a chorale tune, as well as plenty of virtuosic display showing vestiges of improvisation. The south German tradition, evident in the chorale prelude of Johann Pachelbel, tempered the Nordic rigor with increased lyricism. The great German organ composer of the next generation, J.S. Bach, would fashion a synthesis of these northern and southern styles.

KEY TERMS

dance suite	bourrée	*scordatura*
allemande	gavotte	Doctrine of Affections
courante	hornpipe	*Abendmusik*
sarabande	program music	chorale fantasia
gigue	"Mystery" Sonatas	chorale prelude
minuet	("Rosary" Sonatas)	

Chapter

35

Music in Paris and at the Court of Versailles: Vocal Music

Today the French are a proud and sometimes prickly lot, though in fairness they have an extraordinary amount about which to be proud and prickly. Their nationalism, belief in the superiority of their culture, and suspicion of foreign influence is not something unique to modern times. In fact, it is built upon ancient cultural icons extending back to the *Marseillaise* of the Revolution, to Joan of Arc, and to the great Gothic cathedrals—all French creations. But no French man or woman was ever grander, prouder, or more regal than King Louis XIV (Fig. 35-1), the Sun King (*Roi soleil*), source of light for all the French people, or so he said.

Louis XIV personified the absolute monarch. Indeed, his exceptionally long and authoritarian reign (1643–1715) inspired the political theory of **absolutism**—that ultimate power in the state rested in the hands of a king who claimed to rule by divine right. Whatever Louis wanted, Louis got. Wherever Louis was, there was the French government. As he himself famously said: "I *am* the State!" ("L'État, c'est moi!"). Louis strengthened and expanded the nation, pushing its borders to their modern limits and making France the leading power in Europe. He set the standard for monarchs across Europe, to the point that the second half of the seventeenth century and early years of the eighteenth have come to be seen as the "Age of Louis XIV" or the "Age of Absolutism."

As an example of the *grandeur* to which Louis aspired, consider **Versailles** (see Part IV timeline). In 1669 the Sun King determined to build a new home for himself and consolidate his power some twelve miles southwest of Paris. Over the course of twenty years, forests were cleared, rivers diverted, lakes created, and a colossal palace—actually, a complete city—was constructed by a workforce approaching 36,000. When finished, Versailles stood as a monumental symbol of the French absolutist

FIGURE 35-1

King Louis XIV as painted by Hyacinthe Rigaud about 1700. The portrait captures the king's sense of majesty and authority.

Bridgeman Art Library

state. It was also home to thousands of governmental officials, courtiers, and artists. Here ballets and operas were staged, orchestral dance suites performed, and Masses and motets sung in the royal chapel. Toward the end of his reign, Louis XIV employed between 150 and 200 musicians at any given time. Louis controlled and centralized the creation of art music, much as he did governmental administration.

Consequently, musical talent was not scattered around the cities of France. It was concentrated at the king's court, whether at Versailles or the several much-smaller royal residences in Paris, such as the Louvre, the Tuileries, and the Palais Royal. Moreover, the royal musicians usually were not Italians, as was the case at many other European courts at this time, but were mostly French men and women.

The extent of French bias against foreign influence can be seen in the people's reaction to Italian opera. Italian opera was gradually conquering most of late-seventeenth-century Europe. Cardinal Mazarin, an Italian-born prelate who directed the French government during Louis XIV's minority, tried to establish an Italian opera company in Paris by bringing Italian opera there several times between 1645 and 1662. But French listeners did not warm to fully sung drama offered in a foreign language (Italian) in which the highest vocal parts were often sung by castrated males (castrati). "We almost died of boredom," said a lady of the court.[1] Instead, the French preferred their own special genre of theatrical music called *ballet de cour*, one that emphasized not vocal virtuosity, but dance, choral singing, and spectacle.

BALLET DE COUR

If the English historically have been obsessed with choral church music and the Italians with opera, the French have been enamored with dance. Indeed, the roots of modern ballet are to be found in a distinctive French genre of theatrical display called *ballet de cour*. A **ballet de cour** (court ballet) was a type of ballet danced at the French royal court from the late sixteenth to the late seventeenth century in which members of the court appeared alongside professional dancers. Sets of dances and choruses, simple airs (called *airs de cour*), instrumental interludes, pantomime, and lavish scenery all combined to project a loosely assembled dramatic theme. Much of the *ballet de cour* was taken up with eye-popping "production numbers" involving large groups of similarly costumed singers and dancers. Invariably, the ballet opened with a prologue in which allegorical figures sang the praises of the king and the wisdom of his rule. And similarly it concluded with a *grand ballet*, a final grand dance in which the *grands seigneurs* (great lords) of the court, and often the king himself, danced. In all, Louis XIV appeared in some eighty roles in forty major ballets. Through such carefully choreographed exercises, Louis could affirm aspects of an elitist culture then important to the French monarchy: rank, formality, protocol, discipline, and a sense of style.

As for the music of the *ballet de cour*: some of it was choral music sung during dances, and some of it was a special type of French solo song called the **air de cour**— a simple, strophic song for single voice or a small group of soloists. In addition to this vocal music, the *ballet de cour* included purely instrumental music involving sets of dances popular at that time (see Chapter 34): galliards, minuets, bourées, courantes, sarabandes, and the like. These were played by the French court orchestra, which was built around a core of string instruments called the **Vingt-quatre violons du roi**: twenty-four instruments of the violin family (six violins, twelve violas, and six *basse de violons* [oversize cellos]). In the tradition of seventeenth-century French orchestral music, the *Vingt-quatre violons* played five-part music consisting of treble and bass as well as three middle parts played by the twelve violas divided into groups of four. To these could be added harpsichords, trumpets, drums, and the *Douze grands hautbois* (twelve great oboes) of the royal wind band. On occasion, the orchestra for the *ballet de cour* grew to eighty instrumentalists, a size appropriate for the lavish spectacles of the Sun King.

The image of Louis as Sun King first appeared publicly in a *ballet de cour* presented on 3 February 1653 in which the fifteen-year-old king danced the role of the Rising Sun (Fig. 35-2). Louis equated himself with the Greek god of the sun, Apollo, who watched over the arts and sciences generally, and music in particular. Appearing alongside the king that evening was a young Italian-born choreographer and musician named Jean-Baptiste Lully. Lully himself would soon create some twenty-six *ballets de cour*, more than any other composer. The association of King Louis and composer Lully, and the meteoric rise of Lully, date from that moment.

🌼 FIGURE 35-2

Louis XIV as the Sun in the *Ballet de la Nuit*, 1653.

 JEAN-BAPTISTE LULLY AND *TRAGÉDIE LYRIQUE*

Giovanni Battista Lulli (1632–1687) was born in Florence and recruited as a youth to serve as an Italian teacher and dancing master to a cousin of the French king. After he caught the attention of Louis XIV in 1653, the king appointed him *Compositeur de la musique instrumentale* (1653). Other titles followed, including *Maître de la musique de la famille royale* (Master of Music for the Royal Family) in 1662. That same year, Lulli became a naturalized French citizen under the name of Jean-Baptiste Lully. With the king's unflinching support, the enterprising and often ruthless Lully gradually gained exclusive authority over public vocal music. Lully's hegemony reached the point that almost no piece of polyphonic art music could be performed before the French aristocracy without his permission. Lully himself had become an absolutist. He might well have said: "La Musique, c'est moi!"

One of the musical institutions over which Lully gained exclusive control was the *Académie royale de musique*. King Louis XIV established this company (under a slightly different name) in 1669 as a way to encourage the growth of French opera, just as he had founded similar academies to foster painting (1648), dance (1661), literature (1663), the sciences (1669), and architecture (1671). The **Académie royale de musique** was, in effect, an opera company directly licensed and indirectly financed by the king. It performed in the center of Paris at the Palais Royal and was, in everything but title, the Paris Opéra. France now had a national opera company, but it had no French operas to perform. During the 1670s, Lully set about to remedy this deficiency, and in so doing created a new and unique genre of theatrical music, French *tragédie lyrique*.

French theater reached its zenith during the second half of the seventeenth century, in the comedies of Molière (1622–1673) and in the classical tragedies of Pierre Corneille (1606–1684) and Jean Racine (1639–1699). For musical theater, the court enjoyed its own special brand of ballet (*ballet de cour*), as we have seen. Now Lully brought a new kind of entertainment to the stage: French opera, first called *tragédie en musique*, then **tragédie lyrique.** To create this distinctly French style of opera, Lully fused classical French tragedy with traditional French ballet (*ballet de cour*). This new genre, French opera, embraced ballet. Accordingly, the action of the opera might be interrupted at any moment by a ***divertissement,*** a lavishly choreographed diversionary interlude with occasional singing. Thus *tragédie lyrique* was not a solo singer's opera, like Italian opera, but a dancing actor's opera. Indeed, the principal singers were called *acteurs* and *actrices* in keeping with the tradition of French classical theatre. Lully's librettist, Philippe Quinault (1635–1688), drew his subjects from ancient Greek and Roman mythology and from tales of medieval chivalry. But no matter what the plot, the aim was always the same: to praise the king and reaffirm the values of the prevailing aristocratic culture.

Perhaps no *tragédie lyrique* better represents this genre than Lully's five-act *Armide* (1686), the last of his thirteen French operas. King Louis XIV, inspired by an earlier Italian poem, suggested this tale of medieval chivalry and magic-induced love to Lully. The stage is set near Jerusalem during the First Crusade (1095–1099). The sorceress Armide reluctantly falls in love with the most heroic of all the crusaders, Renaud, and then captures his affection by means of a magic spell. Ultimately, Renaud (a shill for King Louis XIV) comes to his senses and rejects Armide, choosing Duty over the illusion of Love.

Armide opens with a **French overture**, a distinctive type of instrumental prelude created by Lully. (Our English word "overture" comes from the French "ouverture," an opening.) A French overture begins with a slow section in duple meter marked by stately dotted rhythms (suggesting the pomp and grandeur of the court), followed by a fast triple-meter section in imitative counterpoint, and finally a return to the slow, stately style of the opening. Because most later composers like Handel and Bach dropped the slow third section, the French overture came to be known as a two-section piece: slow and dotted, then fast and fugal. Thereafter, throughout the remainder of the Baroque period, a French overture could be used to introduce an opera, ballet, oratorio, or instrumental dance suite.

Following the French overture and a prologue obliquely praising the king, the action begins. In Lully's day, *Armide* was known as "the lady's opera" because sorceress Armide dominates the stage. To love or to kill the hero Renaud, that is her dilemma. Armide's inner conflict is most clearly evident at the end of Act II in a scene beginning "Enfin il est en ma puissance" ("Finally, he is in my power"). Here she intends to stab the sleeping Renaud, but love holds her back. Armide expresses her uncertainty in a new type of singing developed by Lully called **récitatif ordinaire** (ordinary recitative). Ironically, this sort of recitative is anything but ordinary. Although still accompanied only by continuo, it is noteworthy for its length, vocal range, and generally dramatic quality. Here we see clearly the difference between Italian recitative of the period and recitative in Lully's *tragédie lyrique*. While the Italian recitative involves rapid declamation within a rather narrow range (see Anthology, No. 91a), French *récitatif ordinaire* is far more elastic. There are rapid passages that recall Italian simple recitative, but also expansive moments that sound much like a florid aria. Notice also the frequent changes of meter. Poet Quinault has fashioned verse with lines of irregular length. Composer Lully sets them within measures of changing length so that the ends of the lines (always stressed in French) come on downbeats (Ex. 35-1). Lully had carefully studied French declamation, as projected on the Parisian stage by actors in the plays of Corneille and Racine. In this example of *récitatif ordinaire*, Lully captures the drama of the moment not only by assigning Armide erratic melodic leaps that suggest confusion but also by inserting unexpected rests that imply hesitation—to kill or not to kill Renaud.

EXAMPLE 35-1

Finally, he is in my power, this superb conqueror. The charm of sleep brings him within my vengeful spell…

For the first performance of *Armide* in 1686, the role of Armide was sung by soprano Marie Le Rochois (1658–1728), who gained something of a cult following because of the way she played this scene. As one fan observed:

> Dagger in hand, ready to pierce the breast of Renaud, Fury animated her features. [Yet] Love took hold of her heart. The one and the other agitated her in turn, pity and tenderness succeeded at the end, and Love was left the victor. What true and beautiful poses! What different movements and expressions in her eyes and on her face during this soliloquy of twenty-nine lines ["Enfin il est en ma puissance"]. . . One can say that it is the greatest piece in all our opera and the most difficult to perform well.[2]

Of course, Armide yields to her heart. To reflect this decision, Lully changes the music from *récitatif ordinaire* to a resolute, yet dance-like air in the style of an *air de cour* (Ex. 35-2). In Lully's French opera, dancers are never far from the center of the action. Moving to the strains of this charming air, magical zephyrs now transport Armide and Renaud to a place where they may enjoy the pleasures of love (Fig. 35-3). Ultimately, Renaud abandons Armide to heed the call of duty. The enraged Armide sets fire to her palace and escapes high across the stage in a flying chariot, bringing the opera to a spectacular end.

❉ FIGURE 35-3

Armide uses her seductive powers to capture the heart of Renaud in a painting by François Boucher, created about 1733.

Lully Kills Himself Conducting

Jean-Baptiste Lully died shortly after the creation of *Armide*, and he did so in a very odd way. On 8 January 1687 Lully went to a Parisian church to conduct a religious work, his *Te Deum*, in a performance involving more than a hundred musicians. To keep them together, he used a large pointed baton to signal the beat, and in so doing he stabbed himself in the foot. The foot became infected and, little more than two months later, Lully died from gangrene. (Ironically, the performance of the *Te Deum* was organized to give thanks for the recent recovery of King Louis XIV from illness.)

While waving a large stick or staff through the air may seem a strange way to set a beat, this was a common practice when conducting religious music in the seventeenth century. With smaller, single choirs of the Renaissance, it was entirely possible to follow visually the motion of the hand of a leader, and many paintings of the period show a choir director manually giving the beat in the air. With the advent of multiple choirs and polychoral music in the Baroque, however, distances between singers increased and coordination of voices became more of a challenge. A large staff, visible at a great distance, was needed. (Even today experienced performers know that, when multiple groups are separated by distance, or perhaps even placed offstage, it is essential not to listen to the sound, which arrives late, but rather to watch the conductor's beat.) At French churches in the seventeenth century, conductors were urged to strike the beat ("Frappez la mesure"). A Frenchman in Rome in 1638 reports that he saw ten choirs held together by a principal conductor who struck the beat (*battoit la principale mesure*) while ten assistant conductors, one with each of the ten choirs, duplicated his motions. This Baroque practice—musicians watching a staff at a great distance—is still used today in marching bands, where performers follow the beat given by a drum major.

EXAMPLE 35-2

Ve-nez, ve - nez, se - con - der mes dé - sirs, dé - mons, trans-formez vous en d'ai - mab - les zé - phirs;

Come, come, support my desires, demons, transform yourselves into favorable winds.

LISTENING CUE

JEAN-BAPTISTE LULLY
Armide (1686)
Overture
"Enfin il est en ma puissance"

CD 5/13–14
Anthology, No. 101a–b

To sum up: French *tragédie lyrique*, created by Jean-Baptiste Lully, was a new genre of opera that fused elements of *ballet de cour* and traditional French tragic theater. Differing markedly from Italian opera, it possessed the following characteristics:

- **Structure**: requires five acts, following the model of traditional French and English tragedy, rather than the three acts of Italian opera
- **Libretto:** draws on mythological or chivalric topics to create a thinly disguised allegory praising the king and reaffirming the elitist values of the court and the aristocracy generally

- **Overture:** begins with a French overture, not an Italian overture (a sinfonia)
- **Singing:** done mainly in *récitatif ordinaire*; involves little of the virtuosic vocal display then coming into Italian opera
- **Voices:** uses female sopranos, never castrati
- **Chorus:** plays a major role in large-scale choral-dance scenes
- **Dance:** is as important as singing to the overall impact of the work; choreographed *divertissements* regularly interrupt the flow of the drama
- **Spectacle and special effects:** brought about by lavish costumes and elaborate stage machinery, all designed to please the audience and satisfy the ego of the king

RELIGIOUS MUSIC

The fact that Jean-Baptiste Lully was mortally wounded when conducting a lengthy motet (his own *Te Deum*) proves, if nothing else, that not all music at the French court was opera and ballet. As King Louis XIV entered old age, he assumed an increasingly pious life, and his court took on a more devout decor. Not just Lully but other, younger composers were now encouraged to provide sacred music for the king and his relatives. Among these composers were Marc-Antoine Charpentier (1643–1704), who wrote eleven Masses and some 207 motets of various sorts, and Michel-Richard de Lalande (1657–1726), who specialized in writing *grands motets* for the court, some seventy-seven in all. Such works might be heard in religious services at the chapel of Versailles, at many of the Jesuit churches and colleges around Paris, or at the king's Sainte-Chapelle on the Île de la Cité, where Charpentier served as music director from 1698 until his death. When monopolistic Lully departed the scene, Italian-style church music had a chance to gain a foothold. Charpentier studied with Giacomo Carissimi for three years in Rome (see Chapter 32), and he introduced Italian oratorio into France. The sacred cantata, also bearing a strongly Italian imprint, likewise came to France at this time, owing in part to the work of Elizabeth Jacquet de La Guerre (1665–1729).

ELIZABETH JACQUET DE LA GUERRE AND THE *CANTATE FRANÇAISE*

King Louis XIV was not averse to hiring talented female artists. There were professional female dancers in his *ballet de cour*, leading *actrices* in the French opera, and even female sopranos in the royal chapel—this at a time when women did not generally appear as solo singers in churches throughout Europe. About 1670 King Louis heard a five-year-old prodigy named Elizabeth Jacquet sing and play harpsichord, and he granted her a place at court as a performing musician under the care of his principal mistress, Madame de Montespan (Louis's piety came later). A journal of the day commented on her ability to compose and to transpose a piece to any key upon demand. At the age of nineteen, Jacquet left Versailles to marry the organist Marin de La Guerre and thereafter assumed the name Elizabeth Jacquet de La Guerre (Fig. 35-4). She established herself in Paris, giving lessons and concerts, and continuing to compose. Jacquet de La Guerre's output was not large, but what she produced was of high quality, notably her suites for solo harpsichord and her violin sonatas. She also wrote an opera, a *tragédie lyrique* entitled *Céphale et Procris* (1694), the first composed in France by a woman. Her twelve cantatas in French on subjects drawn from the Old Testament are testimony to the growing popularity of the cantata in France in the early years of the eighteenth century.

✿ FIGURE 35-4
Posthumous medallion honoring Elizabeth Jacquet de La Guerre, created in 1732. The reverse of the portrait shows her seated at a harpsichord with the motto "I competed for the prize against the great musicians," implying that she was the equal of her male competitors.

"One talks only of cantatas, only cantatas are advertised at the street corners," said an observer of contemporary Parisian life.[3] Here is evidence that early eighteenth-century France witnessed a flowering of the cantata, both secular and sacred. The cantata, like its instrumental counterpart the sonata, was a product of Italy that by 1700 had made its way over the Alps. By 1730, some 1,200 cantatas had appeared in print in France. Needless to say, the **cantate française,** as it was called, set a French, not an Italian, text. But, in other ways, it was identical to the late seventeenth-century Italian cantata (see Anthology No. 91a–b). A soloist told a story in simple recitative and then, intermittently, the same singer reflected upon these events in ensemble-accompanied arias or in arias with basso continuo only. Succumbing to the Italian rage for the *da capo* aria developed by Alessandro Scarlatti, most of the arias were in **ABA** form. Librettists drew upon either classical mythology (for the secular cantata) or scripture (for the sacred cantata). These were dramas in miniature, for a single character, occasionally two. Thus a *cantate française* can be defined as a piece of chamber music projecting a short mythological or scriptural drama; the story, sung in French, unfolds in a succession of recitatives and arias for solo voice (or duet) accompanied by basso continuo and, occasionally, a small orchestra.

Elizabeth Jacquet de La Guerre published three books of *cantates françaises,* in 1708, 1711, and 1715, respectively. Both of the first two are entitled *Cantates françaises sur des sujets tirez de l'Ecriture (French cantatas drawn from subjects from Scripture).* Both portray events in the lives of heroes and heroines of the Old Testament, and both were dedicated to the grandest of all contemporary patrons, King Louis XIV. Like all sacred cantatas, they were intended to provide music for private spiritual reflection, be it in a grand salon or a modest home.

Perhaps it is not surprising that Jacquet de La Guerre, a woman working in the mostly male profession of music, had a special fondness for heroic female characters in biblical history and therefore named cantatas after them: the daughter of Jephte, Judith, Esther, Rachel, and Suzanna, to be specific. We have met the dutiful daughter of Jephte before in Giacomo Carissimi's oratorio of that name (see Chapter 32). Jacquet de La Guerre goes over the same thematic ground as Carissimi but uses neither multiple characters nor a chorus to comment on the action; hers is a cantata, not an oratorio. Her libretto is not in Italian but French, a French that has a certain restrained quality owing to its third-person narrative. Jacquet de La Guerre adopts for all her arias the Italian-born *da capo* aria form (**ABA**). Moreover, she creates luxuriant Italian-style vocal lines with lengthy melismas in the arias (Ex. 35-3) and supports the rapidly shifting emotions of the recitative with rich, Italianate harmonic changes (Ex. 35-4). In sum, Jacquet de La Guerre effects an impressive synthesis of Italian "passion" and French "cool." French musicians of the time referred to this union as *"les goûts réunis"* (the two styles united).

EXAMPLE 35-3

mm. 32-37

Jeph - té re - vient com - blé de gloi - - - - - - -

Jeph - té re - vient com - blé de gloi - - - - - - -

Jephté returns full of glory...

EXAMPLE 35-4

The daughter of Jephté, full of joy, exits from the palace and hastens before him; you will see her all too soon, unfortunate father, alas!

 LISTENING CUE

ELIZABETH JACQUET DE LA GUERRE   CD 5/15–16
Jephté (1711)   Anthology, No. 102a-b
Aria, "Jephté revient"
Recitative, "La Fille de Jepthé"

SUMMARY

French musical institutions flourished, both in Paris and at the royal palace of Versailles, during the long and absolute rule of King Louis XIV (1643–1715). French *ballet de cour* was a unique blend of ballet and choral singing, interspersed with airs and instrumental interludes, all of which was intended to glorify the monarchy. Beginning in 1673, Jean-Baptiste Lully created a new genre of musical theater called *tragédie lyrique*, French national opera with a distinctly Gallic flavor. Noticeably different from the then-dominant Italian opera, French *tragédie lyrique*, typified by Lully's *Armide* (1686), begins with a French overture and is marked by a style of vocal music in which the singer carefully declaims a French text in a flexible and expansive style of recitative called *récitatif ordinaire*. The heroic-tragic drama is regularly interrupted by *divertissements* involving ballet, solo and choral singing, and instrumental dances. *Tragédie lyrique* depends less on virtuoso singers and more on actors who can sing and dance. Both *ballet de cour* and *tragédie lyrique* employed complex machinery and lavish costumes to create visual effects that astonished and moved their audiences while affirming princely power.

The cantata in the French language (*cantate française*), setting either a religious or a secular subject, enjoyed a brief vogue in the salons of early eighteenth-century Paris. Among the principal creators of the *cantate française* was Elizabeth Jacquet de La Guerre, who delighted in bringing to life the stories of heroic women of the Old Testament. In a French cantata, as with an Italian one of this period, a single performer, or two at most, relates a tale from scripture or classical mythology by means of a series of recitatives and arias. It is thus a drama in miniature, lasting only about ten minutes. Unlike French *tragédie lyrique*, which kept its distance from Italian opera, the *cantate française* borrowed heavily from the Italian vocal idiom, particularly the form and virtuoso style of singing of the *da capo* aria.

KEY TERMS

absolutism	*Vingt-quatre violons du roi*	*divertissement*
Versailles	Académie royale de	French overture
ballet de cour	musique	*récitatif ordinaire*
air de cour	*tragédie lyrique*	*cantate française*

Chapter 36

Music in Paris and at the Court of Versailles: Instrumental Music

For the French royal court and the well-to-do of Paris, the seventeenth century witnessed a flowering of vocal music within the new genres of *ballet de cour*, French opera (called *tragédie lyrique*), and the *cantate française*. Yet the Baroque era was also a golden age for instrumental music in France. In this period the French were leaders in the construction of lutes, harpsichords, and organs. Music for the lute, and for the harpsichord in particular, reached a zenith, not only in the history of French Baroque music but also in Baroque music generally.

THE GAULTIERS: FRENCH LUTE MUSIC

During the late Renaissance, the lute had been the most popular of all "learned" musical instruments, considered to be the descendent of the Greek lyre of Apollo and Orpheus. Recall, for example, that for Renaissance Paris roughly ten times more music was published for the lute than for the harpsichord (Chapter 23). The lute continued to enjoy favor during the early Baroque era, especially at the French royal court. Queen Anne (wife of Louis XIII) took up the instrument and so too did Cardinal Richelieu, leader of the French government during the regency of this young king. "It would be difficult to imagine anything more ridiculous than to see him [Richelieu] take his lessons from [lutenist] Gaultier." Though a lute-playing cardinal seemed absurd to this contemporary observer, Richelieu's lessons suggest how pervasive the lute had become in seventeenth-century French aristocratic circles. For the French courtier, playing lute and dancing were two necessary social graces.

The teacher of Cardinal Richelieu, Ennemond Gaultier (1575–1651), was one of a half-dozen musicians working at this time in and around Paris named Gaultier (or Gautier). Equally famous was his younger cousin Denis Gaultier (1597?–1672). The older, and then the younger, Gaultier dominated lute playing in Parisian salons at mid-century. Both seem to have composed only for lute and both seem to have written mainly dance pieces belonging to suites for lute.

The dance suite in France grew out of the practice of pairing dances such as the pavane and galliard during the Renaissance (see Chapter 22). The vogue of the *ballet de cour* (see Chapter 35) made dancing fashionable and brought new dances to prominence, including the allemande, courante, sarabande, and gigue (see Chapter 34). By 1630 these had spread to the repertory for lute and were grouped together in loosely organized suites according to key and/or tuning.

Throughout the Renaissance the standard tuning for the lute involved mainly fourths (G-c-f-a-d'-g'), much like today's guitar tuning (E-A-d-g-b-e'). During the seventeenth century, however, other tunings emerged. Perhaps more important, strings were added to the bass to generate the pitches F, E, Eb, D, and perhaps C'—this so that the lute could participate more effectively as a basso continuo instrument. At mid-century a suite of dances was often preceded by an indication of the tuning appropriate for the group of pieces to follow.

Denis Gaultier's *La Rhétorique des dieux* (*The Rhetoric of the Gods;* c1652) is a sumptuous culmination of the long history of French music for the lute (Fig. 36-1). *La Rhétorique des dieux* is not a widely disseminated print of lute music, but a unique manuscript put together by a group of music-loving admirers of Denis Gaultier. Here are found twelve suites by Gaultier (some incomplete) arranged in pairs of modes—Dorian and Hypodorian, Phrygian and Hypophrygian, and so on—covering all twelve of the late Renaissance church modes. Most of the pieces are dances, but some have emblematic titles and descriptions suggesting to the listener the meaning of the music. For example, one piece is entitled *Apollo the Orator* and is followed by the following lines: "Apollo [god of music] having assumed the human form of Gaultier, displays here all the powers of his eloquence, and by force of his [musical] persuasion makes his listeners pay the keenest attention." Gaultier is the musical "orator" through whom the gods communicate to those on earth.

Commencing the third suite of *La Rhétorique des dieux* is an allemande with the title *Tombeau de Madamoiselle Gaultier* (correctly translated *Lament for Gaultier's Wife*). Here Gaultier speaks to his wife, but only after he is dead! A **tombeau** (French for "tomb") is an instrumental piece commemorating someone's death. Gaultier wanted to commemorate his own demise and leave his wife a brief musical monument of himself; she did, in fact, outlive the composer. The Gaultiers (Ennemond and Denis) were the first to write *tombeaux*, though the tradition continued in France well into the twentieth century. For

❋ FIGURE 36-1

The title page of *La Rhétorique des dieux* (c1652), in which one god holds the title of the work interlined with lute tablature and another plays a lute containing as many as ten strings and/or courses (pairs of strings).

Staatliche Museen du Berlin

this *tombeau* in honor of himself, Denis selected the Phrygian mode, an apposite choice considering the long association of the Phrygian mode and lamentation (see, for example, Josquin's *Miserere*, Chapter 21). But there is more, for Gaultier begins and ends in F♯ minor. In the Baroque era F♯ minor was a highly remote and indeed unusual key, which would have sounded out of tune and thus painful.[1] The full impact of the Phrygian mode, however, may have been lessened by the addition of chromatic inflections and leading tones which have the effect of transforming the Phrygian mode into the more modern melodic minor scale, here transposed to F♯. In fact, the music throughout *La Rhétorique des dieux* conforms more to the newly emerging major-minor tonality than it does to the older sound of the twelve church modes.

A glance at the score of Denis Gaultier's *Tombeau* reveals a musical texture typical of lute music of the period, one called *style brisé*. **Style brisé** (literally "broken style") is a modern term for a type of discontinuous texture in which chords are broken apart and the notes enter one by one. Voices seem to dart in and out. Such a texture is inherent in lute music because the sounds of the lute are delicate and quickly evaporate. Consider the opening of the *Tombeau* (Ex. 36-1). Sometimes there seem to be four voices in the texture, sometimes only two or just one, as on the downbeat of bar four. We hear a bit of plucking here, a bit there—as appropriate to the lute. Yet, in this fragmented environment, a compelling melody is not easily established. In bars 15–17, for example, melody seems to be sacrificed to the pleasures of chordal strumming (Ex. 36-2). Such a style is well suited to the lighter sound and generally lighter musical repertory of the lute, though musicians soon came to adopt it as well for the harpsichord. J.S. Bach's famous opening prelude to the first book of The Well-Tempered Clavier (Ex. 36-3) adopts *style brisé* but transforms it into particularly German rigid arpeggio patterns.

EXAMPLE 36-1

EXAMPLE 36-2

EXAMPLE 36-3

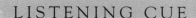

LISTENING CUE

DENIS GAULTIER
La Rhétorique des dieux (c1652)
Tombeau de Madamoiselle Gaultier

CD 5/17
Anthology, No. 103

Adding more and more strings to its lower range made the already-difficult lute even more challenging to play. Larger lutes had as many as twenty-one strings to tune, a time-consuming process. "I have had the pleasure of hearing many a lute tuned, but few played," remarked an exasperated listener of the day. In the second half of the seventeenth century the easily strummed guitar and the colorful, powerful harpsichord replaced the lute as the chamber instrument of choice in France.

THE COUPERINS: FRENCH HARPSICHORD MUSIC

After the Bach family, the Couperin clan forms the most illustrious of all musical dynasties. During the reign of Louis XIV and beyond there were at least a dozen Couperins, both male and female, who made a living as organists, string players, harpsichordists, and composers in Paris. Of these, the most distinguished were Louis Couperin (1626–1661) and his nephew François (1668–1733) called Le Grand ("the Great"). The professional seat of the Couperin family was the parish church of St. Gervais, still standing on the Right Bank of Paris near the Seine River. For nearly 175 years, one Couperin or another served as organist at this splendid Baroque church. In addition, the more talented among them, including Louis and François, were instrumentalists at the royal court.

Louis Couperin is remembered today for one important achievement: he popularized the unmeasured prelude. An **unmeasured prelude** (*prélude non mesuré*) is an opening piece without indications for rhythmic duration or metrical organization. In other words, it has no bar lines and is rhythmically free. The ancestor of the unmeasured prelude for harpsichord was the unmeasured lute prelude. Here a performer moved his fingers freely over the strings to warm up and check the tuning. By the mid seventeenth century, harpsichord composers had adopted the genre as an effective way to open their keyboard suites.

Louis Couperin's unmeasured Prelude in A Minor is the best known of the fourteen that survive under his name. Inspiration for it likely came from the German composer Johann Froberger, for a manuscript preserving this Prelude in A Minor calls it "Prélude à l'imitation de Monsieur Froberger." Froberger, it will be recalled, visited Paris in 1651–1652 and helped standardize the harpsichord suite (see Chapter 34). The opening of the first section of Couperin's prelude (Ex. 35-5), in fact, seems to be an "unmeasuring" of the opening of Froberger's Toccata No. 1 in A Minor (compare Exs. 36-4 and 36-5). Here the unmeasured prelude loosens the already loose toccata.

EXAMPLE 36-4

EXAMPLE 36-5

Publishers eventually tired of dealing with the bizarre-looking notation of the unmeasured prelude. Composers, however, continued to embrace the newfound freedom of the genre in various ways throughout the eighteenth century. J.S. Bach's well-known Chromatic Fantasy was conceived in this freer spirit, and his son C.P.E. Bach wrote unbarred fantasias (see Chapter 43). A French composer summed up the main virtue of the unmeasured prelude when he said "because it is unmeasured, one plays it as one wishes."[2]

It was with good reason François Couperin (1668–1733) was called Le Grand ("the Great"). He surely was the greatest of the Couperins and, arguably, of all French Baroque instrumental composers. J.S. Bach copied Couperin's harpsichord music into the keyboard tutorial he prepared for his wife (the Anna Magdalena Bach Book); Johannes Brahms was one of the co-editors of the first complete edition of Couperin's harpsichord music; and both Debussy and Ravel composed pieces in his honor, the latter writing a belated *Tombeau de Couperin* (see Chapter 67).

François Couperin was born and died in Paris and, like his forebears and descendants, served as organist at the church of St. Gervais. But he also was a leading musician at the court of Louis XIV during the declining days of the Sun King, serving as *organiste du roi* and then as the king's personal harpsichordist. Couperin composed most of his sacred music—including the exquisitely beautiful *Leçons de ténèbre* for Holy Week—for the king's chapel at Versailles. Likewise, Couperin wrote most of his chamber music for the court, including his *Concerts royaux* (*Royal Concerts*, 1722) and *Les Goûts réunis* (*The Tastes United*, 1724), an exercise in melding Italian and French musical idioms. Couperin further showed his love of the Italian style in a trio sonata entitled *Apothéose de Corelli* (1724), yet he quickly followed this with one complimentary to the French style called *Apothéose de Lully* (1725).

In his day François Couperin was considered second to none as a teacher of the harpsichord, and among his pupils were the children and grandchildren of the king. In 1716 Couperin published the fruit of his years of teaching: *L'Art de toucher le clavecin* (*The Art of Playing the Harpsichord*). The **clavecin** (French for harpsichord) was then the favorite chamber keyboard instrument, and some French *clavecins* of the period were large and ornate (see Box, p. 317). **The Art of Playing the Harpsichord** is a pedagogical manual in which Couperin leads the *clavecin* student through a discussion of fingering, ornamentation, and other aspects of performance. His comments on fingering show him to be of the old school, in which the third finger crosses over the second or fourth running down or up the scale (the thumb still does not pass under). But most important is Couperin's discussion of ornamentation.

Ornamentation is an indispensable part of almost all Baroque music. Generally speaking, Baroque ornamentation falls into two broad types: that in which an entire line of music is embellished (as in Italian vocal music, for example); and that in which individual notes are decorated (as in French lute and harpsichord music, for example). No musical repertory was more heavily ornamented than French harpsichord music. The ornaments, what the French call **agréments,** are not written out in full in the keyboard score. Rather, they are indicated by a variety of symbols, and it is up to the performer to insert these *agréments* into the music. Couperin's manual tells the performer how to do it. Below are just a few of the *agréments* Couperin presents.

EXAMPLE 36-6

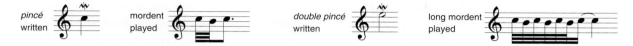

The length of the mordent can be adjusted to the fit the length of the note to which it is applied: the longer the note, the longer the mordent. Most important, the mordent starts on the note, not above it.

EXAMPLE 36-7

Contrary to the mordent, the trill starts above the note. It, too, is to be adjusted to the length of the note it ornaments.

EXAMPLE 36-8

The *port de voix* is a lower, and the *coulé* an upper, appoggiatura. The first note, written as a smaller grace note, is a dissonant note against the bass and must assume at least half of the duration of the larger written note that follows. Finally, all of these ornaments start on the beat, never before it.

In addition to these *agréments,* Couperin discusses performance techniques that are part of the unwritten tradition in French Baroque music. Foremost among these are **notes inégales** in which a succession of equal notes moving rapidly up or down the scale are played somewhat unequally, such as "long-short, long-short." Related to this is the practice of **overdotting,** in which a dotted note is made longer than written, while its complementary short note(s) is made shorter. The performance of *notes inégales* and overdotting appears to have involved more art than science, and was likely much less mathematically exact than the following examples suggest. Couperin does not explain either technique in precise detail, but he makes clear that in French Baroque music, what you see on the page is not always what you play.

> We [French] write [music] differently from the way we play it, which causes foreigners to play our music less well than we play theirs. On the other hand, the Italians write their music in the true note values in which they intended them [to be played]. For example, we dot groups of eighth-notes moving by step [*notes inégales*] despite the fact that we write them as equal notes.[3]

EXAMPLE 36-9

Deciding how to interpret the *agréments* and whether to utilize the practices of *notes inégales* and overdotting are just some of the decisions that a performer must make when engaging Couperin's harpsichord music. Below is one possible realization of two sections of a Prelude by Couperin (Exs. 36-10a and 36-10b). Couperin's original, with his ornamental symbols, appears in the lower system. *Agréments*, *notes inégales*, and overdotting have been applied in the upper one. This realization suggests just how highly nuanced French Baroque harpsichord music can be, and offers a good example of French rococo style. **Rococo** is a term used to describe the decorative arts and the music of mid eighteenth-century France, with all their lightness, grace, and highly ornate surfaces (Fig. 36-3). Perhaps because of the airy yet brilliant sound of the harpsichord, Couperin's rococo style is very idiomatic to this keyboard instrument.

EXAMPLE 36-10A

EXAMPLE 36-10B

The graceful lines of Couperin's art can best be found in the four collections of harpsichord music he published during his lifetime, each entitled *Pièces de clavecin* (1713, 1717, 1722, and 1730). Containing a total of two hundred twenty pieces, these four books constitute the bulk of the harpsichord music that Couperin wrote and that made him famous in his day. Each book is comprised of a handful of suites (called *ordres*), made up mostly of dance pieces. Like the suite, an "***ordre***" is a group of pieces loosely associated by feeling and key. Couperin's *ordres*, however, differ from the usual suite in that they are filled not only with the standard keyboard dances but also with numerous character pieces—pieces that try to capture the personality of an individual, a place, or an aspect of nature or society.

Take *La Favorite* (piece for the Favorite One) from Couperin's third *ordre* (*Pièces de clavecin*, Book I, 1713). The Favorite One may have been the Dauphin, the much

The Eighteenth-Century French Harpsichord

The harpsichord, as we have seen (Chapter 23), first appeared in the Low Countries around 1440 and soon spread south to neighboring France. By the mid eighteenth century, Paris had replaced Antwerp as the European center of harpsichord fabrication and restoration. Among the notable makers of Parisian harpsichords were Jean and Claude Jacquet, earlier relatives of composer Elizabeth Jacquet de La Guerre (see Chapter 35). The Jacquets were succeeded by four generations of the Blanchet family, who started building harpsichords in Paris in 1689 and continued until the Revolution (1789).

While the basic mechanism of the harpsichord remained unchanged—depressing a key caused a plectrum of quill or leather to pluck a metal string—the instrument became increasingly large and complex during the seventeenth and eighteenth centuries. Parisian harpsichord makers were among the first to standardize a two-manual instrument. A second (upper) keyboard was particularly useful in executing pieces involving cross-handed playing (left hand moving over or on top of the right), a technique often required in the music of both Louis and François Couperin. In addition, the bottom keyboard was equipped with two sets of strings: a larger one (called 8',

though the length of the longest string was actually less than eight feet) and a smaller one (called 4', and sounding an octave higher). The upper keyboard had its own set of 8' strings. Moreover, the two keyboards could be made to play together by means of a "coupler." Thus the large French harpsichord of the eighteenth century might play with one of five string sets or combinations and produce as many sound colors: 8' alone (bottom or top); two 8' together (top and bottom manuals coupled); 8' and 4' together (bottom); 8', 8' and 4' together (bottom and top coupled); or 4' alone (bottom). Finally, the keyboard of the instrument was gradually enlarged from four octaves (C to c"') to five (F' to f"'). Some of François Couperin's earliest *ordres* require such a five-octave instrument.

Figure 36-2 shows a five-octave, two-manual harpsichord made by François Blanchet the Elder in Paris about 1740. It typifies the kind of *clavecin* on which Couperin would have played. The notes of his *La Favorite*, for example, would fit easily within its five-octave compass. Moreover, a performer could clearly elucidate the rondeau structure of *La Favorite* by playing the refrain with the keyboards coupled together, while executing the contrasting "couplets" on a single manual that produced a softer sound.

Yale University Collection of Musical Instruments

❀ FIGURE 36-2

A two-manual harpsichord built by François Blanchet the Elder in Paris c1740.

loved eldest son of Louis XIV, who died of the measles in 1712. A sense of loss is conveyed by the bass line of the main theme, which is a chromatic descending tetrachord, a traditional sign of lamentation throughout the Baroque era (see Chapter 31). The piece, as stated by Couperin himself, is a chaconne in the form of a rondeau—"chaconne" because the tetrachord returns repeatedly and thus forms a chaconne bass, yet "rondeau" because the chaconne bass disappears from time to time to allow other musical ideas to come forward. A **rondeau** in the Baroque era is therefore a composition based on the alternation of a main theme (refrain) with subsidiary sections called **couplets** (couplets) to allow musical diversity. Here the refrain and the various couplets create the pattern **ABACADAEAFA.** Couperin's magnificent chaconne-rondeau, four minutes in length, shows that French harpsichord music of the period is not just marked by abundant surface decoration but, if need be, it can project monumental gravity as well.

LISTENING CUE

FRANÇOIS COUPERIN
Pièces de clavecin . . . premier livre (1713)
La Favorite

CD 5/18
Anthology, No. 104

A dancing bear, a beehive, the pleasures of St. Germain-en-Laye, and a famous opera soprano—these are a few of the people, places, and things François Couperin brings to life in the character pieces found within his twenty-seven *ordres*. He also pokes fun at the king's mistresses, the secret societies of the idle rich, and the pretensions of the musicians' union in Paris. One of Couperin's most arresting miniature portraits is his *L'Arlequine* from the twenty-third *ordre* (*Pièces de clavecin*, Book IV, 1730).

Harlequin is a clown from the tradition of Italian *Commedia dell'arte* (improvised slapstick comedy). A troupe of *Commedia dell'arte* players, with clowns Harlequin, Columbine, and Pierrot, was in residence in Paris in the early decades of the eighteenth century. All three clowns wore masks to be funny, certainly, but also to hide a buffoon's pain and humiliation. In a world in which the aristocracy had little to do—the absolute king ran the government absolutely—courtiers tried to while away the hours by creating a make-believe world. This they did with clowns and masks. Harlequin was both comical and grotesque, his smile frightening (Fig. 36-3). Perhaps that is why Couperin has marked his *L'Arlequine* to be performed "*grotesquement.*" The piece starts cheerfully enough. But it ends with a swing around the circle of fifths that includes three successive major seventh chords—a shockingly dissonant sound to eighteenth-century ears and a very modern one to ours. Surely, Couperin inserts this unusual harmonic moment to emphasize the grotesque nature of Harlequin's persona. In character pieces such as *L'Arlequine*, Couperin shows himself to be not only a composer of superb music but also a sharp critic of the courtly society, one full of pretension and masquerade.

Art Institute of Chicago

✿ FIGURE 36-3

"The Harlequin Family" by J. J. Kändler, c1740, a superb example of rococo decoration. Here the passage of time is surrounded by an elegant embellishment and the figures of Harlequin (right) and Columbine (left). Harlequin's smile is somewhat grotesque; the mask of Columbine is that of a bird.

🔘 LISTENING CUE

FRANÇOIS COUPERIN
Pièces de clavecin . . . quatrième livre (1730)
L'Arlequine

CD 5/19
Anthology, No. 105

 SUMMARY

Large volumes, both printed and in manuscript, of high-quality lute music were created in mid seventeenth-century France by Ennemond and Denis Gaultier. The Gaultiers wrote mainly dance pieces, grouped in loosely organized suites, which were often marked by *style brisé*, a broken texture in which the notes of chords are played one after the other and the musical lines dart in and out. *Style brisé* was well suited to the evanescent sound of the lute, yet it was soon brought into the repertory of the harpsichord as well.

French harpsichord music of the late seventeenth and eighteenth centuries is one of the glories of that country's musical patrimony. Members of the Couperin family, Louis and François, set the standard. Louis popularized the unmeasured prelude, a genre that allowed the performer great interpretive freedom. His more important nephew, François Couperin, developed the *ordre*—a suite-like collection of dances and character pieces as well. For his *Pièces de clavecin* Couperin composed two hundred twenty harpsichord works arranged into twenty-seven *ordres* and published in four separate books (1713, 1717, 1722, and 1730). His *Art of Playing the Harpsichord* is a teaching manual that sets out in detail the master's recommended manner of fingering and ornamenting these pieces. Couperin's harpsichord works are always elegant and carefully crafted, sometimes monumental, and sometimes filled with musical irony that serves as social commentary on the aristocratic society of eighteenth-century France.

KEY TERMS

tombeau	*The Art of Playing the Harpsichord*	rococo
style brisé	*agréments*	*ordre*
unmeasured prelude	*notes inégales*	rondeau
clavecin	overdotting	*couplet*

Musical Interlude

From Ancient to Modern: Aspects of Baroque Music Theory

During the seventeenth century, scientists and philosophers revolutionized some of the most fundamental concepts of Western intellectual thought. In this century, Johannes Kepler (1571–1630) formulated the laws of planetary motion; Galileo Galilei (1564–1642), the son of a musician, posited a heliocentric universe; René Descartes (1596–1650) argued for a mathematically based understanding of the material word; and Isaac Newton (1642–1727) discovered the laws of gravity and optics. So significant was this scientific and philosophical revolution that historians call this the **Age of Reason** and mark the seventeenth century as the beginning of the "modern era" in Western history.

In music, too, old modes of thinking about musical structure were replaced by new paradigms during the seventeenth and early eighteenth centuries. This revolution can be seen as a transition from the ancient to the modern world, for most of the theoretical models put forth by Baroque musicians—musical systems and the terms to describe them—are still used by students and professional musicians when they discuss music today. As in most moments in the history of music, Baroque theorists were simply attempting to formulate a rational explanation for the new music they heard. Much of the theory they posited, however, remains with us today.

MODALITY YIELDS TO TONALITY

The modal scales grew out of the eight tones used for singing the psalms in the medieval church, though their names (Dorian, Phrygian, and the like) had been borrowed from the ancient Greeks. Initially there were eight church modes, but these were expanded to twelve during the late Renaissance. Similarly, the modes were first used as a way of defining and directing monophonic chant, though by the Renaissance they provided a framework and direction for polyphonic compositions, both vocal and instrumental. Pieces composed modally seem, to modern ears, to "float" in harmonic space, shifting side to side and cadencing on unexpected pitches. A piece need not even end with the final or fundamental pitch of the mode sounding in the bass.

During the seventeenth century, however, composers increasingly limited their compositions to just two modes: Ionian on C and Aeolian on A. French music theorists were the first to call these two patterns **major** (*majeure*) and **minor** (*mineur*), because the former scale began with a larger third than the latter. They also recognized that the two patterns might be transposed to other pitches so long as accidentals were included to keep the major or minor scale pattern intact. Around 1650, Denis Gaultier wrote a minor-key piece transposed to F♯, for example (see Anthology, No. 103). By 1725 almost all art music was written in either a major or minor key. Even the esteemed George Frideric Handel noticed that the older church modes had become totally obsolete, as he wrote to a friend around 1725:

> As concerns the Greek modes [church modes], I find that you have said everything that there is to say. Their knowledge is doubtless necessary to those who want to practice and perform ancient music [the music of the sixteenth and seventeenth centuries], which formerly was composed according to such modes; however, since now we have been freed from the narrow bounds of ancient music, I cannot perceive what use the Greek modes [church modes] have in today's music.[1]

When defining a central pitch within a melody, theorists began to replace the old Latin term "*finalis*" with words such as "tone" and "key" (in English), "*tonique*" (French), and "*tuono*" (Italian). That central tone was the first note of a seven-note scale (repeating at the octave). Even this concept of a seven-note unit was revolutionary from a pedagogical perspective, for the old way of teaching music involved the ancient system of Guidonian hexachords organized around six-note units (see Chapter 4). During the seventeenth century the natural, soft, and hard hexachords were challenged by a single seven-note pattern (the term for the seventh pitch was "pha," "si," or "ti," among others). A century later, "do" replaced "ut" as the opening syllable, to complete our present system of "do, re, mi, fa, so, la, ti, do."

✿ CHORD INVERSION, FUNCTIONAL HARMONY, AND THE CIRCLE OF FIFTHS: A CLOSED MUSICAL UNIVERSE

During the Baroque era, musical space, like the physical universe observed by Kepler, Galileo, and Newton, became organized in a systematic way that was radically new. Many musical thinkers were involved in this process of reformulating the sonic world of music. But the most innovative and comprehensive thinker about musical harmony was **Jean Philippe Rameau** (1683–1764). Rameau was a composer as well as a theorist. Indeed, his nearly thirty works for the French musical stage and numerous *Pièces de clavecin* rank him as the most important composer in France of the generation after François Couperin. Because Rameau was a composer, he felt himself well positioned to conceptualize and explain to his fellow musicians the new tonal music of the eighteenth century:

> I could not help thinking that it would be desirable (as someone said to me one day while I was praising the perfection of our modern music) for the knowledge of musi-

cians of this century to equal the beauties of their compositions. It is not enough to feel the effects of a science or an art. Rather, one must fashion a theory in order to render them intelligible.[2]

The foundation of Rameau's theory is set forth in his lengthy **Treatise on Harmony** (*Traité de l'harmonie*), which he published in 1722. Just as Newton had approached the physical sciences through mathematics (*Mathematical Principles of Natural Philosophy*, 1687), so Rameau embraced sounding number, the physical division of string, and later the overtone series, as a way to determine what he called the fundamental bass (root) of a collection of pitches in a chord. In a group of pitches involving two consecutive thirds, such as E, G, C, E, G, C, for example, the fundamental pitch, no matter what actually sounded in the bass, was always C (the bottom note of the only perfect fifth in the aggregate). What Rameau codified was the revolutionary principal of **chord inversion** (Ex. 5-1). To this he added other corollaries, in his *Treatise on Harmony* and later works: that the primary chords in music are the triad and seventh chord; that the basic movement within a succession of chords proceeds through fundamental bass notes a fifth apart; that the fundamental tone (tonic) exerts an almost gravitational force that pulls chords to it; that cadences are perfect or imperfect to the degree that they yield to this force of the pulling fifths. Explicit or strongly implied in Rameau's theory were concepts such as the triad, seventh chord, perfect and imperfect cadences, tonic, dominant, subdominant, and mediant pitches, functional harmonic progressions, and chord inversions—all terms and concepts commonly used by later music theorists.

EXAMPLE 5-1

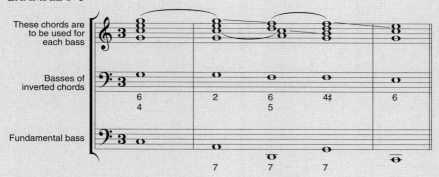

As the eighteenth century progressed, Rameau and other theorists gradually came to adopt an equal tempering of the scale, and this facilitated the completion of a uniform theory of harmony based on the **circle of fifths.** In his *Treatise on Harmony*, Rameau had emphasized the importance of the interval of the fifth as the primary catalyst for moving the fundamental bass through a harmonic progression. In 1711, and then again in 1728, the German composer and theorist Johann David Heinichen (1683–1729) published a "Musical Circle," showing how a composer might proceed around the tonal globe moving by fifths (with relative minor keys interspersed; Fig. 1). Such a movement by fifths, however, might occur only if the scale were "well tempered" or, even better, tuned to equal temperament in which there is exact enharmonic equivalence (F♯ equals G♭, for example). A closed musical circle such as Heinichen's shows the desire of early eighteenth-century composers to play chords and chord progressions in all possible keys.

FIGURE 1

Johann David Heinichen's "Musicalischer Circul" from his *Der General-Bass in der Composition* (1728) demonstrates visually the process of moving around the circle of fifths.

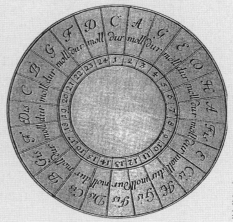

Yale University

SUMMARY

The seventeenth and early eighteenth century witnessed a radical reformation of the way in which the pitch content of music was organized and explained. Teachers of music began to replace the hexachord with the octave as the standard unit of measure, and composers gradually reduced the twelve church modes to just two tonalities (major and minor). At the same time, composers also began to transpose these two tonalities to all twelve pitches of the chromatic scale. This created a self-contained tonal universe regulated by movements of a fifth. Within each key, chords a distance a fifth apart pulled toward one another. By means of modulation, a tonal center could be moved to another center a fifth away and then to another, also a fifth away, and so on, allowing a journey that passed through all twelve chromatic keys of the scale and miraculously arrived back at the beginning (because twelve superimposed fifths result in a unison in equal temperament). This early eighteenth-century organization of tonal space into twenty-four keys (twelve major and twelve minor) revolving around a circle of fifths was as revolutionary for music as was Newton's theory of gravity or Kepler's theory of planetary motion for astrophysics. Indeed, Rameau, influenced by the work of Newton, spoke of a gravitational pull moving the subdominant and dominant to the tonic. And, like most of Newton's laws, this remarkable eighteenth-century construct—a closed network of twenty-four keys forming a unified harmonic system—has endured down to the present day.

KEY TERMS

Age of Reason	Jean Philippe Rameau	chord inversion
major	*Treatise on Harmony*	circle of fifths
minor		

Music in London: Henry Purcell

The seventeenth century was a tumultuous time in English politics. In 1649 the English Parliament seized the king (Charles I) and had him beheaded. Civil war raged between the forces favoring a monarchy and those supporting a more democratic form of government. The royalists regained power in 1660, only to have Parliament depose another king (James II) in 1688, this time by forcing him into exile. Now Parliament invited new rulers, William and Mary, to mount the throne as king and queen. The power of the king and the court was greatly curtailed, while that of Parliament, with its House of Lords and House of Commons, grew proportionally. Individual liberties and democratic self-government expanded (although women were not allowed to vote until 1928!). By the end of the seventeenth century, England had established the first broadly representative government in the West since ancient Greece.

The partial transfer of power from court to commoner that marked the seventeenth century eventually affected music in the Baroque period. Serious opera, for example, rarely flourished in England, in part because it was expensive to produce and received little support from the weakened court. Oratorio, on the other hand, did thrive, because it was less costly to mount and thus appealed to the practical English Puritans. So, too, public concerts and public theaters prospered, because they brought in revenue from daily ticket sales and attracted the increasingly affluent middle class. By 1700 the center of social and artistic life had shifted from the court to public houses (pubs) and public theaters.

London, of course, was the capital and center of art and music for all of England. Its population now numbered nearly 500,000, making it by far the largest city in Europe. Musical life in London was concentrated in three areas. West of the city center was the area of Westminster, where Parliament met. Here, too, stood an old Benedictine monastery called **Westminster Abbey,** providing a venue for ceremonies of state, all with appropriate musical pomp. To the east of Westminster Abbey was Whitehall, where the king and his court resided and entertained, and where the royal chapel sang. Closer to the center of London, then as now, was the theater district. Plays with music, and the occasional opera, were performed here in theaters such as Dorset Garden and Drury Lane, which still exists today.

✿ HENRY PURCELL AND THEATER MUSIC

Henry Purcell (1659–1695) was a child of this changing political and musical environment. Purcell's father was a singer in the royal chapel, and the young Henry too began his career as a chorister in this choir. Here he received instruction in singing, notation, theory, composition, and playing keyboard instruments. After his voice broke in 1673, Purcell became keeper of the royal instruments, then organist at Westminster Abbey and the royal chapel, and finally "composer-in-ordinary" to the court. Toward the end of his life, as the political power and musical interest of the king and queen declined, Purcell increasingly turned his attention to theater music outside the court, where there was more money to be made.

The history of opera in England is somewhat different from that of opera on the European Continent. The Italians and Germans had cultivated opera since the early decades of the seventeenth century. But the English, particularly the Puritans, were skeptical about all-sung opera. Non-stop singing in a theater seemed unnatural to the practical English, especially when it happened in a foreign language. Moreover, the English enjoyed a rich history of purely spoken drama, best exemplified by the plays of Shakespeare. Instead of opera, the English preferred spoken plays (with incidental songs), masques, and semi-operas. The **masque** was an elaborate courtly entertainment using music, dance, and drama to portray an allegorical story that shed a favorable light on the royal family; thus, in many ways, the masque was similar to French *ballet de cour* (see Chapter 35). The **semi-opera** was a spoken play in which the more exotic, amorous, or even supernatural moments in the story were sung or danced. Only rarely was there fully sung opera, such as the excellent *Venus and Adonis* (1685) by John Blow, Purcell's teacher.

Henry Purcell likely acquired his love of the theater at a young age. Since the Middle Ages the roles of women in theatrical productions in Europe had invariably been performed by boys dressed as women; not until 1660 did a woman appear on the public stage in England. For theatrical productions at the English court, the choirboys of the royal chapel often served as female impersonators, and the young Purcell may have got his start in such a role. Regardless of what brought him there, Purcell's compositions for the stage are considerable. They run the gamut of musical theater genres, from simple songs inserted into plays, to incidental music, to semi-opera and fully sung opera. The best known of these today is his only fully sung opera, *Dido and Aeneas*.

Dido and Aeneas (1689)

Purcell's *Dido and Aeneas* apparently received its first performance in 1689 at a school for young women in the London suburb of Chelsea. The school was run by Josias Priest, a friend of Purcell, who was also a choreographer and man of the London theater. The girls presented one major stage production annually, something akin to the senior class play of today, and Priest seems to have provided a role for each and every pupil. They sang in the numerous choruses or danced in the equally frequent dance numbers. All nine solo parts save one (the role of Aeneas) were written for female voices, with the more important solo roles featuring professional singers imported from nearby London.

Appropriately for a school curriculum steeped in classical Latin, the libretto of *Dido and Aeneas* is drawn from Virgil's *Aeneid*. Surely the girls had studied this epic poem in Latin class, and even memorized parts of it. Surely too they knew the story of the soldier-of-fortune Aeneas who seduces proud Dido, queen of Carthage, but then deserts her to fulfill his destiny—sailing on to found the city of Rome. The tale concludes as the abandoned Dido sings an exceptionally beautiful lament, and then runs herself through with a sword (Fig. 37-1). All that remains is for a final chorus to lament her fate.

Dido and Aeneas is an opera in miniature, a chamber opera lasting little more than an hour. Within the three brief acts the music glides quickly between recitative, arioso, and full-blown aria. The climax of the opera comes in the final scene, which culminates in Dido's death. It begins with a brief recitative, "Thy hand, Belinda." Normally recitative is a business-like process that moves the dialogue along through direct, simple declamation. But this one is special. In the stepwise scale that descends an octave, touching almost every chromatic note along the way, we can feel the resignation of the abandoned Dido as she sinks into the arms of her servant Belinda. Here, too, we glimpse one of Purcell's greatest skills: the magical way he sets the English language. He understood where the accents fell in the text of his libretto and gave these stressed syllables greater length and metrical weight in the music; here, the accented syllables generally come on beats one and three, as can be seen in the opening lines "Thy hand, Belinda! Darkness shades me."

🌿 FIGURE 37-1

A detail from the painting *The Death of Dido* by Guercino (1599–1666). The servant Belinda bends over the dying Dido, who has fallen on her sword, atop what will become her funeral pyre.

EXAMPLE 37-1

The aria that follows, known as Dido's lament, is one of the most famous pieces in operatic literature. It is constructed of two beautifully shaped musical phrases that carry the following two lines of text:

> When I am laid in earth, may my wrongs create
> no trouble in thy breast.
> Remember me, but ah! forget my fate.

Each of the two lines is repeated, as are many individual words and pairs. Such repetition of text is typical of an aria, but not a recitative. It is one means by which the composer depicts emotion. The heroine can vocalize, but cannot clearly articulate her feelings in complete sentences. The listener cares less about proper grammar and more that the text and music are emotionally charged. No fewer than six times does Dido plead with Belinda, and with us, to remember her. And, indeed, we do remember, for Dido's plaintive lament is one of the most moving arias in all of opera.

Purcell constructed the lament "When I am laid in earth" on a *basso ostinato*. As we have seen (see Chapter 31), the term *basso ostinato* is an extension of the Italian word *ostinato*, meaning "obstinate," "stubborn," or "pig-headed." In this case, it refers to the fact that the bass line repeats over and over. English composers of Purcell's day called the *basso ostinato* the **ground bass,** because the repetitive bass provided a solid foundation on which an entire composition could be built, or grounded. The repeating pattern might be only a few notes, or several measures, in length.

The ground bass Purcell composed for Dido's lament is five measures long and is heard eleven times. Note that the first half of the musical pattern consists of a chromatic descent that passes through a tetrachord (G, F♯, F, E, E♭, D); the second half moves the harmony from dominant back to tonic. As we have seen (Chapter 31), composers of the Baroque period often used a descending tetrachordal bass as a musical symbol to suggest grief, lamentation, and impending death. Thus, when the basso continuo alone played the descending tetrachord at the beginning of this aria, the audience would have understood the tragic character of the music even before the singer uttered a word. Eight statements of the ground bass then support the repeating phrases of the voice. At the end of Dido's final line, the singer breaks off, as if unable to articulate her sorrow further. But the strings press on, carrying Dido's inconsolable grief across two final statements of the ground bass.

EXAMPLE 37-2

LISTENING CUE

HENRY PURCELL   CD 5/20–21
Dido and Aeneas (1689)   Anthology, No. 106a-b
Recitative, "Thy hand, Belinda"
Aria, "When I am laid in earth"

PURCELL'S ODES AND FUNERAL MUSIC FOR QUEEN MARY

William and Mary (for whom the College of William and Mary is named) were crowned king and queen of England in Westminster Abbey on 11 April 1689. Purcell marched in the procession, composed some of the coronation music, and played organ during the sacral ceremonies. Indeed, Purcell was a busy man that day. It seems that his organ loft gave a good view of the king and queen below, and Purcell made the enormous sum of five hundred pounds selling admission. But the treasurer of the abbey asked for the money back when he learned of the composer's unsanctioned activity. Purcell was not punished further because, as the authorities of the abbey noted, he was "in truth the most excellent musician of his time."

As the years went by, neither William nor Mary proved to be a generous patron of music. Parliament drew their purse strings tight. Moreover, William was a Calvinist (generally called a Puritan in England), and this rather austere branch of Protestantism had little love of music in or out of church. For only one event annually, the queen's birthday, was Purcell required to compose a work for the court.

Art Music Displaced by Folk Music

The music of Henry Purcell belongs to the repertory of what we now call "classical music." Although in its day this kind of brilliant orchestral music and virtuosic singing was appreciated by most of the populace, it was still very much "high art." Yet, even high-born royalty sometimes longed for more commonplace music, if we can trust a story told about Purcell and Queen Mary.

> Having in mind one afternoon to be entertained with music [Queen Mary] sent Mr. Gostling [a singer in the royal chapel] to Henry Purcell and Mrs. Arabella Hunt [see Fig. 37-2], who had a very fine voice, and an admirable hand on the lute, with a request to attend her; [and] they obeyed her commands. Mr. Gostling and Mrs. Hunt sang several compositions of Purcell, who accompanied them on the harpsichord; at length the queen beginning to grow tired, asked Mrs. Hunt if she could not sing the old Scots ballad *Cold and Raw*. Mrs. Hunt answered yes, and sang it to her lute. Purcell was all the while sitting at the harpsichord unemployed, and not a little nettled [annoyed] at the queen's preference of a vulgar ballad to his music.[1]

This anecdote reminds us that a rich tradition of largely unwritten popular music, much of it what we now call Anglo-Irish folk music, coexisted with written art music in England at this time. The Scottish folksong *Cold and Raw,* which apparently originated in the 1500s, was passed along orally for centuries and eventually written down. Several versions of it are currently audible via the internet, some played by electronic synthesizers! To hear one or more of these, simply search under the song title *Cold and Raw*. If the queen found it a pleasant diversion from high art music, you may too.

National Portrait Gallery

❄ FIGURE 37-2
Mrs. Arabella Hunt, a much admired soprano in her day, and performing partner of Henry Purcell.

When writing for the royal court, whether for the birthday, wedding, or welcoming of a ruler, English composers traditionally employed a genre of music called the ode. The **ode** is a multi-movement composition, usually lasting about twenty minutes, containing an instrumental introduction, choruses, duets, and solo arias. The ode has no recitative, however, because there is no drama or action to narrate. Instead, the successive movements offer lyrical hymns of praise to a member of the royal family. In a few cases, odes were also written in honor of St. Cecilia, the patron saint of music.

Henry Purcell composed twenty odes for the English royal family and four in praise of St. Cecilia. Six of the royal odes mark the birthday of Queen Mary (30 April), one for each of the six years Mary ruled. The best of these is the last, *Come, ye sons of art* (1694). The text was newly created by Nahum Tate, who had also fashioned the libretto for Purcell's *Dido and Aeneas.* In successive movements it invites "ye sons of art" (musicians) to celebrate Mary's "triumphant day." First the trumpet, then the "hautboy" (oboe), viol, lute, harp, flute, and finally Nature herself are asked to bring forth their special sounds of praise for the queen. The trumpet is represented by two altos who step forward to sing the duet "Sound the trumpet." On either side of the duet Purcell places the title chorus "Come, ye sons of art" to serve as a spirited choral refrain. In Purcell's day, as was the tradition in the Middle Ages and Renaissance, the alto voice was sung by a male in head voice, or falsetto. Today this high, falsetto alto part is performed by a singer called a **countertenor.** Here two countertenors sing music that is appropriately full of major-key fanfare motifs of the sort usually played by trumpets.

But there is irony in the duet "Sound the trumpet." No trumpets actually sound. Instead, as the countertenors sing in trumpet style, the two trumpeters of the orchestra sit silent. Purcell intended this to be an "in joke," for in his day the two royal trumpeters were named John and William Shore, which surely brought a smile at the words "you make the list'ning shores rebound." More-modern musicians, however, have put the trumpet back in Purcell's vocal duet; the music has been arranged for soprano and trumpet and recorded by, among others, trumpeter Wynton Marsalis.

EXAMPLE 37-3

LISTENING CUE

HENRY PURCELL

Come, ye sons of art (1694)
Chorus, "Come, ye sons of art"
Duet, "Sound the trumpet"
Chorus, "Come, ye sons of art"

CD 5/22–23
Anthology, No. 107a-b

Despite Purcell's best wishes, Queen Mary did not live long. An epidemic of smallpox swept London in the fall of 1694, and on 21 December the queen fell ill.

Doctors prescribed various draughts and potions, subjected her to bleeding, and applied red-hot irons to blister her temples. Not withstanding (or perhaps because of) these treatments, she died a week later. The solemn task of composing the music for her funeral fell to Purcell. Like most of her subjects, Purcell seems to have been sincerely fond of his patron and queen. Indeed, her burial occasioned the same sort of outpouring of national grief as did the funeral of Princess Diana in 1997, which was also held in Westminster Abbey, where Purcell's music fittingly was heard once again. For Mary's service the composer fashioned some of the most beautiful burial music ever written. At the center of the service stood an English choral anthem, the famous *Thou knowest Lord, the secrets of our Hearts*. Preceding and concluding the anthem was a march and a canzona. The march is worthy of special attention, for it is the earliest instrumental funeral march to survive.

Purcell's funeral march is noteworthy also for the instruments that played it: four flat trumpets. The **flat trumpet** was a slide trumpet (like the early trombone), but one for which the sliding tube extended backward over the player's left shoulder, rather than extending forward from the right. Actually, little is known about the flat trumpet and no original survives today. Apparently, the name derives from the fact that the slide made it easier for the trumpet to play in minor keys, which employ a "flat" third scale degree. Surely the capacity to play in minor as well as major accounts for the appearance of the flat trumpet in the funeral music for Queen Mary; the traditional non-slide natural trumpet playing in the usual brilliant keys of C, D, or E♭ major would have been out of place at this somber event. Purcell's march is nothing more than five homophonic chord progressions, each three bars in length. Why then did it bring "tears from all," as an eyewitness reported? Likely because of the rich harmonies, the slow and stately tempo, and the mournful tones of the flat trumpets. The more sprightly canzona sounds less like a funeral dirge than a dance, owing to the rapidly moving notes and lightly imitative texture. Its dance-like character is occasioned by an age-old tradition that holds that burials should end with hopeful, lively music, because the dead are said to dance with the angels in heaven in the life beyond. On our accompanying CD recording, modern reproductions of flat trumpets can be heard.

LISTENING CUE

HENRY PURCELL
Funeral Music for Queen Mary (1695)
March and Canzona

CD 5/24–25
Anthology, No. 108a-b

Less than a year after the death of Queen Mary, Purcell himself died, possibly of tuberculosis. He was barely thirty-six and at the height of his powers. Once again, Purcell's funeral music sounded forth, this time for his own obsequies in Westminster Abbey. He was buried at the foot of the organ, where his memorial plaque can still be read today.

 ## SUMMARY

Like Mozart and Schubert, Henry Purcell composed a remarkable amount of music during his tragically short life. A fully sung opera, *Dido and Aeneas*, numerous semi-operas, and incidental interludes and songs for plays constitute the bulk of his music for the theater. For the English royal family he composed church anthems, twenty birthday odes, and music for Queen Mary's funeral. Whether writing for theater or court, Purcell's scores show his special gifts for melody, infectious dance rhythms, impeccable handling of the English language, and an unfailing freshness of sound. Like his successor, Handel, much of Purcell's finest writing is to be found in his choruses.

KEY TERMS

Westminster Abbey	ground bass	countertenor
masque	ode	flat trumpet
semi-opera		

Chapter  38

Music in London: George Frideric Handel

George Frideric Handel was German-born but spent most of his life in London, becoming in his time a beloved English institution. Handel and his music were arguably the single most important force for cultural unity in England during the entire eighteenth century, even following the composer's death in 1759.

Handel was born in Halle, Germany, in 1685, the same year as J.S. Bach. His father, a surgeon-barber (the two professions were often joined in Handel's day), wanted the son to be a lawyer. But the young Handel's love and obvious talent for music soon led to a change in plans and a rigorous musical education as organist, harpsichordist, and composer. At eighteen Handel moved to the populous north German city of Hamburg, where he played second violin and then harpsichord in the opera orchestra. There he began to study German opera, which was then heavily influenced by the musical style and theatrical conventions of Italian opera. His principal mentor was Reinhard Keiser (1674–1739), the foremost composer of opera in the German language. In 1706 Handel set off for Italy to learn the Italian traditions firsthand, and there he remained for four years, listening to and composing cantatas and operas in Italian. This Italian experience, one not shared by his contemporary, Bach, gave to Handel's subsequent vocal music an accent thoroughly Italianate. Back in Germany in 1710, Handel accepted a position at the court of the elector of Hanover at an annual salary of 1,000 thaler. The terms of his employment allowed for ample travel, so the composer soon set off for England.

As a friend of Handel said in 1713: "In these times, whoever wishes to be eminent in music goes to England. In France and Italy there is something to learn, but in London there is something to earn."[1] Indeed, the already-famous Handel arrived in England with the aim of making money by bringing Italian opera to London. As we have seen, London, with its population of 500,000, was the largest city in Europe. But opera in England had had a checkered history, owing, among other things, to the English aversion to all-sung drama (see Chapter 37). Yet public demand for real opera sung by top-flight Italian virtuosi was starting to grow, and in 1711 Handel satisfied it with *Rinaldo*, the first fully sung Italian opera designed specifically for London and the first to use an all-Italian cast. Conveniently forgetting his obligations in Germany, Handel remained in London, writing Italian opera and using his music to ingratiate himself with the ruling monarch, Queen Anne. But Anne died in the summer of 1714. As fate would have it, Handel's employer in Germany, the elector of Hanover, acceded to the English throne as King George I. Thus were patron and errant musician reunited. Now the most famous composer in England was a German, and so was the king.

Given his connections to the royals, Handel naturally was the first composer called upon when need arose for festive music to entertain the court or to mark its progress. Thus Handel wrote odes and anthems and, ultimately, the *Coronation Service* for the royal family. Among the purely instrumental works Handel composed for the court are his *Water Music* (1717) and *Music for the Royal Fireworks* (1749). For the general public he published sets of concerti grossi, solo concertos for organ and orchestra, and numerous keyboard suites. All the while, Handel worked tirelessly to make Italian opera a staple of English musical life. Encountering increasing financial problems with opera, however, the composer eventually turned his attention to oratorio. Through oratorio, Handel won the hearts and minds of the court and the well-to-do (mostly high-church Anglicans) as well as the common people of England (mostly Puritans). By the time of his death in 1759, Handel had become a cultural monument to which most people could relate with enthusiasm, albeit a few with cynicism (Fig. 38-1). Embracing his ceremonial music for the English monarchy as well as his ever-popular oratorios, the English developed a special bond with Handel's music and responded to it as one people.

✿ FIGURE 38-1

Handel did not do things in moderation—he composed 42 operas and at least 22 full-length oratorios. He consumed food and drink with the same enthusiasm as he soaked up national musical styles. This caricature by Joseph Goupy, done in 1754, pokes fun at the composer for his gluttony (food and wine cask) and his penchant for loud music (trumpet, horn, and drum by his left foot).

✿ HANDEL AND THE DANCE SUITE

The versatile Handel composed in virtually every genre of music known in Western Europe during the early eighteenth century. Aside from *Messiah*, today his most popular composition is his dance suite *Water Music*. Recall that a **dance suite** is a collection of dances all in a single key for one instrument or another, be it a solo instrument or a full orchestra (see Chapter 34); moreover, in the Baroque era the dances of a suite were almost invariably in binary form, **AB.** The suite may begin with a prelude or a French overture, and then continue with a succession of dances, usually ranging in number from four to seven. Of course, listeners did not actually dance to these pieces; they were stylized abstractions. But it was the job of the composer to bring each one to life, making it recognizable to the audience by incorporating the salient elements of rhythm and style from each particular dance.

Bach wrote dance suites for orchestra, for harpsichord, and for solo cello. Handel composed suites for orchestra, specifically *Water Music* and *Music for the Royal Fireworks*. He also published eight suites for harpsichord in 1720 and nine more in 1733. (Handel's famous *The Harmonious Blacksmith*, a title bestowed in the nineteenth century, appears in the fifth suite of the first collection.) Both collections for harpsi-chord are entitled *Suite de Pièces*, reminding us that our English word "suite" comes directly from the French word of the same spelling, meaning "succession" of pieces.

Water Music (1717)

The English royal family, historically, has had a problem with its image. To win favor with the public, the monarchy has traditionally given outdoor concerts, as Queen Elizabeth II did by inviting pop musicians to perform at Buckingham Palace in 2002. Handel's *Water Music* was created for an earlier bit of royal image-building. In 1717 King George I, a direct ancestor of the present queen, was an unpopular monarch. He refused to speak a word of English, preferring his native German. He fought with his son, the Prince of Wales, and banned him from court. London thought King George dimwitted, "an honest blockhead," as one contemporary put it.

To improve his standing in the eyes of his subjects, the king's ministers planned a program of public entertainments, including an evening of music that all the people of London could hear and enjoy. Thus on 17 July 1717, the king and his court traveled by boat up the Thames River. Indeed, so numerous were the boats that it seemed "the whole River in a manner was cover'd." Next to the king's boat was a barge carrying about fifty musicians. As an eyewitness reports, they included "trumpets, horns, hautboys [oboes], bassoons, German flutes [transverse flutes], French flutes [recorders], violins and basses." The account continues: "The music had been composed specially by the famous Handel, a native of Halle [Germany], and His Majesty's principal Court Composer. His Majesty approved of it so greatly that he caused it to be repeated three times in all, although each performance lasted an hour—namely twice before and once after supper."[2] The king and his party did not return to London and the royal residence at St. James until nearly four-thirty in the morning.

To create an hour of music Handel wrote three successive dance suites: one in F major featuring the horn, one in D major highlighting the trumpet, and one in G major and minor centering on the flute. Yet because Handel's complete autograph score of *Water Music* has been lost, and because the surviving contemporary manuscript copies and the early prints do not agree, modern editions differ in the number of movements, titles, and keys. A commonly accepted sequence for the entire work follows.

Suite No. 1 in F Major	Suite No. 2 in D Major	Suite No. 3 in G Major and Minor
1. Overture	10. (Overture)	15. (Sarabande)
2. Adagio e staccato	11. Alla hornpipe	16. Raguadon
3. (Allegro)-Andante-(Allegro)	12. Minuet	17. Minuet
4. (Minuet)	13. Lentement	18. (Andante)
5. Air	14. Bourrée	19. (Country Dance I/II)
6. Minuet (and trio)		
7. Bourrée		
8. Hornpipe		
9. (Allegro)		

The sound of Handel's *Water Music* is both distinctive and historic. It is one of the first English scores to include parts for horn. Although horns had been welcomed into orchestras in Germany, France, and Italy well before 1700, the instrument was introduced into English ensembles only after this date. Oddly, although the home of the horn was Germany and Bohemia (Czech Republic), the English came to call the instrument the **French horn,** having become acquainted with it during visits to the French court of King Louis XIV. Only in the English language is it so named (it is known simply as "the horn" in other countries). The early eighteenth-century French horn was a natural instrument (with no valves) and had a smaller bell, and thus a smaller sound, than the modern horn. Composers frequently assigned a characteristic musical figure called **horn fifths** to the French horn and trumpet, in which the instruments slide back and forth through sixths, fifths, and thirds, sometimes ornamenting along the way as can be seen in Example 38-1 from the Minuet of Suite No. 1. Needless to say, both the French horn and trumpet are featured in *Water Music* because the sound of these brass instruments carries well across outdoor expanses.

EXAMPLE 38-1

> ## LISTENING CUE
>
> **GEORGE FRIDERIC HANDEL**   CD 5/26–27
> *Water Music*, Suite No. 1 (1717)   Anthology, No. 109a-b
> Minuet and Trio
> Hornpipe

Water Music proved to be immensely popular; it was played in pubs and in public gardens in London and throughout the British Isles. The work was arranged for small ensemble, for flute and harpsichord, and for solo harpsichord. In short, it conquered England. Today, Handel's *Water Music*, Bach's Brandenburg Concertos, and Vivaldi's *The Four Seasons* constitute the most popular instrumental music of the first half of the eighteenth century.

HANDEL AND OPERA

Handel enjoyed great success when he became one of the first to bring all-sung Italian opera to London during the years 1711–1717, and this inspired a bolder venture. In 1719 he became the musical force behind a remarkable capitalistic enterprise: the formation of a publicly-held stock company for the production of Italian opera. The principal investor was the king, and thus Handel's opera company was called the **Royal Academy of Music.** Handel wrote most of his best operas for the Academy, yet it went bankrupt in 1728 and again in 1734. To understand how this could happen, we must understand something of the economics of Baroque opera, specifically *opera seria.*

Handel composed some forty-two operas, most of which fall into the category of *opera seria.* **Opera seria** (literally, serious opera, as opposed to comic opera) was fully sung Italian opera of the most elaborate and expensive sort. The plots of *opera*

The Castrato in Handel's Operas

Today pop singers make fortunes, and each star has his or her fanatics. Opera singers have cult followings too, and they earn the most money among "serious" musicians. Over the years, tenor Luciano Pavarotti has commanded a hundred thousand dollars for each appearance at Madison Square Garden or Foxwoods Casino, and soprano Renée Fleming (see Fig. 48-2) appears regularly on the David Letterman Show.

Yet the cult of the singer is not new. In the late Baroque era, star singers were the most adored, and by far the best paid, of musicians. Among the men, the most prized was the virtuoso castrato. The castrato, as we have seen, was a male singer who had been castrated, usually between the age of eight and ten; his body would grow but his larynx and vocal cords would remain small, like those of a woman—all this in hopes that he could be trained to sing beautifully in the soprano or alto range. Audiences on the Continent were greatly enamored with the sound of the castrato, for it combined the high range of a female voice with the power of the male frame. Some could hold a note for a full minute and had a range of an incredible three octaves. The popularity of the castrato was enhanced by the fact that on the Baroque stage, high standing was represented by singers, whether male or female, of high vocal range; the roles of Julius Caesar and Alexander the Great, for example, were sung by castrati, and basses and tenors were usually given only minor parts. Castrati gradually disappeared from the operatic stage during the second half of the eighteenth century, but they continued to sing in Italian churches throughout the nineteenth. The last castrato, papal singer Alessandro Moreschi, died in 1921.

Among the most famous castrati of Handel's day was Francesco Bernardi, called **Senesino** (c1690–1759) because he came from Siena, Italy (Fig. 38-2). Senesino was engaged to sing at the Dresden opera in 1717, where he received a carriage—the eighteenth-century equiva-

lent of a limousine—and an annual salary of 7,000 thalers (Bach's base salary about that time was 400 thalers). Senesino's temper tantrums got him fired from the opera at Dresden, and he moved on to London. In the course of the next two decades he sang heroic roles in some twenty operas by Handel, including that of Caesar in *Giulio Cesare*. Opinion of the English public was divided about Senesino, and castrati in general. One observer noted that "Senesino is daily voted the greatest man that ever lived," while another referred to him as a "squeaking Italian." Today the role of Caesar is sung in one of three ways: by a male in chest voice with the part transposed down an octave, by a male singing in falsetto voice (a countertenor), or by a low female voice called **contralto** (a low alto).

🌼 FIGURE 38-2

A caricature of the principal singers in a scene from an opera by Handel showing the castrato Senesino (left) and soprano Cuzzoni (center).

seria are usually derived from historical events or mythology, and involve larger-than-life figures—kings, queens, gods, and goddesses. There is little drama on stage. The action is often not seen by the audience, but reported by third parties, generally in the form of recitatives. The leading characters do not act so much as react. One after the other, they step forward to sing a self-contained aria, each expressing one of several stock emotions—hope, anger, hate, frenzy, despair, and vengeance, among others. Above all, *opera seria* is a singers' opera. In Handel's day it provided a platform for those singers who possessed the vocal equipment to quiet a restless, often noisy crowd by the power, range, and beauty of their singing. For this to occur, highly trained virtuosi—the best in the world—were needed. But virtuoso singers, then as now, are expensive. The great sopranos and castrati were each paid £1,500

per season, far more than Handel himself. It was Handel's job to recruit these virtuosi (all Italian) from opera houses around Europe. English money was used to buy
the best vocal talent Italy had to offer.

Giulio Cesare (*Julius Caesar*, 1724)

The greatest Italian voices of the day sang the leads in *Giulio Cesare*, an unusually
successful *opera seria* that Handel composed in 1724 for his Royal Academy in London. The libretto recounts an episode in Caesar's life in which he pursues and then
defeats his rival Pompey, in Egypt. Cleopatra, who rules Egypt jointly with her
brother Ptolemy, conspires to seduce the newly arrived Caesar and gain his help in
eliminating her despised brother. All this Cleopatra accomplishes, aided by a generous supply of confidants, servants, disguises, and theatrical tricks. By the end of this
nearly three-hour opera, she becomes queen to a Roman emperor.

In the 1724 production of *Giulio Cesare*, the famous castrato Senesino (see Box
and Fig. 38-2) sang the soprano part of Caesar, while the equally famous female soprano Francesca Cuzzoni sang the role of Cleopatra. In the aria "V'adoro, pupille"
("I Adore You, O Eyes") from Act II of *Giulio Cesare*, Cleopatra must exert all her
charms to win the heart of Caesar, and her music, accordingly, must enchant and
captivate. To create seductive sounds, Handel not only constructed an exquisite
melody but also called for unusual orchestral instruments—the *viola da gamba*, the
theorbo (a large, lute-like instrument), and the harp for heavenly accompaniment.
As is true for most arias in *opera seria*, "V'adoro, pupille" is a *da capo* aria (**ABA**; see
Chapter 32), though here the return to **A** is interrupted by a bit of recitative delivered by the now-enraptured Caesar. Conventions of the *da capo* aria required the
singer portraying Cleopatra to ornament the reprise of **A** to add variety as well as to
show off her voice. Example 38-2 gives the beginning of **A** as Handel wrote it (top)
and suggests how a singer might have ornamented it (bottom).

EXAMPLE 38-2

LISTENING CUE

GEORGE FRIDERIC HANDEL
Giulio Cesare (1724)
Aria, "V'adoro, pupille"

CD 5/28
Anthology, No. 110

With beauty such as this, how could Handel's opera company have gone bankrupt?
The exorbitant cost of the principal singers has already been mentioned, but there
were other factors contributing to the demise of fully sung opera. Among these was
the rise of ballad opera (see Chapter 41), a genre of musical theater alternating spoken

Opera Then and Now

In some ways eighteenth century opera was similar to opera today. Handel's company was funded by a combination of subscriptions and daily ticket sales. Operas were given in a public theater to a paying audience during a season that ran from November into June. Singers were expensive and temperamental. Handel constantly fought with his leading castrato, Senesino; he threatened to throw the diva Cuzzoni out a window when she refused to sing an aria he had written; and Cuzzoni and another prima donna, Bordoni (see Chapter 41), once engaged in a hair-pulling fight onstage. Much was spent on costumes and scenery, but comparatively little on the orchestra. Opera's main drawing cards, then as now, were social glamour and star singers.

There were important differences as well. Most operas performed by Handel's Royal Academy of Music were new works, often composed by Handel himself. Today, opera companies mostly perform "revivals" of previously composed operas—by Handel, Mozart, Verdi, or Wagner, for example.

Moreover, in Handel's day the composer was expected to tailor the music to the voices of the singers in a particular production. If an aria was too high or too low, too difficult or not showy enough, Handel would quickly take up the pen to change it. Today's composers, needless to say, are less accommodating.

Finally, what went on in the opera house was much different. The opening overture was played to call the audience to its seats, not when the audience was seated and quiet. The curtain stayed up between the acts, because other performers stepped on stage to play or dance during intermission. Handel is known to have performed his organ concertos between the acts of his oratorios, and Vivaldi played violin concertos between the acts of his operas. How much of this the audience took in is anyone's guess. Clearly, walking and talking during the performance were more tolerated then; to make a mundane comparison, Handel's opera audience probably behaved like the crowd at a baseball game today.

dialogue with traditional ballads. The popularity of ballad opera, the eighteenth-century counterpart of today's Broadway musical, lured people away from Handel's more high-brow art. Finally, in 1733 a second *opera seria* company, called the "Opera of the Nobility," began operation in London in direct competition with Handel's Academy. Eventually both companies failed, and Handel increasingly turned his attention to oratorio.

HANDEL AND ORATORIO

Oratorio, like opera, was born in seventeenth-century Italy. The very name "oratorio" suggests that it originated in an oratory, a large chapel for prayer. As we have seen (see Chapter 32), an oratorio was a large-scale, multi-movement composition setting a sacred text. Oratorio was not part of the regular worship services of the church, but provided extra-liturgical enlightenment and, especially, enjoyment for the faithful. Indeed, by the time of Handel, the oratorio had become in most ways little more than an unstaged opera with a religious subject. Handel originally intended his oratorios to be spiritual substitutes for opera during the six-week Lenten season before Easter, when secular entertainments such as opera were usually not permitted.

To be sure, oratorio and opera in eighteenth-century London had much in common. Oratorio, like opera, was performed in a public theater before a paying audience. Both usually begin with an overture, are divided into three acts, and consist mostly of recitatives and arias. Finally, both oratorio and opera tell a dramatic story by using individual characters and a chorus.

But there are important differences between oratorio and opera. First of all, oratorio, unlike *opera seria*, is not sung in Italian but in the language of the local people.

In the case of Handel's oratorios, they were sung in English. Moreover, oratorio does not involve staging, costumes, or acting; instead, the audience must picture in its mind's eye the drama that is described on stage. Similarly, oratorio does not require expensive operatic voices and the vocal writing generally is less extravagant than in opera. Finally, oratorio, unlike opera, does not draw upon historical events or tales from classical mythology, but on religious subjects, usually those recorded in scripture. The religious nature of oratorio requires moralizing, and this is done best by the collective forces of a chorus; thus, in oratorio, the chorus is generally far more important than in opera.

Given these qualities, it is easy to see why oratorio appealed to Handel. He could do away with the irascible and expensive castrati and prima donnas. He no longer had to pay for elaborate sets and costumes. He could draw on the English love of choral music, a tradition that extended well back into the Middle Ages (see Chapter 16). In addition, social forces were favoring oratorio. The aristocracy and its wealth, the support network for opera from its inception, was weakening in England. Increasing in importance was a new, untapped market of middle-class consumers—the faithful of the Puritan, Methodist, and growing evangelical sects in England, who viewed the pleasures of foreign opera with distrust, even contempt. Similarly, the subject matter of English oratorio—biblical stories of oppressed peoples who threw off the shackles of domination—was not lost on this rising middle class, who saw themselves overburdened by a corrupt government. The enterprising Handel was quick to see that oratorio was a cost-effective way to use music to bring religious enlightenment to his countrymen, remain politically correct, and still make a handsome profit.

Messiah (1741)

Between 1732 and 1751, when he stopped composing because of blindness, Handel wrote twenty-two oratorios. The majority of these depict heroic figures from the Old Testament, among them Joseph, Susanna, Samson, Esther, Joshua, and the people of Israel captive in Egypt. Yet Handel's most popular oratorio, then as now, is Messiah, which draws on passages from the Old and New Testament concerning the idea of a messiah. Handel composed Messiah in only three-and-a-half weeks during the summer of 1741. It was first performed in Dublin, Ireland, the following April as part of a charity benefit, with Handel conducting. Having heard the dress rehearsal, the local press waxed enthusiastic about the new oratorio, saying that it "far surpasses anything of that Nature, which has been performed in this or any other Kingdom." Such a large crowd was expected for the work of the famous Handel that ladies were urged not to wear hoopskirts, and gentlemen were admonished to leave their swords at home. In this way an audience of 700 could be squeezed into a hall possessing only 600 seats!

Pleased with his artistic and financial success in Dublin, Handel took Messiah back to London, made minor alterations, and performed it in the public theater at Covent Garden. In 1750 he again offered Messiah, this time in the chapel of the Foundling Hospital for orphans, and again there was much popular acclaim for Handel, as well as much profit for charity. In time, Handel gave a conducting score and instrumental parts of Messiah to the hospital and paid for an organ there, so that the oratorio might be given annually. The performances of Messiah at the Foundling Hospital did much to convince the public that Handel's oratorios were appropriate for churches and for charitable fund-raisers. As the music historian and friend of

Handel, Charles Burney, said at the time: "[*Messiah*] has fed the hungry, clothed the naked, fostered the orphan, and enriched succeeding managers of Oratorios, more than any single musical production of this or any country."[3] And so it does to the present day.

In a general way, *Messiah* tells the story of the life of Christ. It is divided into three parts (instead of three acts): (1) the prophecy and birth of Christ; (2) his crucifixion, descent into Hell, and resurrection; and (3) the Day of Judgment and the promise of eternal life. Handel usually performed *Messiah* immediately after Easter. Today it is also offered during the season of Advent before Christmas.

Messiah is comprised of fifty-three musical numbers. Nineteen are for chorus, sixteen are solo arias, sixteen are recitatives, and two are purely instrumental pieces. The large number of choruses reflects the importance of the chorus generally in Handel's oratorios. By contrast, while the arias are important, they tend not to be the big *da capo* show pieces heard in Handel's operas. Ornamentation and vocal display was less important in oratorio than opera, and consequently Handel ultimately included only two *da capo* arias in the entire score. Instead, Handel created for *Messiah* a variety of smaller aria forms in which he tried to create a musical shape and mood appropriate for each aria text.

Typical of the simpler text-specific arias in *Messiah* is the lovely "He shall feed his flock," which invokes the image of Christ, the gentle shepherd of his flock, and of shepherds generally. For this calm and comforting text, Handel fashioned appropriately soothing music. Indeed, "He shall feed his flock" is a perfect example of what is called a **pastoral aria,** a slow aria with several distinctive characteristics: parallel thirds that glide mainly in step-wise motion, a lilting rhythm in compound meter, and a harmony that changes slowly and employs many subdominant chords. The tradition of the pastoral in music extends well back into the seventeenth century and includes, among other pieces, Corelli's "Christmas" concerto from his Opus 6. Bach and later composers, among them Beethoven and Schumann, would also compose pastoral works. Thus Handel's aria "He shall feed his flock" is part of a long continuum in music history in which shepherds, and particularly those of Christmas, are supplied with a lilting style of music called the pastoral.

EXAMPLE 38-3

He shall feed his flock like a shep - herd, and he shall ga - ther the lambs with his arm,

---

LISTENING CUE

GEORGE FRIDERIC HANDEL
Messiah (1741)
Aria, "He shall feed his flock"

CD 6/1
Anthology, No. 111a

Despite the beauty of its arias, the true glory of *Messiah* is to be found in its choruses. Handel was arguably the finest composer for chorus who ever lived. Nowhere is his choral mastery more evident than in the justly famous "Hallelujah" chorus, which concludes Part II of *Messiah* (Fig. 38-3). Here the multitude shouts for joy, for Christ has been victorious on the cross and has ascended triumphantly to reign in heaven.

The power of the "Hallelujah" chorus is generated by several forces: the rhythmically incisive setting of the word "Hallelujah" makes for an exciting exclamation; the repetition of this word throughout builds a feeling of communal participation in a great dramatic pageant; and a variety of choral styles— unison, chordal, fugal, and chordal and fugal together—creates a kaleidoscope of colors and textures. The music is at once complex and very clear. So moved was King George II when he first heard the great opening chords, as the story goes, that he rose to his feet in admiration, thereby establishing the tradition of the audience standing for the "Hallelujah" chorus—for no one sat while the king stood. With its brilliant writing for trumpets in the bright key of D major, this movement might well serve as a royal coronation march, though in *Messiah*, of course, it is Christ the King who is crowned.

The British Library

❀ FIGURE 38-3

The autograph of the full score of Handel's *Messiah* showing the beginning of the "Hallelujah" chorus.

LISTENING CUE

GEORGE FRIDERIC HANDEL
Messiah (1741)
"Hallelujah" chorus

CD 6/2
Anthology, No. 111b

For the first performance of *Messiah* in 1742, Handel's musical forces were rather diminutive: an orchestra of about twenty (mostly strings) and a chorus of eight choirboys for the soprano and five adult males on each of the alto, tenor, and bass lines. As for the soloists, women sang the alto and soprano solos in *Messiah*, and indeed in all Handel's oratorios. (By contrast, the soprano solos in Bach's religious music were invariably sung by a choirboy.) For the performances of *Messiah* at the Foundling Hospital in London during the 1750s, the orchestra grew to thirty-eight players by the addition of doubling instruments (oboes, bassoons, and horns). Later, for the Handel Commemoration of 1785 in Westminster Abbey, about five hundred performers participated, equally divided between chorus and orchestra. In the course of the next hundred years, the chorus swelled to as many as four thousand, with a balancing orchestra of five hundred.

So too grew Handel's stature in the hearts and minds of the English. When he died in April 1759, he left an enormous estate of 20,000 pounds, much of which he bequeathed to charity. He was buried with full honors in Westminster Abbey, with three thousand persons in attendance. Today a sculpture of the composer holding an aria from *Messiah* stands in the Abbey directly opposite a memorial to another giant of English cultural history, William Shakespeare.

SUMMARY

In some ways the music of George Frideric Handel represents a continuation of the English musical tradition. Henry Purcell and his generation wrote wonderfully expressive choral anthems for the church and brilliant trumpet parts to adorn court festivals, as well as evocative music for the theater. But Handel greatly enriched this tradition. As a world traveler with an unsurpassed ear, he had grown up with the sound of the densely contrapuntal German fugue; when in Rome he absorbed the cohesive harmonic language and well-directed basses of Corelli; and, again in Rome, he embraced the Italianate vocal style of the cantata, opera, and oratorio. By combining these sounds with the English choral tradition, Handel achieved a remarkably rich synthesis of national styles. His oratorios in particular show a melding of English choral traditions with the operatic conventions of aria and recitative. Most important, Handel had a flair for the dramatic gained from a lifetime in the theater. He could seize the emotional core of any text, convert it to musical expression, and maintain it with intensity over long spans of time. The vividness, intensity, and grandeur of Handel's music mark it as a positive, life-affirming force.

KEY TERMS

dance suite	Royal Academy of Music	contralto
French horn	*opera seria*	oratorio
horn fifths	Senesino	pastoral aria

Chapter 39

Johann Sebastian Bach: Instrumental Music in Weimar and Cöthen

Johann Sebastian Bach and George Frideric Handel are today the best-known composers of Baroque music. Yet their lives could hardly have been more different. Handel was a man of the world, traveling freely around the European Continent and back and forth to England. Handel had no children, indeed never married. His base of operation was London, a city of a half-million inhabitants. Bach, by contrast, was a devoted father to twenty children and something of a stay-at-home, rarely venturing beyond his familial roots in central Germany. He worked in towns with as few as 3,500 citizens. Handel was a man of the theater, while Bach remained mainly within the precincts of the church.

Yet Bach was keenly attuned to the musical currents of his day, taking great pains to keep in touch with changing musical styles and shape them according to his own intensely rigorous musical intellect. Perhaps more than Handel, Bach used strict constructivist processes to create musical projects of almost superhuman design, such as his Brandenburg Concertos and The Art of Fugue. Whereas Handel wanted his music to sound good, to be heard and enjoyed by all, Bach wanted his music to be good in an almost divinely perfect way; he composed, so he said, "for the greater glory of God alone." By means of intellectual rigor and supreme technical mastery, Bach brought Baroque music to a glorious culmination.[†]

Johann Sebastian Bach came from a long line of musicians who lived and worked in central Germany (Map 39-1). A family tree of this clan includes nearly sixty musical Bachs, extending from the late sixteenth century into the nineteenth. Of these, Johann Sebastian was simply the most talented and industrious. Bach was born in the small town of Eisenach, Germany, in 1685. His father, Ambrosius, directed a town band of five wind players. Bach senior also played the violin, and seems to have taught his son violin, viola, and cello. Young Bach also learned to play the organ, and by the age of fifteen was already composing for that instrument. When Johann Sebastian's parents both died prematurely, he was sent to live with his older brother Johann Christoph in the nearby town of Ohrdruf. There he seems to have learned his trade by secretly copying the works of the masters from a book his brother kept shut away in a cupboard.

As a youth, Johann Sebastian Bach studied music, the humanities, and theology in private Lutheran church schools at Eisenach, Orhdruf, and finally Lüneburg in northern Germany. In all, Bach received twelve years of formal education, more than any other Bach until that time. To pay his way, Bach sang as a choral scholar in various church-school choirs. At Lüneburg, for example, he was a soprano, and then a bass after his voice broke at age fifteen (puberty came later in those earlier centuries). With his formal education completed at the age of seventeen, Bach went forth to make his way in the musical world.

Over the course of the next six years (1702–1708), Bach worked in a number of musical positions, including that of church organist in the small town of Arnstadt (see Map. 39-1). His desire to learn the latest styles resulted in a now-famous story. At age twenty, Bach asked for a leave of absence from his job as organist in Arnstadt

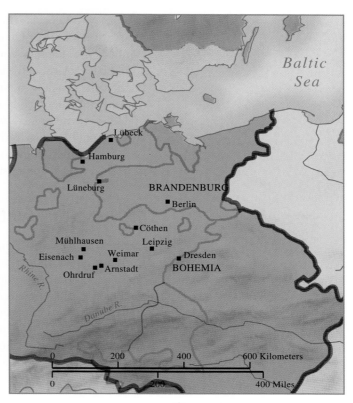

※ MAP 39-1
Central and north Germany in Bach's day.

[†]Like Handel, Bach composed a large number of pieces, more than 1,200. Handel's most important works are vocal compositions and thus are identified simply by their title. Bach, however, wrote a great deal of instrumental music. To avoid confusion among these pieces, twentieth-century musicologists developed a system of grouping his compositions by genre and numbering them. Thus when we buy music by Bach or attend a performance, we usually see an identifying number for the piece in question preceded by the letters **BWV (Bach Werke Verzeichnis),** which is simply German for "Bach Work List." The BWV number for Bach functions much like the "K." numbers used for Mozart's works (see Chapter 47).

to journey to Lübeck, where he could hear the newest organ pieces as well as the famous *Abendmusik* of Dieterich Buxtehude (see Chapter 34). Accordingly, in November 1705, Bach set forth to walk the entire 280-mile distance between Arnstadt and Lübeck. Although his superiors in Arnstadt had given him a leave of a month, Bach walked back into Arnstadt four months after he had left. He was reprimanded not only for truancy but also for the elaborate way he was now playing his chorale preludes on the organ—with so much ornamentation no one could recognize the chorale tune! Evidently, the small town authorities did not like the fancy stuff young Bach had learned from Buxtehude in the big city. Eventually, Bach left Arnstadt and moved on to more promising positions, first in Mühlhausen and then in Weimar.

❀ BACH IN WEIMAR: THE ORGAN MUSIC

During his years in the city of Weimar (1708–1717), Bach wrote most of his great works for organ. In fact, in his day Bach was known more as a virtuoso organist and organ expert than as a composer. At the time, the organ had come to occupy a central place in the religious music of the Lutheran church and in German society generally. In the Lutheran service the organ accompanied the choir and congregation, yet also sounded as a solo instrument, one that could rival a full orchestra in volume and tone color. Moreover, the Germans, then as now, had a tradition of excellence in the manufacture of precision instruments, and they produced pipe organs of the highest quality.

The *Orgelbüchlein*

Among Bach's organ compositions dating from his nine years in Weimar is the **Orgelbüchlein,** a collection of forty-six pieces written mostly between 1708 and 1713. It is called the *Orgelbüchlein* (*Little Organ Book*) because the manuscript measures only 6 x 7 inches. Each of the forty-six pieces is a **chorale prelude,** which, as we have seen (Chapter 34), is an ornamental setting of a pre-existing chorale tune intended to be played on the organ before the singing of the chorale by the full congregation. The performance of the prelude served to recall the chorale tune in the minds of the faithful before they tried to sing it themselves. The title page of the *Orgelbüchlein* suggests that Bach intended to achieve three things with this collection of chorale preludes: (1) to provide the organist with a repertory of pieces to play in church; (2) to show the organist-composer how to construct a chorale prelude on a given tune by providing multiple examples; and (3) to develop the technical facility of the organist by requiring an extensive use of the pedal. In organ music prior to the *Orgelbüchlein*, the bass line could, if the performer wished, be played manually (by the hands) not *pedaliter* (by the feet). Here, in all forty-six pieces, at least one voice must be played by the pedals. Thus users of the *Orgelbüchlein* learned how to coordinate hands and feet, perhaps the most difficult organ technique of all.

Just how challenging a chorale prelude within the *Orgelbüchlein* might be can be seen in "In dulci jubilo" ("In Sweet Jubilation"), a piece intended for Christmas. Originally the melody of "In dulci jubilo" was a Gregorian chant, a hymn sung in Latin in the Roman Catholic Church. In the sixteenth century, the Lutheran Protestants transformed it into a chorale tune by replacing the Latin text with one that combined German and Latin. Even today this jaunty Christmas carol is sung around the world, most often to the English words "Good Christian men rejoice."

The Organ in Bach's Day

The pipe organ, as is well known, makes sounds when air is forced through graduated rows of pipes, usually constructed of metal but sometimes of wood. Pipes of the same type are grouped together and produce a particular sound, and each group of similar-sounding pipes is called a **rank.** Some ranks are made to sound like violins, others like trumpets or horns, and still others like flutes or oboes. Every rank of pipes is activated by pulling out a small wooden knob called a **stop.** A rank of pipes can sound by itself or in combination with other ranks. Thus the fullest sound is made by "pulling out all the stops." The rows, or ranks, of pipes were placed in wooden chests, and one chest usually contained the big pipes for the lowest bass notes. Each of the chests was linked to one or more keyboards at the console of the organ, and a foot (pedal) keyboard was supplied for the bass notes. In Bach's day an assistant was needed to pump the bellows and thereby force air into the pipes, a task nowadays performed by an electrical pump.

Figures 39-1 and 39-2 show the organ at the New Church in Arnstadt, Germany. Dating from the early eighteenth century, it is the only organ Bach himself played that survives to the present day. The organ possesses two manuals and a pedal keyboard, and thus is a mid-size instrument by Bach's standards. A few large north German organs in Bach's time included more than fifty ranks of pipes and four manual keyboards plus one for the feet. One particular virtue of the organ rests in its multiple keyboards, which facilitate playing contrapuntal pieces. By assigning a particular rank of pipes with a distinctive tone color to a particular keyboard, the composer could project three, four, or five individual lines at once, all clearly differentiated from one another by means of their contrasting timbres.

FIGURE 39-1
The console of the organ on which Bach played in the New Church at Arnstadt, Germany, now preserved in a local museum. The console with its keyboards served as the "central processor" for the instrument and sent information to the pipes indicating which were to sound.

FIGURE 39-2
The pipes of the organ at Arnstadt remain today as they were in Bach's day, although the console of the instrument (Fig. 39-1) with its keyboards has been removed and replaced with a more modern one.

When Bach composed a chorale prelude, he usually placed the tune in the soprano and embellished it, lightly or heavily, with appropriate counterpoint. Here, the melody is indeed in the soprano and Bach does supply counterpoint, but he adds one other important element: canon. In truth, Bach was not the first to set "In dulci jubilo" in canon; earlier German composers had recognized that this melody could easily be set against itself at the distance of a measure because each downbeat is a member of the tonic triad. But Bach was not a man to allow himself to be outdone by any composer. Thus, for his setting of "In dulci jubilo," he created two canons—one between the soprano and bass featuring the chorale melody, and another between the alto and tenor serving as counterpoint against the tune. "In dulci jubilo" is one of the earliest manifestations of Bach's lifelong interest in canon.

EXAMPLE 39-1

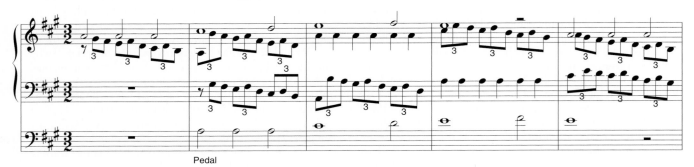

At the end of "In dulci jubilo," Bach appends a brief coda in which the parts undulate above a constantly held low note played on the pedal keyboard of the organ. Because of its original association with the pedal of the organ, any such sustained or continually repeated pitch, usually placed in the bass and sounding while the harmonies change around it, is called a **pedal point.** Bach often concludes his keyboard works with such a sustained or repeating bass. Here a pedal point begins in the tenor range and three measures later the left hand adds its own "pedal point" an octave lower.

EXAMPLE 39-2

LISTENING CUE

JOHANN SEBASTIAN BACH
Orgelbüchlein (c1710)
"In dulci jubilo" (BWV 608)

CD 6/3
Anthology, No. 112

Musical symbolism was an important part of Bach's expressive world. In the chorale prelude "In dulci jubilo" he surely chose to include a canon, indeed a double canon, because the text of the original Latin hymn ended with the plea to Christ: "Trahe me post te" ("Lead me after you"). Bach employs a different sort of musical symbolism in another famous chorale prelude from the *Orgelbüchlein,* "Durch Adams Fall ist ganz verderbt" ("Through Adam's Fall All Mankind Fell"). As the chorale tune sounds on high in the soprano, the alto and tenor provide contrapuntal embellishment below. The bass, however, has a different agendum. It falls precipitously in jagged, dissonant sevenths, thereby playing out through music Adam's "fall" into sin.

EXAMPLE 39-3

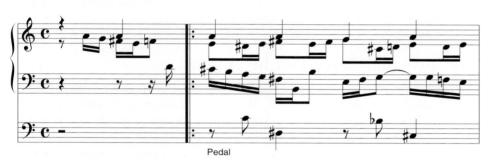

LISTENING CUE

JOHANN SEBASTIAN BACH
Orgelbüchlein (c1710)
"Durch Adams Fall ist ganz verderbt"
(BWV 637)

CD 6/4
Anthology, No. 113

❊ BACH IN CÖTHEN: CHAMBER AND ORCHESTRAL MUSIC

By 1717 Bach had attained full maturity as a musician. He was also an ambitious man fully aware of his talents and his responsibility to his increasingly large family. To better his station in life, Bach now traveled to the court town of Cöthen (see Map 39-1) and successfully auditioned for the job of director of music. When Bach returned to Weimar to collect his family and possessions, Duke Wilhelm of Weimar had him thrown in jail for a month. The duke was not pleased that his musician had "jumped ship" to another court without ducal permission; musicians before Beethoven were little more than indentured servants. When released from jail on 2 December 1717, Bach fled to the court of Cöthen, where he remained for the next six years (1717–1723).

The position Bach assumed at Cöthen was very much a step up for him. He was appointed **Kapellmeister,** the term used in the Baroque and Classical periods to refer to the chief musician, not just of the chapel, but of the entire court. Cöthen, with a population of only 3,500, was not a big city. Nevertheless, it was ruled by an enlightened prince, Leopold of Anhalt-Cöthen, who loved music, played violin, and sang a passably good bass. Having served primarily as an organist at Weimar, Bach was engaged at Cöthen mainly to compose instrumental music. Indeed, his finest chamber and orchestral music dates from these years.

The Two- and Three-Part Inventions

Early in his career, Bach developed a reputation as a superb teacher. Even in Weimar he had attracted nearly a dozen pupils, some coming from great distances and boarding in the master's home. Not coincidentally, as teaching became an important part of his musical life, Bach began to assemble volumes of pedagogical materials for his pupils to play. The *Orgelbüchlein* was one such musical primer for organists. During the years 1720–1723 he compiled another collection of didactic pieces for keyboard players, which we now call the Two- and Three-Part Inventions (the Three-Part Inventions are also called the Sinfonia). The **Two- and Three-Part Inventions** (1723) are two sets of contrapuntal pieces along the lines of simple fugues. Each collection contains fifteen works and each of these is in a separate key (Bach avoids the keys farthest harmonically from C major). These "mini-fugues" require the player to develop a lyrical playing style and to use all five fingers equally; up to this time keyboardists had neglected the thumb (see Chapters 23 and 27). But Bach had a larger pedagogical plan in mind: having mastered two-voice and then three-voice contrapuntal pieces, the student would progress to even more digitally demanding material, the preludes and fugues of The Well-Tempered Clavier.

The Well-Tempered Clavier

Ever since its creation, The Well-Tempered Clavier (*Das wohltemperirte Clavier* in German) has served as the holy grail for harpsichordists and pianists; it is music of such rarified beauty and technical challenge that mastery of it can be a lifelong quest. **The Well-Tempered Clavier** is a collection of preludes and fugues by Bach in two books, one composed in Cöthen about 1720–1722 and the other in Leipzig during the late 1730s. Each volume contains twenty-four pairs of preludes and fugues arranged by key in ascending order—a prelude and fugue in C major is followed by one in C minor, and in turn by one in C♯ major and then C♯ minor, and so on. In this way all twelve pitches of the octave are supplied with a prelude and fugue in a major and minor key. The title implies that Bach now believed a keyboard instrument could, and indeed should, be tuned to play in all tonalities. Bach was gradually moving from a system of unequal temperament to something close to **equal temperament**—a division of the octave into twelve equal half-steps such as we have on the keyboard today (see Box, p. 349). By "clavier" Bach most likely intended to specify the harpsichord, although a performer in his day might try these pieces on the organ or clavichord as well.

To focus on only one prelude and fugue from The Well-Tempered Clavier is to do an injustice to the great variety of styles and designs throughout the collection. Yet the prelude and fugue in C minor from Book I deserves special attention. The prelude begins with blazing sixteenth notes in perpetual-motion style, giving the impression of a highly skilled player improvising a toccata on the spot. The arpeggiated chords change relentlessly, and the performer must jump with a wing and a prayer in hopes of landing on the right notes to begin each new figural pattern. Thumb and fifth finger in particular get a workout here. Finally, although the prelude is in a minor key, it concludes with a bright-sounding major triad. Such a shift from minor to major at the end of a piece is called a **Picardy third.** Musicologists don't know where or why this term was first used, but Baroque composers frequently ended minor-key pieces with a tonic major chord.

To this prelude Bach joined a companion fugue in C minor, a contrapuntal classic that has been analyzed by many musicians, including Bach himself. It begins with a theme, which in the case of a fugue we call the **subject.** This subject is an energetic one, its lively rhythms reminiscent of Italian instrumental music of the day. Typical of fugal composition, each voice presents the subject in turn in an opening section called the **exposition.** Sounding against this subject from time to time is a unit of thematically distinctive material called the **countersubject,** a counterpoint to the subject (Ex. 39-4). The fugue in C minor is a three-voice fugue (in this case alto, soprano, and bass), so once all three voices have presented the subject the exposition is complete. Next comes a free section, called an **episode,** based on motives derived from the subject. Episodes usually involve melodic sequences and

EXAMPLE 39-4

EXAMPLE 39-5

modulation, and this one carries the tonality by step from the tonic C minor up to the relative major E♭. Thereafter, single statements of the subject in different keys alternate with modulating episodes. The epicenter of this particular fugue is found in the episode at measures 17–19, where Bach composes **invertible counterpoint**; the motive which had been in the bass (A) is moved to the alto and the alto motive (B) is placed in the bass (Ex. 39-5). Notice also that motive B is none other than the original countersubject. Finally, the tonality swings around the circle of fifths before the bass and then soprano return with two statements of the subject in a last affirmation of the tonic key. Bach concludes this keyboard work, once again, with a pedal point and a Picardy third. Because no two fugues are alike, they are difficult to define. But a working definition of the term **fugue** might be as follows: a contrapuntal composition for two, three, four, or five voices, which begins with a presentation of a subject in imitation in each voice (exposition), continues with modulating passages of free counterpoint (episodes) and further appearances of the subject, and ends with a strong affirmation of the tonic key. Below is a visual approximation of how this C-minor fugue by Bach unfolds.

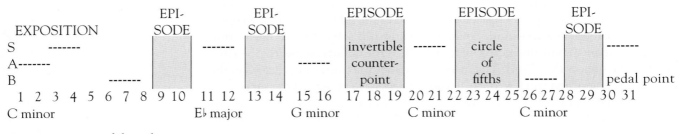

------- statement of the subject

LISTENING CUE

JOHANN SEBASTIAN BACH
The Well-Tempered Clavier (1722)
Prelude and Fugue in C Minor (BWV 847)

CD 6/5–6
Anthology, No. 114

Other Chamber Music

Much of Bach's chamber and orchestral music was written during his years in Cöthen (1717–1723). His position as Kapellmeister required that he compose for, as well as lead, the court orchestra, and that he also provide music for solo performances. In Bach's musical world, solo pieces, works for small ensembles, and even orchestral

Pitch and Tuning in Bach's Day

In Bach's day there was no such thing as standardized pitch. Indeed, the "rule" that concert pitch should be built around an "A" vibrating 440 times per second was not universally mandated until the International Organization for Standardization did so in 1955. The pitch A above middle C was set in Paris in Lully's time (c1675) at about 410 vibrations per second. A tuning fork associated with Handel gives the same A at 422.5. Things were even more variable in Bach's Germany, for here there was one pitch for the organs in church, and another for the instruments of the court or town orchestra. Yet despite the lack of a uniform standard for tuning (A 440, for example), a general trend emerged during the eighteenth century. Tuning slowly evolved from a tuning or temperament with unequal intervals in the various keys (see Musical Interludes 4 and 5) to one of equal temperament with equal intervals.

There were advantages and disadvantages to both the old and new system of tuning. In unequal temperaments, each key had its own distinctive sound because its intervals were slightly different from those belonging to the next key. In most Baroque music, a modulation from the purity of C major to the tension of E major, for example, was a more exciting journey than today. Similarly, a piece in F major sounded very different from one in A major. But the newer equal temperament had its advantages. The composer could modulate through many different keys, indeed all of them, without encountering unpleasant dissonance. Moreover, enharmonic equivalence was now possible; the key of C♯ major sounded exactly like that of D♭ major. Equal temperament was more bland, but more versatile.

In truth, we do not know if Bach's expression "well-tempered" means equal-tempered, or just something very close to equal-tempered. But The Well-Tempered Clavier is an important milestone in the long transition from a scale tuned in unequal intervals to the one tuned in equal intervals that we use today.

compositions were considered to be chamber music because all such music was performed in a domestic music room, or chamber (Fig. 39-3).

Among Bach's chamber pieces are a set of six sonatas for violin, another collection of three sonatas for *viola da gamba*, and yet another group of three for flute, all accompanied by obbligato harpsichord. The term **obbligato** (obliged or mandatory) indicates that a composer has written a specific part for an instrument and intends it to be played as written. Apparently, Bach was reluctant to allow other musicians to realize the figured bass parts to his sonatas. Instead, he often wrote out his own demanding keyboard accompaniments. For violinists and cellists, however, Bach's most important chamber music is to be found in his unaccompanied suites, sonatas, and partitas (**partita** is simply a word that Bach used as a synonym for suite). Here the string instrument is entirely alone.

The six unaccompanied violin sonatas and partitas are especially important. They provide violinists today with a basic repertory for both teaching and performance, just as The Well-Tempered Clavier does today for pianists and the six cello suites for cellists, and no self-respecting violinist can be without the set. Bach himself was a violinist, and his son C.P.E. Bach said that even into his old age his father played the instrument "cleanly and penetratingly." Bach's aim in his set of six works for solo violin is to build technique. Among other things, the player must learn to execute double, triple, and even quadruple stops (to play two, three, or four notes almost

✿ FIGURE 39-3
The recently refurbished Crystal Room at the palace of Cöthen where Bach's Brandenburg Concerto No. 5 was first performed.

simultaneously), as well as to maintain several polyphonic lines at once. Bach was determined to show that the violin could play a multi-voice fugue just as effectively as a keyboard instrument, so he made the second movement of each solo sonata a fugue. As Example 39-6 shows, while demonstrating that a violin can play a fugue, Bach also forces the performer to improve technique by stretching to get several notes in tune at once.

EXAMPLE 39-6

The Brandenburg Concertos

Among the concertos Bach composed while in Cöthen is a justly famous set of six called the **Brandenburg Concertos.** Bach's job at Cöthen required him to lead the court orchestra, conducting either from the harpsichord or the first violinist's desk. The Cöthen orchestra consisted of a group of about fifteen specialists, many of whom had come from the area of Berlin (see Map 39-1). In March 1719, Bach himself went to Berlin to pick up a large new harpsichord that Prince Leopold had ordered. While there, he met the Margrave Christian Ludwig of Brandenburg (1677–1734)—Brandenburg is a territory very near Berlin—who expressed an interest in Bach's music. When he returned to Cöthen, Bach assembled a set of six concerti grossi (some written earlier) and eventually sent them to the Margrave with a flowery dedication. Here Bach writes in French, the courtly language of the period, and with a groveling yet *gallant* tone typical of dedications at this time.

> As I [Bach] had the pleasure a couple of years ago of being heard by Your Royal Highness, in accordance with your commands, and observing that you took some delight in the small musical talent that Heaven has granted me, and as, when I took my leave of Your Royal Highness, you did me the honor of requesting that I send you some of my compositions, I have therefore followed your most gracious commands and taken the liberty of discharging my humble obligation to Your Royal Highness with the present concertos which I have adapted to several instruments. I beg you mostly humbly not to judge their imperfections by the standards of that refined and delicate taste in music that everyone knows you to possess, but rather to accept, with benign consideration, the profound respect and most humble devotion that I attempt to show by this means. . . . I desire nothing more than to be employed on occasions more worthy of you and your service, being with unparalleled zeal,
>   Sire,
>   Your Royal Highness's
>   most humble and most obedient servant,
> Cöthen, 24 March 1721   Jean Sebastien Bach[1]

Most likely, the always-ambitious Bach was angling for a better job. Although no offer of employment was forthcoming from the Margrave, the collection of six concertos still today carries the name "Brandenburg."

In his dedication Bach refers to "the present concertos which I have adapted to several instruments." These words allude to the fact that he designed the Brandenburg Concertos to showcase a variety of orchestral colors. Recall that the concerto grosso consists of a basic orchestra of all players, called the *ripieno* (full) or tutti (all), and from this emerges a small core of soloists, called the *concertino*, to develop and decorate the primary musical themes (see Chapter 33). The various solo groups Bach features in the six Brandenburg Concertos (1721) are as follows.

Key	Movements	Concertino
No. 1 (BWV 1046) F major	[Allegro]-Adagio-Allegro-Minuet	2 horns, 3 oboes, bassoon and *violino piccolo*
No. 2 (BWV 1047) F major	[Allegro]-Andante-Allegro	Trumpet, recorder, oboe, and violin
No. 3 (BWV 1048) G major	[Allegro]-Adagio-Allegro	3 violins, 3 violas, and 3 cellos
No. 4 (BWV 1049) G major	[Allegro]-Andante-Presto	Violin and 2 recorders
No. 5 (BWV 1050) D major	Allegro-Affettuoso-Allegro	Harpsichord, violin, and flute
No. 6 (BWV 1051) B♭ major	[Allegro]-Adagio-Allegro	2 violas, 2 *viole da gamba,* and cello

Let us concentrate on Concerto No. 5, for in this work Bach himself surely functioned as the harpsichord soloist during performances at Cöthen. Concerto No. 5 pits the full orchestra against a *concertino,* consisting of harpsichord, violin, and flute. As with most concerti grossi, the first movement is written in ritornello form, a musical plan popularized by Corelli and Vivaldi. In principle, ritornello form demands that the *ripieno* (tutti) play the ritornello while the *concertino* executes either motives derived from the ritornello or free material that complements it. With Bach, however, the separation between ritornello theme and concertino excursion is not as clear-cut as it had been with Corelli and Vivaldi (see Chapter 33). In Bach's more complex design, the distinction between the large ensemble and the small group of soloists is less pronounced. Nonetheless, Bach's ritornello theme is typical of Baroque melodies in three distinctive ways (Ex. 39-7): it is idiomatic to the violin (repeated notes are easy to play on string instruments); it is lengthy and somewhat asymmetrical; and it possesses a driving rhythm that propels the music forward. As the first movement proceeds, the violin and flute gradually fall by the wayside to allow the harpsichord to carry all the solo material. What had started as a concerto grosso has become a showpiece for solo harpsichord. Bach has written, in fact if not in name, the first true solo concerto for keyboard. Only a virtuoso of the highest order can play the extremely difficult passage-work found toward the end of the movement. But Bach was just this sort of keyboard virtuoso. Picture in your mind's eye the orchestra at Cöthen playing in the prince's music room (see Fig. 39-3). At the center of it all was Bach, seated at the large, new harpsichord he had brought from Berlin, and astounding the members of the court with his bravura playing.

EXAMPLE 39-7

LISTENING CUE

JOHANN SEBASTIAN BACH
Brandenburg Concerto No. 5 in D Major
(BWV 1050; 1721)
First movement

CD 6/7
Anthology, No. 115

SUMMARY

Johann Sebastian Bach wrote many important vocal works, including some three hundred cantatas for the Lutheran church. But the majority of his nearly 1,100 works are for instruments of one kind or another. In his day Bach was known more as a virtuoso organist than as a composer. Bach also played cello, viola, and violin, and early in his career was hired at a court as a violinist. Throughout his life Bach was also a renowned teacher. Many of his best-known instrumental pieces were conceived of, and are still used today, as sets of instructional works. They intend to develop the technical skills and overall musical understanding of the performer. Among Bach's pedagogical projects are the *Orgelbüchlein* (a series of chorale preludes intended to cover the entire church year), the Two- and Three-Part Inventions, the two books of The Well-Tempered Clavier, the six violin sonatas and partitas, and the six cello suites. Bach's complete understanding of the idiomatic capabilities and distinctive colors of the instruments of the Baroque orchestra can best be seen in his Brandenburg Concertos. In this one collection of six concerti grossi, Bach demonstrates a mastery of virtually every instrumental combination and type of orchestral scoring known in his day.

KEY TERMS

BWV (Bach Werke
    Verzeichnis)
Orgelbüchlein
chorale prelude
rank
stop
pedal point
Kapellmeister

Two- and Three-Part
    Inventions
The Well-Tempered
    Clavier
equal temperament
Picardy third
subject
exposition

countersubject
episode
invertible counterpoint
fugue
obbligato
partita
Brandenburg Concertos

Chapter

40

Johann Sebastian Bach: Vocal Music in Leipzig

In the spring of 1723, Bach moved to the city of Leipzig, and there he remained until his death in 1750. Leipzig, with 30,000 inhabitants, was a large German city by the standards of the day, and it boasted an important university where Bach's sons (but not daughters) might enroll. The position that Bach assumed in Leipzig was that of **cantor** (director of church music) at the St. Thomas Church, the largest and most important church in this Lutheran city. While the post of cantor was a prestigious one, the incumbent was nonetheless a civil servant selected by and answerable to the Leipzig town council. Surprisingly, Bach was not the first choice of the city fathers. Only after the well-known composer Georg Philipp Telemann (1681–1767) and the now obscure Christoph Graupner (1683–1760) declined the post, did the members of the town council reluctantly turn to Bach. When he assumed the position in Leipzig, it was understood that Bach would henceforth turn his attention away from instrumental music for the court and would instead concentrate on religious vocal music for the church.

Bach's job in Leipzig was not an easy one. He was required to play the organ at weddings and funerals, teach music and sometimes even Latin grammar to the boys of the choir school of St. Thomas, and superintend the liturgical music of the four principal churches of the city. But by far the most demanding duty of his position as cantor was to provide about a half-hour of new music for the church each Sunday and religious holiday, a total of about sixty days a year. In so doing, Bach brought an important genre of religious music, the Lutheran chorale cantata, to the highest point of its development.

✿ THE LUTHERAN CHORALE CANTATA

When Bach arrived in Leipzig in 1723, he set about composing a cycle of cantatas for the entire church year. In fact, over the next few years he created five such cycles, nearly 300 cantatas in total (although only about two hundred of these survive today). The cantata was the musical high point of the Sunday service. In Bach's time, St. Thomas Church celebrated a Sunday Mass as prescribed two centuries earlier by Martin Luther (1483–1546). Attended by some 2,000 of the faithful, the St. Thomas service began at seven o'clock in the morning and lasted nearly four hours. Following a few introductory chants and prayers, a celebrant read the day's scriptural message from the Gospel. The organist then played a chorale prelude to remind the congregation of the chorale melody of the day and give the instrumentalists an opportunity to tune. At this point, the choir and instrumentalists performed the cantata under Bach's direction. The cantata served as a musical elaboration upon the spiritual theme of the Gospel. Thereafter, a preacher ascended the pulpit (Fig. 40-1) to offer an hour-long sermon discussing the moral and practical implications of this spiritual message. Later that afternoon, the choir and instrumentalists repeated the cantata at a Vespers service at the St. Nicolas Church across town, where an equally large congregation awaited Bach's music.

Typical of the cantatas Bach composed for Leipzig is *Wachet auf, ruft uns die Stimme* (*Awake, A Voice Is Calling*; BWV 140), a work built upon a chorale tune of the same name. A chorale, as we have seen (see Chapter 24), is simply the German version of what most English-speaking communities would call a hymn. *Wachet auf* is a texted chorale tune written in the sixteenth century and widely used by musicians in the Lutheran church before Bach took it up. The structure of the tune is typical of chorale melodies (Ex. 40-1). It is

✿ FIGURE 40-1

Interior of the St. Thomas Church in the mid nineteenth century, looking across the parishioners' pews toward the high altar. Notice the pulpit on the right from which the sermon would be delivered.

St. Thomas's Church, Leipzig

composed of seven phrases that unfold in a pattern **AAB,** specifically **A** (1, 2, 3), **A** (1, 2, 3) **B** (4-7, 3).

EXAMPLE 40-1

A. Awake, a voice is calling
   From the watchmen from high in the tower
   Awake, Jerusalem!
   Midnight is the hour
   They call us with a clarion voice
   Where are the Wise Virgins?

B. Get up, the Bridegroom comes
   Stand up and take your lamps
   Alleluia
   Prepare yourselves
   For the wedding
   You must go forth to meet him!

Because it is based upon a chorale tune, Bach's *Wachet auf* is called a chorale cantata, a genre of music that arose in Germany in the late seventeenth century. The **chorale cantata** is a sacred vocal genre that employs the text and tune of a pre-existing Lutheran chorale in all or several of its movements. *Wachet auf* makes use of a traditional chorale melody during each of its three choral movements, which present the hymn's three textual stanzas in succession. The intervening movements, consisting of recitatives and duet-arias, represent Bach's newly composed settings of the lyrical poems by one of his contemporaries, and use neither the chorale tune nor its text. Thus, Bach creates a formal symmetry, with the chorale-based choral movements at the beginning, middle, and end, flanking each of the recitative-aria pairs and providing a structural framework for the composition as a whole.

Movement:						
1	2	3	4	5	6	7
Chorus	Recitative	Aria (duet)	Chorus	Recitative	Aria (duet)	Chorus
1st stanza			2nd stanza			3rd stanza

Bach was a devoted husband, a loving father to twenty children, and a respected burgher of Leipzig. His cantata *Wachet auf* clearly shows his faith in the religious traditions of his German Lutheran community. Bach composed it in 1731 for a service on a Sunday immediately before Advent (four Sundays before Christmas). The text of the cantata announces the coming of a bridegroom toward his hopeful bride. Christ is the groom. A group of ten virgins represents the bride and, by extension, the entire Christian community. Their story, the Parable of the Wise and Foolish Virgins, is told in the Gospel of St. Matthew (25:1–13); five of the Virgins have brought oil for their lamps and are prepared to meet the coming Christ, but five have not. Both the Gospel and Bach's cantata proclaim this central message: Here

Bach's Choir and Orchestra: Where Were the Ladies?

During the seventeenth century, women frequently appeared as soloists on the operatic stage and occasionally in vocal and instrumental music-making at court. As the eighteenth century progressed, women also began to sing religious music in churches and theaters. But the Lutheran church was a conservative institution in Bach's day. Aside from a few small rural churches where ladies were allowed to appear as "choral adjuncts," women played no role in the performance of Lutheran church music. Ultimately, this traditionalist attitude affected the way the Bach family conducted its business.

When Bach arrived in Leipzig in 1723, he was accompanied by his four children and his second wife, Anna Magdalena Bach (his first wife had died unexpectedly in 1720). Anna Magdalena was a gifted singer who had been employed by the court of Cöthen at a salary almost as great as that of her new husband. But moving to the Lutheran church position in Leipzig forced her to give up her career as a performer. Henceforth, Anna Magdalena would serve as the nucleus of what might be termed "Bach Incorporated"—that industrious group of some dozen or so children, relatives, and students who copied each new Bach cantata and all the necessary parts in preparation for the coming Sunday service. In their quarters next to the St. Thomas Church (Fig. 40-2), Anna Magdalena copied manuscript after manuscript for her husband. She may have assisted him with rehearsals as well.

The actual public performance of a cantata by Bach, however, was an all-male affair. In 1730 Bach stipulated clearly the nature of the orchestra and chorus he required for his sacred vocal music. He drew his instrumentalists from a pool of a dozen string and wind players employed by the town, and these men were supplemented by students from the (all-male) University of Leipzig. Although Bach wanted an orchestra of some twenty players, fifteen seems to have been the norm, and sometimes even fewer were on hand. As to the singers, for the standard four-part choir Bach required at least three singers on each part, though he said he preferred four for a total of sixteen singers. Often, however, many fewer were actually on hand. All of the vocalists—soloists as well as choral singers—were boys or young men from the St. Thomas choir school or the nearby university. Thus the alto and soprano choral parts in Bach's sacred music were sung by males (young men in falsetto voice and boys), and the difficult soprano solos were executed by a solitary choirboy. Indeed, the ladies never did get a fair hearing.

Bach-Archiv, Leipzig

FIGURE 40-2

Leipzig, the St. Thomas Church (center), and the choir school (left), from an engraving of 1723, the year in which Bach moved to the city. Bach and his large family occupied two floors of the choir school, and it was here that the composing, copying, and rehearsing of his music took place.

in the season of Advent all good citizens of Leipzig should put their spiritual houses in order, for Christ will soon be with them.

The spiritually attuned listener can hear the inexorable march of Christ in the opening movement of cantata *Wachet auf*. Here Bach creates a chorale fantasy that is both dramatic and monumental. First the orchestra announces Christ's arrival by means of a three-part ritornello (Ex. 40-2). The ritornello conveys a feeling of growing anticipation. The increasingly numerous sixteenth notes suggest the urgent movement of the faithful surging forward to meet the coming Christ. Then the ancient chorale melody enters on high in the sopranos; it is the voice of tradition, perhaps the voice of God. In long, steady notes, it enjoins the populace to prepare to receive the Lord. Beneath this the voices of the people—the altos, tenors, and basses—scurry in rapid counterpoint, eager to meet their savior. Lowest of all is the bass of the basso continuo. It moves steadily ahead, mainly in stepwise motion in notes of similar value. This walking bass enhances the meaning of the text, underscoring the steady approach of the Lord. The enormous complexity of the movement, with its dense textural layering and rich symbolism, shows why musicians, then and now, view Bach as the greatest contrapuntalist who ever lived.

EXAMPLE 40-2

LISTENING CUE

JOHANN SEBASTIAN BACH
Cantata BWV 140, *Wachet auf, ruft uns die Stimme* (1731)
Movement 1

CD 6/8
Anthology, No. 116a

Movement 2 is a recitative for tenor solo, a narrator who announces the imminent arrival of Christ, the bridegroom. This is an example of simple recitative because the accompaniment is limited to a basso continuo, featuring in this case the organ and bassoon. Generally speaking, in his sacred vocal works Bach assigns the role of the narrator, or evangelist, to a tenor.

Movement 3 is a lengthy duet for soprano (the Soul) and bass (Christ). In German sacred music of the Baroque period, the role of Christ is traditionally assigned to a bass. Here Bach ornaments the charming soprano-bass duet with a lengthy ritornello played by a ***violino piccolo*** (a small violin usually tuned a minor third higher than the normal violin).

Movement 4 calls upon the chorale melody once again. Now Bach places the tune (and the second stanza of the chorale text) in long notes in the tenor voice alone. The tenors are the watchmen of Zion who call Jerusalem (Leipzig) to awake. Beneath this chorale the bass plods forward, mostly in unwavering quarter notes. This classic example of a Baroque walking bass again suggests the inevitable coming of Christ. Against the tenor and bass the violins and violas play a hauntingly beautiful ritornello (Ex. 40-3). It is exactly twelve bars long and subdivided into six two-bar groups—an unusually symmetrical construction for Bach. Perhaps because of the symmetrical, lyrical style of the ritornello, this movement has become one of Bach's most beloved compositions. Indeed, it was one of Bach's favorites too, for it was the only cantata movement that he published.[1] All the rest of his Leipzig cantatas were left in handwritten scores at the time of his death.

EXAMPLE 40-3

LISTENING CUE

JOHANN SEBASTIAN BACH
Cantata, *Wachet auf, ruft uns die Stimme*
Movements 2, 3, and 4

CD 6/9–10 and
Book Companion Website (http://schirmer.wadsworth.com/wright_1e)
Anthology, No. 116b-d

Movement 5 is an **accompanied recitative** in which the bass soloist (representing Christ) invites the anguished Soul to find comfort in him. Unlike the tenor's simple recitative (movement 2), this movement features strings providing a lush chordal accompaniment, creating a halo-like effect to surround the words of Christ—another example of musical symbolism in Bach.

Movement 6 is a duet between Christ and the Soul, who are once again represented by the bass and soprano soloists. Bach wrote no operas, and indeed by the time he arrived in 1723 the Leipzig opera house had closed for good. But he frequently went to nearby Dresden (see Map 39-1), where the court sponsored a flourishing opera, one of the best in Europe. In movement 6, Bach comes as close as he ever will to composing an operatic love duet. In fact, the piece is a perfect *da capo* aria of the sort that might be found in a Baroque *opera seria*.

Movement 7 is a four-part harmonization of the chorale tune that sets the third and final stanza of the chorale text. Here the full congregation joined in the singing of the chorale, likely not by reading from a hymnal but by singing the tune from memory. In this concluding movement, all of the instrumental parts double the vocal lines, a technique termed ***colla parte*** (with the part). Here too all the spiritual energy of Leipzig was united in Bach's simple but expressive harmony.

EXAMPLE 40-4

May glory be sung to you...
The gates are of twelve pearls...

Bach's Four-Part Chorale Harmonizations and Teaching Music Theory Today

Today in colleges, universities, and music conservatories around the world, the study of music theory is grounded in a thorough investigation of four-voice chorale harmonizations by Johann Sebastian Bach. Almost all students majoring in music, for example, study Bach chorales to learn how to write, and thereby understand, proper chord progressions, modulations, and voice leadings. They compose the "missing" three voices (bass, tenor, and alto) below ancient chorale melodies in the style of Bach. Thus the model of Bach, established nearly three hundred years ago, lies at the core of much theory pedagogy today. But would Bach have approved?

Indeed, he would have, for this was precisely the method of teaching Bach himself employed. C.P.E. Bach, the mas-

ter's second son, said this about his father's approach to teaching harmony: "His pupils had to begin their studies by learning pure four-part thorough [figured] bass. From this he went to chorales; first he added the basses to them himself, and they had to invent the alto and the tenor. Then he taught them to devise the basses themselves."[2] Bach also encouraged his students to copy into their notebooks four-part chorale settings from his passions and cantatas (such as, for example, the final movement of the cantata *Wachet auf*). Owing in part to these notebooks of Bach's students, 371 of Bach's chorale settings have been preserved for us to study today. Thus, in a sense, we are all students of Bach.

LISTENING CUE

JOHANN SEBASTIAN BACH
Cantata, *Wachet auf, ruft uns die Stimme*
Movements 5, 6, and 7

CD 6/11–13
Anthology, No. 116e-g

In addition to some three hundred cantatas, Johann Sebastian Bach is said to have composed five passions and a Christmas oratorio, all large-scale works. A **passion** is a musical depiction of Christ's crucifixion as recorded in the Gospels; it is traditionally performed on Good Friday. By Bach's time, a passion had become virtually identical to an oratorio, except that it dealt with just one subject, the death of Christ. Of Bach's five passions, only two survive, the St. John Passion (1724) and the St. Matthew Passion (1727). The former requires about two hours to perform, and the latter two-and-a-half. Perhaps for that reason, members of the Bach family called the St. Matthew setting the "Great Passion." It requires three choirs and two small orchestras, each with a colorful variety of instruments. Many believe the St. Matthew Passion, with no fewer than sixty-eight expressive movements, to be Bach's greatest dramatic work.

BACH'S LATER MUSICAL PROJECTS

By 1730 Bach had tired of the weekly grind of creating new music for the church each Sunday. He did not relinquish his position at the St. Thomas Church, but gave it less time as he turned his attention to other musical activities. In late March 1729, Bach assumed directorship of the Collegium Musicum in Leipzig. A **collegium musicum** was an association of musicians, usually university students, who came together voluntarily to play the latest music before the public in a large café or beer hall. (The name "collegium" is still used today by performing groups in colleges and universities, although now the emphasis is not on a repertory of modern music, but on early music as played on reproductions of historical instruments.) Bach directed the Collegium Musicum of Leipzig, on and off, for at least a dozen years. It provided an opportunity for him to compose and perform orchestral music—concertos and orchestral suites—something that his recent preoccupation with church music in Leipzig had not allowed him to do.

Not only did Bach turn to projects beyond the St. Thomas Church in his last decades but he also looked beyond the city limits of Leipzig. In 1733 he composed a *Kyrie* and *Gloria* for the court in Dresden, which would later serve as the opening movements of his great B-Minor Mass (see below). Another work destined for Dresden at this time is Bach's **Goldberg Variations** (BWV 988), a virtuosic set of thirty variations preceded and concluded by a simple air, the air and each variation based on the same thirty-two-bar harmonic pattern. The collection derives its name from a gifted pupil of Bach, Johann Goldberg, who worked for one of Bach's patrons in Dresden. It seems that the patron was something of an insomniac and asked Bach for music that Goldberg might play to alleviate the tedium of his sleepless nights.

In 1747 Bach undertook his last substantial journey, a trip to Berlin to visit his son, Carl Philipp Emanuel Bach. C.P.E. Bach was employed as a keyboardist at the court of King Frederick the Great of Prussia (1712–1786), who himself was a musical enthusiast, being a skilled flautist. Bach arrived in the evening, when Frederick, as was his custom, was playing chamber music with his court musicians. Immediately the king went to a keyboard to play a melody he had composed, and asked Bach to improvise a fugue on it on the spot. This Bach did in a way such that the king and his courtiers alike "were seized with astonishment," as a newspaper of the day reported. But Bach himself was not satisfied. When he returned home to Leipzig he set about making the royal theme serve as the unifying element, not merely in a single fugue, but in a collection of pieces: a trio sonata, two fugues (called ricercars), and ten puzzle canons. Bach called his royally inspired collection **The Musical Offering** (BWV 1079) and dedicated it to His Majesty with appropriately inflated praise of the king's musical talent. In truth, however, The Musical Offering reveals how the genius of Bach was needed to unlock the full musical potential of the king's original idea.

Bach's other great encyclopedic work is The Art of Fugue, which he began about 1740 and had not quite finished at the time of his death a decade later. **The Art of Fugue** (BWV 1080) is a collection of fugues and canons, all derived from the same subject (Bach's own) and all apparently intended for keyboard. Here we see exemplified almost every contrapuntal technique known to musicians. When published after his death, it consisted of fourteen fugues and four canons, all written in score and most for four voices. Bach intended the final fugue to be a quadruple fugue, but it breaks off shortly after the exposition of the fourth subject. Appropriately, this last subject is built upon the four pitches B♭, A, C, B♮, which in German musical notation spells the word BACH.

The Goldberg Variations, The Musical Offering, and The Art of Fugue demonstrate Bach's focus on large-scale musical projects during the last decade of his life. In each of these he brought one particular form of composition—variation, puzzle canon, or fugue—to a level of excellence that was never surpassed.

B-Minor Mass

Bach's last composition, his **B-Minor Mass** (BWV 232), is perhaps the grandest of all of these large-scale projects, for here he brought the tradition of the Baroque Latin Mass to a glorious culmination. As we have seen, Bach had composed the *Kyrie* and *Gloria* for the court of Catholic Dresden back in 1733. Now, in 1748, in old age and declining health, the master determined to extend the work by adding a *Credo, Sanctus,* and *Agnus,* and thus create a complete setting of the Ordinary of the Mass as sung for centuries in the Roman Catholic Church. For these additional movements, Bach did not compose entirely new music. Instead, he refashioned movements of cantatas and Masses that he had written years before. For example, a *Sanctus* written in 1724 became the opening of the *Sanctus* of the B-Minor Mass; a movement of a cantata of 1714 (*Weinen, Klagen [To Whine and Wail,* BWV 12]) was reworked to serve as the "Crucifixus" of the *Credo.* Bach borrowed from this earlier cantata because its subject matter (weeping) was signalled by a descending tetrachordal bass, the Baroque emblem of mourning. The vocal parts of the "Crucifixus" are thus filled with dissonant, painful tritones and augmented seconds, all created in the score by the use of many sharps (but no flats). The sharp, of course, is cruciform or cross-like, in shape; this is the way Bach's musical symbolism works.

EXAMPLE 40-5

Today we may be scandalized that Bach chose to re-use so much previously written material in what would be his last great work. But virtually all composers of the Baroque period engaged in this practice. (Handel was an especially notorious "borrower.") It gave the artist a chance to review an earlier work, revise it, and thereby improve the score. For Bach in particular, this process of musical review provided yet another opportunity to perfect his art, and Bach was nothing if not a perfectionist.

LISTENING CUE

JOHANN SEBASTIAN BACH
B-Minor Mass (BWV 232; 1749)
Credo, "Crucifixus" (begun 1714; final form 1749)

CD 6/14
Anthology, No. 117a

The turn to the relative major at the end of the "Crucifixus" sounds a note of hope to be realized in the next movement, "Et resurrexit" ("And He arose").

The theme of Christ's resurrection now receives an appropriately triumphant setting. With large orchestra and brilliant trumpets sounding in a sprightly triple meter, the music seems to dance joyfully toward heaven. Unlike the "Crucifixus," which was refashioned from much-earlier music, the "Et resurrexit" was apparently newly composed. Indeed, these notes must have been among the last that Bach wrote. Thus what we call the great B-Minor Mass is a compilation of pieces that Bach had composed over the course of three decades. It represents a culmination of all that he had learned about writing sacred music for the church.

LISTENING CUE

JOHANN SEBASTIAN BACH
B-Minor Mass (1749)
Credo, "Et resurrexit" (1749)

CD 6/15
Anthology, No. 117b

Bach's B-Minor Mass is a massive five-movement sacred work that takes some two hours to perform. During the composer's lifetime, the Mass was never heard in its entirety. It was inappropriate for the Lutheran church because it contains portions of the Mass text not used in the Lutheran service; likewise, it was unsuitable for the Catholic liturgy due to its length and the freedoms taken with the text. Nor could it have been sung simply as a concert—concerts of purely religious music as we know them did not exist in Bach's day. Today the B-Minor Mass is performed in concert halls around the world. It is appreciated less as a Catholic Mass and more as a work that transcends denominations. Like Beethoven's Ninth Symphony, Bach's B-Minor Mass is his ecumenical gift to all humanity.

SUMMARY

When Johann Sebastian Bach died during the summer of 1750, apparently of a stroke, he and his music were soon forgotten. With its heavy reliance on traditional chorale tunes and dense counterpoint, his creations were thought to be too old-fashioned and rigid, even pedantic. Yes, Bach's music is often difficult. He was intent on discovering and exploiting the musical potential of every idea, and he took no shortcuts. In so doing, Bach created grand projects that demonstrate the special qualities of almost every musical genre and form except opera—organ prelude, prelude and fugue, solo sonata, concerto grosso, cantata, passion, variation set, puzzle canon, and Latin Mass. These encyclopedic projects offer a splendid summation of music of the Baroque era.

But as early as the 1730s new musical currents were in the air, those of the Enlightenment. The public wanted lighter textures, simple phrasing, and tuneful melodies. Although Bach's sons adjusted to the tastes of the day, "the old Wig," as one of them irreverently called him, did so only sporadically. Thus, shortly after 1750, the mention of the name "Bach" would likely have conjured up the image of one or the other of his fashionable sons, not the great polyphonic master. Yet, a small group of musicians, including Mozart, Beethoven, Schumann, and Mendelssohn, kept the knowledge of Bach's extraordinary music alive. When Mendelssohn performed Bach's St. Matthew Passion in 1829 as part of a centenary commemoration, a "Bach revival" was underway. From that time on, musicians have never ceased to admire Bach's music for its internal integrity, grand design, and superhuman craftsmanship.

KEY TERMS

cantor	*colla parte*	The Musical Offering
chorale cantata	passion	The Art of Fugue
violino piccolo	collegium musicum	B-Minor Mass
accompanied recitative	Goldberg Variations	

THE ENLIGHTENMENT AND THE CLASSICAL ERA

$\mathcal{H}$istory is a seamless flow. When politicians act, artists create, and philosophers think, they do so without concern for periodicity. Historians look back and group together earlier leaders, artists, and thinkers within a fixed historical period because common themes seem to unite their aims and modes of expression—ones distinctly different from what came before and after. Music historians, for example, find it convenient to mark the end of the Baroque period at 1750 with the death of Bach. But choosing this or any other year oversimplifies an evolutionary process. Need-

1650	1700	1750

BAROQUE PERIOD (1600–1750)   **ENLIGHTENMENT**

Tsar Peter the Great (r. 1682–1725)

King Frederick

Antoine Watteau (1684–1721), French painter

Domenico Scarlatti (1685–1757), Italian composer

• c1700 Bartolomeo Cristofori (1655–1732) invents the piano in Florence, Italy

Giovanni Battista Sammartini (c1700–1775), leader in creation of concert

Johann Stamitz (1717–1757), composer and

Empress Maria Theresa of Austria (1717–1780)

1725 *Concert spirituel* founded in Paris

Johann Christian Bach

Carl Ditters von

Giovanni Paisiello

André Grétry

Joseph Haydn (1732–1809)

Bridgeman Art Library

Wolfgang Amadeus Mozart (1756–1791)

CORBIS

Ludwig van Beethoven (1770–1827)

CORBIS

less to say, composers did not stop writing in one musical style one day and start in a new one the next. Often elements of baroque music coexisted with those of the emerging Classical style. The decades from 1730 to 1770 were a time of gradual transition. This period of musical change coincided with an intellectual era called the Enlightenment, a philosophical, scientific, and political movement that dominated eighteenth-century thought. Similarly, the years 1770–1820 encompass the music of Haydn, Mozart, and Beethoven, three composers with sometimes very different musical styles. Yet their modes of expression, which build upon traditional principles of balance and proportion, have much in common. The music of all these composers comprises the Classical era.

Part

V

1750	1800	1850

| (1730–1770) | CLASSICAL PERIOD (1770–1820) | |

the Great of Prussia (r. 1740–1786)

Franz Schubert (1797–1828), composer

Napoleon Bonaparte (1769–1821)

1776 Adam Smith publishes *Wealth of Nations*

1796–1815 Napoleonic Wars

symphony

Carl Czerny (1791–1857), composer and one of Beethoven's best students

conductor of Mannheim orchestra

1805 *Fidelio* premieres at the Theater-an-der-Wien

1810 Metronome invented in Vienna

1814–1815 Congress of Vienna

(1735–1782), composer (son of J. S. Bach)

Dittersdorf (1739–1799), composer and friend of Mozart

(1740–1816), composer of Italian *opera buffa*

(1741–1813), French opera composer

Johann Wolfgang von Goethe (1749–1832), German poet

Lorenzo da Ponte (1749–1838), librettist

Antonio Rosetti (1750–1792), composer of symphonies

Antonio Salieri (1750–1825), official court composer to Emperor Joseph II

Muzio Clementi (1752–1832), pianist and rival to Mozart

Ignace Pleyel (1757–1831), pupil of Haydn and composer

Luigi Cherubini (1760–1842), composer of opera

Catherine the Great (r. 1762–1796)

Chapter 41

Music in the Age of Enlightenment: Opera

The **Enlightenment** was a philosophical, scientific, and political movement that dominated eighteenth-century thought. Ultimately, it brought about wholesale social revolution, transforming a society that had been ruled mainly by court and church into one governed by more democratic institutions. During the Enlightenment, also called the Age of Reason, scientists gave free rein to the pursuit of truth and the discovery of natural laws. Faith in human reason replaced faith in divine intervention. This era saw the rise of a natural religion called Deism, the belief that a Creator made the world, set it in motion, and left it alone thereafter. Much of this philosophy sprang from the *Principia mathematica* (*Mathematical Principles*) of Isaac Newton (1642–1727), which postulates that the universe runs according to natural laws such as gravity. Social scientists like Hume in England and Voltaire in France tried to extend these natural scientific laws into the realm of political action. They attacked the privileges and abuses of the established court and church. Gradually, age-old customs and beliefs (or superstitions) were pruned away. In many French churches, medieval stained glass was removed in favor of clear glass, a literal act of "enlightenment."

Most important, the principles of the Enlightenment incited a revolt against the monarchy and the *status quo*. At first the attack came from the written word, not the sword. A French *Encyclopédie*, by far the most comprehensive work of its kind to date, was produced between 1751 and 1772; the first *Encyclopedia Britannica* appeared in 1768. The twenty-eight volume *Encyclopédie* was compiled by a group of French freethinkers called **les philosophes,** including the important trio Denis Diderot (1713–1784), Jean-Jacques Rousseau (1712–1778), and François-Marie Arouet, known as Voltaire (1694–1778). They espoused the principles of social justice, equality, religious tolerance, and freedom of speech. Voltaire, in particular, made fun of the habits and privileges of both clergy and aristocracy. The frilled cuffs, pink stockings, and powdered wig of the courtier were an easy target for his pen. A more natural appearance, one appropriate to a tradesman, merchant, or manufacturer, was his ideal. Pretension and privilege should yield to common sense and social equality, although some (women and slaves) would still be decidedly less equal.

Needless to say, the notion that all persons (or at least free men) were created equal put the thinkers of the Enlightenment on a collision course with the defenders of the existing social order. Spurred on by economic self-interest and the principles of the philosophers, an increasingly numerous and self-confident middle class in America and France rebelled against the monarchy. The American Revolution began in 1776 and the French Revolution in 1789. The Enlightenment philosophers had done their work.

Jean-Jacques Rousseau, a leading Enlightenment philosopher, advocated that all government should be based on the consent of the governed rather than the divine right of kings. For Rousseau, nature was the source of all good art, and the "noble savage" was far superior to the civilized courtier. Rousseau was also a musician. As a youth he taught music and worked as a music copyist when money was scarce. He later wrote the articles on music for the *Encyclopédie* and compiled a *Dictionnaire de musique* (1768) with 900 entries, the first modern musical dictionary. Throughout his *Dictionnaire*, Rousseau argued that musical expression should be simple and natural, relying on melody as the main vehicle of communication. For Rousseau, issues of the heart were equal to those of the head.

But Rousseau, not satisfied to be a musical philosopher, also tried his hand at composition. Among his surviving works is a comic opera called *Le Devin du village* (*The Village Soothsayer*, 1752), for which he created both libretto and music. Rousseau's story line, in which true love (assisted by a bit of magic) triumphs over wealth and status, reflects his democratic leanings. The overture ends with a simple dance (a piano reduction is given in Ex. 41-1). Rousseau's phrases are short and arranged in neat four-bar units. His texture is light, being concentrated on the outer voices; the first and second violins generally skip along in pleasing parallel thirds. Finally, with the expression mark "Gai" he asks the performers to play with a carefree spirit.

EXAMPLE 41-1

Music historians use the French term **galant style** (rather than "Enlightenment style") to describe eighteenth-century music such as this, music that is graceful, light in texture, and generally symmetrical in melodic structure. The *galant* ideal of a graceful melody with a simple accompaniment is indeed fully harmonious with the Enlightenment values of naturalness, clarity, and simplicity. But the *galant* idiom was just one of many styles to be heard during the Enlightenment.

✿ MUSIC OF THE ESTABLISHMENT: ENLIGHTENMENT *OPERA SERIA*

To appreciate the plurality of musical styles that existed during the Enlightenment, we begin by visiting the electoral-royal court of Dresden, Germany. Dresden was seat of the Elector of Saxony.[†] In the early eighteenth century, the elector was

[†]As we have seen, in German history, an elector was one of nine powerful princes with the right to vote in the election to choose the Holy Roman Emperor.

Gemäldegalerie, Dresden

❧ FIGURE 41-1

Soprano Faustina Bordoni, wife
of composer Johann Hasse, who
sang the title role in his opera
Cleofide. She and her rival
Francesca Cuzzoni developed the
stereotype of the *prima donna*: a
singer with a superb voice, a high
salary, and a demanding and often
difficult temperament.

named August the Strong, and he held the titles king of Poland
and duke of Saxony. In 1719 Elector August built a new opera
house seating 2,000 spectators. He also hired the best singers he
could find (all Italian), including an expensive castrato called
Senesino (see Box in Chapter 38). In 1731 August engaged what
might be called the first "power couple" in the history of music,
composer Johann Hasse (1699–1783) and his wife, soprano
Faustina Bordoni (1697–1781). Hasse was a north German educated in Italy, whose services as a composer of opera were in demand throughout much of the Continent; Bordoni (Fig. 41-1)
was the leading soprano, the great ***prima donna*** (leading lady)
of the age, and she commanded fees far greater than his.

Hasse and Bordoni made their operatic debut in Dresden in
1731 with an *opera seria* entitled *Cleofide*. Not only was *Cleofide*
Hasse's first opera for Dresden, it was also one of the first in
which he would set a text by **Pietro Metastasio** (1698–1782),
the principal librettist for eighteenth-century *opera seria*. Like
Gilbert and Sullivan in the nineteenth century and Rodgers and
Hammerstein in the twentieth, Metastasio and Hasse worked as
a team to create many works for the musical stage—in this case,
nearly thirty operas. Metastasio's strength was his ability to fashion clearly shaped drama and equally crystalline poetry. But
Metastasio did not provide texts only for Hasse. His libretti were
set nearly four hundred times by other composers of eighteenth-
century *opera seria*, including Handel, Gluck, and even Mozart on occasion.

The libretto of Hasse's *Cleofide* concerns the life of Alexander the Great, and like
many *opere serie*, the plot is a thinly disguised allegory that praises the virtues of a
magnanimous ruler. When the ancient warrior-king Alexander the Great stepped
on stage in Dresden, the audience was encouraged to see the modern warrior-king
August the Strong, for both had territorial ambitions to the east. The heroine Cleofide (sung by Bordoni), queen of a region of India, is in love with Poro, king of another region of India. Cleofide confesses her love in a famous aria, "Digli ch'io son
fedele" ("Tell him that I am faithful"), not knowing that he, disguised as his own
general, hears her confession. The magnanimous Alexander (sung by a castrato)
agrees to their marriage, even though he fancies the bride for himself. All of this is
typical of late-Baroque *opera seria*; the plots are complicated, characters appear in
disguise, and male leads usually have high, womanly voices. As the eighteenth century progressed, Metastasio himself worked to reduce the number of characters and
simplify the plot, bringing the libretto more in line with Enlightenment ideals of
clarity and simplicity. As to the music, it centered on the *da capo* aria and the vocal
ability of the soprano and castrato. *Cleofide* is very much a singer's opera. Essential
characteristics of Enlightenment *opera seria* include the following.

- The libretto is a thinly disguised allegory that praises the heroic actions of the
ruler.
- The opera has a happy ending (*lieto fine* in Italian), thanks to the intervention of
a god or a magnanimous monarch.
- Elaborate scenery is required, sometimes including horses, elephants, and camels
on stage.
- Castrati sing the roles of young romantic leads; tenors or basses sing the parts of
male authority figures such as fathers.

- The music consists almost exclusively of simple recitatives and florid *da capo* arias.
- Attention is focused on beautiful melodies and the vocal skill of the leading singers.
- The *prima donna* and the castrato reign supreme, receiving fees many times that of the composer.

The premiere of Hasse's *Cleofide* in Dresden on 13 September 1731 was a gala event. In the audience were two significant guests: Johann Sebastian Bach and the future King Frederick (the Great) of Prussia. Bach, as we have seen, was then cantor in nearby Leipzig, and he took every opportunity to go to the Dresden opera house to hear what he called "the lovely Dresden ditties." Frederick of Prussia, as we will see, was a music-loving monarch who took up the flute as well as composition. Later, Frederick established his own opera company in Berlin and composed an ornamented version of "Digli ch'io son fedele" for a performance of *Cleofide*. In fact, we possess three versions of this aria: Hasse's original (Ex. 41-2, top), a slightly ornamented version said to have been created by Faustina Bordoni herself (Ex. 41-2, middle), and the king's even more florid rendition (Ex. 41-2, bottom). We now call such florid figuration assigned to the soprano voice **coloratura,** and refer to singers of such passagework as coloratura sopranos.

EXAMPLE 41-2

Tell him that I am faithful, tell him that he is my treasure, tell him that he is my treasure…

LISTENING CUE

JOHANN ADOLF HASSE
Cleofide, (1731)
Aria, "Digli ch'io son fedele"

CD 6/16
Anthology, No. 118

Although librettist Metastasio reduced the number of characters found in Baroque *opera seria* and simplified the plot in accordance with the spirit of Enlightenment, *opera seria* was still a serious art form for the elite. Above all, Metastasio's libretti reaffirmed the values of the ruling aristocracy: loyalty, benevolence, and enlightened rule. Perhaps as an antidote to this high-art seriousness, a new genre of musical theater arose that we now broadly call comic opera. Throughout the eighteenth century these two types of opera—traditional *opera seria* and the newer, lighter comic opera—would vie for supremacy on the operatic stage.

❋ MUSIC AND SOCIAL CHANGE: COMIC OPERA

Comic opera was a simpler, more direct type of musical theater that made use of comic characters, dealt with everyday social issues, and emphasized values more in step with those of the middle class. Arising in several countries in Europe at the same time, comic opera went under various names: ballad opera (England), *opera buffa* (Italy), *opéra comique* (France), and *Singspiel* (Germany). In each of these countries, comic opera assumed a distinctly local form. Whereas *opera seria* was sung only in Italian, comic opera was usually performed in the native tongue. Using the local language brought comic opera closer to the ordinary citizen.

English Ballad Opera: *The Beggar's Opera*

The first important challenge to the *opera seria* establishment was John Gay's *The Beggar's Opera*, produced in London in 1728. In this three-act work, John Gay (1685–1732) populates the stage, not with heroic kings but common criminals. The criminals must be able to sing simple tunes, but need not trouble themselves with recitative because Gay's dialogue is simply spoken in the vernacular of the audience. At the outset a beggar steps forward and speaks for Gay himself: "I hope I may be forgiven, that I have not made my Opera throughout unnatural, like those in vogue; for I have no Recitative." The "unnatural" opera then "in vogue" in London was, of course, the *opera seria* of Handel that was playing at the King's Theater.

The Beggar's Opera poked fun at aristocratic Italian opera and the established government. Whereas *opera seria* began with a formal three-section sinfonia or a two-part French overture, the overture to *The Beggar's Opera* quotes the tune *The Happy Clown*, a satirical lampoon of reigning prime minister Robert Walpole. While *opera seria* had lengthy *da capo* arias, *The Beggar's Opera* uses popular songs. Many of the tunes are English, Scottish, or Irish folk songs, generally called ballads. A **ballad** is a traditional, usually strophic, song that tells a lengthy story. *The Beggar's Opera* is a **ballad opera**—a comic opera using re-texted ballads (or other popular songs) and spoken dialogue rather than recitative.

The plot of *The Beggar's Opera* concerns the love of Polly Peachum for handsome Captain Macheath. It unfolds within the world of lowlife London, where there is no honor among thieves, and less among the nobility. Polly's mother is a prostitute, her father a fence and an informer, and Macheath a mugger. Mr. and Mrs. Peachum are scandalized to find that Polly has married Macheath. They fear that his criminal line of work, though praiseworthy, will not prove lucrative enough for her (and them). What is worse, a lawyer will now be needed to settle Polly's dowry. To the tune of *A Soldier and a Sailor*, Mr. Peachum pillories the legal profession:

Your wife may steal your rest, sir,
A thief your goods and plate . . .
If lawyer's hand is fee'd, sir,
He steals your whole estate.

And so fly the verbal barbs in this satire of eighteenth-century law and morality. As to the music, it charms through the innocence and timeless beauty of the ballad melodies. Polly's song "Oh, ponder well! be not severe" is a re-texting of the English ballad "The children in the wood," which had been well-known since Shakespeare's time (Ex. 41-3). The ballad melody is only eight bars long and the vocal range quite limited; in Gay's ballad operas, the leads need not be great singers, just good actors.

EXAMPLE 41-3

Oh, pon-der well! be not se-vere; So save a wretch - ed

wife! For on the rope that hangs my Dear, de-pends poor Pol-ly's life.

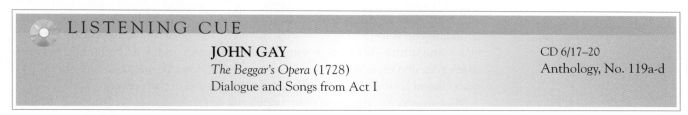

LISTENING CUE

JOHN GAY
The Beggar's Opera (1728)
Dialogue and Songs from Act I

CD 6/17–20
Anthology, No. 119a-d

The Beggar's Opera was a huge success. It ran for sixty-two performances (then a record) in a West End London theater operated by one John Rich (wags said that Rich had been made gay and Gay rich). By the end of the century, Gay's ballad opera had been carried to colonial cities such as Boston, Philadelphia, Richmond, Charlestown, and Williamsburg (it was said to be George Washington's favorite opera). In 1928 Bertold Brecht and Kurt Weill built their *Dreigroschenoper* (*Threepenny Opera*) on Gay's story and characters (see Chapter 70), and made Macheath famous through his song "Mac the Knife."

Opera Buffa

If the English had their ballad opera in this period, the Italians had **opera buffa.** Literally, *opera buffa* means buffoonish (comic) opera. In the seventeenth century, comic operas had been few and far between. There were, however, comic scenes played out by lower-caste characters within Italian serious opera, just as earlier there had been scenes of comic relief within Shakespeare's plays. Around 1700 separate comic scenes came to be performed between the acts of an *opera seria*. A musical diversion between the acts of an opera or a play is called an **intermezzo.** By 1710 full-length comic operas had appeared in Naples. In contrast to *opera seria*, *opera buffa* involved a wide spectrum of social classes, from peasants and servants to noblemen. Moreover, it usually included a comic bass part, but no high-flying castrato (except in Rome where women were banned from the stage and castrati assumed their roles). The musical high points featured short airs, as opposed to lengthy *da capo* arias. Of the many comic operas originating in Italy at this time, by far the best-known today is Pergolesi's *La serva padrona* (*The Maid Made Mistress*, 1733).

Small, sickly, and crippled Giovanni Battista Pergolesi lived only twenty-six years (1710–1736). After his premature death from tuberculosis, greedy music publishers and sympathetic music historians attributed more music to Pergolesi than he had actually written. In truth, his musical output comprised only a handful of operas, four cantatas, a few sonatas, and some religious music, including a well-known *Stabat Mater* (1736). Pergolesi composed *La serva padrona* as a brief two-act intermezzo to be played between the acts of one of his longer, serious operas. *La serva padrona* has only two singing characters: Serpina (soprano), a clever chamber maid, and Uberto (bass), her elderly, lecherous lord. In the course of this fast-moving farce, the impertinent Serpina dupes Uberto into marrying her and thus becomes "The Maid Made Mistress." Here comic opera turns the established social order on its head.

The interplay between the maid and the master is at its best toward the end of Act I. In a spirited recitative the two protagonists exchange insults. In *opera buffa*, unlike ballad opera, the dialogue is not spoken but is delivered in fast-paced simple recitative. Recitative periodically yields to lyrical singing, however, as can be seen in a duet, "Lo conosco a quegl'occhietti" ("I see it in your eyes"), that typifies Pergolesi's naturally effervescent style. Employing a carefree *galant* idiom, Pergolesi captures in music the spirit of the two characters: she is high-strung, flighty, yet supremely self-confident; he is lowdown, slow-witted, and not so resolute, equivocating between major and minor. With its driving rhythmic energy, quick interchanges between characters, and rapid shifts between major and minor, this duet foreshadows the glorious ensemble finales fashioned by Mozart at the end of the century.

Most important, the immediate popularity of *La serva padrona* announced that a new musical genre, *opera buffa*, had arrived. The appeal of English ballad opera was limited to England and its colonies. Italian *opera buffa*, on the other hand, soon spread throughout continental Europe and beyond, gradually becoming a serious rival to *opera seria* for the public's affection. By 1760 *La serva padrona* had been staged in more than sixty theaters in cities as disparate as St. Petersburg and Barcelona, Vienna and Baltimore. In this case, an upstart maid (*opera buffa*) had become mistress of the opera house.

LISTENING CUE

GIOVANNI BATTISTA PERGOLESI	CD 6/21–22
La serva padrona (1733)	Anthology, No. 120a-b
Recitative, "Io non só chi mi tien!"	
Duet, "Lo conosco a quegl'occhietti"	

The War of the Buffoons: *Opéra Comique*

In 1752 a troupe of traveling Italian players carried *La serva padrona* to Paris, capital of the Enlightenment. Here Pergolesi's *opera buffa* ignited, not merely a controversy but a paper war over the relative merits of Italian and French musical style. The battle came to be called **La Guerre des Bouffons** (The War of the Buffoons—drawn from the term "clownish" in *opera buffa*) and it raged, on and off, for several years. More than sixty pamphlets were written, on one side or the other, by the major social critics of the day. The issue was this: What sort of opera was appropriate for the French stage? Should it be the traditional opera of the French court (the old *tragédie lyrique*; see Chapter 35), or the newer, lighter-style opera (Italian *opera buffa*) that portrayed everyday characters? On the conservative side were King Louis XV, the followers of Lully and Rameau, and the defenders of French classical theater; on the populist side were the freethinking *philosophes* and the social egalitarians.

Not surprisingly, liberal Jean-Jacques Rousseau marched into these opera wars on the progressive (pro-Italian) side. Indeed, he did something unusual for a Frenchman: he criticized the French language as being unmusical. In a pamphlet entitled *Lettre sur la musique française* (1753), Rousseau opined that French vocal music ran the risk of being "insipid and monotonous." In his view, the high-flown language of French classical drama had too many mute syllables and too few sonorous vowels; Italian was a more musical language. A year earlier Rousseau had demonstrated how a simpler poetic style and a more natural melody might better serve the French musical stage. He created a light opera entitled *Le Devin du village* (*The Village Sooth-sayer*, 1752), one of the first of a type that we now call *opéra comique*. French **opéra comique,** similar to its Italian cousin *opera buffa,* has characters from the everyday world. They sing in a fresh, natural style, and the dialogue is generally spoken, but sometimes (as in *Le Devin du village*) it is delivered in recitative. The principals sing either simple airs or popular melodies called *vaudevilles* (whence the English term "vaudeville" for a popular review or show). Consider Rousseau's simple air (here a duet) for the principals of *Le Devin du village,* the shepherds Colin and Colette. Most of the time they sing basic triads or skip down the scale in a dance-like rhythm. These are not psychologically differentiated characters; they have almost the same name and say almost the same words. Moreover, they sing almost the same music, Colin's usually duplicating Colette's at the interval of a sixth (Ex. 41-4). Rousseau even allows parallel octaves (see bar 7). In Rousseau's rustic *opéra comique,* academic rules of counterpoint were out of place. Indeed, counterpoint itself was judged "unnatural" by Rousseau.

Example 41-4

(continued on next page)

coeur   et ma   foi. Qu'un doux ma - ri - a - ge m'u - nisse a - vec toi.

coeur   et sa   foi. Qu'un doux ma - ri - a - ge m'u - nisse a - vec toi.

Forever, Colin pledges my (his) heart and faith; in this sweet marriage I am united with you…

LISTENING CUE

JEAN-JACQUES ROUSSEAU
Le Devin du village (1752)
Duet, "À jamais Colin"

CD 6/23
Anthology, No. 121

The opera wars flared up again in Paris during the 1770s. An Italian composer, one Niccolò Piccinni (1728–1800), had been brought to Paris to create an Italianate alternative to the *tragédies lyriques* that continued to play on the Parisian stage. In response, the pro-French party brought in a champion of its own, Christoph Willibald Gluck, to revitalize French music drama. The "Piccinnists" now did battle with the "Gluckists" in notes and words. The quarrel even caught the attention of the American minister to France, Benjamin Franklin, who said wryly: "Happy people! thought I, you live certainly under a wise, just, and mild government, since you have no public grievances to complain of, nor any subject of contention but the perfections and imperfections of foreign music."[1] Franklin does not say if he was a Piccinnist or a Gluckist.

❀ FIGURE 41-2
Christoph Willibald Gluck
composing at a clavichord.

Bridgeman Art Library

❀ THE REFORM OPERAS OF GLUCK

Christoph Willibald Gluck (1714–1787; Fig. 41-2), though born in what is now the Czech Republic, seems to have lived as a citizen of all Europe. At least he spent extended periods in all the operatic capitals of Europe, including Vienna, Milan, Naples, London, Prague, Dresden, Hamburg, and Paris. Gluck composed almost nothing but opera, about forty-five in all. In 1752 Gluck settled more or less permanently in Vienna, where he came to occupy official musical positions at the court of Empress Maria Theresa (1717–1780). It was here that he helped to create a new style of opera—serious opera, in Italian, but opera very different from Baroque *opera seria*.

By 1760 Vienna had become a remarkably cosmopolitan city. Italian opera had long dominated the Viennese court. Indeed, Pietro Metastasio, the greatest *opera seria* librettist of the eighteenth century (see above), was the official court poet. In 1761 Vienna became home to another important Italian librettist, Ranieri Calzabigi (1714–1795). At the same time, French culture had made strong inroads in Vienna, for here, as elsewhere throughout Europe, the French language enjoyed the status of the primary language of cultured society. In 1755 Gluck had become director of a French opera and dance company installed at the Viennese court. Calzabigi himself had spent a decade in Paris and knew well French *tragédie lyrique*, which placed great weight on the ballet and the chorus. In 1762 Gluck and Calzabigi teamed up to create a new type of opera that historians call "reform opera." **Reform opera** sought to combine the best features of the Italian and French traditions, to yoke Italian lyricism to the French concern for intense dramatic expression.

The first of the reform operas by Gluck and Calzabigi carried the title *Orfeo ed Euridice*. The plot is familiar. Indeed, it is yet another telling of the story with which opera had begun more than a hundred and fifty years earlier: the Orpheus legend (see Chapter 30). The Italian libretto crafted by Calzabigi, however, distilled the action down to its essential elements. The opera starts, not by introducing Orfeo and Euridice but by his mourning her death. Calzabigi also reduced the number of characters to just three (Orfeo, Euridice, and Cupid). Gluck's contribution was no less radical. He did away with the old *da capo* aria and greatly reduced the importance of elaborate, coloratura singing. As Gluck said about his new approach to opera:

> I resolved to free [opera] from all the abuses which have crept in either through ill-advised vanity on the part of the singers or through excessive complaisance on the part of composers, with the result that for some time Italian opera [*opera seria*] has been disfigured and far from being the most splendid and most beautiful of all stage performances has been made the most ridiculous and most wearisome.[2]

As the role of the virtuoso soloist diminished, that of the chorus increased greatly. Equally important, Gluck exploited a type of recitative new to the eighteenth century: obbligato recitative. As its name implies, in **obbligato recitative** (also known as **accompanied recitative**) the orchestra is necessary (obligatory) to the desired musical effect. Not only does the orchestra provide accompaniment for the singer but it also plays significant musical motives on its own. Throughout Gluck's *Orfeo ed Euridice*, the orchestra accompanies all arias and all recitatives. Thus the boundary between aria and recitative is less distinct, and the contrast between the sections, or "numbers," within the opera is less clear. *Orfeo ed Euridice* unfolds continually, one number flowing almost imperceptibly into the next, leaving the audience little opportunity to applaud (and stop the action). Attention is focused on the musically enhanced drama rather than on the vocal displays of the soloists, and clarity and direct expression of the text assume paramount importance. The extent to which Gluck transformed opera can be gauged by comparing the qualities of Hasse's earlier Enlightenment opera *Cleofide* (see above) with Gluck's reform opera *Orfeo ed Euridice*. Qualities of Gluck's reform opera include the following.

- The overture generally sets the mood of the opera to follow.
- The vocal style is far less florid, with little improvised ornamentation.
- The focus is on the expressive potential of the text.
- *Da capo* arias are eliminated and strophic forms favored.
- Obbligato recitative (accompanied recitative) is used extensively.
- Arias and recitatives are less strictly separated.
- The plot of the libretto is simplified, the number of characters reduced.
- The chorus assumes an important role and participates in the drama.
- Dance assumes a dramatic role.
- The orchestra is more important and provides more varied sounds.

In many ways, Gluck's reforms gave back to opera the character it possessed at the very beginning of its history (c1600): restrained, yet expressive singing is fully integrated with choral music and dance.

The most dramatic moment in *Orfeo ed Euridice* occurs at the beginning of Act II, as Orfeo descends into the Underworld to reclaim his beloved Euridice. For this inferno scene, Gluck assembled an uncommonly large and colorful orchestra. In addition to the expected strings and winds (pairs of oboes, bassoons, and horns), he includes unusual instruments such as the harp and two ancient wind instruments, namely the cornett and trombone. The sweet-sounding harp accompanies Orfeo as he pleads with the furies, who block his way in the Underworld. They in turn are supported by the demonic sounds of blaring cornett and trombone. When the chorus of furies rebuffs Orfeo with shouts of "no, no," these wind instruments contribute to the cacophony with biting diminished-seventh chords. For the eighteenth century, this was literally the sound and fury of Hell. Ultimately, Orfeo's musical pleading softens the demonic spirits; the trombones withdraw and the infernal voices become quiet. Expressive, yet controlled, singing has vanquished the hellish sounds of chorus and orchestra, and Orfeo is free to pass.

LISTENING CUE

CHRISTOPH WILLIBALD GLUCK
Orfeo ed Euridice (1762)
Aria, "Deh placatevi"
Chorus, "Misero giovane"

CD 7/1–2
Anthology, No. 122a-b

Toward the end of *Orfeo ed Euridice*, the hero succumbs to his human failing. Fearful that Euridice does not follow, he turns to see if she is there—the single act expressly forbidden by Cupid. Again, the gods carry Euridice away. Orfeo laments his loss, first in an obbligato recitative and then in a full-blown aria. The aria, the famous "Che farò senza Euridice" ("What will I do without Euridice"), rejects *da capo* form and vocal display. Instead, this strophic song is full of what Gluck himself called "beautiful simplicity" that captures the poignancy of the moment. Orfeo's overweening curiosity—a very human failing—has stripped him of his prize. Ultimately, the god Cupid takes pity on these mortals and reunites them, an act of clemency that would have been appreciated by Enlightenment audiences.

LISTENING CUE

CHRISTOPH WILLIBALD GLUCK
Orfeo ed Euridice (1762)
Obbligato recitative, "Ahimè! Dove trascorsi?"
Aria, "Che farò senza Euridice"

CD 7/3–4
Anthology, Nos. 122c-d

Within ten years Gluck's *Orfeo ed Euridice* had made its way to theaters in Italy, Germany, Sweden, and England, and the composer had become a celebrity. In 1774 he brought *Orfeo ed Euridice* to Paris and added more ballets to please Parisian taste. Knowing the French aversion to the castrato voice, he also transposed the alto castrato part of Orfeo down into the range of high tenor. Paris loved this new French arrangement, now titled *Orphée et Eurydice*. Here was opera that combined the best of both Italian and French music drama. It had melody, but melody that was dignified; it had chorus and ballet, but both were integrated in the drama, not merely spectacular interruptions. Even the critical Jean-Jacques Rousseau praised the opera:

"To spend a couple of hours in the enjoyment of so great a pleasure persuades me that life is worth living."³

SUMMARY

Italian *opera seria*—the traditional opera of the established aristocratic court—continued to thrive throughout the Enlightenment but was not uncontested. *Opera seria* glorified the status quo and the absolute ruler. Its stage was decorated with expensive sets and populated with high-priced castrati and divas who specialized in vocal virtuosity. Librettist Pietro Metastasio, often working with composer Johann Hasse, attempted to reduce the number of characters, simplify the plot, and concentrate the action. Their Enlightenment *opera seria*, however, was still informed by, and strongly reinforced, aristocratic values. By 1730 a rival to *opera seria* appeared on the stage in several European countries: comic opera. Although comic opera assumed a distinctly different guise in each country in which it appeared, the various national forms nonetheless had many common characteristics. They

- Were designed to appeal to more middle-class sensibilities.
- Had characters from everyday life, even lowlife, populate the stage.
- Satirized the upper classes or foreigners who threatened the simple, honest way of life.
- Contained spoken dialogue (or rapid-fire simple recitative) in the native language of the country.
- Preferred actors who could sing to expensive singers who could act.
- Abounded with pantomime and slapstick comedy.

The differences among the national dialects of comic opera were: English ballad opera employed simple tunes, many of them ballads (traditional folk songs), to which new text was added as appropriate for the plot; Italian *opera buffa* did not use spoken dialogue but fast-moving simple recitative; French *opéra comique* preferred pre-existing airs and popular melodies called *vaudevilles*; and German *Singspiel* (see Chapter 48) frequently employed folk songs for the sung portions and sometimes favored magical or supernatural events in the plot.

Comic opera, a new and different genre, attacked *opera seria* from without. The reform opera of Christoph Willibald Gluck tried to alter it from within. True to the spirit of the Enlightenment, the reform opera of Gluck emphasized simple design and natural expression. Reform opera was still serious grand opera with characters of noble intentions. Yet in reform opera the dictates of dignity and moderation created a drama centered on the expression of intense human emotions, rather than the vocal exploits of star singers.

KEY TERMS

Enlightenment	coloratura	*La Guerre des Bouffons*
les philosophes	comic opera	*opéra comique*
galant style	ballad	reform opera
Faustina Bordoni	ballad opera	obbligato recitative
prima donna	*opera buffa*	(accompanied
Pietro Metastasio	intermezzo	recitative)

Chapter 42

Music in the Age of Enlightenment: Orchestral Music

Society underwent profound changes during the Enlightenment as power and wealth increasingly devolved from the aristocracy to the middle class. The introduction of comic opera with characters from all ranks of society, as we have seen, was a musical reaction against exclusively aristocratic *opera seria*. In the field of instrumental music, too, social transformation led to change in the type of music produced and the kind of person who played and heard it. By the mid eighteenth century, economic progress had brought prosperity to the growing middle class. Now the bookkeeper, physician, cloth merchant, stock trader, and student collectively had enough disposable income to organize and patronize their own concerts. High art music, which we call "classical music," moved beyond the court and church to become popular entertainment. The day of the public concert had arrived.

PUBLIC CONCERTS

The city of Paris, home to Voltaire, Rousseau, and other freethinking egalitarians, was the epicenter of the Enlightenment. Not surprisingly, therefore, Paris saw the first and most numerous public concert series. Foremost among these was the **Concert spirituel** founded in 1725. Originally formed to give a public hearing to religious music sung in Latin, its repertory soon came to emphasize purely instrumental symphonies and concertos. Concerts were advertised to the public by means of flyers distributed in the streets. To make its offerings accessible to several strata of society, it also instituted a two-tiered system of prices (four *livres* for boxes and two *livres* for the pit), with children under fifteen admitted at half price. Women were almost as numerous in the audience as men. Thus, we can trace to the mid eighteenth century the practice of middle-class citizens buying tickets and attending public performances of high art music.

London, too, participated in the advent of public concerts during the eighteenth century. Here, concerts were at first centered in the Vauxhall Gardens, something akin to an eighteenth-century theme park located on the south bank of the Thames River. Visitors paid a daily admission fee, bought exorbitantly priced food and drink, and wandered freely among various amusements. The musical fare included free concerts in a centrally located bandstand. Leopold Mozart, father of Wolfgang, took his family to the Vauxhall Gardens when visiting London in 1762. Here he found both pleasing music and a new spirit of democracy in the air:

> In the middle is a kind of high open summerhouse in which is to be heard an organ and music on trumpets, drums and all instruments. . . . Here each person pays only one shilling and for this shilling has the delight of seeing many thousands of people and the most beautifully illuminated garden; and of hearing beautiful music. More than six thousand people were present when I attended. . . . Here everyone is equal, and no lord allows any person to uncover [doff a hat] before him; having paid their money [to enter], all are upon equal terms.[1]

In Vienna, the music of Wolfgang Mozart, as well as Haydn and Beethoven, would later sound at public concerts in the Burgtheater (Court Theater). This Viennese hall, which had opened in 1741, welcomed paying customers of whatever class, as long as they dressed and behaved properly. Although the nobility still occupied the best seats (Fig. 42-1), opening the doors of culture to the general public fostered a leveling between classes. The featured artists were usually composer-performers who offered the public a variety of music: their latest symphony, a concerto, and an aria or two, and perhaps a fantasia or set of variations for solo keyboard.

THE EARLY SYMPHONY: GIOVANNI BATTISTA SAMMARTINI IN MILAN

The word "symphony" descends from the ancient Latin term *symphonia*, which connotes a harmonious sound. By the 1620s, the Italian term "sinfonia" was applied more specifically to an instrumental ritornello at the beginning or in the middle of a vocal work. Soon the title "*sinfonia avanti l'opera*" became a simple way to designate the opening instrumental overture to an opera. Thereafter, for the next hundred years, the symphony developed mainly in the context of the Italian opera overture. By the late seventeenth century, the typical Italian symphony/overture had acquired three sections that came in immediate succession, fast/slow/fast. The middle portion was very brief and in a contrasting key, whereas the finale often made use of a light dance idiom. Finally, by the 1730s, composers in Italy had begun to write symphonies as free-standing instrumental works, a development that signaled the decline of the Baroque concerto grosso. Thus the **concert symphony** as we know it today—a three- or four-movement instrumental work projecting the unified sounds of an orchestra—was a creation of the more egalitarian Enlightenment. The emphasis shifted from just a few "stars" of the Baroque concerto grosso to the larger orchestral team of the Enlightenment symphony. Henceforth the symphony would constitute the weightiest composition at a public orchestral concert. So closely associated did the orchestra become with the genre of the concert symphony that still today we call it a "symphony orchestra."

The leader in the creation of the concert symphony was Giovanni Battista Sammartini (c1700–1775). Despite his very Italian-sounding name, Sammartini was the son of a French oboist (Saint-Martin) who had immigrated to Milan, Italy. The son too played oboe, and violin and organ as well. Sammartini spent his entire career in Milan as a church musician. Toward the end of his life he held the post of *maestro di cappella* (director of church music) at no fewer than eight churches simultaneously. Sammartini's activity in the church did not preclude him from writing symphonies. Indeed, in this period, symphonies and even concertos were often included as preludes to or interludes during religious services. Sammartini's symphonies were also heard at outdoor public concerts that he himself directed.

In all, Sammartini left some eighty symphonies. Most are in three movements (fast/slow/fast), with the last movement often a minuet finale. Some of his early symphonies from the 1730s are "trio symphonies"—symphonies with only two independent violin parts and a bass line for viola, cello, and double bass, each playing the same notes an octave apart in its own register. More common is the four-part symphony for four independent string parts, with the cellos and basses doubling on the bass line. If a woodwind sound was desired, oboes or flutes would simply double the violin parts. Only in the symphonies from the last decade of his life (1765–1775)

FIGURE 42-1

A performance at the Burgtheater in Vienna in 1785. The nobility occupied the frontmost seats on the floor, but the area behind (to the left of) the partition was open to all. So, too, in the galleries, the aristocracy bought boxes low and close to the stage, while commoners occupied higher rungs as well as the standing room in the fourth gallery. Ticket prices depended, then as now, on proximity to the performers.

did Sammartini write independent oboe parts and separate the cellos and basses into two independent lines.

Sammartini's Symphony in D Major (J-C 14)† is a fine example of the *galant* symphony in its formative stages. Each of the three movements is brief, lasting approximately three minutes, a minute-and-a-half, and two minutes, respectively. Typically, the first movement is the longest and most substantive. Its form is binary, as in the movements of the Baroque dance suite. But there are two innovations here. First, Sammartini introduces a clear-cut second theme coinciding with the appearance of the dominant key. Second, and perhaps more important, the beginning of part **B** is greatly expanded; the first theme and transitional material are transformed as the music pushes through two related keys. This creates what might be called "expanded binary form," with part **B** now being significantly longer than part **A** (fifty-two measures, compared to twenty-eight). The beginning of part **B,** in fact, is similar to what we will later call a "development section" because of its elaboration of earlier themes. This portion of binary form will take on increasing importance throughout the eighteenth century. The first movement of Sammartini's Symphony in D Major can be diagrammed as follows:

Theme:	‖: 1st	transition	2nd	:‖:	1st	1st and trans. developed		2nd :‖
Key:	D major		A major		A major	B minor	E major	D major
Part:	‖: A			:‖:	B			:‖
Measure:	1–8	9–20	21–28	:‖:	29–36	37–72		73–80 :‖

As to the *galant* features of this movement, notice the first theme at the very opening of the movement (Ex. 42-1). It is a simple D major triad set out as a descending arpeggio and played in unison. The pattern is immediately repeated in halved note values and then halved again as the theme gains rhythmic energy. These opening four bars, which end on the dominant, form an **antecedent phrase**; it is immediately answered by a four-bar complementary unit called the **consequent phrase** that returns the music to the tonic. Such symmetrical phrasing is typical of the *galant* idiom as well as the Classical style to come.

EXAMPLE 42-1

†J-C refers to the system for numbering Sammartini's symphonies provided in Newell Jenkins and Bathia Churgin, *Thematic Catalogue of the Works of Giovanni Battista Sammartini* (Cambridge, Massachusetts, 1976).

Playing in an Eighteenth-Century Orchestra

Needless to say, the orchestra in the age of Enlightenment was smaller than the modern symphony orchestra; even the biggest ensemble generally had no more than forty players. The more subdued timbre of the string instruments resulted in part from the strings themselves, which were made of animal gut, not of wire, and from the design of the bridge, which put less tension on the strings. Furthermore, bows had less horsehair and were more "bowed" (convex rather than concave) in shape. There were other important differences as well, as implied in Johann Quantz's **Essay on Playing the Flute** (*Versuch einer Anweisung die Flöte traversière zu spielen*) of 1752, a three-hundred page treasure trove of information about mid eighteenth-century performance practices.

   Johann Quantz (1697–1773) was one of the great flautists of the age. He had spent long years associated with orchestras in Dresden and Berlin. He had also traveled widely, to London and Paris, among other places, and had heard Sammartini's orchestra in Milan. Here are a few of the differences between playing in an orchestra then and now, as suggested by Quantz:

- The principal violinist should serve as conductor (a nonplaying conductor, baton in hand, doesn't appear before the orchestra until the nineteenth century).

- A keyboardist (harpsichord or piano) fills out a figured bass to give the orchestral sound more body (a harpsichord or piano continued to play with the symphony orchestra into the 1790s).
- The principal violinist gets the pitch from the keyboard (not the oboe) and then sounds it for the other players.
- The pitch varies greatly from region to region; pitch is lower in France and Italy, for example, than in Germany, but even in Germany what they called an A in concert orchestras was approximately a full step lower than our A 440 today.
- The orchestra should memorize the first few bars of the piece so as to watch the conductor and effect a cleaner, more emphatic beginning.
- The players should add ornaments (trills and appoggiaturas, for example) to the written score, but these must be carefully rehearsed by the conductor.
- The players should stand during an orchestral concert; only those who must sit (the keyboardist and cellos) may do so.
- The players should tap the beat with the front of the foot, even during rests, to keep a steady tempo.

Finally, Quantz provides a seating chart for a mid-size orchestra (below). Presumably, this was just one of several possibilities at the time.

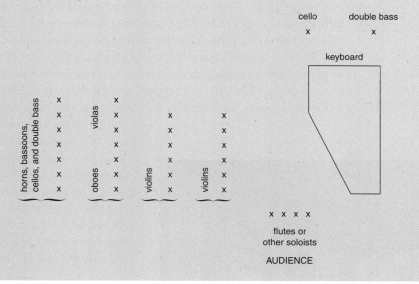

LISTENING CUE

GIOVANNI BATTISTA SAMMARTINI
Symphony in D Major (c1740)
First movement, *Allegro*

CD 7/5
Anthology, No. 123

❀ THE RISE OF ORCHESTRAL DISCIPLINE: JOHANN STAMITZ IN MANNHEIM

By the 1750s, the Italian symphony had moved north across the Alps. Here it took deep root and grew into the Classical symphony as we know it today. One important northern center for its development was Mannheim, Germany. In the mid eighteenth century, Mannheim was the capital of the Palatine, a territory running south-north along the Rhine River. Its ruler was Elector Carl Theodore (1724–1799), a lover of music and books. The palace from which Carl Theodore governed is an impressive complex (it now houses the University of Mannheim). At its center is a grand stairway leading up some two-hundred steps to the Hall of Knights (*Rittersaal*; Fig. 42-2), where concerts were held.

The Mannheim orchestra in the mid eighteenth century boasted a distinguished conductor and composer, Johann Stamitz (1717–1757). The Czech-born Stamitz had come to Mannheim in 1741 to be a violinist in the court orchestra. Indeed, Stamitz was apparently a virtuoso on all string instruments; at a concert in June 1742 he was the featured soloist, in turn, on violin, viola, cello, and double bass. Within a decade, Stamitz became director of the orchestra at Mannheim and distinguished himself as a composer. His works number fifty-eight symphonies and nearly two dozen concertos, including twelve for solo flute and one for clarinet, probably the first clarinet concerto ever written.

At Mannheim, Stamitz assembled an all-star orchestra. He hired a number of celebrated woodwind players and entire families of Czech hornists and trumpeters—the area around Prague was renowned for its brass players at this time. Stamitz taught and coached until he molded the orchestra into the most disciplined ensemble in Europe. The fame of the Mannheim orchestra lasted well beyond Stamitz's premature death. One observer of the day called it "an army of generals." Mozart's father said of it in 1763: "Ah if only the court music [at Salzburg] were regulated as it is in Mannheim! The discipline that reigns in that orchestra!"[2]

What was this orchestral discipline of which the elder Mozart speaks? Observers of the day mention the precise playing, and particularly the uniform bowing among the strings. In addition, the orchestra specialized in novel dynamic effects: *fortissimo* followed by *piano*, for example. At Mannheim, the louds seem to have been louder and the softs softer. But nothing impressed listeners in the Hall of Knights more than what is called a **Mannheim *crescendo,*** a gradual increase from very soft to very loud with a repeating figure over a pedal point. Another special effect was the **Mannheim rocket,** as it was later called—a triadic theme that bursts forth as a rising arpeggio. Orchestral gestures such as these, when precisely executed, were known to bring the audience to its feet.

Dramatic orchestral effects are clearly audible in Johann Stamitz's own symphonies, but other distinctive features are noteworthy as well. First, Stamitz was the earliest composer consistently to incorporate a fourth moment in his symphonies. After the opening *allegro* and the slow second movement, he

❀ FIGURE 42-2

Hall of Knights at Mannheim. In the mid eighteenth century this lavish two-story room served as a concert hall for the twice-weekly, semi-public concerts of the Mannheim court.

inserted a minuet and trio (see Chapter 45), which he followed with a fast finale (*presto* or *prestissimo*). Second, Stamitz expanded the orchestral score, making the winds obligatory. His symphonies of the 1750s are set out for eight parts: four strings, two horns, and two oboes (flutes or clarinets may substitute for the oboes). His horns not only provide a harmonic backdrop for the strings, but often step forth with solos. Similarly, whereas most previous composers used the oboes simply to double the violins, Stamitz frequently gives them their own independent lines. Later, Mozart would sometimes call for four woodwind instruments simultaneously: clarinets, flutes, and bassoons, as well as oboes. Mozart, who had spent much time in Mannheim as a youth and would go on to write superb orchestral parts for woodwinds, learned much about orchestration from Mannheim composers such as Stamitz.

Stamitz's Symphony in E♭ Major was published in 1758 in a collection of six symphonies called *La Melodia Germanica*. Here neither binary form nor any expansion of it shapes the music. Instead, thematic ideas seem to be conceived as orchestral gestures. They appear, and then reappear, in an unpredictable order so as to dramatize the effects of precision playing. Example 42-2 shows a portion of the first theme, in which the melodic material seems to be generated solely to service an orchestral effect; the strings churn away while the dynamic level rises from *pianissimo* to *fortissimo*—a fine example of a Mannheim *crescendo*.

EXAMPLE 42-2

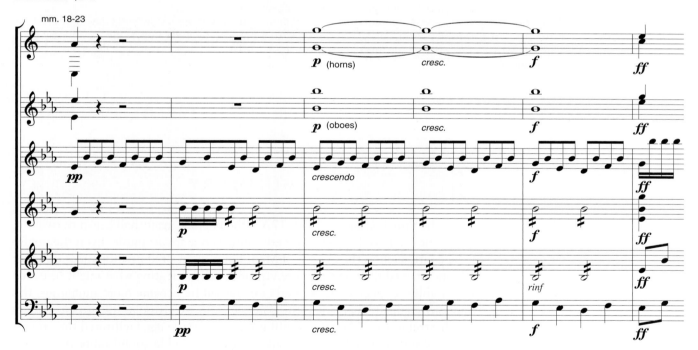

LISTENING CUE

JOHANN STAMITZ
La Melodia Germanica, No. 3 (c1755)
Symphony in E♭ Major
First movement, *Allegro assai*

CD 7/6
Anthology, No. 124

How Fast Is *Allegro*?

Composers began placing tempo markings in music during the seventeenth century. As time progressed, the instructions became more elaborate, so that by 1750 expressions such as *Allegro ma non troppo, Adagio spiritoso,* and *Adagio pesante,* among others, were used. But how fast is *Allegro,* and how slow *Adagio*? Even in the scientific age of the Enlightenment, a standardized mechanism for measuring musical time had yet to be devised. Johann Quantz (see earlier Box), an experienced orchestral player, proposed using a device that musicians had employed since at least 1500 for setting a beat in a musical performance: the human pulse. The musician checked his pulse and then set the beat by getting it in sync with a specific note value (half-, quarter-, or eighth-note) depending on the tempo marking of the composer.

To simplify things, Quantz set out four basic categories for tempos: *Allegro assai* (very fast), *Allegretto* (moving), *Adagio cantabile* (a songful *adagio*), and *Adagio assai* (very slow). All other tempo markings, he stipulated, were more "an expression of the dominant passions in each piece than a real tempo marking." He did, however, allow for a moderate middle tempo between the first two, which resulted in five primary tempos. To each of these he assigned a speed according to "the pulse beat at the hand of a healthy person," or 80 beats per minute. The modern equivalents of Quantz's tempo markings can be summarized as:

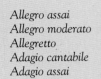

Allegro assai	160 beats per minute
Allegro moderato	120 beats per minute
Allegretto	80 beats per minute
Adagio cantabile	40 beats per minute
Adagio assai	20 beats per minute

Quantz was quick to admit that his system lacked uniformity. He knew that in every musician the pulse changed according to the time of day, the amount of that person's activity and food consumed, and other variables. A rate of 80 pulse beats per minute was most likely to be found, he said, "in a jovial and high-spirited yet rather fiery and volatile person" after he had eaten lunch! A musician who was "low-spirited, or melancholy, or cold and sluggish" could set the tempo slightly faster than his pulse. Quantz knew that this was not very scientific, and he concluded his discussion of tempo with the following remark: "Beyond this, if someone could discover a simpler, more accurate, and more convenient device [than the pulse] for learning and establishing tempos, he would do well to communicate it to the public immediately."

This "more convenient device" would come, but musicians had to wait until the invention of the metronome in Vienna around 1810.

SUMMARY

During the Enlightenment (1730–1770), the public concert hall began to rival the aristocratic salon as the preferred performing venue for art music. Even the nobles of the court, such as the elector of Mannheim, sponsored performances in larger halls and opened the doors to more visitors, thereby creating what might be called "semi-public" concerts. As concerts for the public became more numerous, the symphony gradually supplanted the Baroque concerto grosso as the principal genre of orchestral music. The more egalitarian spirit of the age facilitated the growth of the orchestra, which emphasized a united ensemble sound more than soloistic skills. The tripartite Italian opera overture grew into the three movement concert symphony (fast/slow/fast), best seen in the eighty-some symphonies of Giovanni Battista Sammartini. By 1750 the Italian symphony had crossed the Alps to German-speaking cities such as Mannheim. Here Johann Stamitz expanded the symphony to four movements, added dramatic effects to the score, and improved ensemble discipline by demanding uniform bowing and precise changes in dynamics.

KEY TERMS

Concert spirituel	consequent phrase	Mannheim *crescendo*
concert symphony	*Essay on Playing the Flute*	Mannheim rocket
antecedent phrase	Johann Quantz	

Music in the Age of Enlightenment: Keyboard Music

In 1776 the Englishman Adam Smith published his *Wealth of Nations*, a landmark study of the creation of capital. Here for the first time was an account of **capitalism,** an economic system in which the means of production of goods are privately owned and bring ever-increasing wealth to private individuals. In the eighteenth century, London was the European center of capitalism, for the English had profitably explored and exploited new markets around the world. They also enjoyed relatively free trade and comparatively little royal control. Other European cities prospered as well. For the newly affluent merchant, lawyer, and stock trader, it was important to create a domestic situation in which the lady of the house did not work; how else might she be distinguished from women of lower social classes? Moreover, the beginning of the Industrial Revolution ushered in an era in which items women had traditionally made at home (soap, candles, and clothes, for example) were increasingly produced in factories and sold in shops. Greater wealth, then, brought with it increased leisure time, which provided middle-class women the opportunity to make music in the home.

 DOMESTIC KEYBOARD MUSIC FOR WOMEN

A smattering of French, an eye for needlepoint, some skill at the keyboard—these were the signs of good breeding necessary to a gentlewoman of the Enlightenment. The spirit of democracy may have been in the air, but this was still very much a sexist age. Serious learning was deemed beyond the ken of a woman, and the notion that a woman might attend university was considered absurd. Only one career awaited, that of wife and mother. To improve marital prospects, domestic refinements were required. And, as a German social critic said in 1773: "Among the *galant* arts that are expected of a young lady, music figures the most important of all."[1]

What sort of music might a young lady perform in those days? Keyboard music, of course. Wind instruments distorted the face. The violin required the upper torso to twist. The cello necessitated the legs to be spread; perish the thought! The guitar and mandolin were decorous enough, but by far the most favored instruments were the harpsichord and piano. Consequently, as almost every painting of the period shows, a woman making domestic music in the mid eighteenth century did so demurely seated at a keyboard, joined perhaps by a singer.

Composers quickly rushed to supply this emerging market with pieces such as "sonatas for the fair sex," "songs particularly adapted for ladies with pianoforte accompaniment," and "keyboard pieces for the cultured lady." It was assumed that ladies would not wish "to bother their pretty little heads with counterpoint and harmony." All that was needed was a tuneful melody and a few supporting chords to flesh it out. In 1775 the accommodating Johann Reichardt published his *Songs for the Fair Sex* with the more difficult notes in smaller note heads to be omitted "if the pretty little hand won't stretch."

Needless to say, a repertory aimed at amateur performers, whether male or female, encouraged a lighter, less complicated style than the more professionally oriented keyboard music of the Baroque era. More melody and less counterpoint was the general trend. In truth, a simpler kind of music had already been produced in Italy around 1730. This Italian *galant* style of keyboard music can be seen in the forty-odd harpsichord sonatas of Domenico Alberti (c1710–1746). Alberti would be forgotten today had not other composers adopted a particular component of this style, an accompaniment pattern we now call the Alberti bass. An **Alberti bass** animates simple triads by playing the notes successively in a pattern, as shown in Example 43-1. For the keyboardist, this was an easy formula to play. Should the Alberti bass prove too difficult, an even simpler method was at hand: repeat the bass note, but in alternating octaves, as shown in Example 43-2. A rumbling octave bass became a favorite technique of both Italian and German composers of the eighteenth century. The Germans called it the **murky bass.** Composers of the eighteenth century, including the young Beethoven, used both the Alberti bass and the murky bass as a way of energizing what was at heart a simple, homophonic accompaniment. Such "bass filler" patterns made the keyboard music of the day more accessible, and made the average amateur performer sound more technically skilled than she was.

EXAMPLE 43-1 Domenico Alberti, Opus 1, No. 3 (1748), first movement

EXAMPLE 43-2 J. C. Bach, Opus 5, No. 1 (1766), third movement

THE ADVENT OF THE PIANO

During the Enlightenment a new instrument, the piano, began to replace the harpsichord as the workhorse of musical performance. The harpsichord, which first appeared in France in the fifteenth century (see Chapter 19), produces sound when strings are plucked, but the plucking always has the same force, and thus produces the same volume of sound. A different kind of keyboard instrument, the piano, was invented in Florence, Italy, around 1700 by Bartolomeo Cristofori (1655–1732). To replace the harpsichord's plucking apparatus, Cristofori invented a mechanism to strike the string with a soft hammer and have it then fall quickly and quietly back to its resting position. Each blow could now be carefully controlled by the force of the player's finger. The instrument could play *piano* as well as *forte*—hence the term **pianoforte** (see Box in Chapter 47).

FIGURE 43-1
Lodovico Giustini, *Sonate da cimbalo di piano, e forte* (Florence, 1732) was the first keyboard score to be intended explicitly for piano. Clearly evident are the markings "*pia.*" and "*for.*" calling for the dynamic levels *piano* and *forte*.

The original piano had a narrow range and a small tone. But its ability to regulate instantly the volume of each note gave it a major advantage over the harpsichord. Successive phrases of a musical "question and answer" could be shaded in varying degrees of soft and loud, which constituted an important factor in a music that increasingly came to be made up of short, complementary phrases. Moreover, the piano could also emphasize the melody at the expense of the accompaniment, something only possible on a harpsichord if the instrument had two keyboards. With a range of articulations including staccato and legato, it also could produce a variety of subtle nuances. Finally, the piano could play gradations of sounds—diminuendos and crescendos—to make the music more exciting.

Figure 43-1 shows a sample page from the first music ever published for piano, Lodovico Giustini's *Sonate da cimbalo di piano, e forte* (Florence, 1732). A glance at the score, covered with marks such as "pia." and "for." and "più for.," confirms that the composer took full advantage of the sonic capabilities of the new instrument. From 1750 onward, most keyboard music was advertised as "appropriate for both harpsichord and piano," even if it were better suited for one than the other. No intelligent publisher could afford to ignore a substantial share of the growing market, and no self-respecting keyboardist could avoid performing on both instruments.

DOMENICO SCARLATTI IN MADRID

Domenico Scarlatti (1685–1757) was born in Naples, the son of opera and cantata composer Alessandro Scarlatti (see Chapter 32). Young Scarlatti's domain, however, was not to be vocal music, but music for the keyboard. In his earliest years, Domenico showed himself to be something of a harpsichord prodigy, and at the age of fifteen he was appointed keyboardist to the king of Naples. In 1719 Scarlatti's career took a surprising turn for an Italian musician deeply steeped in Italian musical ways: he became composer to King João V of Portugal and moved to Lisbon. Scarlatti's principal charge at the Portuguese court was to serve as music teacher and mentor to the king's daughter, Maria Barbara. A marriage in 1729 placed Maria Barbara in line to be queen of Spain, and both she and Scarlatti moved to Madrid. Scarlatti spent his last decades in the Spanish capital writing keyboard sonatas for his patroness and other members of the royal court, creating some 555 sonatas in all.

Most surprising for a keyboard prodigy such as Scarlatti, he published no music for keyboard until he was fifty-three years old! His first publication, called *Essercizi* (1738), contains thirty sonatas, each of only one movement. The title *Essercizi* suggests that these pieces were to serve as exercises to develop specific keyboard skills, much as would the etude in later centuries. (Similarly, in this period the English often called their sonatas "lessons," implying that some technical advantage was to be gained from the study of such pieces.) In the preface to his *Essercizi*, however, Scarlatti downplays the difficulties of these works and suggests that his temperament, as his contemporaries noted, was congenial with the more playful mood of the *galant* age: "Do not expect, whether you are an amateur or a professional, to find any profound intention in these compositions, but rather an ingenious jesting with art by means of which you may attain freedom in harpsichord playing."

Scarlatti's "ingenious jesting with art" is fully evident in his Sonata in A Major (Kirkpatrick No. 26[†]) from the *Essercizi*. As with almost all of Scarlatti's sonatas, the form here is binary (**AB**), with both sections repeated. The harmonic plan, too, has the conventional movement of I-V in **A** and V-I in **B**. Scarlatti's playfulness can be heard at the very beginning, where a downbeat sounds like an upbeat in an off-kilter example of metrical displacement (Ex. 43-3A). But the real surprises come at the junctions between I and V in part **A** and between V and I in part **B.** At the first of these moments Scarlatti includes crunching downbeat dissonances (Ex. 43-3B). This is the famous Scarlatti **acciaccatura.** In Italian, "acciaccatura" denotes something bruised or battered, and here the composer batters the listener with these dissonant downbeat chords. Scarlatti experts believe he derived this unusual effect from hearing dissonant chords strummed on Spanish guitars. Indeed, few composers fell more deeply under the intoxicating spell of the Spanish guitar music than Scarlatti. Likewise, the juncture between V and I in part **B** has a distinctly Spanish sound. Here the harmony rocks back and forth between two chords built on bass notes a major second apart, a sure sign of modal music indigenous to old Spain (Ex. 43-3C). Finally, everywhere throughout this sonata we see another hallmark of Scarlatti's flamboyant style, **hand-crossing.** Continually, the left hand must cross over the right to create an exciting three-level texture (left hand, right hand, and left over). Hand-crossing looks difficult but is often rather easy to do, and it gives to the music the appearance of playful daring.

EXAMPLE 43-3A

[†]While there are at least three numbering systems for the sonatas of Domenico Scarlatti, the most widely recognized one is that of Ralph Kirkpatrick, which appeared in his book *Domenico Scarlatti* (Princeton, 1953).

EXAMPLE 43-3B

EXAMPLE 43-3C

Did Scarlatti intend his sonatas for the harpsichord or piano? The preface to the *Essercizi* explicitly mentions the harpsichord, perhaps because at that time the piano was a relative newcomer. Yet Scarlatti's patroness and protégé, Queen Maria Barbara of Spain, owned three pianos on which her music master surely played. Thus, although Scarlatti expected his sonatas to be played on the harpsichord, it is not historically inaccurate to play them on the piano.

LISTENING CUE

DOMENICO SCARLATTI
Essercizi (1738)
Sonata No. 26 in A Major

CD 7/7
Anthology, No. 125

THE CLAVICHORD IN BERLIN: CARL PHILIPP EMANUEL BACH

During a long reign (1740–1786), King **Frederick the Great** made his realm, the north German kingdom of Prussia, a major player in European affairs. He also transformed Berlin (see Map 39-1) from a sleepy hamlet of 10,000 into a cosmopolitan capital of 100,000, full of art and learning. Frederick was an enlightened leader who spoke French fluently, wrote poetry and music, and brought the philosopher Voltaire to his court. He also built an opera house on a site that the Berlin Opera has occupied ever since. Yet Frederick also became a great military leader, one whose territorial acquisitions laid the foundation for the modern state of Germany. From the age of seven, Frederick received lessons in keyboard playing and figured bass realization. Eventually he even tried his hand at composition (see Chapters 40 and 41). Frederick also played the flute, and, when he became king in 1740, one of his first acts was to lure the flautist Johann Quantz (see Chapter 42) to the royal court in Berlin. The next year he engaged as keyboardist C.P.E. Bach, one of J.S. Bach's talented sons. During the day, King Frederick drilled his troops. Each evening, between the

🌿 FIGURE 43-2
Flautist and monarch Frederick
the Great plays chamber music at
his court. Carl Philipp Emanuel
Bach is at the keyboard, and the
king's teacher, Johann Quantz,
stands on the extreme right.

hours of seven and nine, however, he played
flute sonatas and concertos (Fig. 43-2), most
composed by his teacher Johann Quantz and
accompanied by C.P.E. Bach at the keyboard.

Carl Philipp Emanuel Bach, the second
son of J.S. Bach, moved from Leipzig to Berlin in 1741 to serve as personal accompanist
to the flute-playing king of Prussia. Here he remained for more than twenty-five years, performing in the monarch's evening musicales,
accompanying in the court opera orchestra,
and composing. Bach wrote in all musical genres of the day except opera and Catholic Mass.
But he had been trained by his father as a keyboardist, and keyboard music lies at the heart
of his creative work.

By the mid eighteenth century, demand for keyboard music for amateurs, and especially women, was increasing. Bach capitalized on this quickening enthusiasm for
middle class music-making by issuing a stream of artistically and commercially successful keyboard sonatas. Principal among these are his *Six Easy Sonatas* (1766), six
sonatas *For Use by Ladies* (1770), and six collections of sonatas *For Connoisseurs and
Amateurs* (1779–1787). The last sets, *For Connoisseurs and Amateurs*, were particularly lucrative—taken together some 6,300 copies were printed, an astonishingly
large number for the eighteenth century.

Coinciding with the growing demand for amateur music was the need for instructional manuals dealing with matters of musical performance. Johann Quantz satisfied the desires of flutists, as we have seen (Chapter 42), with his *Essay on Playing
the Flute* (1752). In 1756 Leopold Mozart, father of Wolfgang, would write a best-
selling violin method. By far the most influential instruction book for keyboard in
the eighteenth century was C.P. E. Bach's two-part **Essay on the True Art of Playing the Keyboard** (*Versuch über die wahre Art das Clavier zu spielen*, 1753 and 1762).
Clementi and Haydn would later learn from Bach's book, as would the young
Beethoven. In his lengthy *Essay*, Bach tries to give both soloist and accompanist all
the practical information the keyboard performer might need concerning musical
intervals, key signatures, figured bass realization, ornamentation, improvisation, accompanying techniques, and fingering. At the end of his method book, Bach appends six three-movement sonatas in ascending order of difficulty that were
designed to develop keyboard technique.

To appeal to the largest number of buyers for his sonatas, C.P.E. Bach referred to
his instrument by the generic term "clavier," meaning simply "keyboard." Sometimes C.P.E. played on the harpsichord and sometimes on the newer piano; his royal
patron owned fifteen! But C.P.E. Bach's favorite instrument was the quieter clavichord, which, while much softer than the harpsichord or piano, allowed for far
greater expressivity. Said an observer of Bach's playing: "To know Bach completely
one must hear the wealth of his imagination, the profound sentiment of his heart,
his constant enthusiasm as he improvises on his clavichord."[2]

Bach's style of playing and his style of composition—his "profound sentiment of
his heart"—came to be associated with the *empfindsamer Stil*. **Empfindsamer Stil**
(German for "Sensitive Style") is a term applied to the hyper-expressivity that

The Clavichord

The clavichord first appeared in the fourteenth century, and its popularity in the West continued unabated until the late eighteenth century (see Chapter 23). The harpsichord and piano produce sound when a device plucks or strikes the string and then falls back. On the clavichord, however, a metal "T" called a tangent pushes against the string and continues to do so as long as the key is depressed. This allows the performer to hold and "wiggle" the key up and down and produce a vibrating sound that the Germans called *Bebung*—"quaking." Composers indicated this trembling effect in the score by placing dots with a slur over them above the note (Ex. 43-4). *Bebung* was the perfect vehicle for expressing the throbbing heart, panting breast, or quivering hand in music in the *empfindsamer Stil*.

The clavichord was smaller than either the piano or the harpsichord and was accordingly less expensive. Usually the clavichord was encased in a rectangular box with strings running at right angles to the keyboard. Because it was smaller, composers could carry one in their baggage when traveling, as Mozart often did. Because it was quiet to the point of being almost inaudible, the clavichord was a good practice instrument in schools, convents, and seminaries. Finally, because of its low volume, the clavichord was the best keyboard instrument for very private music-making by the solitary soul. It could express the quiet grief so dear to sensitive hearts in the age of *Empfindsamkeit* (sensitivity). The following *Ode to My Clavier* (here, meaning clavichord) was published in Germany the year after Part I of Bach's *Essay* on keyboard playing. It is not a great poem, but it expresses well the "heart on sleeve" sentimentality that marked the poetry and music of the *empfindsamer Stil*.

Ode To My Clavichord by Wilhelm Zachariae (1754)

Oh Echo of my sighing soul,
My faithful strings set in array,
Now troubling day gives way
To night—all sorrow's goal.

Help me, gentle strings,
Help remove these painful things.
But no! leave me to my pain,
Comfort I do distain.

Yes, sadness I condone.
I love the saddest part,
And if I cry alone,
I vent my loving heart.[3]

affected northern European arts generally in the second half of the eighteenth century. True to the Enlightenment, this "cult of feeling" was not inspired by religious ecstasy but by ordinary domestic experience. Jane Austen's later *Sense and Sensibility*—full of heart-rending family scenes and dramatic reconciliations—typifies the sentimental style in English literature. In music, this intimate and often passionate voice can best be heard in the keyboard pieces of C.P.E. Bach. As he said toward the end of his autobiography: "I believe that music must, first and foremost, stir the heart." True to his vow, when Bach played, "He looked like one inspired. His eyes were fixed, his under-lip fell, and drops of effervescence distilled from his countenance." [4]

Another fine example of *empfindsamer Stil* can be found in C.P.E. Bach's Fantasia in C Minor (Helm No. 75/iii and Wotquenne No. 63.6/iii[†]). It appears as the final movement of the last of six sonatas appended to his keyboard method book. The **fantasia** of the eighteenth century is a rhapsodic, improvisatory work, often unbarred, in which the composer gives free rein to the musical imagination without concern for conventional musical forms. It is in the fantasia that we most fully experience C.P.E. Bach's *Empfindsamkeit*: long asymmetrical lines, unpredictable rhythms, abrupt harmonic shifts, and sudden dynamic changes. In truth, C.P.E. Bach is not a typical composer of the *galant* style. His long, irregular phrases often go against the grain of the simpler *galant*, with its short, balanced, repeating phrases. Bach was known to

[†]There are two standard catalogues of the works of C.P.E. Bach, that of E.E. Helm, *Thematic Catalogue of the Works of Carl Philipp Emanuel Bach* (New Haven, CT, 1989), and an earlier one of A. Wotquenne: *Thematisches Verzeichnis der Werke von Carl Philipp Emanuel Bach (1714–1788)* (Leipzig, 1905).

improvise at the clavichord for hours on end, and indeed the Fantasia in C Minor sounds like an expressive improvisation committed to paper (Ex. 43-4). We can be sure that he intended it for the clavichord because the score contains signs calling for *Bebung*, a trembling ornament that can only be played on a clavichord.

EXAMPLE 43-4

* asterisk indicates *Bebung*

LISTENING CUE

CARL PHILIPP EMANUEL BACH
Fantasia in C Minor for clavichord (1753)

CD 7/8
Anthology, No. 126

Growing tired of King Frederick's increasingly conservative musical taste, and having seen no increase in his pay for a sixteen-year period, C.P.E. Bach left Berlin and moved to Hamburg in 1768. Here he took charge of the music in the five major Protestant churches of this north German city. On the side, Bach instituted a series of public subscription concerts (six or twelve concerts in each series), in which he featured himself at the keyboard. While he was promoting public concerts for a paying audience in Hamburg, his half-brother J.C. Bach was doing the same in London.

✻ THE PIANO IN LONDON: JOHANN CHRISTIAN BACH

C.P.E. Bach was known as "the Berlin Bach," while his half-brother J.C. Bach was called "the London Bach." Although he was the youngest son of J.S. Bach, Johann Christian Bach (1735–1782) was anything but a chip off the old Bach: the son moved to Italy, converted from Lutheran to Catholic, wrote operas, and ended up composing tuneful piano pieces in London. As this famously practical Bach said, "My brother (C.P.E.) lives to compose, but I (J.C.) compose to live."

Arriving in London in 1762, J.C. Bach used his German connections to get himself appointed music master to the English royal family, itself of German descent. And, just as his brother accompanied the flute-playing Frederick the Great in Berlin, so J.C. Bach sometimes accompanied the flute-playing English king George III (against whom the American colonies would soon rebel). In 1764 J.C. Bach and another German musician, Carl Abel, began a series of public concerts in London. A music lover could buy a ticket to a subscription series of up to fifteen concerts, at which the two featured their most recent compositions, along with those of other fashionable composers. The **Bach-Abel concerts** continued for nearly twenty years, and became a model for the public concert series in London and elsewhere throughout Europe. Also in 1764, J.C. Bach met and befriended the Mozarts, who were in London as part of a European tour to showcase the seven-year-old Wolfgang's talents. Bach and Mozart played together on a single keyboard, Wolfgang sitting on Bach's lap: "Herr Johann Christian Bach, the Queen's teacher, took the son between his legs, the former played a few bars, and the other continued, and in this way they played a whole sonata."[5] Young Mozart studied the music of J.C. Bach and later acknowledged the artistic debt he owed him. Indeed, there was a great affinity between the emerging Classical style of Mozart and the *galant* style of J.C. Bach.

Johann Christian Bach's music represents the essence of the *galant* style. His melodies are smooth and graceful, his accompaniments simple, and his textures light and airy. Moreover, Bach's melodies are not technically difficult, a fact that was seen as appealing to amateurs. Said an Englishman of the time: "In general his compositions for the piano forte are such as ladies can execute with little trouble; and the allegros [more] resemble bravura songs, than instrumental pieces."[6] In his keyboard music, J.C. Bach rarely calls on the right hand to play more than a single melodic line, and this produces a *cantabile* (singing) melody, as can be seen in Example 43-5. An Italianate Alberti bass in the left hand, providing a simple, direct harmonic accompaniment, supports the easily flowing tune in the right. Although the rapidly moving bass looks difficult, it is really rather simple, since very few chords are involved and thus few changes of hand position are required. In fact, the thumb of the left hand plays only two notes.

EXAMPLE 43-5

Soon after arriving in London, J.C. Bach took advantage of the flourishing music trade to publish collections of symphonies, keyboard concertos, and keyboard sonatas. Among these, the six he issued as Opus 5 in 1766 represent a landmark—they are the first sonatas published in London to indicate on the title page the option of performance by piano. Moreover, Bach was the first musician to play the piano as a solo instrument in public in England, which he did at one of the Bach-Abel concerts in 1768. As Bach's friend, the historian Charles Burney, observed: "After the arrival of John Christian Bach in this country, and the establishment of his concert[s] . . . all the harpsichord makers tried their mechanical powers at piano-fortes."

Of the sonatas in J.C. Bach's Opus 5, the second in D major shows particular evidence of being conceived for piano rather than harpsichord. Not only are there marks of "piano" and "forte" written in the score, but there are also striking contrasts of texture that can best be brought out on the piano. The opening movement, for example, alternates dramatic chordal units with a quieter two-bar *cantabile* melody (Ex. 43-6). Perhaps most important, Bach lengthens the binary form considerably, a harbinger of the longer piano sonata of the Classical era. There are two distinctly different themes in section **A,** and the beginning of section **B** is expanded

The Piano Comes to England

In 1760 London was not only Europe's most populous city but it was also the richest. Exploration, free trade, and emerging capitalism caused commerce to flourish. The gentrified middle class had money and time to spare for the finer things in life. One thing many well-to-do Londoners came to covet was a pianoforte. In 1750 the piano was almost unknown in England; by 1800 it had replaced the harpsichord entirely, putting harpsichord makers out of business. Part of the attraction of the piano was its size and price. During the 1760s an enterprising German émigré, Johannes Zumpe, began to manufacture what is known as the **square piano,** a small box-shaped piano with strings running at right angles to the keys that could be set upon a table or a simple stand (Fig. 43-3). Zumpe's diminutive pianos sold for less than half the price of large harpsichords. Said an observer of the day: "There was scarcely a house in the kingdom where a keyed instrument had ever had admission, but was supplied with one of Zumpe's piano-fortes for which there was nearly as much call in France as in England. In short he could not make them fast enough to gratify the craving of the public."[7]

During this time the English term "grand" piano originated, and it did so in a strange way. In 1777 Robert Stodart applied for an English patent for a combination piano and harpsichord. He called his instrument "grand" to distinguish it from the smaller square model of Zumpe. Almost immediately, however, the term **grand piano** was applied solely to a large piano with sturdy legs and strings running roughly in

the same direction as the keys. By the 1780s, the English piano-maker John Broadwood referred to his five- or six-foot-long pianos as "grands," and the term has remained in use ever since.

🌸 FIGURE 43-3

Johann Zoffany's painting of 1775 represents members of two British families as they gather for music-making. The woman plays a square piano by Johannes Zumpe and the man a cello.

into a full-blown development. In fact, this movement is written not in Baroque binary form, but instead in one that will dominate the Classical period: sonata form (see Chapter 44).

EXAMPLE 43-6

LISTENING CUE

JOHANN CHRISTIAN BACH
Piano Sonata in D Major, Opus 5, No. 2 (1766)
First movement, *Allegro di molto*

Book Companion Website (http://schirmer.
wadsworth.com/wright_1e)
Anthology, No. 127

Later, in 1772, Wolfgang Amadeus Mozart paid homage to his early mentor, J.C. Bach. He arranged three of the Opus 5 sonatas (Nos. 2–4) as piano concertos, thereby creating what are now known and enumerated as Mozart concertos K. 107, 1–3. Mozart's alterations were by no means elaborate; he mainly provided Bach's keyboard score with accompanying orchestral parts and added cadenzas for the soloist. Needless to say, if Mozart could make a Classical concerto out of a *galant* sonata, there was little distinction between late *galant* and early Classical styles. At this moment in music history, Classical style simply emerged from the *galant*.

  SUMMARY

Amateur music-making flourished during the Enlightenment as the middle class grew with an expanding European economy. Keyboard music in particular enjoyed favor with women who had increased leisure time. The harpsichord ceded pride of place during the eighteenth century to the pianoforte, owing to the piano's greater capacity for contrasts and shadings of volume as well as nuanced articulation. The leading keyboard genre was the sonata, whether the one-movement type associated with Domenico Scarlatti or the far more common three-movement kind of C.P.E. Bach and his younger brother, J.C. Bach. Scarlatti and C.P.E. Bach project two distinctly personal views of *galant* style. The former's writing is flamboyant and extroverted, showing off the skills of the performer including hand-crossing; the latter is more introverted and often unpredictable, with long themes and irregular phrases. The compositional style of J.C. Bach is closer to the core of *galant* style, with its graceful, balanced phrases composed of short motivic ideas supported by simple harmonies. There is a great affinity between the *galant* style of J.C. Bach and the emerging language of Classical music, especially as expressed by Mozart.

  KEY TERMS

capitalism	hand-crossing	*Bebung*
Alberti bass	Frederick the Great	fantasia
murky bass	*Essay on the True Art of*	Bach-Abel concerts
pianoforte	*Playing the Keyboard*	square piano
acciaccatura	*empfindsamer Stil*	grand piano

Chapter 44

Classical Music in Vienna

The music of Haydn, Mozart, and the young Beethoven dominates our view of the late eighteenth century. These composers, along with Franz Schubert (1797–1828), form what historians refer to as the **Viennese School,** for indeed all four of these great musicians capped their careers in Vienna. Perhaps at no time in the history of music were so many extraordinary composers found within the walls of a single city. What is more, these composers interacted with one another in a variety of ways: Mozart was a close friend of Haydn; Haydn taught Beethoven; and Schubert was a torchbearer at Beethoven's funeral.

Musical style, too, had a cohesion rarely found in the history of music. Universal musical principles were at work in an age that greatly valued universal ideals. Composers working in Naples, Madrid, Berlin, Paris, and London, influenced by those in Vienna, tacitly reached a consensus as to how music was supposed to sound. The style they created we now call "Classical" music.[1] Whereas "classical" (lower case "c") suggests all Western art music, "Classical" (with a capital "C") has come to denote the high art music of the period roughly 1770–1820. In no city did that art music reach a higher level than in Vienna.

Vienna was then the capital of the old Holy Roman Empire (see Map 49-1). As such, it served as the administrative center for a large part of Europe, including portions of modern-day Germany, Italy, Croatia, Bosnia, Serbia, Slovakia, Poland, Czech Republic, and Hungary, in addition to all of Austria. Vienna was surrounded by vast agricultural lands, with no other large cities for hundreds of miles. The aristocracy from disparate territories, even Russia, congregated in Vienna, especially during the long winter months when there was little agricultural work to be supervised. In 1790, the heyday of Haydn and Mozart, Vienna had a population of roughly 215,000. The nobility numbered about 3,250, and they were attended to by some 40,000 footmen, maids, and other servants. The unusually high percentage of aristocrats among the population may partly account for the fact that art music was so intensely cultivated in the city. The nobles patronized music, often enjoying it together with middle-class citizens at public or semi-public concerts.

With so much patronage to offer, Vienna attracted musicians from throughout Europe, including Christoph Willibald Gluck (1714–1787) from Bohemia (Czech Republic), Antonio Salieri (1750–1825) from Italy, Joseph Haydn (1732–1809) from Rohrau in lower Austria, Wolfgang Amadeus Mozart (1756–1791) from Salzburg in upper Austria, and Ludwig van Beethoven (1770–1827) from the German Rhineland. Vienna was a crossroads for human transit and thus a melting pot of culture. Here high art music from many regions coalesced into a universal musical style that would set the standard for all of Europe.

❖ CLASSICAL STYLE

What are the musical characteristics of Classical style? Many are the same as those found in *galant* music of the earlier Enlightenment: clarity, simplicity, formal balance, and naturalness. Formal patterns are clearly articulated and readily apparent to the ear. Architecture of the late eighteenth century conveys many of these same qualities to the eye. It too is marked by balance, harmonious proportions, and an absence of ornate decoration. Because the designs of many eighteenth-century public buildings were taken directly from classical Rome, this style is called **Neoclassical architecture** (Fig. 44-1). Around the turn of the nineteenth century, Neoclassical architecture was carried to the United States by Thomas Jefferson and others. Today it can be seen in many state capitols, universities, and government buildings, particularly in Washington, D.C. Just as this architectural style has become "classic," continuing to give pleasure to succeeding generations, so too has the music of Haydn, Mozart, and Beethoven.

An excerpt from the famous *Andante* middle movement of Mozart's Piano Concerto No. 21 in C Major (K. 467) exemplifies the clarity, expressive grace, noble simplicity, and balanced contrasts that characterize the Classical style in music. Here Mozart fashions two three-bar phrases: the first is an antecedent phrase that carries the music forward and ends on the dominant harmony, while the second unit is a consequent phrase that complements the first three bars but brings the music back home to the tonic (Ex. 44-1). Subsequent phrases are grouped in three two-bar phrases. The piano presents a melody that is light and airy, yet perfectly balanced. It is also both singable and memorable; indeed, this melody was turned into a popular movie theme (the "love song" from *Elvira Madigan*). A light harmonic support is fashioned by repeating, first a tonic triad, then a dominant-seventh chord, and finally the tonic triad again. This accompaniment supports, but does not interfere with, the graceful melody. Gone entirely is the heavy bass line of the Baroque basso continuo. Gone too is the sometimes-asymmetrical melody of the Baroque that was often more instrumental than vocal in character.

Bridgeman Art Library

🌸 FIGURE 44-1

The façade of Schoenbrunn Palace near Vienna was completed in 1744–1749 with the encouragement of Austria Empress Maria Theresa (1717–1780). The symmetrical units, long lines, and freedom from excessive ornaments are typical of Neoclassical architecture.

EXAMPLE 44-1

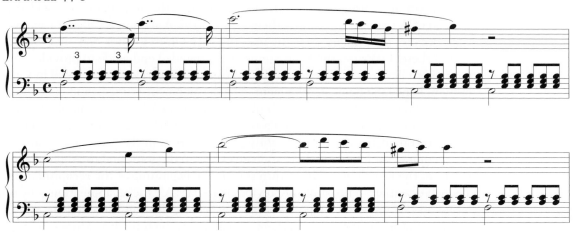

🌸 CLASSICAL FORMS

Classical music resounds with pleasing proportions, owing to balanced lines and uncluttered textures. In addition, large-scale musical forms are at work. In the Classical era, perhaps more so than any other period, certain tried-and-true musical forms regulated nearly all art music. Rare was the symphony, concerto, or sonata written during the period 1770–1820 that was not shaped according to a conventional musical form. Most of these forms, however, were not new. Some, such as rondo form and theme-and-variations form, go back to the Middle Ages, while ternary form and rounded binary form flourished during the Baroque period. Only one new form, sonata, emerged during the second half of the eighteenth century. Yet it came to dominate musical structure during the Classical period and continued to be an important formal procedure into the twentieth century.

Rounded Binary Form

Baroque composers usually used binary form (**AB**) in their sonatas and dances. Classical composers generally preferred rounded binary form (**ABA'**). Here **A** ends by establishing a new key (usually the dominant or relative major), while **B,** beginning in a non-tonic key, at first contrasts with **A** but gradually gives way to an altered reprise of **A** (hence **A'**) with a return to the tonic key. In the Classical period, minuets and scherzos are almost always written in rounded binary form, with **A** and then **BA'** repeated (‖:A:‖:BA':‖). Perhaps more important, it is from rounded binary form that the larger sonata form emerged.

Sonata Form

The most important formal innovation of the Classical period is **sonata form.** Classical composers most often employed this form when writing a fast (*allegro*) first movement of a Classical sonata, quartet, or symphony. They also often invoked it when writing fast finales and, less frequently, slow second movements. Sonata form can best be understood as an expansion of rounded binary form. Composers began to extend the **A** portion of rounded binary form by including a second, often contrasting, theme in the dominant (or, in minor-key pieces, relative major) key. The passage of modulation between the tonic and the new key in sonata form we call the **transition** or **bridge.** Often too some distinctive thematic material is added at the end of **A** to serve as a closing theme. The entire **A** section is called the **exposition,** because the primary thematic material of the movement is "exposed" or presented there. Likewise, the **B** section is now expanded and made to provide more contrast to **A.** Here the themes of the exposition are varied or developed in some fashion, hence the name **development.** The development is usually full of counterpoint and rapid modulations, much like an episode in a fugue. Harmonically, it is the most unstable section of sonata form. Only toward the end of the development, in the **retransition,** does tonal stability return, often in the form of a dominant pedal point. The dominant chord then gives way to the tonic and the simultaneous return of the first theme. This return signals the beginning of the **recapitulation.** Though essentially a revisiting of previous material (**A**), the recapitulation is by no means an exact repeat. Composers invariably rewrote the transition in the recapitulation to ensure that the second theme remained in the tonic key. Moreover, most composers took advantage of the recapitulation to offer a "second pass" at the thematic material—to vary it by means of slight thematic alterations or enrich it by adding complementary contrapuntal lines. It was the convention in the eighteenth century in both binary and sonata form movements to repeat both **A** (exposition) and then **BA** (development and recapitulation). Today, however, performers do not always honor such repeats (see Box).

   Finally, optional elements may appear at either end of sonata form. Many of the mature symphonies of Mozart, and especially Haydn, have brief introductions before the exposition. Almost without exception these are slow, stately prefaces full of provocative or puzzling chords designed to set the listener wondering what sort of

Should I Repeat?

Symphonies, quartets, and sonatas in the Classical period began, and often ended, with a movement in sonata form. Almost all call for a repeat of the exposition by means of repeat signs, and many require a repeat of the development-recapitulation as well. Today performers and conductors usually honor the first repeat, but rarely the second. Does dropping the second repeat conform to eighteenth-century practice? In some cases, yes. To be specific, a few musicians of the day were growing impatient with this practice of a double repetition, as the French opera composer André Grétry (1741–1813) implied in 1797:

> A sonata is a speech. What would we think of someone who, dividing his speech in half, delivered each half twice? [For example:] "I came to your house this morning; yes, I came to your house this morning; to talk with you about some business; to talk with you about some business." This is nearly the effect that musical repeats have.[1]

As early as the 1780s, Haydn and Mozart began to dispense with the second repeat (development and recapitula-

tion) in some, but not all, of their works. The autograph of Mozart's Symphony in G Minor (No. 40), for example, indicates a second repeat in the finale but not in the first movement. Similarly, Mozart calls for the second repeat in the first movement of his Piano Sonata in B♭ Major (K. 570), but gives no such indication in the first movement of his Sonata in D Major (K. 576). Such omissions are likely intentional, but should not be taken as a license to omit all written repeats. Because Mozart carefully specified his intentions in his scores, a performer who wishes to be faithful to him should use a historically accurate edition and follow the composer's repeat signs as indicated.

By the nineteenth century, the second repeat had almost entirely disappeared. The mature Beethoven usually required a repeat of the exposition, but not the development and recapitulation. The tradition of the first repeat, however, long held firm. Composers such as Brahms and Dvořák were still calling for a repeat of the exposition in sonata-form movements as late as the 1880s.

musical adventure is about to unfold. A **coda** (Italian for "tail"), on the other hand, might be appended to the recapitulation. Its function is to add extra weight to the end of the movement to give it a feeling of conclusion. Like tails, codas may be short or long; however, they always end in the tonic key.

The diagram of sonata form, below, aims to show the basic principles underpinning sonata form. As with all models of this sort, it represents a simplified abstraction of what is in fact a lengthy, complex, and often unpredictable musical process. In practice, most pieces do not conform to this model in all particulars. The ensuing chapters discuss many movements in sonata form within string quartets, symphonies, and sonatas of Haydn, Mozart, and Beethoven—yet the application of sonata form within each work is unique.

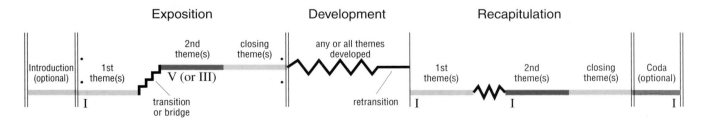

Ternary Form

In the Classical period, composers made frequent use of strict ternary form (**ABA**), as well as a more varied version of it. In strict ternary form, the **A** section begins and ends in the tonic; this is different from binary and rounded binary form, in which **A** ends in the dominant. **B** carries the music to a complementary key such as the dominant, relative major, or parallel minor, and the returning **A** repeats the first section (**A**) note for note. Strict ternary form, broadly applied, was especially favored by Classical composers for the third movements of symphonies and string quartets, in which minuet-trio-minuet or scherzo-trio-scherzo sequences were common. In the more varied version of ternary form, the reprise of **A** was considerably rewritten. Classical composers often employed varied ternary form for their slow movements, as did Beethoven in his Symphony No. 3, The "Eroica" (Anthology, No. 141).

Theme-and-Variations Form

In theme-and-variations form, the composer chooses a theme and then varies it, by altering the melody, harmony, and/or rhythm, or by ornamenting or embellishing around it. Composers of the Classical period preferred to write variations on simple tunes—popular or patriotic songs, folk melodies, or tunes of their own making. Mozart, for example, wrote variations on what we now call "Twinkle, Twinkle Little Star," while Beethoven composed a set on "God Save the King." The simplicity of such melodies as these allowed composers greater freedom in the process of variation. Originally, a work in theme-and-variations form was a one-movement, free-standing piece. But, in the 1760s, Haydn had brought theme-and-variation form into the multi-movement symphony and quartet. Here it usually served as a formal plan for fast finales, and was sometimes found in slow movements, as is the case in Haydn's famous Symphony No. 94, The "Surprise" (Anthology, No. 130).

Rondo Form

The rondo of the Classical period perpetuates a formal procedure that extends back into the Middle Ages (see Chapter 12). During the Baroque era, the "rondeau" was popular, particularly in France, as a one-movement instrumental dance or keyboard piece (see Anthology, No. 104). Enlightenment composers such as J.C. Bach brought the form into the multi-movement symphony and sonata. A typical Classical **rondo** sets a refrain (**A**) against contrasting material (**B, C,** or **D**) to create a pattern such as **ABACA, ABACABA,** or even **ABACADA.** Almost all true rondos include at least three statements of the primary structural unit or refrain (**A**) and at least two contrasting sections (**B** and **C**). The rondo usually projects a playful, exuberant mood, and for that reason the form often served as the last movement of a sonata or symphony, to bid a happy farewell to the audience. Mozart, for example, wrote four concertos for French horn, and the finale of each is in rondo form. Similarly, Beethoven used rondo form in the finales of all five of his piano concertos (see Chapter 49).

CLASSICAL GENRES

Form regulates the flow of most art music, and Classical music is no exception. Classical composers Haydn, Mozart, and Beethoven carefully positioned all of the elements of musical expression—themes, harmonic relationships, instrumental colors, textures, and dynamics—in ways that enhance formal clarity. Form provides a structure for each movement. But most compositions of the Classical period are multi-movement works. Classical composers grouped movements together to conform to an established genre—a broad category, or type, of music. Among other things, a musical genre implied a particular performing force as well as a place of performance. The symphony, for example, was usually performed by a full orchestra in a large princely chamber or public concert hall, while the quartet was played by four soloists in the home. Following are brief descriptions of the principal genres of Classical instrumental music. Genres of vocal music, namely, opera, oratorio, and Mass, will be discussed in Chapters 46 and 48.

Symphony

During the eighteenth century, the symphony gradually replaced the solo concerto and concerto grosso as the leading genre of large-scale instrumental music. Haydn, Mozart, and Beethoven each wrote more symphonies than concertos, and concerts featuring the music of these masters would invariably begin and end with one of their symphonies. Beethoven, for example, in his public debut in Vienna on 2 April 1800, presented a concert that began with a symphony by Mozart and ended with his own Symphony No. 1. The overall symphonic output of the eighteenth century was immense; one scholar has catalogued more than 12,000 symphonies produced between about 1720 and 1810. From the mid eighteenth century onward, the symphony formed the heart and soul of almost every orchestral concert. That is why the large orchestral ensemble is still called a symphony orchestra.

Concerto

During the Baroque era, two types of concertos could be found: the solo concerto and the concerto grosso. During the Classical period, the concerto grosso largely disappeared, leaving only the solo concerto, which Classical composers preferred to write for solo violin or keyboard. By the time Mozart arrived in Vienna in 1781, the piano was well on its way to replacing the harpsichord as the solo instrument in the keyboard concerto. Haydn, Mozart, and Beethoven all wrote concertos for piano as well as for violin. Of the piano concertos, the twenty-three concertos of Mozart and the five of Beethoven are the best known today (see Anthology, Nos. 136 and 140).

Divertimento and Serenade

Originally the term "divertimento" simply meant a musical diversion and comprised a variety of types of chamber music including the string quartet. But, in time, the **divertimento** came to imply a lighter style of music and a five-movement format: fast/minuet and trio/slow/minuet and trio/fast. The term **serenade** was generally used interchangeably with divertimento. Both types were played not only indoors but also outdoors as evening entertainment. Open-air concerts in the summer helped give Vienna its reputation as a musical city. The term "serenade" also implied that the music was appropriate for serenading a lady on her birthday or name day. Early in his career young Haydn earned money by serenading in the streets of Vienna.

Some divertimenti and serenades were composed for strings alone. One such piece is Mozart's famous *Eine kleine Nachtmusik* (*A Little Night Music*, 1787). It was originally written in five movements (the first minuet has been ripped out of the autograph score) for four string parts: two violins, viola, and cello, with double bass perhaps doubling the cello. But wind ensembles were also active participants in this genre (Fig. 44-2) because their sounds project well outdoors. At first, pairs of oboes, French horns, and bassoons formed the standard ensemble; later, after 1780, a pair

✿ FIGURE 44-2

A large *Harmonie* employed at the German court of Oettingen-Wallerstein consisting of pairs of flutes, clarinets, oboes, and French horns, supported by bassoon and double bass. Musicologist Sterling Murray, an expert on Oettingen-Wallerstein, dates this silhouette to 1783–1784 because a second bassoonist joined the ensemble in 1785.

of clarinets was added. Because in the eighteenth-century orchestra the winds played mostly harmony (German "Harmonie") and not melody, such an independent wind band came to be called a **Harmonie** in late eighteenth-century Vienna, and the music for it was designated **Harmoniemusik.** Mozart wrote a number of excellent divertimenti and serenades for *Harmonie*, including his Serenade in C Minor, created in 1782 for the emperor's wind band.

String Quartet

Joseph Haydn wrote his first string quartets in the late 1750s, and would bring the genre to its first maturity. With the addition of a viola line to the old Baroque trio sonata texture, along with an animated cello part, the quartet featured four more-or-less evenly matched instrumental parts. The function of a string quartet was somewhat different from that of the symphony or concerto, in that it was designed for a private or semiprivate performance in the aristocratic salon or the middle-class parlor. This domestic music, always played one-on-a-part, came to be called "chamber music."

Sonata

The Classical **sonata** was a type of domestic instrumental chamber music in two, three, or, more rarely, four movements for soloist or small ensemble. In Vienna in particular, young women of refinement were expected to play the piano. They acquired, and then demonstrated, their skills by playing piano sonatas. The easiest and shortest of these was sometimes dubbed **sonatina** (Italian for "little sonata"). Sonatas and sonatinas by Haydn, Mozart, Clementi, and others flooded the market. Although most were intended as teaching pieces, Beethoven designed many of his piano sonatas to serve as vehicles to showcase his own virtuosity. Accordingly, his sonatas are more technically demanding than those of Haydn or Mozart. In addition, Haydn, Mozart, and Beethoven all wrote violin sonatas. Yet, here again a distinction must be made. The accompanied sonatas of Haydn and Mozart often demand more of the keyboard player than the violinist. Indeed, in Mozart's earliest sonatas for violin and piano, the violin is optional (Ex. 44-2). Not until the violin sonatas and cello sonatas of Beethoven do the soloist and pianist consistently behave as equal partners.

EXAMPLE 44-2 Mozart, Violin Sonata in G Major (K. 9), III

In the Classical era, each of these instrumental genres carried implications with regard to form. To illustrate the relationship between genre and form in Classical music, a list of well-known compositions by the Classical masters follows, along with an indication of their forms, movement by movement. The symphony and string quartet usually consisted of four movements, whereas the sonata and concerto usually had just three. In all of these genres, the first movement was almost always in sonata form. In the four-movement genres (symphony and quartet), the third movement was usually a ternary-form dance (minuet-trio-minuet or scherzo-trio-scherzo), each section of which (minuet, scherzo, or trio) was in rounded binary form. The pieces listed below demonstrate how the three foremost Classical composers—Haydn, Mozart, and Beethoven—chose to allocate musical form within the various genres of instrumental music.

Genre of Composition		Form of Composition		
Symphony, Quartet, and Serenade	*1st movement*	*2nd movement*	*3rd movement*	*4th movement*
Haydn, Symphony No. 94, the "Surprise"	sonata	theme & variations	ternary	sonata
Haydn, String Quartet, the "Emperor"	sonata	theme & variations	ternary	sonata
Mozart, Symphony in G Minor (K. 550)	sonata	sonata	ternary	sonata
Mozart, Serenade, *Eine kleine Nachtmusik*	sonata	ternary	ternary	rondo
Beethoven, Symphony No. 3, the "Eroica"	sonata	ternary	ternary	theme & variations
Piano sonata	*1st movement*	*2nd movement*	*3rd movement*	
Haydn, Sonata No. 52 in E♭ Major	sonata	ternary	sonata	
Beethoven, the "Pathétique"	sonata	rondo	rondo	
Piano concerto	*1st movement*	*2nd movement*	*3rd movement*	
Mozart Piano Concerto in G Major (K. 453)	sonata	ternary	theme & variations	

✤ THE CLASSICAL ORCHESTRA

The story of the Western orchestra between 1750 and 1820 is essentially one of growth. A typical orchestra around 1750 included strings, two oboes, two bassoons, and two horns, as well as an accompanying keyboard instrument (then the harpsichord), and to this ensemble could be added trumpets and timpani on festive occasions. Joseph Haydn's experience with several Classical orchestras may be taken as representative. When Haydn first signed on at the Esterházy court in 1761, his princely patron's orchestra numbered only about sixteen players, though this ensemble was gradually increased to twenty-five; in the 1780s, Haydn's symphonies were played in public concerts in Paris by a group of more than seventy; for his concerts

Photograph courtesy of Richard J. Martz Horn Collection

✻ FIGURE 44-3

The natural French horn of the eighteenth century with crooks that, when inserted, alter the pitch of the instrument.

in London in 1795, an orchestra of about sixty was on hand. Obviously, as the performance site for the symphony moved from the private salon to the public auditorium, the volume of sound needed to be increased to fill the larger hall.

Most of this increase occurred in the string section. Mozart mentions an orchestra of some eighty players including forty violins, ten violas, eight cellos, and ten double basses, for a public concert at the Burgtheater in Vienna in 1781. Although this was an exceptionally large ensemble brought together for a special benefit concert, it suggests that, for times of public display, the Baroque orchestra with two or three string players per part would no longer please.

Color was added to the ensemble through the addition of more woodwinds. The orchestra at Mannheim had led the way in this regard (see Chapter 42). Instead of a pair of oboes (or flutes or clarinets) and bassoons, now pairs of oboes, clarinets, flutes, and bassoons became the norm for the largest ensembles. The woodwinds gave variety to the sound and could be used to add contrapuntal weight to the texture. Mozart in particular exhibited great care in his woodwind parts, usually composing a separate line for each instrument within the pair, rather than having both instruments double on one line.

As to the brasses, two French horns were part of every ensemble, although occasionally four horns were required. These horns were still natural instruments, without valves (Fig. 44-3). Chromatic pitches could be played by inserting the hand into the bell of the instrument (hand-stopping). If the player needed to change key, he inserted a **crook** (a small piece of pipe) that altered the length of tubing within the instrument and consequently its pitch. Finally, to create an especially festive, brilliant sound, trumpets and drums might appear. Trumpets too were natural instruments that were usually pitched in the "bright" keys of D or C.

In sum, private aristocratic orchestras in the Classical period remained small, but ensembles for public halls, especially in Vienna, Paris, and London, sometimes became quite large, featuring as many as eighty musicians in special cases. But, what was the norm? Perhaps the orchestra Mozart assembled for his public concerts in Vienna in 1783 can be taken as the typical "mid-size" orchestra. The ensemble counted six first violins, six seconds, four violas, three cellos, and three double basses; to these were added pairs of flutes, oboes, clarinets, and bassoons, four horns, two trumpets, and timpani—a total of thirty-seven players.

CLASSICAL COMPOSERS

Viewed from a modern perspective, the Classical period was dominated by three composers: Haydn, Mozart, and Beethoven. There were, of course, many other artists active at the time, some of whom were very successful. While Haydn's music was widely disseminated and respected, Mozart's was less well known. Even in Vienna, Mozart's operas were less popular than those of such now-obscure figures as Vicente Martín y Soler (1754–1806) and Giovanni Paisiello (1740–1816). Haydn and Mozart had their competitors. Mozart's nemesis, as portrayed in the film *Amadeus*, was Antonio Salieri (1750–1825), who served as official court composer to Emperor Joseph II. Mozart also had a rival in Muzio Clementi (1752–1832), and the two engaged in a famous keyboard duel in 1781. Clementi has left us many sonatas and sonatinas, which most beginning and intermediate pianists still play today. Other important figures of the day include Ignace Pleyel (1757–1831), Haydn's pupil and sometime rival, and Antonio Rosetti (1750–1792), whose Requiem Mass was performed at a memorial service for Mozart. To these can be added Carl Ditters von Dittersdorf (1739–1799), who sometimes played string quartets with Mozart and Haydn in Vienna, and Haydn's younger brother Michael (1737–1806), who for years worked in Salzburg with Wolfgang and Leopold Mozart. Michael Haydn's Symphony in G Major (1783) was long thought (mistakenly) to be a symphony by Mozart. As this confusion shows, these were able musicians whose compositional skill was not that much less than the great Viennese masters. The best compositions of Haydn, Mozart, and Beethoven, however, reached a level all their own.

SUMMARY

The term "Classical period" denotes the art music composed during the late eighteenth and early nineteenth centuries, roughly 1770–1820. The epicenter for the Classical style was Vienna. Haydn, Mozart, Beethoven, and Schubert collectively have come to be called the Viennese School. Classical composers were remarkably consistent with regard to the musical genres they adopted and the musical forms they employed within these genres. Of the forms, the newest and most important is sonata. It became the structural backbone of almost all first movements within the instrumental genres, and of many final movements as well. The genres and forms popularized in the second half of the eighteenth century remained important throughout the nineteenth and even into the twentieth century. The orchestra increased in size and color during the Classical period, owing in particular to the addition of woodwinds. The orchestral showpiece was the symphony, and from the Classical period onward it is possible to speak in terms of the "symphony orchestra." Joseph Haydn was a great innovator in the genres of string quartet and symphony; Wolfgang Amadeus Mozart created works of extraordinary beauty in every genre; and Ludwig van Beethoven took the genres and forms created by his predecessors and gave them unheard-of expressive powers.

KEY TERMS

Viennese School	retransition	*Harmonie*
Neoclassical architecture	recapitulation	*Harmoniemusik*
sonata form	coda	sonata
transition (bridge)	rondo	sonatina
exposition	divertimento	
development	serenade	

Joseph Haydn: Instrumental Music

The story of Joseph Haydn's life is a rags-to-riches tale spanning many decades. Haydn was born into humble circumstances, yet by dint of talent and hard work became the most famous composer in Western Europe. His long career bridged the span between the late Baroque and early Romantic periods; he started composing while J.S. Bach was still working on his B-Minor Mass and lived to hear Beethoven's early-Romantic symphonies. Haydn excelled in writing instrumental music, single-handedly creating what we now call the string quartet, and accelerating the development of the symphony, making it the showpiece of the public concert hall.

THE LIFE OF JOSEPH HAYDN (1732–1809)

Joseph Haydn was born in 1732 in a farmhouse in Rohrau, Austria, about twenty-five miles east of Vienna (Map 45-1). His father, a wheelwright, played the harp but could not read music. When the choir director of St. Stephen's Cathedral in Vienna happened to be scouting for talent in the provinces, he heard the boy soprano Haydn sing, and brought him back to the cathedral in Vienna. Here Haydn remained as a choirboy, studying the rudiments of composition and learning to play the violin and keyboard. When his voice broke at the age of seventeen, he was abruptly dismissed. During the next eight years Haydn eked out what he called "a wretched existence," working as a freelance performer and teacher in Vienna. In 1761 Haydn's years of struggle ended when he was engaged as director of music at the Esterházy court.

The **Esterházy family** was the richest and most influential among the German-speaking aristocrats of Hungary, with estates covering some ten million acres southeast of Vienna. Over a period of more than thirty years, Haydn worked for three Esterházy princes, the most important of which was Nikolaus Esterházy, who played

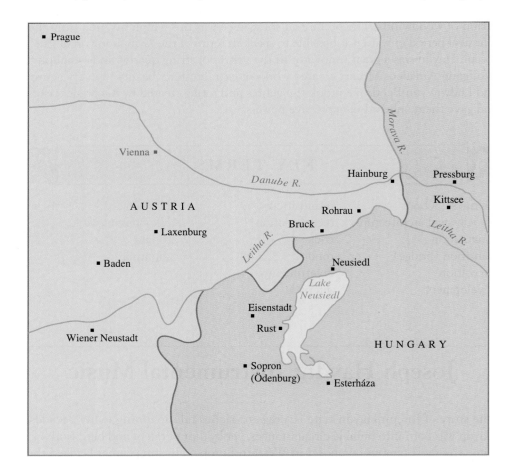

✳ MAP 45-1

Haydn's world.

the **baryton** (a *viola da gamba*–like instrument with six strings) and for whom Haydn wrote 126 baryton trios. The contract Haydn signed at the Esterházy court in 1761 provided a handsome salary, lodging, board at the table of court staff, and the blue and gold servant's livery of court employees (Fig. 45-1). It also regulated Haydn's musical activities:

> [He] and all the musicians shall appear in uniform, and the said Joseph Haydn shall take care that he and all the members of the orchestra follow the instructions given, and appear in white stocking, white linen, powdered, and with either a pigtail or a tiewig . . . .
>
> The said [Haydn] shall be under obligation to compose such music as his Serene Highness may command, and neither to communicate such compositions to any other person, nor to allow them to be copied, but he shall retain them for the absolute use of his Highness, and not compose for any other person without the knowledge and permission of his Highness.[1]

As the contract makes clear, Haydn could compose only for his Esterházy patron, and the works he produced belonged to the prince, not the composer—such was the subservient position of composers generally in eighteenth-century society. Yet Haydn was more than satisfied with his position at the Esterházy court. Except for a few weeks during the winter season when the ruler and his retainers visited Vienna, the court resided in the princely estates southeast of the city. This mostly isolated life away from the musical world forced Haydn to become inventive, as he noted when recalling his days with Prince Nikolaus: "I was cut off from the world, nobody in my vicinity could upset my self-confidence or annoy me, and so I had no choice but to become original."[2] The desire to "take risks" and create novel effects never deserted the composer.

For most of the 1760s, Haydn wrote mainly instrumental music for the Esterházy court—symphonies, concertos, and baryton trios in which Prince Nikolaus could perform. During the 1770s, however, Haydn turned his attention increasingly to opera. Here, too, he composed according to the tastes of his patron, for during this decade Prince Nikolaus undertook to complete a massive new court complex called Esterháza south of Vienna (see Map 45-1). When finished, Esterháza would approach in size the colossal palace of Versailles and boast a large, free-standing opera house (Fig. 45-2) for which Haydn composed some dozen operas in Italian. But, despite his success with opera and his later Masses and oratorios, Joseph Haydn is remembered today primarily as a composer of instrumental music: symphonies, string quartets, concertos, and keyboard sonatas.

 FIGURE 45-1

Portrait of Joseph Haydn at about the age of thirty, wearing a wig and the blue livery of the Esterházy court. With the kind permission of Professor Daniel Heartz.

HAYDN'S EARLY AND MIDDLE SYMPHONIES†

Joseph Haydn has been called the "father of the symphony," but this honor is not entirely merited. As we have seen (see Chapter 42), many other composers were actively writing symphonies during the 1740s and 1750s. Nonetheless, Haydn wrote

---

†As is true for Bach and Mozart, there is a thematic catalogue of the compositions of Joseph Haydn, in this case one prepared by the Dutch musicologist Anthony Hoboken (1887–1983): *Joseph Haydn: thematisch-bibliographisches Werkverzeichnis* (Mainz, 1957–1978), 3 vols. Thus, a work of Haydn is often identified in the literature by a **Hoboken (Hob.) number.** For the symphonies of Haydn, however, the Hoboken numbering system has been so commonly adopted (Haydn Symphony No. 104 equates to Hob.I:104) that usually no Hoboken number appears. Finally, Hoboken has classified the works of Haydn chronologically by genre; roman number I stands for the symphonies and III for the string quartets, for example.

Pesci, Esterhása Castle, Orszagos Müemleki Felügeloség

FIGURE 45-2
The palace of the Esterházy family southeast of Vienna, where Joseph Haydn lived 1766–1790. It was modeled on the grand French palace of Versailles west of Paris.

more works in this genre than any other composer, 108 in all. Haydn's first symphonies (1757–1760) are in three movements (fast/slow/fast). By the time Haydn joined the Esterházy court in 1761, however, a four-movement format had become his norm. Following the example of Johann Stamitz at Mannheim, Haydn inserted a minuet in third position. Originally a **minuet** was a triple-meter dance that was often added toward the end of the Baroque dance suite (see Chapter 34). In the Classical period, this dance was invariably written in rounded-binary form and coupled with a matching rounded-binary movement called the trio, to form a **minuet and trio** (at first the trio was more lightly scored than the minuet, being often written for just three instruments, hence its name). Thus, Haydn's usual sequence of movements within a symphony proceeded fast/slow/minuet and trio/fast.

Typical of the best of Haydn's early symphonies is a set of three (Nos. 6–8) that he composed in 1761, soon after arriving at the Esterházy court. He named them *Le Matin* (*Morning*), *Le Midi* (*Noon*), and *Le Soir* (*Evening*), and in each he sought to create an appropriate musical mood for the corresponding time of the day. *Le Matin*, for example, opens with a slow introduction that depicts a sunrise; the upper parts slowly rise and then hold on high, as the dynamic level grows from *pianissimo* to *fortissimo*. Writing a slow introduction to the fast opening movement of a symphony becomes common with Haydn at this time, and in his late symphonies it becomes the norm. In addition, Haydn composed his symphonies Nos. 6–8 in a special orchestral style called **concertante,** a concerto-like approach in which individual instruments regularly emerge from the orchestral texture to function as soloists. The newly instituted orchestra at Esterházy was small, consisting of only about sixteen musicians, including the string section, two horn players, a bassoonist, and two oboists who might also double on flute. Evidently, Haydn wanted to please his patron by writing in a way that best displayed the talents of the orchestra. In *Le Matin*, for example, the main theme of the first movement is carried by a solo flute (Ex. 45-1), and the return to it at the recapitulation is announced by a jaunty French horn solo. In the context of the modest Esterházy orchestra, these wind solos would have projected particularly well.

EXAMPLE 45-1

LISTENING CUE

JOSEPH HAYDN
Symphony No. 6 in D Major,
Le Matin (1761)
First movement, *Adagio; Allegro*

CD 7/9
Anthology, No. 128

Clearly, Haydn's aim in his "times-of-the day" symphonies was to create a descriptive set along the lines of Vivaldi's earlier *Four Seasons*. This was not the only occasion on which Haydn would call upon extra-musical phenomena to inform his symphonies. Various later symphonies also suggest an outside stimulus, judging from their nicknames (given by later commentators). Among these are the "Hornsignal" (Symphony No. 31), "Funeral" (No. 44), "Farewell" (No. 45), "Passion" (No. 49), and "Fire" (No. 59). The **"Farewell" Symphony** is today the best known of these programmatic works, perhaps owing to the anecdote that gave rise to its title. It seems that Prince Nikolaus had stayed at Esterháza longer than expected, and his musicians were eager to return to their wives and families closer to Vienna. To make the point, Haydn concludes the symphony by asking the players, one by one, to extinguish their candles and walk off the stage, leaving only two violinists to play at the end. The prince got the message, as the story goes, and the musicians were soon allowed to return to their winter quarters.

Haydn Goes Hunting

What did the great composers do for recreation and amusement? Beethoven took long walks, musical sketchbook in hand, almost daily, no matter how foul the weather. Mozart played endless games of billiards (he had a billiard table in his bedroom) and went horseback riding in the Prater Park in Vienna for exercise. Joseph Haydn too tried horseback riding, but when he took a nasty spill in 1760 he vowed never to remount. Haydn was small and unassuming, and his physical stature sometimes disappointed those who loved his music. Once Haydn was singled out in a crowd of admirers, but at least one person refused to believe the small man could be the great composer: "That's not Haydn—it can't possibly be! Haydn must be a fine, big, handsome man and not that insignificant little one you've got there in the middle."[3]

In his old age Haydn was fond of telling stories about his earlier days on the Esterházy estates. His first biographer, G. A. Griesinger, says the following about his outdoor activities: "Hunting and fishing were Haydn's favorite pastimes during his stay in Hungary, and he never forgot that he once brought down with one shot three hazel-hens, which later appeared on the dinner table of the Empress Maria Theresa (1717–1780). Another time he aimed at a hare, but only shot off its tail; yet the bullet continued and killed a pheasant that chanced to be close by; then Haydn's dog, pursuing the hare, strangled itself in a snare." Evidently, hunting with Haydn could be dangerous sport.[4]

Aside from the unusual nature of its programmatic content, the "Farewell" Symphony is also important in the history of music because its style typifies a group of Haydn's works dating from the late 1760s and early 1770s, whose expressive character has been called *Sturm und Drang*. The term **Sturm und Drang** ("Storm and Stress") originated not in music but in German literature. It suggests a mode of expression that sought to frighten, stun, and overcome with emotion. Its anti-rational approach was, of course, at variance with the Enlightenment emphasis on order and rational thought in all things. In fact, the *Sturm und Drang* movement had less affinity to the balanced Classical idioms of the eighteenth century than to the more passionate Romantic art of the nineteenth century. As a specifically musical term, *Sturm und Drang* refers to a small but significant group of works written around 1770 that are marked by agitated, impassioned writing, such as Mozart's Symphony No. 25 and Haydn's symphonies Nos. 44, 45, and 49. All are characterized by minor keys, angular themes, syncopation, string tremolos, sudden dynamic shifts, and violin lines that race up and down the scale. In Haydn's case, this intense, stressful sound gradually disappears as he turns increasingly to opera during the later 1770s.

HAYDN'S STRING QUARTETS

Joseph Haydn is also called the "father of the string quartet," and here the honor is entirely justified, for Haydn almost single-handedly fashioned the genre in its modern form. In all, he composed sixty-eight quartets scored for two violins, viola, and cello. To appreciate Haydn's accomplishment, we must recall that small-ensemble writing at the end of the Baroque era was dominated by the string trio sonata—usually two violins over a basso continuo (bass line with chordal support by the harpsichord). The first violin carried the melody above a heavy bass. Between 1750 and 1770, Haydn gradually refashioned what was essentially a "top and bottom" texture into one with four more-or-less equal voices, the lowest of which was a cello; the old basso continuo was reduced to a single cello line.

Haydn also brought a new mood to the string quartet. His earliest quartets of the 1750s have the feel of the light, outdoor, five-movement divertimento. By the 1770s, however, the tone of his quartets had become more serious and the individual movements more weighty. Like the symphony, the quartet now consisted of four movements, including a minuet in either second, or, increasingly, third position. Yet, unlike the symphony, which often excels in dramatic effects that only a large orchestra can create, the string quartet emphasizes a continual motivic development, and this motivic working out occurs almost equally in all four parts.

Haydn's set of six string quartets Opus 20, written around 1772, was something of a landmark for the genre, exhibiting the two most prominent characteristics of the Classical string quartet: an approximately equal-voiced texture and a generally serious tone. Two of the six (Nos. 3 and 5) are in minor keys, and the generally dark quality of the set places it firmly within Haydn's *Sturm und Drang* period of the early 1770s. Moreover, three of the quartets (Nos. 2, 5, and 6) have fugal finales. The use of fugal procedure within the string quartet makes these works sound both serious and "learned." Haydn was not only a playful, capricious composer but also, when he chose to be, a very cerebral one. The finale of Opus 20, No. 5, is, in Haydn's words, a "Fuga a due soggetti" ("Fugue with two subjects"), while the fugal finale of No. 6 has three subjects, and No. 2 has four. In these finales, Haydn displays such erudite contrapuntal techniques as musical inversion, canon, and stretto.

Almost ten years elapsed before Haydn issued his next collection of string quartets, a set of six numbered Opus 33. In 1779 Haydn had signed a new contract with Prince Nikolaus Esterházy that allowed him to sell his music to whomever he wished. The Opus 33 quartets seem to be a product of this new arrangement. Haydn himself solicited sales of the set by writing to potential buyers, advertising that the quartets were "written in an entirely new and special way." Now, for the first time in his quartets, the movement that had been called "minuet" is entitled **scherzo** (Italian for "joke" or "jest"). These scherzi, in fact, do play jokes on the listener, because the downbeat of the dance is frequently placed out of sync with the minuet's three-beat meter, creating syncopations and hemiolas. The Opus 33 quartets are Haydn's first mature quartets to be imbued with this playful, more popular, style. Opus 33, No. 2, for example, is referred to as the "Joke" Quartet because it concludes unexpectedly in the middle of a phrase; the players simply stop, leaving listeners to wonder if the piece is really at an end. Opus 33, No. 3, is nicknamed the **"Bird" Quartet** because the strings sound distinctly like birds chirping and pecking their way across the musical landscape.

Despite its playful tone, the opening movement of the "Bird" Quartet (Opus 33, No. 3) is a carefully crafted composition in sonata form. At the outset, melody and harmony are set forth in a way that blurs the distinction between leading voice and accompaniment; this greater integration of melody and accompaniment is one of the hallmarks of quartet style. The exposition contains three themes (first, second, and closing), each of equal weight yet each presenting "the sprightly bird" in a distinctly different pose. The substantive development makes use of all three themes and is almost as long as the exposition itself. Everywhere, well-proportioned sections support a melodic unfolding full of light-hearted charm. What is characterized as the "popular" quality of Haydn's music can perhaps best be seen in his closing theme (Ex. 45-2). Here a tuneful, stepwise melody sounds forth in the first violin, with the quick grace-notes adding avian charm to the sound.

EXAMPLE 45-2

Finally, in the coda, Haydn drives to the end with the opening bars of the first theme, a gambit that his pupil Beethoven will later exploit in his own symphonies and sonatas. The Opus 33 quartets influenced Mozart as well, for they served as a point of departure for a set of six that Mozart wrote during 1782–1785 (see Chapter 47) and, appropriately enough, dedicated to his good friend Joseph Haydn.

LISTENING CUE

JOSEPH HAYDN
Opus 33, No. 3, The "Bird" Quartet
(Hob.III:39; 1781)
First movement, *Allegro moderato*

CD 7/10
Anthology, No. 129

Haydn continued to write string quartets to the very end of his composing years. Indeed, the incomplete string quartet Opus 103, which he abandoned in 1803, marks his last composition in any genre. Among the late quartets is a set of six, Opus 76, composed in 1797, which includes the so-called Emperor Quartet.

The **"Emperor" Quartet** (Opus 76, No. 3) reflects the political and military events of the Napoleonic Wars (1796–1815), which made their way right to Haydn's doorstep. In 1796 the armies of Napoleon invaded the Austrian Empire and this, in turn, ignited a firestorm of patriotism in Vienna, the Austrian capital. But the Austrians were at a musical disadvantage: the French had their *Marseillaise* and the English their *God Save the King* (which Haydn had heard repeatedly in London), but the Austrians had no national anthem around which to rally. Thus Haydn was commissioned to compose an appropriate tune, and he created the melody for the text *Gott erhalte Franz den Kaiser* (God Preserve Emperor Franz) in honor of the reigning Austrian Emperor Franz II (Ex. 45-3). Called **The Emperor's Hymn,** it was first sung in theaters throughout the Austrian realm on the Emperor's birthday, 12 February 1797.

EXAMPLE 45-3

Gott er-hal-te Franz den Kai-ser, Uns-ern gu-ten Kai-ser_ Franz!
Lan-ge le-be Franz der Kai-ser, In des Glück-es hell-stem_ Glanz!

Ihm er-blü-hen Lor-ber-rei-ser, Wo er geht zum Eh-ren-kranz.

Gott er-hal-te Franz den Kai-ser, Uns-ern gu-ten Kai-ser Franz!

God preserve Emperor Franz, our good Emperor Franz.
Long life to Emperor Franz, in the brightest splendor of happiness.
Garlands of laurel bloom for him wherever he goes, as a wreath of honor.
God preserve Emperor Franz, our good Emperor Franz.

Capitalizing on the popularity of his tune, Haydn soon made it serve as a basis of a theme-and-variations set in the second movement of his string quartet Opus 76, No. 3 (Hob.III:77), now called the "Emperor" Quartet. In this movement the theme is stated by the first violin and harmonized by simple chords. Then four variations follow. In these the second violin, cello, viola, and again first violin each has its turn to present the tune amidst increasingly ornate embellishment.

As we might suspect, Haydn's patriotism was not sufficient to keep Napoleon's armies at bay. Nor was the Austrian army. The French had surrounded Vienna in 1805 and would do so again in 1809. Indeed, in the spring of 1809 a cannon ball fell adjacent to Haydn's house, shaking the composer and terrifying his servants. But Haydn retained faith in his emperor and his tune, and he played a piano arrangement of it daily. In fact, *The Emperor's Hymn* was the last music Haydn played before he died in the early hours of 31 May 1809.

The popularity of *The Emperor's Hymn* ended neither with Haydn's death nor with the final defeat of Napoleon in 1815, nor even with the death of Emperor Franz II in 1835. So alluring was Haydn's melody that, with altered text, it became a Protestant hymn and then, in 1853, the national anthem of Austria. Austria gave up the tune after its defeat in World War II, but, with amended text, Germany took it up in 1950! And so today Haydn's timeless melody serves as the German national anthem.

HAYDN'S SONATAS AND CONCERTOS

Today Joseph Haydn is known primarily for his string quartets and symphonies. But he also wrote more than sixty keyboard sonatas and more than thirty concertos for various instruments. In Haydn's case, we say "keyboard" sonatas because it is not always certain whether a particular sonata was composed for the harpsichord, clavichord, or pianoforte. Haydn seems to have switched to the newer piano in the early 1770s. One sonata in particular, No. 20 in C minor (Hob.XVI:20; 1771), includes a rapid alternation of pianos and fortes, which could be executed on the piano (or clavichord), but not on the harpsichord (Ex. 45-4). This passage also reveals a characteristic feature of Haydn's keyboard sonatas: highly variegated rhythms. In general Haydn's writing for solo keyboard is marked by frequent changes of note values and rhythmic patterns. So too Haydn's sonatas tend to be freer and more unpredictable in the unfolding of the melodic material; they belong more to the expressive tradition of the north German sonata and fantasia of C.P.E. Bach than to the smooth, elegant Italian-style sonata of J.C. Bach.

EXAMPLE 45-4

Although Haydn's keyboard sonatas are now played less often in recital than those of his younger contemporaries Mozart and Beethoven, they do have strong advocates among professional pianists today. Most favored among these are the aforementioned No. 20 in C minor, a passionate work belonging to the composer's *Sturm und Drang* period, and No. 52 in E♭ major (Hob.XVI:52). This last sonata, which dates from Haydn's final stay in London in 1794, was written for the female virtuoso Therese Jansen Bartolozzi. When this work was finally published in London in 1800, it was entitled "Grand Sonata for the Piano Forte," and its proportions are indeed grand. Remarkable for a sonata in E♭, it has a slow movement in the key of E major (Ex. 45-5). The pianist ends the first movement on a solid E♭ major triad and directly proceeds to open the middle movement with an equally solid, but entirely shocking, E major triad. Haydn may have been a grandfatherly figure by 1794, but he could still behave like an *enfant terrible*.

EXAMPLE 45-5

Surviving from Haydn's hand are ten solo concertos for various string and woodwind instruments (at least seven others have been lost). Most important among these are the Cello Concerto in D Major of 1784 and the Trumpet Concerto in E♭ of 1796. The latter piece is especially well known today, owing to a Grammy-winning recording by Wynton Marsalis. Haydn also composed more than a dozen keyboard concertos, most of which are early works of the 1750s and 1760s that were conceived for the harpsichord rather than piano. Mozart augmented his income by mounting concerts at which he would be the featured soloist in one of his own piano concertos. Haydn, while a competent pianist, was no virtuoso, and, as we shall see, filled his purse during the 1780s and 1790s, not by writing concertos but mainly by composing symphonies.

SUMMARY

Joseph Haydn wrote a great deal of vocal music in his long career, including at least fifteen Italian operas, fourteen Latin Masses, and two important oratorios. Yet he is remembered today primarily for his instrumental music: his sixty-eight string quartets, 108 symphonies, fifty-two piano sonatas, and numerous concertos, including a celebrated one for cello and another for trumpet. Haydn created the modern string quartet, transforming the old trio sonata into a new genre, and converting what had been a top-bottom texture held together by a basso continuo into a sonority of four more-or-less equal lines. Homophony now blends with counterpoint so as to lessen the distinction between melody and accompaniment. After Haydn, the string quartet remained the most common form of chamber music, and nearly every important subsequent composer wrote for this medium.

Haydn did not create the symphony, but in the course of forty years managed to revolutionize it. In 1750 the symphony had only begun to emerge as an independent instrumental genre. By the end of the century, it had become the preeminent means of musical expression for a large ensemble, one rivaled only by opera. Most of Haydn's early symphonies were written at the Esterházy court for a small orchestra of sixteen, and they often have no more than three or four independent lines playing at once (the remaining instruments simply doubled). During the 1770s, Haydn composed his symphonies, in particular, in an emotional style called *Sturm und Drang*, and these works are marked by minor keys, angular themes, syncopation, string tremolos, and sudden dynamic shifts. Haydn enjoyed a long and productive career, and he continued to compose quartets, symphonies, and sonatas until the age of seventy.

KEY TERMS

Esterházy family	minuet and trio	scherzo
baryton	concertante	"Bird" Quartet
Hoboken (Hob.) number	"Farewell" Symphony	"Emperor" Quartet
minuet	*Sturm und Drang*	*The Emperor's Hymn*

Joseph Haydn: Late Symphonies and Vocal Music

Chapter 46

By 1780 Joseph Haydn had become one of the foremost composers in Europe, primarily through pirated copies of his music. The previous year, Haydn had signed a new, less restrictive, contract with his patron, Prince Nikolaus Esterházy, which freed the composer from his prior obligation to compose solely for the prince. Free to write for anyone and publish wherever he wished, he now sold his music to publishers in a number of prominent European cities, including Vienna, Paris, and London. The opportunity to publish abroad brought Haydn handsome fees, and growing fame brought him equally remunerative commissions. Consequently, in his maturity and old age Haydn enjoyed fame and, if not fortune, at least considerable financial security (Fig. 46-1). His first important foreign commission came from Paris, and it occupied much of Haydn's time during the mid-1780s.

🌼 FIGURE 46-1

The mature Joseph Haydn in the act of composition. His left hand tries out an idea at the keyboard (likely a clavichord), while his right hand is poised to write it down. Haydn said the following about his compositional process: "I sat down and began to fantasize, according to whether my mood was sad or happy, serious or playful."

🌸 THE PARIS SYMPHONIES

Haydn's music had been known in Paris since the 1760s. By the 1780s, his symphonies were played there far more than those of any other composer, and in 1785 he received a lucrative commission from the *Loge Olympique*, a society of musically inclined Freemasons. These artistically enlightened Parisian amateurs requested six symphonies to be performed by their orchestra. For each symphony, Haydn would receive twenty-four Louis d'Or and an additional five Louis d'Or for publication rights. The six symphonies Haydn subsequently created (Nos. 82–87) are now called the **Paris Symphonies.**

The orchestra of the *Loge Olympique* in Paris was more than three times the size of that of Haydn's Esterházy patron back in Austria. The Paris ensemble counted nearly seventy strings, including forty violins and ten double basses, as well as pairs of winds. Perhaps for this reason, the Paris Symphonies show a Haydn eager to replace complex counterpoint with dramatic orchestral effects. From time to time the violins suddenly surge forward *fortissimo* and the textures and dynamics shift radically. Of course, the Paris Symphonies were intended, not for a private salon but for a large public concert hall and a paying audience. This may account for the broadly popular nature of many of the themes. Phrasing tends to be uncomplicated, even folksy, often fashioned in two- or four-measure pairs. Indeed, the slow movement of Symphony No. 85 is a set of variations built on an old French folk song, *La gentille et jeune Lisette* (*Young, Sweet Lisette*), itself a model of classical balance (Ex. 46-1).

EXAMPLE 46-1

Symphony No. 85 became the favorite of Reine (Queen) Marie-Antoinette (who was later to lose her head during the Revolution of 1789–1799), and thus it is known as "La Reine." Two other Paris Symphonies also acquired fanciful names: Symphony No. 82 is known as "L'Ours" ("The Bear"), because the finale is said to suggest the lumbering dance of a circus bear; while No. 83 is called "La Poule" ("The Hen"), reputedly because of the "clucking" sound of the violins in the first movement. Clearly, Haydn was playing to popular taste in these Parisian works. Haydn's next five symphonies (Nos. 88–92) also have connections to Paris, although the last of these (No. 92) has come to be called the "Oxford" Symphony because it was performed in July 1791 when Haydn received an honorary degree at Oxford University in England.

 ## THE LONDON SYMPHONIES

How did Haydn come to be in England? In 1790 Haydn's long-time patron Nikolaus Esterházy died and, after nearly thirty years of service, Haydn was now a free man— he was "pensioned off." Immediately, Haydn was approached by a foreign musician who knocked at his door and declared: "I am Salomon of London and have come to fetch you. Tomorrow we will arrange a contract."[1] The visitor was Johann Salomon, a German violinist and concert promoter living in London, who proposed that Haydn travel to London and participate in a venture that promised both financial gain and public acclaim. Thus, the aging Haydn, now nearly sixty, departed Vienna in December 1790; those seeing him off in a tearful farewell included Wolfgang Amadeus Mozart. Haydn resided in London during 1791–1792 and again in 1794–1795. His principal assignment there was to provide Salomon with twelve new symphonies. Haydn was to be paid both for the performances and the publication rights. These twelve symphonies, which Haydn composed from 1791 to 1795, have come to be called the **London Symphonies.** From his activities in London, Haydn netted 24,000 Austrian gulden, the equivalent of more than twenty years' salary at the Esterházy court. His trips to London made him financially secure for life, and the London Symphonies crowned his career as a symphonic composer.

As with the earlier Paris Symphonies, several of the London Symphonies have received fanciful titles. No. 100 is called the "Military" Symphony, for example, because the score requires instruments from a military band, namely cymbals, triangle, and bass drum; No. 101 is named the "Clock" owing to the "tick-tock" accompaniment in the *Andante* movement; and No. 96 takes its name the "Miracle" supposedly because a large chandelier crashed during the premiere in London and—miraculously—no one was hurt! But among the "titled" London Symphonies, none is better known than the "Surprise" Symphony.

The **"Surprise" Symphony** (No. 94) was exceptionally well received by the London audience at its premiere on 23 March 1792. The first movement provides a vivacious dance in $\frac{6}{8}$ meter; the third movement is a rollicking minuet with trio; and the brilliant finale forms an appropriately rousing conclusion. Yet both the name and the fame of the symphony come from its second movement marked *Andante*. In his last years, Haydn gave his biographers two different accounts as to why he had hidden a "surprise" inside this movement. In one, the composer says that he wanted simply "to surprise the public with something new, and to make a [London] début in a brilliant manner. . . ." In the second account, Haydn says more specifically that during the second half of the Salomon concerts, the London audience was prone to fall asleep. To call it to attention, he prescribed that the full orchestra play a sudden *fortissimo* at the end of the very quiet first phrase. "The sudden thunder of the whole orchestra shocked the sleepers, all awoke and looked at each other with surprised expressions"—whence the acquired title.[2]

Reviewers of the day were struck not only by this novel effect but also by the "simple, profound and sublime" quality of music. Haydn's *Andante* does indeed embody a simple binary theme (**AB**), beginning with a tonic triad followed by a dominant seventh chord (Ex. 46-2), which serves as the basis for a set of variations. Yet this commonplace opening allows for a shocking change of harmony and mood in the exact middle of the movement, the location of which creates an overall balance despite radical contrast.

EXAMPLE 46-2

LISTENING CUE

JOSEPH HAYDN
Symphony No. 94, The "Surprise" (1791–1792)
Second movement, *Andante*

CD 7/11
Anthology, No. 130

When Joseph Haydn returned to London in February 1794 for an additional series of Salomon's concerts, he opened the season with a new symphony in E♭ major, No. 99. The critic of the *Morning Chronicle* could barely contain his enthusiasm: "[The new symphony] is one of the grandest efforts of art that we ever witnessed. It abounds with ideas, as new in music as they are grand and impressive; it rouses and affects every emotion of the soul; [and] it was received with rapturous applause."[3] Perhaps it was the elegiac slow movement, or the pleasing minuet, or even the contrapuntally complex finale that delighted the London critic. But when the program was repeated a week later, the first movement gave such special pleasure that it was immediately encored; in the eighteenth century, the audience not only applauded after each symphonic movement but also demanded the immediate repeat of a movement it found exceptionally pleasing.

What might have been the "new ideas" that impressed the London critic? In the first movement, the novelty is not in the construction of the melodies, but in the orchestration and the unusual, even eccentric, approach to harmony and form. Here, for the first time (1794), Haydn makes use of clarinets in a symphony (though Mozart had done so as early as 1778). These, in addition to pairs of flutes, oboes, bassoons, horns, and trumpets, as well as timpani, help create a rich, imposing orchestral sound. The movement's numerous harmonic and formal surprises include a dominant pedal point in the introduction that sits on the "wrong" note for the key of E♭; an expected "second theme" in the dominant key that turns out to be none other than the first theme transposed (a technique not uncommon to Haydn's sonata-form compositions); and a recapitulation that omits almost entirely the all-important first theme. But most striking here are the abrupt contrasts between stable passages of music (the tonally secure first theme and closing theme, for example) and those that are unstable owing either to syncopated accents marked *sforzando* or to chromatically sliding chords. Once again with Haydn, unity is born of diversity and contrast.

LISTENING CUE

JOSEPH HAYDN
Symphony No. 99 in E♭ Major (1794)
First movement, *Adagio; Vivace assai*

CD 7/12
Anthology, No. 131

Haydn Wins Over His Orchestra

Great artists are often known for their tempers, eccentricities, and egos. Beethoven was legendary for having tantrums in front of musicians and patrons alike. Gustav Mahler was reputed to be a tyrannical conductor. Even the composer of serene sacred music, Josquin des Prez, would fly into a rage when singers tampered with the notes he had composed. By contrast, Haydn seems to have been more diplomatic—or perhaps more cunning!—than most great artists.

When Haydn arrived in London he spoke scarcely a word of English. His principal charge was to compose and perform his new symphonies before a large paying audience at the Hanover Square Rooms in central London. Haydn himself conducted the orchestra of seasoned freelance professionals, including many Germans and Italians, from his position seated at the keyboard. (A keyboard instrument, either harpsichord or piano, still sometimes accompanied the symphony orchestra, a legacy of the Baroque basso continuo.) Professional orchestral players, then as now, are a notoriously hard-nosed, unsympathetic group. As reported in an early biography, one dictated by Haydn himself, the composer used almost every trick imaginable to get the London musicians to play their best.

[Haydn] had set out a symphony that began with a short *Adagio*, three identical-sounding notes opening the music. Now when the orchestra played the three notes too emphatically, Haydn interrupted with nods and "Sh!

Sh!" The orchestra stopped, and [Johann] Salomon had to interpret for Haydn. They then played the three notes again but with no happier result. Haydn interrupted again with "Sh! Sh!." In the ensuing silence a German cellist quite near to Haydn expressed his opinion to his neighbor, saying in German, "If he doesn't like even the first three notes, how will it be with the rest!" Haydn was happy to hear Germans speaking, took these words as a warning, and said with the greatest courtesy that he was requesting as a favor something that lay wholly within their power, and that he was very sorry that he could not express himself in English. Perhaps they would allow him to demonstrate his meaning on an instrument. Whereupon he took a violin and made himself so clear by the repeated playing of the three tones that the orchestra understood him perfectly. Haydn did not in the future let the matter rest there. He implored, as small children do, by holding up both hands, called now this one, now that one "my treasure" or "my angel." He often invited the most important players to dinner, so that they appeared gladly for private rehearsals in his home. He praised them and interwove reprimand, when it was necessary, with praise in the subtlest fashion. Such behavior won him the affection of all musicians with whom he came in contact, so that out of love for him they rose to the level of inspiration required for a performance of a Haydn work.[4]

THE LATE VOCAL MUSIC

Joseph Haydn received his first formal musical instruction at the Cathedral of St. Stephen in Vienna while serving as a choirboy during the 1740s. From this experience he gained a thorough knowledge of the music and liturgy of the Roman Catholic Church. Haydn, Mozart, and Beethoven all lived in Catholic Austria and followed, with different degrees of fervor, the Roman Catholic faith. Thus, throughout his long life Haydn composed sacred music for the church, including Latin motets and full settings of the Ordinary of the Mass. As did Mozart and Beethoven, Haydn gave special attention to religious music toward the end of his life.

When Haydn returned to Vienna in September 1795, he resumed his relations with the Esterházy court. His responsibilities were less demanding than before, now being reduced to a single requirement: each year he was to produce a polyphonic Mass for the name-day of Maria Esterházy, wife of the prince. Thus, he composed and directed a total of six Masses for the Esterházy court, which were performed annually on 8 September (the Feast of the Nativity of the Virgin Mary). These Masses are large-scale works requiring full orchestra and chorus with soprano, alto, tenor, and bass soloists. A Mass with orchestra and chorus in eighteenth-century Austria was as much a festive concert as it was a religious service. This was especially true of these late Masses of Haydn, in which the orchestra often adopts both symphonic style and symphonic forms. Best known today among Haydn's Masses are his *Mass in the Time of War* (1796) and *Lord Nelson Mass* (1798), both associated in the public mind with events of the Napoleonic Wars that then engulfed Austria.

Toward the end of his creative life, Haydn composed two sacred oratorios, **The Creation** (1796–1798) and *The Seasons* (1801). During his stay in London, Haydn had been impressed by the massive choral performances of Handel's oratorios in Westminster Abbey. This experience encouraged him to try his hand at English oratorio; indeed, he brought the original English-language libretto of *The Creation* with him when he returned from London to Vienna in 1795. For the next three years he fine-tuned the libretto and composed the score, setting the words in both English and German and thereby creating a bilingual work that could be performed in either language to suit the audience. *The Creation* received its first public performance on 19 March 1799, in the Burgtheater in Vienna (see Fig. 42-1). Like Handel's *Messiah*, Haydn's *The Creation* became a staple of charity fund-raising; Haydn himself frequently conducted subsequent performances to raise money for worthy causes.

As its name suggests, *The Creation* recounts the story of the creation of the world as told in the Book of Genesis. Like Handel's *Messiah*, it is divided into three parts, each of which consists of various choruses, arias, and recitatives. Moreover, each part ends with a rousing chorus, in which the multitudes proclaim the glory of God. "The Heavens Are Telling," which concludes Part One, can be taken to be Haydn's response to Handelian choral writing. The declamation is clear and forceful, passages of homophony alternate with those of imitative polyphony, and a textual refrain ("the heavens are telling") serves to unify the movement. Haydn had carried the genre of the large-scale symphony to England; in return he brought English oratorio to the Continent.

EXAMPLE 46-3

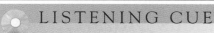

LISTENING CUE

JOSEPH HAYDN
The Creation (1796–1798)
"The Heavens Are Telling"

CD 7/13
Anthology, No. 132

In the same year that Haydn conducted the premiere of *The Creation*, he complained to his German publisher about his declining health and waning powers of concentration:

> Some days my enfeebled memory and the un-strung state of my nerves crush me to the earth to such an extent that I fall prey to the worst sort of depression, and am quite incapable of finding even a single idea for many days there-after; until at last Providence revives me, and I can again sit down at the pianoforte and begin to scratch away.[5]

Indeed, Haydn's productivity diminished and, after giving up work on his last string quartet in 1803, he composed no more. The public, however, continued to shower him with praise and various honors, including a performance of *The Creation* in 1808 to mark his seventy-sixth birthday (Fig. 46-2). When Haydn finally expired on 31 May 1809, Europe lost a beloved cultural icon.

 FIGURE 46-2

Haydn's farewell. This watercolor records the performance of *The Creation*, conducted by Antonio Salieri, given in Vienna on 27 March 1808 to mark Haydn's 76th birthday. Haydn himself attended, but had to be transported into the hall in a chair (he is the seated figure in lowest center to which all eyes are turned). Haydn stayed up to the end of Part I, ending with "The Heavens Are Telling," and then, old and frail, asked to be carried from the hall. This was his last public appearance.

SUMMARY

The late symphonies of Joseph Haydn consist mainly of the Paris Symphonies (Nos. 82–87) and the London Symphonies (Nos. 93–104), which date from the 1780s and 1790s, respectively. All are large-scale, four-movement symphonies remarkable for their variety and sometimes for their formal and harmonic daring. Haydn's Paris and London Symphonies were performed in those cities by large orchestras, sometimes consisting of seventy or more players. Taking full advantage of these big ensembles, his scores now reflect a richer, more spacious texture, sometimes with as many as ten or twelve independent lines sounding together. They also call for unexpected orchestral effects, such as the sudden *fortissimo* in the midst of the quiet opening of the "Surprise" Symphony. The critical acclaim that greeted Haydn's Paris and London Symphonies cemented his position as the most renowned composer in Europe. During the 1790s and early 1800s, Haydn, now in his sixties, still managed to create six large polyphonic Masses and two full-length oratorios. In these late symphonies, Masses, and oratorios, Haydn once again reveals his unique gift. He could combine the conventional with the unexpected, the serious with the jocular, and the learned with the popular, thereby creating music that appealed to prince and commoner alike.

KEY TERMS

Paris Symphonies
London Symphonies

"Surprise" Symphony
The Creation

Chapter 47

Wolfgang Amadeus Mozart: Instrumental Music

Mozart lived barely thirty-six years. Yet, because he had an insatiable appetite for composing, he left us an astonishing amount of music.[†] The published complete edition of Mozart's music includes some one hundred twenty often-thick volumes. Mozart seems to have composed in his head far faster than he could write the notes on paper. Moreover, he excelled in all genres of music of his day, composing operas, piano concertos, symphonies, and chamber works that must be counted among the greatest works ever written in these categories. For this reason, Mozart has been rightly called "the most universal composer in the history of Western music."[1]

❀ THE LIFE OF WOLFGANG AMADEUS MOZART (1756–1791)

Mozart was a child prodigy. Unlike Haydn, whose career developed slowly and lasted long, Mozart's star shot suddenly across the musical firmament and disappeared just as quickly. He was born in 1756 in the mountain town of Salzburg, Austria, and died in 1791 in Vienna. Whereas Haydn's father could not read music, Mozart's father, Leopold, was a composer and well-known violin pedagogue, and his older sister Nannerl was a talented keyboard performer. Leopold noticed almost immediately that his son had an extraordinary ear and a preternatural facility for music generally. At the age of six, the young Mozart was playing the piano, violin, and organ, as well as composing. Soon Leopold abandoned his own ambitions and focused the energies of the entire family on nurturing the talent of their *Wunderkind* Wolfgang.

In 1763 the Mozart family began a show tour—part educational, part moneymaking—around the major capitals of Europe. In Vienna, Wolfgang played for and sat on the lap of Empress Maria Theresa. Then the family went to Munich, Brussels, Paris, London, Amsterdam, and Geneva, playing for royalty all along the way. At times the "traveling Mozarts" came perilously close to resembling a circus act. On demand, Wolfgang would sight-read difficult music, improvise on a tune requested by the audience, or play blindfolded or with the keyboard covered with a cloth. After three years the Mozarts made their way back to Salzburg. But father and son soon departed on multi-year visits to the major cities of Italy, and in each the boy gave at least one concert to cover expenses. In Rome, in 1770, Pope Clement XIV dubbed the fourteen-year-old Mozart a Knight of the Golden Spur, the first musician in two hundred years to be so honored. Although the aim of this globe-trotting was to acquire fame and fortune, the result was that Mozart, unlike Haydn, was exposed at an early age to a wealth of musical styles—French Baroque, English choral, German polyphonic, and Italian vocal. His keen ear absorbed them all, and ultimately they increased both the substance and the universal appeal of his music.

Mozart spent most of the 1770s in his native Salzburg. Still a prodigy but no longer a child, he earned a living from his position as violinist and organist for the Archbishop of Salzburg. The reigning Archbishop Colloredo, however, did not

---

[†]More than six hundred compositions survive from Mozart's pen. In 1784 he began to keep track of them in a little book he called "Verzeichnis aller meiner Werke" ("List of all my works"). This thematic catalogue later served as the basis for a more complete inventory of Mozart's works done by the German botanist and mineralogist Ludwig von Köchel (1800–1877). A Köchel or "K" number identifies Mozart's compositions in roughly chronological order.

spend generously on the arts and had little appreciation of Mozart, genius or not (the composer referred to his patron as the "Archboobie"). Provided only with a place in the orchestra, a small salary, and his board, Mozart at Salzburg, like Haydn at Esterháza, ate with the cooks and valets. For a Knight of the Golden Spur who had dazzled kings and queens, this was humble fare indeed, and Mozart chafed under this system of aristocratic patronage. After several unpleasant scenes in the spring of 1781, the twenty-five-year-old composer cut himself free of the archbishop and set out to make a living as a freelance musician in Vienna.

The mid-1780s witnessed the peak of Mozart's productivity and the creation of many of his greatest works. He had a full complement of pupils (all female), played several concerts a week, and enjoyed lucrative commissions as a composer. Piano concertos, string quartets, and symphonies flowed from his pen seemingly as fast as he could write them down. In little more than a year (1786–1787) he created two of the greatest operas ever written: *Le nozze di Figaro* (*The Marriage of Figaro*) and *Don Giovanni*.

Mozart died unexpectedly on 5 December 1791. Several theories—kidney failure and rheumatic fever among them—have been put forward as possible causes. Despite later rumors, Mozart was not poisoned by Antonio Salieri or anyone else. Mozart's early death is all the more tragic because in 1791 his career was flourishing. His *Singspiel* (German comic opera), *Die Zauberflöte* (*The Magic Flute*), had been a hit with middle-class patrons at a suburban Vienna theater; his *opera seria*, *La clemenza di Tito* (*The Clemency of Tito*), was well received by the court in Prague; and his Requiem Mass, for which a mysterious patron had made a handsome down payment, was nearly completed. The astonishing grandeur and pathos of the Requiem, left unfinished at the time of Mozart's death, suggest an artist still in full command of his creative powers.

SYMPHONIES

Mozart composed symphonies throughout his life, completing a total of forty-one, according to the traditional count.[2] Many of these he wrote as a mere youth during his travels about Europe. Numerous others were the products of his years as a frustrated court employee in Salzburg. His final six symphonies came into being in Vienna between 1782 and 1788. They, along with the late symphonies of Haydn, represent the culmination of the Viennese symphonic style.

The Oscar-winning film *Amadeus* begins with the opening of Mozart's striking Symphony No. 25 in G Minor (K. 183), known as the **"Little" G-Minor Symphony** (to distinguish it from the later, longer Symphony No. 40 in G Minor; K. 550). This selection, written in Salzburg in 1773, provides an appropriate way to introduce Mozart, for in this work the young composer exhibits his own distinctive voice in the genre of the symphony. The piece represents Mozart's first symphony in a minor key. Indeed, the minor mode, agitated syncopations of the strings, and dramatic fall of a diminished seventh (Ex. 47-1) all show Mozart writing in the *Sturm und Drang* style of the early 1770s. But more important is Mozart's approach to the instruments of the orchestra. The urgent, jagged first theme almost immediately transforms into a lyrical melody for solo oboe—a wonderful example of the "dramatic" quality of Classical music by which one mood can quickly give way to another. In addition, Mozart writes for four natural French horns (see Fig. 44-3), one pair in G and the other in B♭; this allows him to modulate to different keys and still include the colorful sound of the horn. With its passion and intensity, rapid shifts between major and minor, and colorful writing for the winds, the "Little" G-Minor Symphony is a small masterpiece. These same Mozartean characteristics would appear more fully developed in his last six symphonies written for Vienna.

EXAMPLE. 47-1

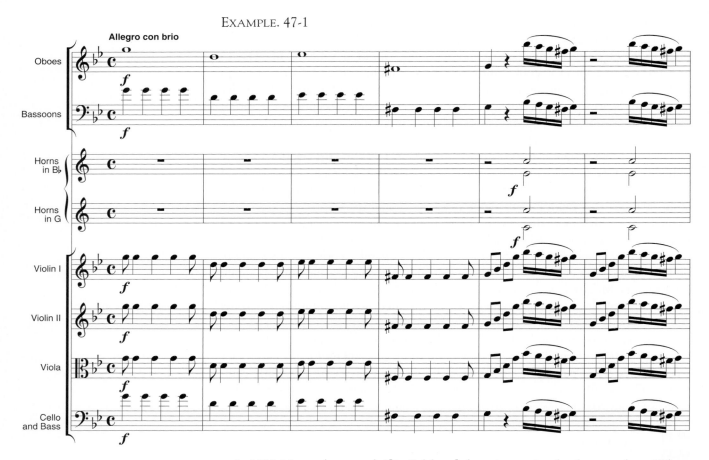

In 1781 Mozart lamented, "[In Salzburg] there is no stimulus for my talent. When I play or when any of my compositions is performed, it is just as if the audience were all tables and chairs."[3] As we have seen, Mozart felt unappreciated in provincial Salzburg, where his patron, the archbishop, placed little value on his talent. Consequently, in the spring of 1781 at the age of twenty-five, Mozart broke loose and established himself as an independent, freelance musician in Vienna. Writing symphonies was only a small part of Mozart's creative life in Vienna, yet the six he produced there can be counted among the finest examples of the Classical symphony. The first three of these later took names from the patron or the city for which the work was destined, while the last two are known by titles given them by later commentators. Mozart's final six symphonies are:

- Symphony No. 35 in D Major, the "Haffner" (K. 385) (written in 1782 for a wealthy Salzburg family)
- Symphony No. 36 in C Major, the "Linz" (K. 425) (written in 1783 for a performance in Linz, Austria)
- Symphony No. 37, in G Major (Only the slow introduction to the first movement is by Mozart, the rest is the work of Michael Haydn, younger brother of Joseph Haydn.)
- Symphony No. 38 in D Major, the "Prague" (K. 504) (written in 1786 for a performance in Prague)
- Symphony No. 39 in E♭ Major (K. 543) (written in 1788, likely for performance at Mozart's subscription concerts in Vienna)
- Symphony No. 40 in G Minor, the "Great" (K. 550) (written in 1788, likely for performance at Mozart's subscription concerts in Vienna)

- Symphony No. 41 in C Major, the "Jupiter" (K. 551) (written in 1788, likely for performance at Mozart's subscription concerts in Vienna)

The people of Prague, now the capital of Czech Republic, had a special love for Mozart's music. Two of his operas (*Don Giovanni* and *La clemenza di Tito*) enjoyed premieres there, and Mozart's **"Prague" Symphony** was destined for that city as well. The first movement of the "Prague" is one of Mozart's finest symphonic creations. Certainly it is one of his most difficult to perform, owing to the density of the texture and the demands placed on the woodwinds. To the usual complement of strings, Mozart adds pairs of flutes, oboes, bassoons, horns, and trumpets, as well as timpani. The winds in particular add contrapuntal density as they weave an intricate polyphonic web around the melodic line carried by the strings. Mozart also injects a new element of chromaticism; again the woodwinds enrich the texture by inserting chromatic scales, as can be seen in bars 28–31 of the first movement (Ex. 47-2).

EXAMPLE 47-2

Mozart's colorful use of woodwinds and his penchant for chromaticism is heard again in his celebrated **Symphony No. 40 in G Minor,** sometimes called the "Great" G-Minor Symphony to distinguish it from the earlier "Little" G-Minor

Symphony (1773). This was one of three symphonies (his last three) that Mozart wrote in the short span of six weeks during the summer of 1788. All three were apparently intended for performance at subscription concerts Mozart planned to give that fall in the casino of Vienna; Mozart often performed there because, then as now, the casino offered large public rooms and attracted people with money.

Symphony No. 40 is one of the most performed of all eighteenth-century symphonies, indeed of all symphonies. It is not a festive composition (and hence features no trumpets or drums), but rather an intensely brooding work that suggests desperation, even tragedy. The first movement starts quietly with an insistent accompaniment that precedes the haunting violin melody. The second theme in particular is a beautifully scored dialogue between strings and woodwinds. Yet the summit of woodwind writing occurs in the re-transition immediately before the recapitulation. Here the strings stop entirely to allow the upper woodwinds to cascade down in a chromatic sequence above a bassoon pedal point, for a rainbow of sound that returns us to the opening theme (Ex. 47-3). Originally the symphony had no clarinets, but Mozart added them later to increase the richness of the wind writing. Indeed, Mozart took great pains with his orchestration, and his scores are more complex than those of any of his Classical contemporaries. The winds in particular are always carefully "voiced," and rarely simply double the string parts. Ultimately, Mozart's colorful writing for winds formed the basis for the orchestration of Haydn's London Symphonies as well as those later composed by Beethoven and Schubert.

EXAMPLE 47-3

LISTENING CUE

WOLFGANG AMADEUS MOZART
Symphony No. 40 in G Minor (K. 550; 1788)
First movement, *Allegro*

CD 7/14
Anthology, No. 133

In what was to prove to be his final symphony, Symphony No. 41 in C Major, Mozart returned to the festive sounds of the large orchestra and a bright major key. The title **"Jupiter" Symphony** was not given by Mozart. Rather, it was bestowed by Haydn's friend Johann Salomon (see Chapter 46), apparently because Mozart's use of trumpets and timpani, as well as stately dotted rhythms, evoked images of nobility and godliness for eighteenth-century listeners. Of the four movements of the "Jupiter," the most famous is the finale, which contains perhaps the greatest technical *tour de force* in all of music. Here Mozart begins as usual in standard sonata form, presenting five themes: two in the first theme group, one in the transition, and two in the second theme group (Ex. 47-4).

EXAMPLE 47-4

In the development section, Mozart marches these five themes through various contrapuntal drills, including musical inversion, invertible counterpoint, and stretto. Yet it is in the coda that a Mozartean miracle occurs: quintuple invertible counterpoint. It turns out that Mozart had designed each of these five themes so that they might all be heard simultaneously and their vertical position continually reshuffled—one great final display of contrapuntal ingenuity. Below is given the superimposition of the themes as Mozart composed it (Ex. 47-5a) and, for clarity of presentation, an abstraction of this transposed to C (Ex. 47-5b).

EXAMPLE 47-5A

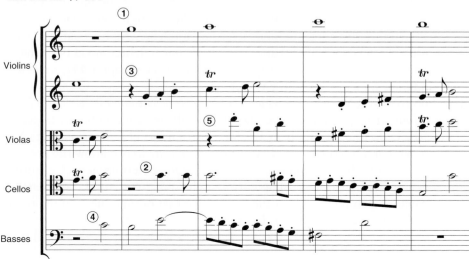

EXAMPLE 47-5B

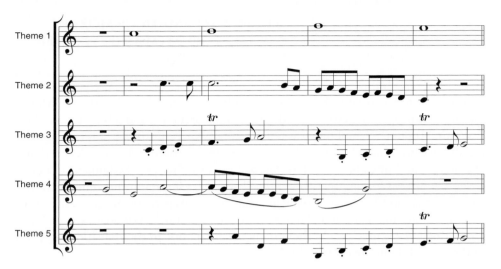

LISTENING CUE

WOLFGANG AMADEUS MOZART
Symphony No. 41 in C Major
(K. 551, 1788)
Fourth movement, *Molto allegro*

CD 7/15
Anthology, No. 134

CHAMBER MUSIC

Today we think of chamber music as music for a small instrumental group, played in a small to mid-size room or hall, with one performer to a part. In Mozart's day, however, the distinction between "chamber" and "orchestral" music was not so easily made. Mozart's small ensemble pieces were played both indoors and outdoors, sometimes with one musician to a part and sometimes with more. Mozart composed a number of divertimenti and serenades for wedding receptions, balls, university celebrations, outdoor serenading, and other sorts of public entertainments. He seems to have used the terms "divertimento" and "serenade" interchangeably to signal a composition usually in five movements and often displaying a lighter mood (see Chapter 44). Some were for winds alone (*Harmoniemusik*; see Chapter 44), some for strings, and some for a mixture of the two groups.

Best-known among Mozart's serenades is his *Eine kleine Nachtmusik* (K. 525, 1787) scored for four string parts. It can be played by a full string ensemble with basses doubling the cello line, or simply by the four instruments of a string quartet. Although the autograph score is dated 10 August 1787, we do not know the precise occasion for which Mozart composed this bit of night entertainment. Certainly nothing demonstrates better the simplicity and pleasurable intent of the serenade than the famous opening melody of the first *Allegro* that outlines first a tonic triad and then a dominant-seventh chord (Ex. 47-6).

EXAMPLE 47-6

Mozart composed some two dozen string quartets, but his six **"Haydn" Quartets** (1782–1785) form the core of his work in this genre. As we have seen (Chapter 45), Joseph Haydn was the creator of the string quartet, and in 1781 he published his influential Opus 33 set of quartets in Vienna. This same year, Mozart moved to Vienna, studied these quartets, and began to compose his own set of six, which he published in 1785 and dedicated to Haydn. Haydn and Mozart had become fast friends in these years, and they sometimes played quartets together in Mozart's apartment. It was at one of these gatherings in early 1785 that Haydn said to Leopold Mozart, then visiting from Salzburg: "Before God and as an honest man, I tell you that your son is the greatest composer known to me either in person or by name."[4]

In his touching dedication to the "Haydn" Quartets, Mozart refers to Haydn as his "very dear friend" and to the quartets as "the fruit of a long and arduous study." Judging from the unusually high number of revisions Mozart made to his manuscripts, he did indeed labor mightily on these quartets in an effort to digest Haydn's method of thematic integration. In the end, Mozart produced a set of six quartets that are distinctly different from one another: K. 387 in G major, K. 421 in D minor, K. 428 in E♭ major, K. 458 in B♭ major (the "Hunt"), K. 464 in A major, and K. 465 in C major (the "Dissonance").

The final work in the collection, the **"Dissonance" Quartet,** derives its title from the *Adagio* introduction to the first movement, a passage famous for its harmonic audacities. Here, Mozart leads the listener through a bizarre harmonic labyrinth as the harmony slides down chromatically by half-steps; the ensuing C-major first theme of the exposition sounds all the more shocking for its tonal clarity. (For study purposes, the opening of this quartet can be found in the Anthology, No. 135.)

Not to be forgotten among Mozart's chamber works are several fine quintets, including K. 452 for piano and winds, K. 581 for clarinet and strings, and K. 515 and 516 for strings alone. This last piece is an extraordinary work, one of only a handful of pieces that Mozart wrote in G minor. As this quintet and his two famous symphonies in the same key show, Mozart saved G minor for pieces of great intensity.

❀ PIANO AND VIOLIN SONATAS

When Mozart moved to Vienna in the spring of 1781, he intended to make his living as a composer. But, like so many other creative musicians throughout history, he soon took on private students as a way to pay the bills. In a letter of early 1782,

Mozart reveals that he had to squeeze composition into the beginning and end of the day, because the best hours were taken up with giving piano lessons:

> My hair is always done by six o'clock in the morning and by seven I am fully dressed. I then compose until nine. From nine to one I give [piano] lessons. Then I lunch unless I am invited to some house where they lunch at two or even three o'clock. . . . I can never work before five or six o'clock in the evening, and even then I am often prevented by a concert. If I am not prevented, I compose until nine.[5]

In these years, Mozart had had three or four pupils at a time, all of them women. Throughout the eighteenth century most keyboard sonatas were directed toward amateurs for performance in the home, and most of these consumers were women (see Chapter 43). For his female pupils, for patrons, and sometimes for himself, Mozart composed a total of eighteen sonatas for solo piano and twenty-eight sonatas for piano and violin. The Piano Sonata in C Major (K. 545) was clearly intended as a teaching piece for beginning students (and is still used as such today); when Mozart entered the piece in his list of compositions in 1788, he labeled it "for beginners." As with most Classical keyboard sonatas, K. 545 is in three movements. At the outset we see Mozart writing in a simple *galant* style typical of the Classical era (Ex. 47-7). The melody is graceful, arranged in units of two-plus-two measures, while the left-hand accompaniment is a standard Alberti bass, and the texture is light. All of these—balanced phrases, Alberti bass, and transparent textures—are musical fingerprints by which we identify the Classical style, and all are found abundantly in Mozart's piano sonatas.

EXAMPLE 47-7

Some of Mozart's best pupils, Barbara Ployer and Josepha Auernhammer among them, were the equals of male performing professionals. For these female virtuosos, and for himself, Mozart wrote more technically demanding sonatas. The Sonata in A Major (K. 331) of 1783 is such a work. The final movement (Ex. 47-8), the famous "Alla Turca," is a rousing rondo in **ABCBAB**+coda form. Here Mozart explicitly aims to imitate the sounds of **Turkish music,** the noise of Turkish military percussion instruments, which were introduced into European music in the eighteenth century during the Turkish Wars. Some pianos of the day were equipped with special devices to effect the sounds of the "Turkish" music, such as bass drum, cymbals, and the like. These could make the Turk sound all the more terrifying.

EXAMPLE 47-8

Pianoforte or Fortepiano?

Does one say "pianoforte" or "fortepiano"? In writings about music, we see both, but which is more correct? The piano was invented around 1700 by Bartolomeo Cristofori in Florence, Italy (see Chapter 43). At first it was called "cimbalo di martelletti" (harpsichord with little hammers) and it could "fa' il piano e il forte" (play soft and loud). Eventually, these words were compressed into a single noun, "pianoforte." During the 1760s, German performers began to reverse the words, creating "fortepiano," but Mozart, judging from his letters, continued to prefer "pianoforte," though he often used the then-generic word "cembalo" (keyboard) as well. But, whether called pianoforte or fortepiano, Mozart's instrument was much smaller and more delicate than the modern concert grand.

Mozart began playing the piano, as opposed to the harpsichord, during the 1770s. He admired the instruments of Andreas Stein of Augsburg for their light, even tone. Stein's instrument also included a knee lever, the forerunner of the modern damper pedal, which empowered the player to raise the dampers and allow the strings to resonate. When Mozart purchased his own instrument in Vienna around 1783, he chose a piano by the Viennese maker Anton Walter. This instrument is preserved today in the Mozart family museum in Salzburg (Fig. 47-1). In 1785 Mozart also acquired a pedal board, with strings and pedal keyboard, that could be positioned beneath his Walter piano (Fig. 47-2). This allowed him to reinforce the bass notes of his keyboard music and extend them by five notes. Mozart played the two instruments together, much as he might an organ. When he performed in Vienna, whether at the municipal theater or casino, movers apparently transported Mozart's piano with pedal board to the concert site.

The piano of the late eighteenth century was rather small by modern standards. Similar in shape, size, and weight to the harpsichord, Mozart's piano had a range of only five octaves (F' to f''') plus five lower notes provided by the pedal. Moreover, the key depth was only about 3 mm, and roughly 10 to 15 grams of force were needed to depress it (as compared to a key depth of 9 mm on a modern piano and a required force of about 55 grams). This would have encouraged a light, rapid style of playing. Finally, the hammer on Mozart's piano was a small wooden one covered with leather (as opposed to the much larger one covered with softer felt on the modern piano). The light hammers and efficient damper mechanism allowed the crisp attacks and subtle nuances of articulation called for in Mozart's keyboard scores.

FIGURE 47-1
Mozart's piano, now preserved in the Mozart Museum, Salzburg. The composer purchased the instrument in Vienna, in about 1783, from the manufacturer, Anton Walter.

FIGURE 47-2
An early piano with pedal keyboard of the type once owned by Mozart. This instrument was made in Salzburg in 1798 by Johann Schmidt.

We must not forget that Mozart was not only a composer and pianist but also a virtuoso violinist who astonished listeners at the age of six. His father Leopold, moreover, was a leading violin pedagogue. Mozart's twenty-eight violin sonatas, as was usual in the Classical period, often placed more technical demands on the pianist than on the violinist. Indeed, Mozart considered the violin, not the piano, to be the accompanying instrument. Perhaps most remarkable is the Sonata in E Minor (K. 304), Mozart's only violin sonata in a minor key. Written during a disastrous trip to Paris in 1778, the final movement is full of pathos and despair. Perhaps Mozart composed it as an act of homage to his mother, who had died in Paris, leaving the son to report the sad news to his father back in Salzburg.

CONCERTOS

The piano concertos take us into the world of Mozart, the public performer. If Mozart created many of his piano sonatas for teaching purposes in the home, he fashioned his piano concertos for himself and his very best students to play in public. A prodigious pianist, Mozart was certainly one of the first in music history to make his mark as a touring virtuoso on the instrument. Although the solo keyboard concerto was known to composers of the late Baroque era, they were few in number. Just as it can be fairly said that Haydn created the string quartet, so Mozart can be considered the father of the modern piano concerto.

The years 1783–1788 marked the high point of Mozart's popularity in Vienna. Not coincidentally, Mozart composed more than half of his twenty-three original piano concertos during these five years. The Viennese musical public wanted to hear brilliant passagework and dazzling displays of keyboard virtuosity. The piano concerto was the test-track for such display. At each of his public concerts Mozart offered one or two of his latest creations. He alone selected the program. He also rented the hall, hired and paid the orchestra, publicized the concert, directed the moving of his piano, and sold tickets from his apartment. Sometimes all went well for concert-promoter Mozart, as suggested by the following review:

> **Vienna, 22 March 1783:** Tonight the famous Knight Herr Mozart held a musical concert for his own benefit at the Burgtheater in which pieces of his own music, which was already very popular, were performed. The concert was honored by the presence of an extraordinarily large audience and the two new concertos and other fantasies which Herr Mozart played on the Forte Piano were received with the loudest approval. Our Monarch [Emperor Joseph II], who contrary to his custom honored the entire concert with his presence, joined in the applause of the public so heartily that one can think of no similar example. The proceeds of the concert are estimated at 1600 gulden.[6]

Like the Baroque keyboard concerto, Mozart's piano concertos are always in three movements (fast/slow/fast). Generally, the first movement sets the substantive tone for the work, the second offers a contrasting lyrical "song," and the third provides a light, dance-like sendoff. Most important to the development of the concerto genre was Mozart's employment of a new form for the fast first movement. The commonly used term "double-exposition" form derives from the fact that the materials of the exposition are played twice, first by the orchestra and then by the pianist with orchestral accompaniment. But one must distinguish between two very different sorts of expositions: one is "passive" and the other "active." Indeed, a better term for the form of the first movements of Mozart's concertos is **concerto-sonata form** (see page 433). First the orchestra presents its exposition entirely in the tonic, and is thus introductory ("passive") in function; then the soloist enters in the tonic but provides the crucial ("active") modulation to the secondary key area, thereby providing the same tonal "drama" found in conventional sonata form. The active solo exposition is a distinctly different section, for here the performer has the freedom to add new themes into the mix, as well as to elaborate (or omit) some of the orchestra's themes. Toward the end of the solo exposition, the full/tutti orchestra returns with selected bits of its opening theme, a throwback to the ritornello principle of both the old Baroque concerto grosso and the *da capo* aria (see Anthology, No. 91b, for example). Thus, Mozart integrates the older ritornello procedure with the new principles of sonata form. The diagram below shows how a movement in concerto-sonata form begins. Remember that this diagram is an abstraction, and many concertos deviate from the model in one way or another.

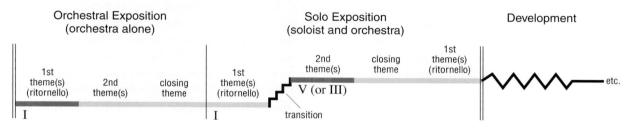

Mozart composed perhaps a half-dozen piano concertos that might rightly appear in any list of the greatest concertos ever written. The serene G major (K. 453), heroic C major (K. 467), demonic D minor (K. 466), wind-dominated E♭ major (K. 482), and tragic C minor (K. 491) are among his very best. Yet surely one of the brightest lights in this shining constellation is the Piano Concerto in A Major (K. 488) of 1786.

Probably written for his star pupil, Barbara Ployer, the Concerto in A Major has always been one of Mozart's most popular compositions. The first movement offers a seemingly endless supply of graceful melodies, and both it and the closing movement appear in the bright key of A major (a particularly resonant key for strings). Yet, for the slow second movement, Mozart chooses a key found almost nowhere else in his oeuvre, the starkly dark key of F♯ minor, whose somber tone contributes to the unearthly beauty of this *Adagio*.

The essence of Mozart's concerto style, however, can be seen in his sparkling musical "dialogues." Lightning-quick exchanges between soloist and accompanying orchestra were entirely new to the concerto. In these, Mozart reveals the full potential of the genre, showing that soloist and orchestra might not simply speak "in turn," but instead banter back and forth in the most playful and pleasing way. "Anything you can do, I can do better." "No you can't." "Yes I can"—the antagonists seem to say. In Mozart's contest between interactive forces there is no winner—except the listener.

 LISTENING CUE

WOLFGANG AMADEUS MOZART
Piano Concerto in A Major (K. 488; 1786)
First movement, *Allegro*

CD 8/1
Anthology, No. 136

 SUMMARY

Mozart was a prolific composer who wrote an astounding amount of music in his fewer than thirty-six years. His compositions, catalogued by Ludwig von Köchel (K), number more than six hundred. They range from early piano sonatas composed at the age of six (1762) to his unfinished Requiem Mass (1791). The traditional numbering system for Mozart's symphonies counts forty-one, though in fact he composed nearly sixty. In addition, he wrote eighteen piano sonatas, twenty-four string quartets, and twenty-three piano concertos. Mozart can rightly be seen as the creator of the piano concerto, and he established concerto-sonata form as the norm for the first movement of that genre.

Mozart's mature concertos and final six symphonies display a rich, distinctly Mozartean array of orchestral sounds. They are dramatic, often because of quick shifts between the major and minor mode, as well as colorful, owing especially to the brilliant woodwind writing. Finally, they frequently show two other characteristics of Mozart's style: intense chromaticism and dense counterpoint. In their drama, color, and intensity, Mozart's late instrumental works not only carry the Viennese Classical style to new heights but they also prefigure the music of the Romantic era.

KEY TERMS

Köchel (K) number
"Little" G-Minor
    Symphony
"Prague" Symphony

Symphony No. 40
    in G Minor
"Jupiter" Symphony
"Haydn" Quartets

"Dissonance" Quartet
Turkish music
concerto-sonata form

Chapter 48
Wolfgang Amadeus Mozart: Vocal Music

Mozart was fascinated by the magic of the theater. Scarcely was there a moment in his career when he was not looking for a good libretto to set, writing an opera, or overseeing the production of one. In all, he composed twenty operas. Eight are of the older Italian *opera seria* kind, seven in the newer Italian comic *opera buffa* style, and five of the simpler German type called **Singspiel,** a German light comic opera with spoken dialogue rather than recitatives. Mozart's first *Singspiel,* entitled *Bastien und Bastienne* (1768), was written when he was twelve and intended for Vienna. It apparently premiered in the summer home of the famous Dr. Franz Anton Mesmer (1733–1815), the inventor of the theory of animal magnetism (whence, "to mesmerize"). Of the operas Mozart composed before moving to Vienna in 1781, the most impressive is *Idomeneo* (1780). *Idomeneo* is an *opera seria*—the plot involves an ancient mythological story and requires both chorus and ballet. Yet Mozart removes the often statue-like stiffness of *opera seria* by giving the characters more natural music to sing. Although *Idomeneo* has been called "the greatest *opera seria* of the eighteenth century," its emphasis on strong character development through music hints at the masterpieces of Mozart's last decade.

Soon after settling for good in Vienna in 1781, Mozart received a commission directly from Emperor Joseph II: he was to create a German opera for the Emperor's German-speaking subjects. Mozart's response was a *Singspiel* entitled *Die Entführung*

Lorenzo da Ponte: Librettist to Mozart

The life story of Lorenzo da Ponte should be the subject of a movie (as Mozart's was for *Amadeus*), because it was filled with extraordinary contradictions and improbable adventures. His birth name was not Lorenzo da Ponte, but Emmanuele Conegliano. Born in northern Italy of Jewish parents, he converted to Catholicism in 1763, adopted the name of the local bishop (Lorenzo da Ponte), entered a seminary, and became a Catholic priest. Having studied Latin and Italian in the seminary, da Ponte took a job as a tutor of literature and languages in Venice, but his love of liberal politics and married women soon got Father da Ponte banned from that city. Making his way to Vienna, he gained an introduction to Emperor Joseph II through Antonio Salieri, imperial court composer and rival of Mozart. Da Ponte soon became the official court librettist ("Poet to the Imperial Theaters"), and both Salieri and Mozart made use of his talents. But when Joseph died in 1790 and Mozart the following year, da Ponte's fortunes declined. For a short

time he lodged with another famous Venetian adventurer and lover, Giacomo Casanova (1725–1798), then made his way to London, where he worked as a librettist at the King's Theater and opened a bookstore. But charges of shady financial dealings were leveled against him, so in 1805 da Ponte stole away from London for America, one step ahead of his creditors. After a brief stop in New York, he established himself in Sunbury, Pennsylvania, as a merchant, distiller, and occasional gunrunner during the War of 1812. Eventually, da Ponte returned to New York City, where in 1826 he mounted a production of Mozart's *Don Giovanni*, the first opera by Mozart to be performed in America. About this same time he also became the first professor of Italian literature at Columbia University. Upon his death in 1838, da Ponte bequeathed his personal library to Columbia, where it remains the nucleus of the Italian collection to the present day.

The Granger Collection, NY

🌿 FIGURE 48-1

Lorenzo da Ponte (1749–1838)

aus dem Serail (*The Abduction from the Seraglio*). Like all operas of the *Singspiel* type, here the dialogue is simply spoken (there are no recitatives). The comic plot concerns the somewhat clumsy rescue of two young women from the harem of a Turkish lord. Obviously Mozart was capitalizing on the fact that in late eighteenth-century Vienna, things Turkish were all the rage. There were Turkish dress styles, Turkish hairdos, Turkish stories, and, as we have seen (Chapter 47), Turkish music. To satisfy the public's appetite for Turkish exoticism, Mozart made sure that his new opera not only had a Turkish plot, but also contained plenty of Turkish music—percussive marches and choruses with bass drum, cymbal, and triangle.

Beginning in 1785 Mozart had the good fortune to join forces with a gifted librettist, the larger-than-life figure **Lorenzo da Ponte** (1749–1838). Ultimately, da Ponte ended up in America selling guns to the British, mounting the first full production of a Mozart opera in the United States, and founding the Italian Department at Columbia University (see Box). But he was first and foremost a poet and librettist. During the 1780s da Ponte and Mozart created three operatic masterpieces, *Le nozze di Figaro* (1786), *Don Giovanni* (1787), and *Così fan tutte* (1790). Each is an *opera buffa*, yet each is infused with a newly serious tone. Social revolution, amorality and murder, and human frailty and infidelity are examined in turn. Mozart's fluid musical style was well suited for blending comedy with tragedy. As often with life (and Mozart), we don't know whether to laugh or cry.

Le nozze di Figaro (*The Marriage of Figaro*) is based on a radical work of the French playwright Beaumarchais, a play that fanned the flames of the French Revolution (1789). For six years the French king's ministers had prevented it from reaching the stage. When it finally did in 1784, the play took Paris by storm. In Austria a frightened Joseph II quickly banned the work from his Empire, but librettist Lorenzo da Ponte convinced him to allow a softened version to come to the stage in Vienna as an opera. What was so seditious about the play and libretto derived from it? In *Le nozze di Figaro* a clever, good-hearted, mostly honest manservant (Figaro) outwits a philandering, mostly dishonest nobleman (Count Almaviva). Perhaps most revolutionary of all is the close friendship between Countess Almaviva and her maid Susanna. It is this unlikely pair of women who ultimately teach the Count a lesson.

Social tension is immediately apparent at the outset of the opera. In the palace of the Count, Figaro has been measuring a bedroom for himself and his betrothed, Susanna. To his dismay, he learns that the room they have been given is right next to the Count's. The Count wishes to exercise his ancient *droit de seigneur*—the lord's claim to sexual favors from a servant's fiancée. In the aria "Se vuol ballare" ("If you want to dance") Figaro tells us that, should the Count wish to fool around, Figaro will call the tune. In fact, Figaro refers to the Count with a derisive diminutive "Signor Contino"—which, given his tone of voice, might be translated roughly as "you little twerp." Musically, the aria begins with straightforward, indeed foursquare music, showing Figaro to be a well-balanced, rational, yet resolute fellow. In the middle section, however, where the libretto reveals that the servant might need trickery to defeat the master, the music accordingly invokes slippery chromaticism and the sinister sound of the minor mode. Finally, in the closing *presto* section, Figaro's anger gets the better of him. Fulminating with rage, he loses control of his deliberate "dance."

LISTENING CUE

WOLFGANG AMADEUS MOZART
Le nozze di Figaro (1786)
Aria, "Se vuol ballare"

CD 8/2
Anthology, No. 137a

In Act II of *Le nozze di Figaro* we meet Countess Almaviva, the victim of the Count's womanizing (Fig. 48-2). What sort of person is she? Mozart tells us in music that she is a woman who bears sorrow with great serenity and dignity. In traditional *opera seria*, a soliloquy such as this would call for dazzling coloratura—a soloist alone on stage needs to do something sensational. But Mozart is not so much interested in vocal display as character development through music. Over long, legato lines of arching beauty, the Countess asks that the god of love bring her relief, "Porgi, amor." The text is simple, not extravagant, and so is the vocal range and style. The Countess's stature is portrayed instead in the richness of the orchestral scoring, most especially in the lush wind writing. Throughout *Le nozze di Figaro* Mozart sets high style against low, fast against slow, loud against soft, major against minor, and male against female. Nowhere in *Le nozze di Figaro* is there an aria in which virtuosic coloratura singing is heard; everywhere there is balance and control, the essence of Classical style.

LISTENING CUE

WOLFGANG AMADEUS MOZART
Le nozze di Figaro (1786)
Aria, "Porgi, amor"

CD 8/3
Anthology, No. 137b

In the subsequent aria, "Voi, che sapete" ("You ladies who know"), Mozart develops yet another character type—the petulant adolescent. Here we meet Cherubino, a lad of fourteen who is in love with the Countess, and with Susanna, and with all women all at once. His music is light, bouncy, and generally charming, yet full of mood swings (to distant keys in the aria's middle). At the climax Cherubino clamors upward in excited melodic sequence, only to dissolve in frustration back to the tonic. The part of adolescent Cherubino was intended by Mozart to be sung by a woman dressed as a man. It is thus called a **trouser role.** Such cross-dressing was common on the eighteenth-century stage, and it brought a certain erotic charge to the action.

The aria "Voi, che sapete" demonstrates another aspect of Mozart's musical genius: the capacity to write music of exquisite beauty from the simplest of materials (Ex. 48-1). It begins with an unremarkable four-bar antecedent phrase, followed by a matching four-bar consequent phrase. Yet together the two form a perfect pair, one made all the richer by the luxuriant accompaniment, again, for woodwinds (here clarinet, oboe, bassoon, and flute). Yet there is more, for when Cherubino enters he (she) inserts a new four-bar phrase in the middle of the previous two. So perfectly crafted is this new phrase that we hardly notice its insertion. All is sublimely beautiful, yet sublimely simple. To paraphrase Mozart's own words, there seems to be "not one note too many, nor one too few."[1]

FIGURE 48-2

Renée Fleming singing the role of Countess Almaviva.

EXAMPLE 48-1

(continued on next page)

You ladies who know about love, tell me if I have it in my heart.

LISTENING CUE

WOLFGANG AMADEUS MOZART
Le nozze di Figaro (1786)
Aria, "Voi, che sapete"

CD 8/4
Anthology, No. 137c

Despite the charm and beauty of his arias, it is in his ensembles that Mozart carries vocal music for the stage to unequaled heights of complexity and intrigue. The ensemble played to Mozart's strengths. As we have seen in his piano concertos (see Chapter 47), no one was better at composing rapid-fire dialogue in music. Likewise, no one was better at handling the intricacies of plot and action as one character after another appeared on stage. Having two, three, four, and more individuals press their points of view simultaneously helped push the dramatic action along; rather than having things happen in succession, they could come all at once. Compared to other operas, fast-paced *Figaro* contains relatively few solo arias and many more vocal ensembles. Three of the four acts end with an energetic **ensemble finale**—a rousing way to bring down the curtain.

To sample just a bit of Mozart's ensemble technique, we examine a section of the ensemble finale that closes Act II, a group song for independent soloists that goes on for an astonishing twenty-five minutes. On stage at this point are Figaro, Susanna, the Count and Countess, and Antonio, the gardener. Antonio is annoyed that someone has trampled his flowers; the Count suspects the culprit is Cherubino, who may have jumped out the Countess's window; Figaro, Susanna, and the Countess have reason to protect Cherubino. Thus there are many points of view to be heard. Here Antonio sings only on a single pitch, showing that he is a rustic fellow of no refinement. Figaro is musically agitated, then triumphant; the Count is triumphant, then agitated. The ladies sing together in interlocking thirds, thereby demonstrating their solidarity through music. Each twist in the plot is underscored in the music by a corresponding change in key and style. These are the musical mechanisms by which Mozart works his magic in his complex ensemble finales.

LISTENING CUE

WOLFGANG AMADEUS MOZART
Le nozze di Figaro (1786)
Ensemble, "Vostre dunque"

CD 8/5
Anthology, No. 137d

Mozart teamed with da Ponte to fashion two other *opere buffe*, *Don Giovanni* and *Così fan tutte* (*Thus do they all*). *Don Giovanni* tells the story of a philandering, indeed murdering Don Juan, a nobleman whose deviant behavior makes the peasants he exploits seem all the more noble. The music Mozart created for this lurid tale may be even more powerful than that of *Le nozze di Figaro*. In fact, many believe *Don Giovanni* to be the greatest opera ever written. While *Così fan tutte*, too, has much beautiful music, the libretto has little of the sensationalism or social bite of *Don Giovanni* or *Le nozze di Figaro*.

In his last year (1791), Mozart composed two operas that show his remarkable versatility. One, *La clemenza di Tito* (*The Clemency of Tito*) is an *opera seria* commissioned for the crowning of Emperor Leopold II in Prague as king of Bohemia; needless to say, for the installation of a king, old-style *opera seria*, and old-style values, were chosen above social revolution. The second opera, *Die Zauberflöte* (*The Magic Flute*), is very different. *Die Zauberflöte* is a German *Singspiel*, yet here the music ranges from the most vocally demanding sounds of Italianate opera to the naively simple style of German folk song. The libretto was the product of actor-singer-showman Emanuel Schikaneder, and he called for all the special effects the eighteenth century could muster—magical instruments, a fire-breathing snake, a flaming temple, and the like. Yet the end has distinctly Masonic overtones that promote universal brotherhood. From the start Mozart and Schikaneder aimed to appeal to a popular rather than a courtly audience. Accordingly, they mounted their production, not at the court theater in central Vienna, but at a suburban theater beyond the city walls in a neighborhood where the tickets were cheaper and the audience sat on wooden benches. This was the Viennese equivalent of "off-Broadway." *Die Zauberflöte* hit the target audience to the financial gain of all, and to this day remains one of Mozart's most universally appealing operas.

❋ REQUIEM MASS

Mozart became ill in the fall of 1791. He took to his bed about 20 November and died in the early morning of 5 December (see also Chapter 47). All fall he had been working on a Requiem Mass, which had been commissioned by a mysterious messenger. (Not until 1964 was it fully revealed that an Austrian nobleman had requested the work with the aim of honoring his recently deceased wife, passing off Mozart's score as his own composition.) Realizing that he was dying, Mozart eventually came to see this requiem as burial music for himself.

The **Requiem Mass** is the funeral music for the Roman Catholic Church. As such it makes use of several movements from the traditional Ordinary and Proper of the Mass that have existed since the Middle Ages (see Chapter 3). To these is added a medieval chant particular to the burial service, the sequence *Dies irae* (*Day of Wrath*). The **Dies irae** (discussed at length in Chapter 5) is by far the longest and most textually expressive movement within the Requiem Mass. Over the centuries many composers have set the requiem in polyphony, paying special attention to the *Dies irae*. Mozart, Berlioz, and Verdi are just a few of the composers to capture in sound the "hellfire and brimstone" quality of this apocalyptic text:

Dies irae, dies illa,	Day of wrath, that day,
Solvet saeclum in favilla,	When the ages shall be reduced to ash
Teste David cum Sibylla.	As foretold by David and the Sibyl Prophet.
Quantus tremor est futurus,	What terror will occur
Quando judex est venturus,	When the eternal Judge arrives,
Cuncta stricte discussurus.	To loosen the chains of those in Hell.

For frightening words such as these, Mozart creates appropriately terrifying music. Subsequent verses, too, have music that does honor to the vivid text. In the verse "Tuba mirum" ("Wondrous trumpet"), for example, Mozart creates what is perhaps the most famous trombone solo in the entire literature. Although the trombone was featured in the unearthly scenes of such operas as Gluck's *Orfeo* and Mozart's *Idomeneo*, it would not be admitted into the symphony orchestra until the time of Beethoven. Yet within the music for the church, it had a long history extending back to the sacred Masses and motets of the Renaissance. Mozart calls for the trombone at this point in his requiem (Ex. 48-2) because the text itself calls for the trumpet (or trombone) to sound the Last Judgment.

EXAMPLE 48-2

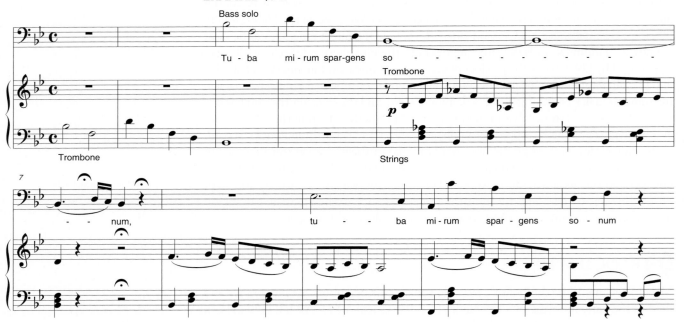

The trumpet sends forth its wondrous sound.

Perhaps the most graphic moment in Mozart's Requiem is found in the "Confutatis" of the *Dies irae*. Here the text erects a contrast between the cries of the hellish pain of the damned ("Confutatis" = those confounded) against the heavenly sounds of the elect ("Benedictis" = those blessed). Mozart places the damned down low in a minor key, supported by an agitated accompaniment. They sing with a jagged vocal line that incorporates a tritone (the *diabolus in musica*, the tonal devil). The elect, on the other hand, dwell in a higher, quieter realm of major, where any dissonance is quickly resolved. In Mozart's vision of the cosmos, there is vivid contrast, yet balance, even between Heaven and Hell.

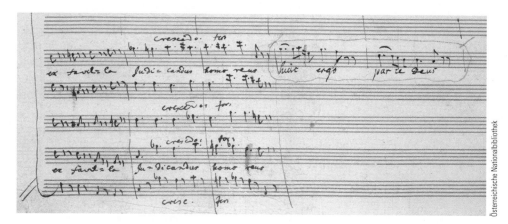

Österreichische Nationalbibliothek

🌿 FIGURE 48-3
The last notes written by
Mozart, toward the opening
of the "Lacrimosa" of the
Requiem Mass.

LISTENING CUE

WOLFGANG AMADEUS MOZART
Requiem Mass (1791)
"Confutatis"

CD 8/6
Anthology, No. 138a

Mozart did not complete his Requiem. It was left to his students, most notably Franz Xaver Süssmayr (1766–1803), to compose a few unfinished portions and flesh out the orchestration. Where Mozart stopped can be determined by a glance at the autograph score (Fig. 48-3), specifically toward the end of the *Dies irae* in a section called "Lacrimosa dies illa" ("Ah, that day of tears and mourning"; Ex. 48-3). Here Mozart writes a melody that ascends in a mostly chromatic scale for more than an octave, like the just man or woman rising from ashes of Hell. At this point death took the pen from the master's hand. The version completed by pupil Süssmayr is generally used in performances today.

EXAMPLE 48-3

(continued on next page)

When the just person rises from the ashes to be judged…

LISTENING CUE

WOLFGANG AMADEUS MOZART
Requiem Mass (1791)
"Lacrimosa" (completed by Süssmayr)

CD 8/7
Anthology, No. 138b

SUMMARY

Given the highly dramatic quality of Mozart's music, it is not surprising that he was attracted to the dramatic potential of musical theater in its most elaborate form: opera. In all, Mozart composed some twenty operas. His universality in this genre can be seen in the fact that he has left us examples of traditional *opera seria*, German *Singspiel*, and *opera buffa*. Moreover, his operas *Le nozze di Figaro*, *Don Giovanni*, and *Così fan tutte*, all with librettos by Lorenzo da Ponte, mix elements of *seria* and *buffa*. Mozart's special gift as an operatic composer was his uncanny ability to portray each dramatic situation and each character vividly through music. The various characters are often united in cumulative fashion in ensemble finales, where the differing points of view are heard simultaneously in a brilliant display of musical and dramatic counterpoint. Mozart also composed much splendid music for the Roman Catholic Church. By far his best-known religious work is his Requiem Mass with its graphic setting of the text of the *Dies irae* movement. Commissioned under mysterious circumstances and composed during his final weeks, Mozart came to look upon this Requiem Mass as music for his own funeral.

KEY TERMS

Singspiel	trouser role	Requiem Mass
Lorenzo da Ponte	ensemble finale	*Dies irae*

Chapter

49

The Early Music of Beethoven

In November 1792, Ludwig van Beethoven, then twenty-one years of age, arrived in Vienna to study with Joseph Haydn and to expand his musical horizons (Map 49-1). He had traveled some five hundred fifty miles from his hometown in Bonn, where he had already showed such prodigious skill as a composer and pianist that his teacher compared him to Mozart. From this time until his death in 1827, Beethoven remained a permanent resident of Vienna. His career there coincided with a period of political and social unrest and changing musical tastes, and it was beset by the composer's own personal adversities.

Despite these distractions, Beethoven created a body of musical works that is recognized throughout the world as unique and enduring. His compositions have

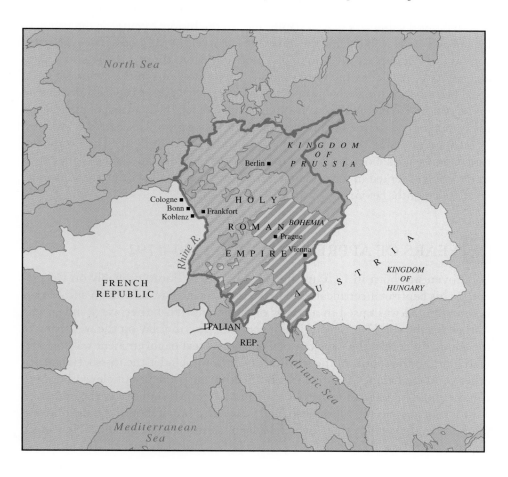

❋ MAP 49-1
Beethoven's world, c1803.

continually delighted and inspired listeners, with no periods of waning interest, no significant revisionist thinking that has questioned their importance, no lessening of their profundity after repeated hearings. His music has shown a universal greatness, equally perceptible to audiences of all periods and in all places. It is as important to classical music in the twenty-first century as it was in the twentieth or nineteenth, and its appeal is as evident to listeners in Asia and Africa as it is to those in Austria, where the music was created.

Why is it that we all like Beethoven's music? One reason is that he wrote music with all of us in mind, whatever our tastes or background. People who are new to classical music will all respond to his Fifth Symphony because he composed this work so that it would be likable by just such listeners. It is full of life (we all know what that's like) and everyone can follow its pacing, marked by passages of rest that erupt into great climaxes, or moments when two conflicting forces seem to have locked horns, ultimately leading to the triumph of the more positive of these opponents.

Beethoven seemed to address more experienced listeners in his string quartets, and others still in works like the *Missa solemnis* and Piano Sonata in C Minor, Op. 111, which hint at some higher universe beyond the one of struggle and conflict so realistically portrayed in the Fifth Symphony. Another appealing thing about Beethoven's music is its balanced mixture of elements, like a fine wine that has just the right proportion of sugar and tartness. One moment Beethoven will write the most exquisite melody—think of the slow movement of the "Pathétique" Piano Sonata—and the next moment he puts any thought of beautiful melody aside so as to concentrate on motion and rhythm, which can erupt in such muscular displays as in the scherzo of the Ninth Symphony. Beethoven wrote music for everyone.

In light of Beethoven's special significance to the history of music, a discussion of his life and works will occupy the next three chapters of this book. These chapters conform to a customary division of his creative life into three periods—early, middle, and late—each of which is set off by important events in the composer's personal life and by distinguishable musical styles. The first period begins at the time of his arrival in Vienna in 1792 and extends until about 1802, a time of crisis when the composer had to face the prospect of losing his hearing. This period is preceded by an apprenticeship during the composer's earlier years in Bonn. The middle period extends from about 1802 until roughly 1814, and the late period—filled with works unprecedented in form and range of expression—follows this and continues until only months before his death on 26 March 1827.

❃ YEARS OF APPRENTICESHIP: 1770–1792

Beethoven was born in 1770 in the German city of Bonn, probably on December 16; his baptismal certificate is dated the following day. Like Bach and Mozart before him, he was raised in a family of musicians. His father was a singer who worked for the ruler (or "elector") of an archdiocese that lay on the west bank of the Rhine River near the large city of Cologne. Its seat of government was some fifteen miles to the south, in the smaller city of Bonn. Under the instruction of another court musician, **Christian Neefe,** Beethoven at the age of eleven began to compose, and he increasingly attracted attention for his skill as a keyboard player.

In 1784 a new elector, Maximilian Franz, came to power in Bonn, and the thirteen-year-old Beethoven was then given a salary as assistant court organist. He seemed destined to follow in the footsteps of his father and grandfather—and those of established musicians like Joseph Haydn—as a court employee. The music-loving Maximilian Franz had strong ties to Vienna and its musicians. He was a brother of the reigning Hapsburg monarch, Joseph II, and he had grown up in Vienna, where he knew and admired Mozart. ("He thinks the world of me," Mozart smugly reported to his father.)

In 1787 the elector sent Beethoven to Vienna to study with Mozart, although Beethoven almost immediately returned, due to the illness of his mother. After her death later in that year, he was forced to take over the guardianship of his two younger brothers and his alcoholic father, although his musical achievements continued. Carl Junker heard Beethoven play in 1791 and published this report:

> I heard him extemporize in private; yes, I was even invited to propose a theme for him to vary. The greatness of this amiable, light-hearted man, as a virtuoso, may in my opinion be safely estimated from his almost inexhaustible wealth of ideas, the altogether characteristic style of expression in his playing, and the great execution which he displays. . . . In short, he is more for the heart—equally great, therefore, as an *adagio* or *allegro* player. Even the members of this remarkable [Bonn] orchestra are, without exception, his admirers, and all ears when he plays.[1]

In 1792 Maximilian Franz again attempted to invest in the future of music at his court by financing another trip for Beethoven to Vienna. Mozart had died the year before, so this time arrangements were made for him to have lessons with Joseph Haydn, who had examined some of Beethoven's recent music on a leg of his first trip to London in 1790–1792. Bonn's young genius left for Vienna in the first days of November, never to return. Just before his departure, Count **Ferdinand Waldstein,** one of his most influential supporters in Bonn, wrote prophetically in Beethoven's album:

> Dear Beethoven! You are going to Vienna in fulfillment of your long frustrated wishes. The genius of Mozart is mourning and weeping over the death of its pupil. It found refuge but no occupation with the inexhaustible Haydn. Through him it wishes to form a union with another. With the help of assiduous labor you will receive *Mozart's spirit from Haydn's hands.*[2]

Waldstein's sentiments show the esteem in which Mozart's works were held in Bonn—an admiration that Beethoven fully shared—but a surprisingly condescending judgment of Haydn, then widely recognized as the world's greatest living composer.

Beethoven was well-advanced as a composer when he went to Haydn. He had written about fifty works during his apprenticeship period in Bonn and, although many of these were published at the time, none is a mature composition. Most involve piano, including sonatas, variations, a concerto, small pieces, and chamber music. There are also works for winds, songs, and arias, and, most important, two cantatas whose texts observe the death in 1790 of Emperor Joseph II and the crowning of his successor, Leopold II. Most of these compositions are now identified by **WoO numbers** (*Werk ohne Opuszahl,* work without opus number), which were assigned to them in the standard catalog of Beethoven's music compiled in 1955 by Georg Kinsky and Hans Halm.

❀ BEETHOVEN'S WORLD IN 1792

Beethoven's trip from Bonn to Vienna in November 1792 coincided with the beginning of a twelve-year period of warfare between France and its European neighbors. Only months before, France was gripped by a general insurrection, after which its monarchy was abolished and a republican form of government established. These measures brought to a climax the **French Revolution,** which had begun in 1789. Armies from German lands, primarily Prussia and Austria, marched on France at this time to try to protect the French king and the Austrian provinces in what is now Belgium, but they failed in both objectives.

Beethoven's trip to Vienna was filled with adventure. The roads on which he traveled to the east were occupied by German soldiers heading west to meet the French. Near the city of Koblenz (just south of Bonn), Beethoven's carriage made a mad dash through army troops, for which Beethoven gratefully gave his driver an extra payment.

When Beethoven reached Vienna after about a week, he was temporarily separated from warfare, although by 1805 French armies had reached even Vienna. His friends in Bonn were not so lucky, since the city was quickly overrun by the French. His former employer Maximilian Franz permanently fled into exile.

VIENNA: 1792–1802

Ferdinand Waldstein's slighting attitude toward the "inexhaustible Haydn" seems to have carried over into Beethoven's studies, which he undertook with Haydn for about one year after arriving in the Austrian capital. Although outwardly maintaining a respectful attitude, Beethoven made it no secret to friends that he was disappointed with the instruction he was receiving from Haydn, and he later sought out more systematic training in counterpoint from Johann Albrechtsberger and Johann Schenk, in violin playing from Ignaz Schuppanzigh, and in vocal composition from Antonio Salieri.

The profession of music in Vienna in 1792 still had many antiquated features when compared to the artistic opportunities available in a city like Paris or London. In Vienna, a serious musical culture existed primarily in the private houses and palaces of the aristocracy. The music-loving nobility sometimes maintained their own private orchestras and chamber ensembles. They hired teachers and coaches, sponsored concerts, presented visiting performers, encouraged new music, and provided a forum for interchange among artists and skilled amateurs. In the public sphere, opera remained the most lucrative genre for a successful composer, and large churches—such as the magnificent Cathedral of St. Stephen in the center of the city—presented music that could be heard by the general public. Public concerts tended to focus on the works of an individual composer or performer, and these were often gala events mixing orchestral and vocal selections in which soloistic playing was typically limited to improvisation. Until well into the nineteenth century, public concerts in Vienna were limited by the lack of a suitable auditorium. Theaters were used for concerts, but they were available only on relatively few dates—primarily during Lent and before Christmas—and they were usually rented directly by a featured artist rather than by any established concert-presenting agency.

Beethoven's preliminary contacts with Bonn's music-loving aristocracy and his irresistible prowess on the piano opened the doors of Vienna's aristocrat musical culture to him. His piano playing—especially his **improvisations**—became legendary. His student **Carl Czerny** recalled his playing:

> Nobody equaled him in the rapidity of his scales, double trills, skips, etc.—not even Hummel. His bearing while playing was masterfully quiet, noble, and beautiful, without the slightest grimace (only bent forward low, as his deafness grew upon him). . . . He made frequent use of the pedals, much more frequent than is indicated in his works.

His playing of the scores of Handel and Gluck and the fugues of Seb. Bach was unique, in that in the former he introduced a full-voicedness and a spirit which gave these works a new shape.[3]

Czerny especially praised Beethoven's legato playing, which he found refreshingly different from the "hammered, detached staccato technique of Mozart's time." Beethoven himself often remarked that he wished to make the piano sing. The instrument that Beethoven preferred during his early period was one made for him by Johann Andreas Streicher and his wife, Nannette Stein. This was considerably smaller and lighter than the modern grand piano, and it used the nuanced "Viennese action" that had small hammers covered with leather and light dampers that were lifted by a knee lever rather than a pedal. Its normal range was from F (two octaves and a fifth below middle C) to F or G five octaves above. The modern piano, by comparison, has a range of more than seven octaves.

PIANO MUSIC AND THE "PATHÉTIQUE" SONATA

During his first decade in Vienna, Beethoven composed primarily for his own instrument, the piano. He wrote twenty of his thirty-two mature piano sonatas between 1794 and 1802, and there are also thirteen sets of variations, numerous small piano pieces, two piano concertos, and chamber music with piano (mainly instrumental sonatas and piano-string trios). The piano sonatas are the centerpieces of this body of works. Here, Beethoven inherited a genre already cultivated by Mozart and Haydn, although from the very beginning—the three sonatas of Opus 2, published in 1796—Beethoven treats the sonata as though confident of his ability to surpass these great forebears. His sonatas have a range of emotion, a diversity of formal structure, and a technical difficulty that is considerably larger than is found in the piano sonatas of Haydn or Mozart. Half of Beethoven's twenty have four movements (the sonatas of Haydn and Mozart never surpass three), and in these cases Beethoven adds a minuet, scherzo, or march as a third movement to enlarge the customary fast/slow/fast three-movement frame. The two sonatas of Opus 27 (the second is the celebrated "Moonlight" Sonata) have the freedom of form characteristic of a **fantasia.** As in the earlier Classical period, most of Beethoven's early piano sonatas are in the major mode, but the six that are in minor keys have an especially passionate character.

One of the most original of the early minor-mode sonatas is the Sonata in C Minor ("Pathétique"), Op. 13, completed in 1798. The title "Pathétique," which was given to the work by Beethoven himself, suggests that the sonata will be emotional and deeply felt, qualities that apparently led Beethoven to introduce many formal novelties. Beethoven's pieces in the key of C minor have certain similarities: most are filled with turbulence and conflict. Frequently—as in the Fifth Symphony and Third Piano Concerto, although not in Opus 13—they end triumphantly in C major. The "Pathétique" Sonata uses the standard sequence of three movements—*allegro* (with slow introduction)/*adagio*/*allegro*—and its first movement is the longest and weightiest of the cycle.

The opening of the first movement was no doubt a surprise for its early listeners. All of the sonatas of Haydn and Mozart, and all of Beethoven's own previous sonatas, begin with a main theme in a fast tempo, but the "Pathétique" Sonata begins instead with a somber and brooding prologue marked *grave.* Haydn's symphonies—an example is his Symphony No. 99 in E♭ Major (see Chapter 46)—often begin with slow introductions that prepare the listener for the principal music to come, but this *grave* is more of an emotive improvisation, one filled with fragmentary ideas, sequences, rapid scales, and harmonies linked by diminished chords. In his opening improvisation, Beethoven uses every inch of the piano keyboard and repeatedly interrupts quiet phrases with *fortissimo* outbursts.

Order is restored at the *allegro molto e con brio*, where a movement in sonata form begins. But Beethoven uses the principle of sonata form in a way that is far from ordinary. An important innovation is his striving for greater continuity throughout the movement and a more seamless integration of its parts, thus avoiding the earlier tendency to compartmentalize a first movement into separate sections. One way that Beethoven achieves this new connectedness is to integrate the slow introduction more fully into the logic of the whole movement. Recall the function of the slow introduction to the first movement of Haydn's Symphony No. 99. Haydn makes the passage introductory, in that its motives only forecast the principal themes that follow in the exposition. They do not explicitly return anywhere in the movement. Beethoven, on the contrary, brings back the *grave* of the "Pathétique" Sonata twice within the body of the movement, just before the development section and before the coda. He also explicitly brings back the first motive from the *grave* within the development section, as shown in Example 49-1, and in this way more fully integrates it into the fabric of the whole movement. In light of these innovations, we must think of the opening *grave* as much a part of the exposition of the sonata form as an introduction to it.

EXAMPLE 49-1

Beethoven's idea of sonata form as a continuous musical argument is also realized in the harmonic dimension, in which the composer finds ways of melding its various parts. For example, in the first movements of Haydn and Mozart, the music normally comes to a full stop at the end of the transition, just before the entrance of the second theme. But, at this point in the "Pathétique" Sonata (measure 51), Beethoven overlays the beginning of the principal second theme with a continuation of harmonic motion that is more characteristic of a transition. As the second theme begins, the fifth degree (B♭) of the new key E♭ is kept in the bass for twelve additional measures as a pedal point, and it arrives on the tonic tone E♭ only at measure 89, with the beginning of another theme.

LISTENING CUE

LUDWIG VAN BEETHOVEN
Piano Sonata in C Minor ("Pathétique," 1798)
First movement, *Grave; Allegro molto e con brio*

CD 8/8
Anthology, No. 139

✿ PIANO CONCERTO NO. 1 IN C MAJOR

In Beethoven's days in Vienna, as earlier in Mozart's, concertos were the primary type of music used by a virtuoso performer in public concerts. These allowed the soloist to show off a command of the instrument, and they revealed the highly prized ability of a player to improvise. For a performer who was also a composer, the genre provided an opportunity to display a full range of creative skills. In each of his major public concerts during his first decade in Vienna, Beethoven played a concerto. During these years he had two of his own concertos at his disposal: Concerto No. 1 in C Major, Op. 15, and Concerto No. 2 in B♭ Major, Op. 19. Confusingly, Concerto No. 2 was composed earlier than Concerto No. 1, but it received the higher number since it was published slightly later. Beethoven gave these early concertos up for publication only after he had used them repeatedly in his concerts, and, after publication, he rarely if ever performed them again.

There are several important differences between the way most modern performers play Beethoven's piano concertos and the way Beethoven himself played them. Judging from the reports of contemporaries, it is likely that Beethoven treated the entire solo part with a greater degree of extemporization than is the case at present, when all performers adhere strictly to the composer's published text and confine improvisation, at most, to cadenzas. Beethoven played his own concertos before they were published, and when he did so, the solo parts were left as incomplete sketches that the composer brought to life in differing ways at the time of a performance. Ignaz von Seyfried recalled turning pages for Beethoven when he first played his Piano Concerto No. 3 in 1803: "He asked me to turn the pages for him; but—heaven help me!—that was easier said than done. I saw almost nothing but empty leaves; at the most on one page or the other a few Egyptian hieroglyphs wholly unintelligible to me scribbled down to serve as clues for him."[4]

Another major difference between then and now is that Beethoven—as well as Mozart and other pianists of the day—played from beginning to end, without falling silent during the passages where the orchestra has the main melodic material. In these tutti sections the soloist became an accompanimental instrument, doubling the basses and playing chords to reinforce the texture. There is much evidence for this practice. Carl Czerny recalled of his first meeting with Beethoven (see Box), during which he played Mozart's Piano Concerto in C Major, K. 503, that Beethoven "played the orchestral melody with his left hand whenever I had purely accompanying passages." This suggests that the normal way of rendering the solo part of a concerto was to play both the principal solo passages and also chords or accompanimental figures during the intervening orchestral moments.

Beethoven's own performances of his concertos were memorable occasions. An impressionable young Czech composer, Václav Tomášek, attended a concert in Prague in 1798 at which Beethoven improvised and performed a concerto. In memoirs published some fifty years later, Tomášek recalled the memories etched by this encounter:

> Beethoven's magnificent playing and particularly the daring flights in his improvisation stirred me strangely to the depths of my soul; indeed I found myself so profoundly bowed down that I did not touch my pianoforte for several days.[5]

The principal work that Tomášek heard at the 1798 concert was Beethoven's Piano Concerto No. 1 in C Major, Op. 15. This composition, like other classical concertos, has three movements—fast/slow/fast—the sequence dominated in weight and length by the first movement. In overall form and character, Beethoven's C-Major Concerto

Carl Czerny Meets Beethoven

Beethoven occasionally taught piano. One of his best students was Carl Czerny (1791–1857), who recalled his initial impressions of Beethoven (Fig. 49-1) when, at the age of ten, he received his first lessons:

. . . His jet-black hair, cut à la Titus, made him look shaggy the way it stood off from his head. Since his beard had not been shaved for several days, the lower part of his swarthy face looked even darker. I also noticed immediately with the power of observation so typical of children that both his ears were stuffed with cotton which seemed to have been dipped in a yellow liquid. But at that time he certainly appeared to be not the least bit hard of hearing. I had to play something right away and since I was too bashful to start with one of his works I played the great C major concerto by Mozart (the one that starts with chords [K. 503]). Beethoven soon took notice, moved close to my chair, and played the orchestral melody with his left hand whenever I had purely accompanying passages. His hands were very hairy and his fingers very broad, especially at the tips. When he expressed satisfaction I felt encouraged enough to play his recently published *Sonate Pathétique* and finally the *Adelaide*, which my father sang with his very respectable tenor voice. When I had finished, Beethoven turned to my father and said, "The boy is talented, I myself want to teach him, and I accept him as my pupil. Let him come several times a week. But most important, get him Emanuel Bach's book on the true

art of clavier playing [*Versuch über die wahre Art das Clavier zu spielen*, 1753–1762], which he must have by the time he comes to see me again. . . ."[6]

Bridgeman Art Library

✺ FIGURE 49-1

Beethoven (age twenty-nine in this engraving) was small in stature and had a dark complexion.

is similar to Mozart's piano concertos from the 1780s (see Chapter 47). Like Mozart, Beethoven brings to his early concertos a great variety of expression. By its very medium, one in which an individual performer interacts with an orchestral group, the concerto has the potential to suggest a drama in which the leading role—played by the soloist—can take on a new persona in every movement.

With its march rhythm, trumpets and drums, and a main theme that begins with a fanfare (Ex. 49-2), the opening movement casts a spotlight on the soloist as a military hero who captures our attention with his swaggering virtuosity. In the slow movement, a passionate *largo* in A♭ major, the soloist exchanges his army uniform for the costume of an operatic diva. Her affective and highly florid melody (Ex. 49-3) melts the very soul of her listeners.

EXAMPLE 49-2

EXAMPLE 49-3

A relatively short and high-spirited finale rounds off the C-Major Concerto, and here the soloist becomes a harlequin in a comic opera, impishly clowning, showing off, and defeating our expectations. The finales of all of Beethoven's concertos—like most of those by Mozart—use a rondo form, or, more accurately, **sonata-rondo form.** Recall the general features of rondo form from Chapter 44. An opening theme returns in the tonic key after each in a series of contrasting themes (called **episodes**). The general design of a rondo is thus **ABAC . . . A.** Rondos were especially favored by French composers during the Baroque period. Their popularity continued throughout the Classical period, at which time they were used both in independent compositions and in movements (especially finales) within longer instrumental cycles. By Beethoven's day, the simple rondo had given way to a more complex design that brought in features of sonata form.

Composers in the Classical period were never in complete agreement as to how this amalgamation of the two forms should occur, but the finale of Beethoven's C-Major Concerto offers a typical example. The top of the following diagram charts the rondo-like features of this movement.

Rondo	A		B	A	C	A	B	A	Coda
Sonata	Exposition:	--------------------				Recap	------		Coda
	main theme	(trans.)	2nd theme						
Key:	I ------ . . .		V ------	I ------	vi ------	I ---			
Measure:	1		66	152	192	311	382	485	505

The rondo theme itself is called **A,** and it is stated four times, each in the tonic key of C major. There are two episodes (**B** and **C**), but only theme **C**—in the minor mode with a dance-like rhythm and heavy beat—has the sharp contrast with its surroundings that we expect of a rondo episode. Compare the beginnings of these three themes in Example 49-4. Theme **B** smoothly fits together with theme **A,** like the two themes in an exposition of a movement in sonata form. But theme **C** makes a clear contrast in comparison to **A,** more in keeping with the tradition of the rondo.

EXAMPLE 49-4

Theme A (mm. 1-6)

Theme B (mm. 65-73, strings only)

Theme C (mm. 191-99, piano only)

ben marcato e sempre stacc.

The outline of sonata form is shown in the lower part of the preceding diagram. Its presence is felt most strongly at the opening and closing of the movement but hardly at all in the middle. Themes **A** and **B** are very similar to the first and second themes of a symphonic exposition, in the tonic and dominant keys, respectively. The middle of the movement has no direct analogy with sonata form, but this re-appears at measure 311 with the beginning of a recapitulation of the principal themes **A** and **B,** both in the home key of C major.

Beethoven reminds us that we are hearing a concerto when he adds a cadenza for the pianist near the movement's end. Beethoven writes this cadenza out, unlike the improvised cadenza in the first movement, and after it we hear one final statement of the rondo theme and an extended coda.

LISTENING CUE

LUDWIG VAN BEETHOVEN
Piano Concerto No. 1 in C Major (1795)
Third Movement, *Allegro*

CD 8/9
Anthology, No. 140

THE ONSET OF DEAFNESS

Around 1798, just when his career as a pianist and composer was thriving as never before, Beethoven came to the terrifying realization that he was losing his hearing. He reported a constant buzzing in his ears, an inability to hear high frequencies, a painful discomfort from loud sounds, and a general lack of clarity in making out spoken words. These are all symptoms of neural degeneration of the inner ear, and their cause in Beethoven's case is unknown.

Understanding of deafness and its treatment was primitive during Beethoven's lifetime. His physicians addressed his condition with warm and cold baths, herbal ointments, and by applying a substance to the arms that made the skin blister. Beethoven himself had heard that galvanism (electric shock) was an effective treatment, and he was convinced that his condition stemmed from his chronic digestive disorders.

Like virtually everyone who has faced a disability, Beethoven primarily feared isolation and the threat of social stigma. At this time, he withdrew into himself and came to live solely in his music, which was still crystal clear in his mind, if no longer so in his ears. Finally, in the summer of 1801, he began to discuss his dilemma with his most trusted acquaintances. He wrote to his childhood friend Franz Wegeler (who had become a physician) in June 1801, describing in detail his symptoms and the treatments he had received.[7] An especially affecting letter was addressed at the same time to his friend Karl Amenda:

> A sad resignation must be my refuge, although indeed I am resolved to rise above every obstacle. But how will it be possible? Yes, Amenda, if my infirmity shows itself to be incurable in half a year, I shall appeal to you. You must abandon everything and come to me. Then I shall travel and you must be my companion (my affliction causes me the least trouble in playing and composing, the most in association with others). . . . *I beg of you to keep the matter of my deafness a profound secret to be confided to nobody no matter whom.*[8]

SUMMARY

In their ability to capture and hold the imagination of listeners throughout the world for more than two centuries, the musical works of Ludwig van Beethoven (1770–1827) are unique in the history of music. Beethoven grew up in the city of Bonn, where he showed prodigious gifts as a pianist (especially in improvisation) and composer. In 1792 he moved to Vienna, where he studied with Joseph Haydn and continue to advance in the path of virtuoso and composer. Beethoven's career is customarily divided into three phases: an early period extends from 1792 until about 1802, a middle period from 1802 until 1812 or somewhat later, and the late period from then until 1826.

In his early period, Beethoven consciously attempted to carry on the styles of music that he had encountered in works by Haydn and Mozart, and he concentrated on compositions for his own instrument, the piano. These include many sonatas, of which the "Pathétique" Sonata, Op. 13, shows the wide range of emotion and formal innovation that would characterize his later music. His Piano Concerto No. 1, Op. 15, adheres closely to the form of the Mozartean piano concerto. Its finale is an example of sonata-rondo form (a mixture of elements from these two standard movement plans), and it exhibits the rollicking high spirits typical of a Classical finale.

KEY TERMS

Christian Neefe	French Revolution	fantasia
Ferdinand Waldstein	improvisation	sonata-rondo form
WoO numbers	Carl Czerny	episode (in a rondo form)

Chapter 50

Beethoven's Middle Period: 1802–1814

Beethoven's anxiety over his deafness only worsened after his appeal to his friends in 1801. In the spring of the following year, at the urging of a physician, he spent time in the quiet town of Heiligenstadt, north of Vienna, and here he wrote a will that he addressed to his two brothers. This document, now known as the **Heiligenstadt Testament,** is far from being a simple instruction for the disposition of property after death, and Beethoven's thoughts were directed not so much to his brothers as to all mankind, present and future. The composer pours out his innermost feelings about himself and his future prospects, explaining his moody and withdrawn personality, his life in the shadow of deafness, and his determination to prevail in the face of such a dire adversity. Excerpts from this remarkable document are presented in the box on the next page.

In addition to explaining his frame of mind, Beethoven also touches in the testament on a view of art that breaks with the past. Art is not a means for providing listeners with a simple pleasure, he says; instead, it is something far higher and more basic to life. Art is what held him back from suicide. His life was not his to take, he says, until he had brought forth the artistic works that he was put on earth to create. Compare this elevated idea of art with the definition of music given by Charles Burney in his 1776 *General History of Music*: "Music is an innocent luxury, unnecessary, indeed, to our existence, but a great improvement and gratification of the sense of hearing."[1] We can only wonder if Beethoven would have turned away from self-destruction if music for him was only "an innocent luxury."

❧ BEETHOVEN'S LIFE AND MUSIC DURING THE MIDDLE PERIOD

It is remarkable that Beethoven in his Heiligenstadt Testament says nothing about deafness being an impediment to his work as a composer. The progress of the disease during his middle period, from about 1802 until about 1814, was slow and intermittent. He continued to play piano in public concerts throughout this time, and at no point during these years was his compositional creativity significantly disrupted. His sometimes depressive and vehement states of mind did not, in general, show through into his music, which continued on the forceful and emotive path that he had already blazed in his "Pathétique" Sonata.

The middle years were Beethoven's most productive and successful period as a composer. Between 1802 and 1814 he wrote seven of his nine symphonies, seven new piano sonatas, the opera *Fidelio,* and some of his most respected chamber music. He continued to write concertos, completing three new piano concertos (for a total of five), and also the Violin Concerto (1806) and Triple Concerto for piano, violin, and cello (1804). This last—a concerto with multiple soloists—is the type of work that Mozart and Haydn called a **symphonie concertante.**

Beethoven continued to make his living as an independent composer and pianist. He sold new works to publishers, gave special gala concerts for his own benefit (the Viennese called these **academies**), and taught piano. In March 1809 his financial prospects were further brightened when he received a substantial lifetime salary from three of his aristocratic patrons, who asked only that he remain a citizen of Vienna.

The Heiligenstadt Testament

Oh you men who think or say that I am malevolent, stubborn, or misanthropic, how greatly do you wrong me. You do not know the secret cause which makes me seem that way to you. From childhood on my heart and soul have been full of the tender feeling of goodwill, and I was ever inclined to accomplish great things. But, think that for six years now I have been hopelessly afflicted, made worse by senseless physicians, from year to year deceived with hopes of improvement, finally compelled to face the prospect of *a lasting malady* (whose cure will take years or perhaps be impossible). Though born with a fiery, active temperament, even susceptible to the diversions of society, I was soon compelled to withdraw myself, to live life alone. If at times I tried to forget all this, oh how harshly was I flung back by the doubly sad experience of my bad hearing. Yet it was impossible for me to say to people, "Speak louder, shout, for I am deaf." Ah, how could I possibly admit an infirmity in the *one sense* which ought to be more perfect in me than in others, a sense which I once possessed in the highest perfection, a perfection such as few in my profession enjoy or ever have enjoyed. . . .

For me there can be no relaxation with my fellow men, no refined conversations, no mutual exchange of ideas. I must live almost alone like one who has been banished, I can mix with society only as much as true necessity demands. If I approach near to people a hot terror seizes upon me and I fear being exposed to the danger that my condition might be noticed. . . . But what a humiliation for me when someone standing next to me heard a flute in the distance and *I heard nothing,* or someone heard a *shepherd singing* and again I heard nothing. Such incidents drove me almost to despair, a little more of that and I would have ended my life—it was only *my art* that held me back. Ah, it seemed to me impossible to leave the world until I had brought forth all that I felt was within me. So I endured this wretched existence—truly wretched for so susceptible a body which can be thrown by a sudden change from the best condition to the very worst. . . .

Recommend *virtue* to your children; it alone, not money, can make them happy. I speak from experience; this was what upheld me in time of misery. Thanks to it and to my art, I did not end my life by suicide— Farewell and love each other.[2]

Giraudon/Art Resource

❀ FIGURE 50-1

Isidor Neugass, portrait of Beethoven, c1806. Although Neugass's portrait shows Beethoven elegantly dressed, the composer was famous for his unkempt appearance.

❀ BEETHOVEN'S SYMPHONIES: NEW PATHS

Beethoven approached the genre of the symphony—the stronghold of Haydn and Mozart—with great caution. He completed his Symphony No. 1 in C Major, a work in the vein of Haydn, only in 1800, toward the end of his first period. Symphony No. 2 in D Major followed in 1802, and much of it was composed at the same time that he wrote his Heiligenstadt Testament, although the symphony reveals none of its angst. Six additional symphonies, Nos. 3–8, followed between 1803 and 1812, and his one remaining symphony, No. 9, comes from the late period, which will be described in the next chapter. In addition to symphonies, Beethoven also wrote orchestral overtures that are performed today as concert works. These include overtures for performances of spoken plays—*Egmont* and *Coriolan* (for plays by Goethe and Heinrich von Collin, respectively) are the best known; four overtures for various versions of his opera *Fidelio*; and an overture to his ballet *Die Geschöpfe des Prometheus* (*The Creatures of Prometheus*, 1801).

In many of the works from his middle period, Beethoven made a conscious effort to go beyond the musical forms and styles of Mozart and Haydn, who heretofore provided his principal models for composition. Carl Czerny recalled a remark that Beethoven had made in 1803: "I am not satisfied with what I have composed up to now. From now on I intend to embark on a new path."[3]

Beethoven's "new path" is especially evident in his symphonies of the middle and late periods, during which the composer rethought almost every aspect of the structure, dimension, and expressive content of the genre as it had earlier existed. For example, he progressively expanded and diversified the makeup of the orchestra itself, giving the medium greater resonance and more diverse color. In the finale of the Fifth Symphony (1808), he brought in three trombones—instruments that earlier were used mainly in operas and church music—and he expanded the woodwind choir by the addition of piccolo and contrabassoon. These instruments also appear in the Ninth Symphony (1824), and here the complement of French horns is expanded to four. Most striking of all in this work is Beethoven's unprecedented use of chorus and solo voices.

The new path is also plain to see in Beethoven's Symphony No. 3 in E♭ Major ("Eroica," or "Heroic," 1802–1805). Its differences from the classical norm are evident primarily in two areas: the enlarged scale on which the work is constructed, and a heightened expressivity that extends into nonmusical areas.

The "Eroica" has the customary four symphonic movements (fast/slow/scherzo/fast) and a conventional large tonal plan, but each movement is far longer than in any previous symphony. The first movement lasts nearly a half-hour, about the same duration as an entire symphony by Mozart or Haydn. The added length is produced by a more thorough probing of basic harmonic and melodic materials, which leads to many formal novelties. The second movement—titled *Marcia funebre* (*Funeral March*)—combines elements of ternary and sonata forms into an extended composite, and the third movement contains the familiar scherzo/trio/scherzo, although with unusual proportions and tonal relationships. The finale consists of an ingenious and high-spirited set of variations upon a theme that Beethoven had used in several earlier compositions, including the ballet *The Creatures of Prometheus*.

The "Eroica" Symphony—by its title clearly a work that deals with heroism—also takes an important step foward in the development of **program music,** that is, instrumental music that overtly expresses nonmusical ideas. Orchestral music in earlier periods sometimes depicted extramusical content. In Antonio Vivaldi's violin concertos called *The Four Seasons* (published c1725) each season is described by a poem printed in the score; the music vividly imitates birds chirping, a thunderstorm, and other natural phenomena. Recall that Haydn's Symphony No. 6—titled *Le Matin* (*Morning*)—contains a witty musical depiction of a sunrise. Carl Ditters von Dittersdorf (1739–1799) wrote symphonies that allude to literary works and other nonmusical matters. But such references are not typical of the classical symphony in general, which, on the surface at least, deals with purely musical issues.

Beethoven's expressive resources in the "Heroic" Symphony go beyond the simple illustrative intentions of his predecessors. Beethoven shaped the poetic content of this symphony at a deeper level by reflecting, both objectively and subjectively, on the idea of the hero. Throughout his life, Beethoven was attracted to stories concerning heroes, exceptional individuals who, through struggle and fearless persistence, improve the lot of mankind. During his middle period, he often used such stories as the basis for musical compositions. His ballet *The Creatures of Prometheus* deals with the Greek mythological figure Prometheus, who stole fire from the gods and presented it to mankind despite ghastly punishments. The opera *Fidelio* (discussed momentarily) focuses on the heroine Leonore, who fearlessly frees her husband from an unjust imprisonment.

Beethoven's interest in the hero came into focus, as it did for many European intellectuals and artists of the day, in the figure of Napoleon Bonaparte (1769–1821). Napoleon had attracted widespread admiration as a commander of French armies in the aftermath of the French Revolution, when France was continually at war with its neighboring countries. The composer's imagination was fired by what Napoleon seemed to represent: a fearless warrior and a new type of political leader who could realize for all mankind the ideals of the Revolution, notably "Liberty, Equality, Brotherhood," its most memorable slogan.

Beethoven composed his Third Symphony as a work, not simply dedicated to Napoleon, but one that would bear his name and contain music embodying aspects of his heroism. By the fall of 1803, the symphony was sufficiently advanced for negotiations to begin on its sale to a publisher. These were undertaken on the composer's behalf by his student Ferdinand Ries, who wrote to the publisher Simrock concerning the new symphony: "In his own testimony it is the greatest work he has yet written," Ries assured. "He will entitle it 'Bonaparte.'"

But in 1804 Beethoven's idealism concerning Napoleon was shattered when Napoleon had himself declared Emperor of France. Beethoven eliminated the title "Bonaparte" and, for the first edition of the symphony in 1806, gave its name (in Italian) as the "Heroic Symphony [*Sinfonia eroica*] . . . Composed to celebrate the memory of a great man." The extent to which the music of the symphony deals specifically with Napoleon or with a more general notion of heroism has been endlessly debated. Certainly, the work's epic length, the presence of a funeral march in which mankind evidently mourns a fallen hero, and the re-use of a theme in the finale from *The Creatures of Prometheus*—a ballet dealing with a hero—relate, though in differing ways, to Beethoven's idealized memory of Napoleon and to the subject of heroism. No specific narrative is spelled out in the music.

The second movement, "Funeral March," is one of the symphony's most distinctive parts, especially in its poetic content. Its music vividly paints an objective image, a funeral march, and at the same time it conveys a personal reaction to that image. Shortly before he began to compose the "Eroica" Symphony, Beethoven had written several funeral marches for piano. The "Funeral March on the Death of a Hero"—the title given to the slow movement of the Piano Sonata in A♭ Major, Op. 26 (1801)—is especially relevant. Both this movement and the symphonic one begin with a theme in the low-to-middle register, in minor mode, with a somber dotted march rhythm. Both movements have a large-scale tonal motion from minor to major and back, and they share evocations of the sound of muffled drums.

These are all objective musical attributes of a funeral. But the symphonic movement goes considerably beyond the piano sonata by representing the sorrowful feelings of an observer who contemplates the funeral. This observer's own emotional response shapes the musical content. For example, the principal theme returns at the end, fragmented and dislocated in meter and accompaniment (Ex. 50-1). This transformation suggests the mood, broken and grieving, of one who follows the hero's casket. In this concluding passage, Beethoven does not simply draw a musical portrait of a funeral but reproduces the image of the hero in the mind of the mourner.

EXAMPLE 50-1

Main Theme: Violin I, mm. 1-8

Adagio assai
sotto voce

Final Appearance: Violin I, mm. 238-46

sotto voce   sempre più **p**

Beethoven's use of the orchestral instruments allows him to convey more vividly the images and feelings associated with a funeral. He uncouples the basses from the cellos (in virtually all of his earlier orchestral music they usually double each other at the octave), and this permits him to manipulate the sound of the basses in several distinctive ways, for example, making groaning noises at the movement's opening. He repeatedly gives plaintive melodies to the oboe, which among all the instruments of the orchestra most evokes the human voice, and this contributes to a personalized tone of bereavement. The form of Beethoven's funeral march is irregular, which is not surprising in a work of such protracted scale. It has the general features of a large ternary form whose middle part is in the major mode, while outer parts are in the minor. But prior to the reprise (m. 173), Beethoven inserts an intense fugato passage that is more at home in sonata form than ternary.

The greatly extended dimensions and striking contrasts of the "Eroica" Symphony baffled its early listeners. Following a performance in 1805 one journalist commented: "This reviewer belongs to Herr van Beethoven's sincerest admirers, but in this composition he must confess that he finds too much that is glaring and bizarre, which hinders greatly one's grasp of the whole, and a sense of unity is almost completely lost."[4] After two hundred years of hearing and studying the work, we no longer share this reviewer's perplexity because we have absorbed many of the ways that Beethoven achieves coherence in the work despite its protracted length and diversity. One of the most important of these unifying elements—also present in the C-Major Piano Concerto—is the interlocking of themes throughout the entire four-movement symphony by underlying common elements. Notice, for example, the relation between the principal subject of the fugato in the Funeral March and the first phrase of this movement's main theme (Ex. 50-2). Although outwardly different, the two phrases have a perceptible similarity created by a common intervallic scaffold, which consists of an ascending fourth followed by an ascending minor third (bracketed in the example). Such underlying relationships also connect themes in different movements. Compare the principal theme from the middle part of the Funeral March with the famous opening theme of the first movement (Ex. 50-3). Here the common element is the ascending major triad. The effect of such latent interrelationships is to bring all moments of the symphony together into a coherent, though varied, musical argument and to make the work—to use Richard Wagner's description of his own operas—something spoken in one breath.

EXAMPLE 50-2

Main Theme: Violin I, mm. 1-2

Fugato Subject: Violin II, mm. 114-117

EXAMPLE 50-3

Funeral March: Oboe, mm. 69-71

First Movement: Cello, mm. 3-6

 LISTENING CUE

LUDWIG VAN BEETHOVEN
Symphony No. 3 ("Eroica," 1802–1805)
Second movement (Funeral March), *Adagio assai*

CD 8/10
Anthology, No. 141

THE OPERA *FIDELIO*

When he began his second decade in Vienna, Beethoven had conquered the world of instrumental music, and he then turned to the new challenge of composing large vocal genres. First he completed an oratorio *Christus am Oelberge* (*Christ on the Mount of Olives*, 1803), and then he took up the writing of opera—the acid test for an ambitious composer of the early nineteenth century. The operas staged in Vienna around 1800 came from an international repertory in which Italian comic works remained, as in Mozart's day, the most popular. Beethoven had little interest in this genre. He later dismissed the comic operas of Gioachino Rossini for their appeal to "the frivolous and sensuous spirit of the time." Operas in German that continued the tradition of *Singspiel*—such as Mozart's ever-popular *Magic Flute*—were increasingly well-received, and Beethoven was more sympathetic to this type. He was also attracted to new French operas, such as those by Luigi Cherubini (1760–1842), which were successfully produced in German translations in Vienna just after the turn of the century.

Synopsis of *Fidelio*

Fidelio is set in a state prison in Spain. Leonora has disguised herself as a man and taken a job as assistant to the jailer, Rocco, hoping to find her husband, Florestan. He has been wrongly imprisoned by his old rival Don Pizarro, the prison governor. At the very sight of the evil Pizarro, Leonore recoils. "Monster!" she mutters. Compassionately, she asks Rocco to let the prisoners walk freely in the courtyard.

The curtain rises on Act 2 to reveal Florestan's underground cell. Rocco and Leonora descend into the cell to clear out an old well to serve as Florestan's grave, since Pizarro has decided to murder him. Rocco signals Pizarro, who enters wearing a cloak, his dagger drawn. Just as he is about to stab Florestan, Leonora rushes forward, flings herself upon her husband, and cries out "First kill his wife!" As Pizarro runs off, the bewildered Florestan asks Leonora "What have you done for me?" "Nothing, my Florestan," she replies.

All reassemble in the courtyard to greet Don Fernando, a minister of state, who has come, he says, as a brother, not a tyrant. He is astonished to find his old friend Florestan, and Pizarro is led away to answer for his treachery. Everyone praises the goodness of God and the heroic bravery of Leonora.

Beethoven would have been especially familiar with Cherubini's opera *Les deux journées* (*The Two Days*, 1800). It was staged in the summer of 1803 simultaneously in Vienna's two leading opera houses, and Beethoven was then residing in one of them, the Theater-an-der-Wien, where he was at work on an opera text by the theater's owner, Emanuel Schikaneder. The libretto of *Les deux journées*, written by Jean-Nicolas Bouilly, apparently attracted the composer on both a personal and an artistic level. Its story—involving conflict among ruthless aristocrats, helpless political prisoners, and honest workers—conjured up recent memories of the revolutionary years. Its leading characters embody the clear-cut virtues that Beethoven said had sustained him during his suicidal crisis at the time of the Heiligenstadt Testament, and these characters engage in an easily understood morality play in which heroic values win over evil ones. The action is filled with derring-do, which was sure to please its audiences. Beethoven must also have seen himself in Bouilly's character Armand, an innocent man who is wrongly persecuted and ultimately imprisoned, just as Beethoven was hounded by his physical disabilities and imprisoned by deafness.

Beethoven put aside Schikaneder's libretto when he found another one by Bouilly called *Léonore, ou l'amour conjugal* (*Leonore, or Conjugal Love*), that was constructed according to the same formula as *Les deux journées*. Even though *Léonore* had already been set to music by several opera composers, Beethoven had it translated into German for his own use, and it became the basis for his opera *Fidelio*, which he completed in 1805.

Fidelio received its premiere at the Theater-an-der-Wien in November 1805, a time when Vienna was occupied by French troops and many of Beethoven's aristocratic patrons were in hiding. The few who heard the work agreed that it was not successful on stage. One reviewer commented: "As a rule there are no new ideas in the vocal pieces, they are mostly too long, the text repeats itself endlessly, and finally the characterization fails remarkably." Even though Beethoven despised music critics, he must have recognized some truth in these remarks. Before its revival some four months later in 1806, he revised the opera and shortened it from three to two acts. But he was still dissatisfied and withdrew the work after only two performances. A second revision was made before its revival in 1814, and this is the version that is generally performed today.

For each of the three versions of the opera, Beethoven wrote a different overture. The original is now called *Leonore* Overture No. 2 (1805); *Leonore* Overture No. 3

was composed for the 1806 production. Both take the title *Leonore* from Beethoven's provisional title for the opera as a whole. *Leonore* Overture No. 1 was composed around 1808 for a planned revival of the opera in the city of Prague, and the definitive 1814 version is begun by the so-called Overture to *Fidelio*. Today, the brilliant *Leonore* Overture No. 3 usually precedes the opera's second act or the final courtyard scene of Act 2. This is a questionable practice that was adopted by German conductors (including Gustav Mahler) in the late nineteenth century.

The musical form of *Fidelio*—unlike the forms encountered in Beethoven's instrumental music—does not deviate from the late classical model encountered in Mozart's *Magic Flute* and his other German operas. Following an overture, the acts of *Fidelio* are subdivided into a succession of distinct musical numbers, primarily aria-like solos, ensembles (duets, trios, and quartets), and choruses. Between these, spoken dialogue advances the story. The texts of the arias reflect on some static idea or emotion, and these are often introduced by a passage set in orchestrally accompanied recitative. The ensembles present contrasting or conflicting viewpoints among several characters, while the choruses offer a unified viewpoint by a group of like-minded people. The acts are each ended by a longer and sectionalized number called a "finale," in which ensemble singing dominates but choral and soloistic passages are often included. In these, the plot is brought to a point of climax or resolution. At the beginning of Act 2, Beethoven writes **melodrama,** a special type of operatic number associated with French theater. Here the voices speak, alternating with or accompanied by short fragments of orchestral music.

Leonora's principal music occurs in her great aria "Abscheulicher!" ("Monster!") from Act 1. She has overheard Pizarro and Rocco talk about murdering the special prisoner who is kept underground, and she is cast into a state of agitation because she suspects the prisoner is her husband. Imagining a beautiful rainbow, she contains her emotions and invites the star of hope to guide her onward. Finally, she takes command of herself and trusts in her own powers of duty and love.

The aria has a two-part design that came into widespread use in operas of the early nineteenth century. This form has no generally accepted name, although "cavatina and cabaletta," "recitative and aria," "scene and aria," and "double aria" have all been tried. The first part begins with an introductory passage in which Leonore's unsettled emotions are depicted by a recitational melody with wide leaps, disjunct phrases, and sudden shifts in tempo, tonality, and mode (Ex. 50-4a). The music then settles into a firm, slow "first tempo" with a lyrical melody and stable key (Ex. 50-4b). The second part of the aria (the **cabaletta**) is fast, virtuosic, and conclusive, and its main melody is heard twice, with connective materials between (Ex. 50-4c).

EXAMPLE 50-4

(continued on next page)

Come, Hope, let the last star not disappear for the weary one.

I follow an inner drive; I waver not; the duty of true conjugal love strengthens me.

This multipartite form allows for an element of dramatic action to enter into the aria—a musical number that usually brought the action of earlier operas to a standstill. The formal succession recitative/slow tempo/fast cabaletta mirrors the transformation of the character Leonore at this moment, as she moves from a tentative condition, racked by emotion, to a state of resolution from which she will not deviate until her husband is freed.

✿ AFFAIRS OF THE HEART: THE IMMORTAL BELOVED

Throughout his early and middle periods, Beethoven was involved in many love affairs. These were usually short in duration, although several led to proposals of marriage. One such was made to Magdalena Willmann, a singer whom Beethoven had known in Bonn. She declined his offer because—according to the recollections of her niece—"he was so ugly, and half crazy!"[5] Later, Beethoven's marriage proposal to a teenage piano student, Therese Malfatti, met with the same negative outcome.

Beethoven's Letter to the Immortal Beloved

Though still in bed, my thoughts go out to you, my Immortal Beloved [*unsterbliche Geliebte*], now and then joyfully, then sadly, waiting to learn whether or not fate will hear us—I can live only wholly with you or not at all— Yes, I am resolved to wander so long away from you until I can fly to your arms and say that I am really at home with you, and can send my soul enwrapped in you into the land of spirits— Yes, unhappily it must be so— You will be the more contained since you know my fidelity to you. No one else can ever possess my heart—never—never— Oh God, why must one be parted from one whom one so loves. And yet my life in V[ienna] is now a wretched life— Your love makes me at once the happiest and the unhappiest of men— At an age I need a steady, quiet life—can that be so in our connection? . . . Be calm, only by a calm consideration of our existence can we achieve our purpose to live together—Be calm—love me—today—yesterday—what tearful longings for you—you—you—my life—my all—farewell.—Oh continue to love me—never misjudge the most faithful heart of your beloved.

ever thine
ever mine   L[udwig].[6]
ever ours

One of Beethoven's most often played piano pieces, "Für Elise," may have been written for Therese Malfatti and titled "Für Therese"—her name then misread when the piece was published in 1867. (Beethoven's handwriting was sometimes virtually illegible.)

In these early affairs of the heart, Beethoven—consciously or not—seems to have directed his interest toward women with whom no lasting relationship was possible. But around 1811, toward the end of the middle period, he became involved in a far different sort of affair. It is known solely from an extraordinary letter found among his papers after his death. In the letter Beethoven addresses an unnamed woman, whom he refers to as **"Immortal Beloved,"** to whom he speaks in a passionate though conflicted voice that sometimes lapses into incoherence (see Box).

The letter long posed a riddle for Beethoven scholars. It is not certain if it was ever actually mailed, no year for it is given, and its recipient is not identified. Who, then, is the Immortal Beloved? A convincing answer came in 1972 from the Beethoven authority Maynard Solomon, who persuasively identified the lady in question as Antonie Brentano (1780–1869; Fig. 50-2). Solomon also confirmed that the letter was written in the summer of 1812. When she met Beethoven in Vienna in 1810, Antonie Brentano had married into a well-known German literary family and was the mother of four children. Beethoven became a regular visitor to the family's Vienna residence, and Antonie developed a deep admiration for him: "He walks godlike among the mortals," she remarked in a letter to her brother-in-law in 1811. No other details of their relationship are known, although the context of the letter suggests that Brentano was prepared to leave her husband and to live with Beethoven, which the composer seems unwilling to accept despite his passionate response to her. Shortly after writing his impassioned letter, Beethoven had a final reunion with her and her family in the Czech resort of Karlsbad. Then, in the fall of 1812, she moved with her husband to Frankfurt and saw no more of the composer.

The significance of the episode of the Immortal Beloved for Beethoven's music is uncertain. In general—as in the crisis of deafness—Beethoven was adept at separating his personal life from his music. But certainly the

🌿 FIGURE 50-2

Joseph Carl Stieler, portrait of Antonie Brentano (1808). Antonie Brentano was Beethoven's "Immortal Beloved," whose willingness to love the composer unconditionally forced him to a new level of self-realization.

affair was deeply significant for Beethoven's consciousness of himself. From this point onward he accepted the fact that he would live alone, and he had no other romantic contacts with women. The incident caused him more than ever to live in his music, especially as deafness continued to descend upon him. His passionate relation with the Immortal Beloved marked for him a moment of self-realization, and it helped to formulate the emotional background for Beethoven's final period of creativity.

SUMMARY

Beethoven's "middle period" extends from about 1802 to 1814. His music of this time includes symphonies, concertos, sonatas, chamber works, and the opera *Fidelio*. In much of this music—the Symphony No. 3 in E♭ Major ("Eroica"), for example—Beethoven consciously set out to write in a novel style that was not so reliant as before on models from Mozart, Haydn, or other predecessors. The "Eroica" Symphony is far longer than earlier symphonies, which requires many formal innovations, and its intense expressivity encompasses extramusical ideas. Specifically, the work expresses Beethoven's admiration for heroism, which he once believed to be embodied by Napoleon Bonaparte. The original title of the symphony was *Bonaparte,* but this was changed to "Heroic" Symphony ("Sinfonia eroica") after Napoleon declared himself emperor.

Beethoven's opera *Fidelio* went through three versions (1805, 1806, and 1814), of which the last is considered the definitive one. Based on a French libretto, the work takes a conservative approach to form and genre that Beethoven inherited from German opera of the late eighteenth century. *Fidelio* consists of a succession of musical numbers—solos, ensembles, and choruses—separated by spoken dialogue.

KEY TERMS

Heiligenstadt Testament	program music	cabaletta
symphonie concertante	melodrama	"Immortal Beloved"
academy		

Chapter 51

After the Congress of Vienna: Beethoven's Late Music

In the spring of 1814, following twelve years of nearly continuous warfare, the allied forces of Austria, Great Britain, Russia, and Prussia finally conquered the armies of France. The French emperor, Napoleon Bonaparte, abdicated his throne and fled to the Mediterranean island of Elba. To celebrate this long-sought victory, Emperor Francis I, King of Austria, invited leaders from all of Europe to meet in Vienna, where they would redraw the boundaries of their continent and reestablish principles of legitimate rule. This **Congress of Vienna** began in September 1814 and lasted into the following summer.

MUSIC AT THE CONGRESS OF VIENNA

The Congress proved to be as much a gala celebration as a diplomatic conference. It brought more than 100,000 visitors to Vienna, then a city of about 250,000, and entertainment was widely available in the form of concerts, masked balls, banquets, and hunting expeditions. The visiting French poet Auguste de La Garde recalled a concert of an orchestra of a hundred pianos, hosted by Emperor Francis in the Imperial Palace:

> In one of the vastest halls, that of the States, there were a hundred pianos on which professors and amateurs performed a concert. [Antonio] Salieri, the composer of *Les Danaides*, was the conductor of that gigantic orchestra. To tell the truth, however, save for the general scene, which in all these fêtes was always dazzling, that matchless charivari, in spite of the superior talent of the maestro directing it, was more like a huge display of strength and skill than a concert of good taste.[1]

For many of the dignitaries, the trip to Vienna was an opportunity to hear the music of and even personally to meet Beethoven, recognized by this time as the world's greatest living composer. They could attend performances of his opera *Fidelio* at the Kärntnertor Theater, and Beethoven obligingly churned out several new works celebrating the occasion of the congress. He was not at all averse to making money from the festive events. On 29 November 1814, he presented a gala concert for his own benefit that filled the huge Redoutensaal (grand ballroom) in the Imperial Palace. Vienna's leading musicians volunteered to play in the orchestra, which Beethoven conducted in a performance of his Symphony No. 7 and two lesser works appropriate to the occasion—his *Battle Symphony* (a musical depiction of Wellington's victory over the French at Vittoria) and a new cantata titled *Der glorreiche Augenblick* (*The Glorious Moment*). Among the royalty present at the concert was Frederick William III, King of Prussia. Louis Spohr played violin in the orchestra that day, and he recalled Beethoven's eccentric way of conducting, no doubt a product of his near total deafness:

> Beethoven had accustomed himself to give the signs of expression to his orchestra by all manner of extraordinary motions of his body. So often as a *Sforzando* occurred, he tore his arms which he had previously crossed upon his breast, with great vehemence asunder. At a *piano*, he bent himself down, and the lower, the softer he wished to have it. Then when a *crescendo* came, he raised himself again by degrees, and upon the commencement of the *forte* sprang bolt upright. To increase the forte yet more, he would sometimes, also, join in with a shout to the orchestra, without being aware of it.[2]

 BEETHOVEN'S LIFE AND WORKS
IN HIS LATE PERIOD

The years around the time of the Congress of Vienna were relatively fallow for Beethoven. Beginning about 1816 his creativity reawakened. He began composing piano sonatas, after which he returned to orchestral works, a Mass, and string quartets. Between 1816 and 1822 Beethoven wrote his last five piano sonatas, then in 1823 an imposing set of Thirty-Three Variations on a Waltz by [Anton] Diabelli (Fig. 51-1). As if to counterbalance the massive scale of these compositions, he also wrote two important collections of small pieces, or **bagatelles,** for piano, Opus 119 and Opus 126 (1822–1824). His *Missa solemnis* (High Mass) in D Major was completed in 1823, just before the epic Symphony No. 9 in 1824. For the first time in the history of the genre of the symphony, Beethoven introduces, into the finale of

FIGURE 51-1

Portrait of Beethoven, by Ferdinand Waldmüller, in 1823, the year that Beethoven composed the *Diabelli* Variations. According to his assistant, Anton Schindler, the composer lacked the patience to sit for this portrait. "He would repeatedly stand up, pace the floor irritably, and go to his writing-table in the next room."

Erich Lessing/Art Resource, NY

the Ninth Symphony, chorus and solo voices. They sing a poem by Friedrich Schiller, "An die Freude" ("To Joy"; the poem is usually referred to as "Ode to Joy"). Beethoven's final compositions were five string quartets, composed from 1824 to 1826. Beethoven left behind no major compositions close to completion, although he had made a few sketches for a string quintet and a symphony. The latter sketches have recently been assembled into a "Symphony No. 10," which was recorded and issued as a work by Beethoven, but in reality has little to do with him.

Beethoven's life during his late period was beset by personal crisis, increased deafness, and failing health. From 1818 his hearing had declined to the point where he could no longer understand speech, so he communicated by way of **conversation books.** A person wishing to speak to him wrote into a notebook and Beethoven responded either orally or, if privacy was desired, in writing. Some one hundred forty of these uniquely important notebooks still exist.

Despite his deafness, the composer still tried to be involved with the making of music. A touching and pathetic incident occurred during the 1824 premiere of his Ninth Symphony, which Beethoven attempted to conduct with an assistant. The pianist Sigismond Thalberg was in the audience, and he related to Alexander Thayer, Beethoven's biographer, that "after the Scherzo of the 9th Symphony B[eethoven] stood turning over the leaves of his score utterly deaf to the immense applause, and [the soloist Caroline] Unger pulled him by the sleeve, and then pointed to the audience, when he turned and bowed."[3]

String Quartet in B♭ Major, Op. 130

Following the premiere of the Ninth Symphony on 7 May 1824, Beethoven devoted his remaining time to the writing of string quartets. Years earlier, between 1800 and 1810, he had written eleven quartets that continued the genre created almost single-handedly by his teacher Haydn, but he had not returned to the quartet medium since. In November 1822 he received a request from one of his Russian admirers, Prince Nicholas Galitzin, to compose "one, two, or three new quartets for which labor I will be glad to pay you what you think proper."

The offer was accepted with a down payment, and by 1825 Beethoven had completed three quartets (in E♭ major, A minor, and B♭ major) that he dedicated to this Russian patron. His interest in quartet writing continued, and in 1826 he completed two additional quartets (in C♯ minor and F major), these being his final compositions.

The last of the Galitzin quartets, Opus 130 in B♭ Major, revives several notable features from Beethoven's earlier music. As in the "Eroica" Symphony, the themes in different movements throughout the quartet are subtly linked by motivic similarities, which compensate below the musical surface for the considerable contrast in character and material above. Like the first movement of the "Pathétique" Sonata, the first movement of the quartet begins with music in a slow tempo that returns repeatedly later in the movement.

There is also much that is new about the B♭ Quartet that is characteristic of Beethoven's late style. The overall design of the work bypasses the classical four-movement norm, which is replaced by six movements each having a different character. The fifth movement, titled **"Cavatina,"** shows the intense lyricism that characterizes many late works, and the original finale, the so-called **Grosse Fuge (Great Fugue),** is the grandest of the many imposing fugal compositions from Beethoven's final period, when his interest in reviving the contrapuntal style of such predecessors as J.S. Bach was evidently keen.

The Great Fugue is the quartet's most unusual part. It is nearly twenty minutes long, almost double the first movement, which earlier was the longest and most dominating movement of a quartet or a symphony. The Great Fugue is almost entirely free in form, markedly dissonant, and uniquely dense in texture for a string quartet to this time. Arnold Schoenberg wrote about it later: "I have heard many a good musician, when listening to Beethoven's *Great Fugue*, cry out: 'This sounds like atonal music.'" After the B♭ Quartet was completed, premiered, and sent to the publisher, Beethoven replaced the Great Fugue with an alternate finale that was shorter and lighter. The Great Fugue was then published separately as Opus 133. Depending on which finale is used, there are two equally authentic versions of the B♭ Quartet, something unique in Beethoven's entire oeuvre.

Although our attention is nowadays drawn to the finale of the B♭ Quartet, Beethoven's heart was in the fifth movement, which he titled "Cavatina." Karl Holz, who was Beethoven's personal assistant at the time, and who played violin in the earliest performances of the work, wrote in 1857 to one of Beethoven's biographers: "For him the crown of all of his quartet movements and his very favorite piece was the Cavatina. . . . Truly, he composed it amid tears of sadness, and he assured me that never before had any of his own music had this effect on him and that even the thinking back on it brought him new tears."[4]

The title Cavatina comes from operatic music. For the German composer of the day it denoted an aria that was slow, lyric, and simple in structure. This describes the Cavatina of the quartet, except that the singer's role is taken over by the first violin. Beethoven even gives the instrument places to breathe and to rest, while the melody is echoed at these moments by the second violin. In the middle of its three sections, the music moves into the key of C♭ major, at the extreme flat side of the tonal spectrum, which for Beethoven is often a sign of maximal affective content. At this point the emotions seem to overwhelm the singer, whose part is marked *beklemmt* (tormented) and whose line dissolves into a rhythm of sobs above throbbing triplets in the accompaniment (Ex. 51-1). We can readily understand Beethoven's own emotional reaction to this music.

EXAMPLE 51-1

🔘 LISTENING CUE

LUDWIG VAN BEETHOVEN   CD 8/11
String Quartet in B♭ Major (1826)   Anthology, No. 142
Fifth movement (Cavatina), *Adagio molto espressivo*

The *Missa solemnis*

In the spring of 1819, Beethoven learned that his student **Archduke Rudolph**—a brother of the Emperor, and long one of Beethoven's most generous patrons—was to be made a cardinal of the Catholic Church and installed as Archbishop of Olomouc, a city north of Vienna. Immediately the composer began planning to honor the Archduke by writing a large-scale Mass—of the type often called "solemn" or "high"—for use at the service of installation, which was to occur on March 9 of the following year. Beethoven wrote to the Archduke: "The day when a high mass of mine shall be performed at the ceremonies for Your Imperial Highness will be for me the most beautiful day of my life."

Of all the major categories of music at this time, however, church music was the one with which Beethoven had the least experience. He had written a Mass in C Major in 1807 and the oratorio *Christ on the Mount of Olives* in 1803, but virtually nothing else. This lack of attention was mainly due to professional circumstances. Unlike Haydn, Beethoven did not work in a situation demanding church music, and his specialities as a composer lay elsewhere. Although nominally a Catholic, Beethoven rarely attended Mass and seemed little interested in enriching music for the liturgy. Still, he maintained an intense and philosophical interest in religions, and he always had a strong spiritual impulse and belief in God as a force in his own life.

As he began to contemplate his new High Mass, or *Missa solemnis*, he apparently studied earlier sacred music—Handel's *Messiah*, Mozart's *Requiem*, works by J.S. Bach, and choral music by Palestrina among other earlier composers—to learn how his predecessors had represented religious ideas musically. His principal formal model was found in the late Masses of Haydn (see Chapter 46), which were large works divided into the five sections of the Ordinary of the Mass (*Kyrie, Gloria, Credo, Sanctus,* and *Agnus dei*). Each of these was subdivided into passages of contrasting tempo, key, and character. The chorus alternates with four solo voices, the latter treated mainly as a small ensemble. Although the richness of orchestral writing suggests a modern style, Haydn often resorts to fugue and counterpoint reminiscent of earlier traditions of church music. Beethoven brought all of these features into his *Missa solemnis.*

Beethoven missed his deadline for the Archduke's service of installation by about three years. The *Missa solemnis* was completed in 1823, and Beethoven—perhaps viewing it as his work for the ages—hatched the idea of holding it back from publication and instead offering manuscript copies to Europe's royalty (at 50 gold ducats each). Louis XVIII of France and Frederick William III of Prussia were among the ten who accepted this offer. Three movements from the *Missa solemnis* were performed at the concert on 7 May 1824, at which the Ninth Symphony also had its premiere, and the first complete performance was arranged a month later by Beethoven's patron, Nicholas Galitzin, in St. Petersburg.

Many listeners to the *Missa solemnis* are first struck by the work's difficulties, sprawling size and tendency toward bombast, and mixture of styles. The *Gloria,* for example, seems almost larger than life, as Beethoven drives the chorus into unrelieved singing in the high register. In the *Agnus dei,* impassioned operatic recitatives stand beside marches and intricate fugatos. Although composed at the same time as the Ninth Symphony and sharing some of the symphony's bravado, the *Missa solemnis* is more complex and idiosyncratic, and for most listeners a harder nut to crack. Beethoven's decidedly experimental frame of mind—always probing the ways that music can relate to the traditional texts of the Mass—mixes unmistakably in this great work with his unrelentingly personal voice. He calls attention to this dichotomy on the very first page of the autograph manuscript (Fig. 51-2). Here he wrote: "Von Herzen—Möge es wieder—zu Herzen gehen!" "From the heart—May it again—go to the heart!"

The first movement, *Kyrie,* is the most conventional of the five. The form is a customary ternary **ABA'**, which follows the tripartite text: Kyrie eleison / Christe eleison / Kyrie eleison (Lord have mercy upon us / Christ have mercy upon us / Lord have mercy upon us). Here and throughout the work, Beethoven uses the interaction of the chorus with the group of four solo voices as a dramatic tool. The chorus suggests the voice of mankind speaking about God—usually exuberant, sometimes full of awe, and almost always unanimous in its sentiments. The solo group represents the voices of individuals, who sometimes echo the excited outcries from the chorus but often produce a more nuanced understanding of God, and seem to teach such thoughts to the chorus.

© Bettmann/CORBIS

❊ FIGURE 51-2

Autograph page from the *Missa solemnis.* Beethoven's musical manuscripts were difficult to read, written in haste and often filled with revisions. The words at the top read "Von Herzen—Möge es wieder—zu [Herzen gehen!]" ("From the heart—May it again—go to the heart!").

LISTENING CUE

LUDWIG VAN BEETHOVEN
Missa solemnis (1823)
Kyrie

CD 8/12
Anthology, No. 143

BEETHOVEN'S DEATH AND FUNERAL

Beethoven's final illness began in December 1826, when his jaundiced appearance suggested liver failure. After writing a will in which he left his entire estate to his nephew, Karl van Beethoven, and after taking the last rites of the Catholic Church, he died in the afternoon of 26 March 1827. On the day of his funeral, a crowd estimated at 20,000 poured into the streets of Vienna to accompany the coffin to the Dreifaltigkeitskirche (Holy Trinity Church) and from there to the cemetery. A funeral oration written by Franz Grillparzer, Austria's leading dramatist, was read:

> . . . He was an artist—and who shall arise to stand beside him? As the rushing behemoth spurns the waves, so did he sweep to the uttermost bounds of his art. From the cooing of the doves to the rolling of thunder, from the craftiest interweaving of well-weighed expedients of art up to that awful pitch where planful design disappears in the lawless whirl of contending natural forces, he had traversed and grasped it all. He who comes after him will not continue him; he must begin anew, for he who went before left off only where art leaves off. [5]

SUMMARY

Beethoven's final period begins from about the time of the Congress of Vienna (1814–1815), which was a celebration of peace and a political conference intended to redraw the political boundaries of Europe following the fall of Napoleon. After this time, Beethoven wrote fewer compositions, but these were in an idiosyncratic style marked by expanded overall designs, intricate fugal composition, lyricism, and an expressivity so intense that it can no longer be restrained by Classical ideas of balance and symmetry. His late compositions include the Ninth Symphony, the *Missa solemnis*, five piano sonatas, the *Diabelli* Variations for piano, and five string quartets.

Summary of Beethoven's Major Compositions
Orchestral Music
    Symphonies Nos. 1–9 (1800–1824)
    5 piano concertos (1795–1811) and 1 concerto for violin (1806)
    Overtures for plays, opera, and ballet, and concert purposes
Chamber Music
    16 string quartets (1800–1826) and the *Grosse Fuge* (1826)
    7 trios for violin, cello, and piano (1795–1811)
    10 sonatas for violin and piano (1798–1815)
    5 sonatas for cello and piano (1796–1818)
Piano Music (solo)
    32 sonatas (1795–1822)
    Variations (including the *Diabelli* Variations, 1823)
Opera and Ballet
    Fidelio (opera: 1805, revised 1806 and 1814)
    The Creatures of Prometheus (ballet: 1801)
Choral Music
    Masses (in C Major 1807, *Missa solemnis* 1823)
    Oratorio: *Christ on the Mount of Olives* 1803
    Symphony No. 9 finale (1824)

KEY TERMS

Congress of Vienna   conversation books   *Grosse Fuge* (*Great Fugue*)
bagatelle   "Cavatina"   Archduke Rudolph

NOTES

Abbreviations

History in Documents   *Music in the Western World: A History in Documents*, ed. Piero Weiss and Richard Taruskin (New York, 1984).

JAMS   *Journal of the American Musicological Society*

Letters of Mozart   Emily Anderson, *The Letters of Mozart and His Family*, ed. and trans. Emily Anderson, 3 vols. (London, 1966).

NG   *The New Grove Dictionary of Music and Musicians*, ed. S. Sadie and J. Tyrrell (London, 2001).

PART IV

Chapter 29   none

Chapter 30   1. This translation to Peri's preface of the score of *Euridice* was kindly provided by Pietro Moretti. 2. The words of Marco da Gagliano (1582-1643) as quoted in *History in Documents*, 176.

Chapter 31   1. Translated from Monteverdi's preface to his eighth book of madrigals as given in the introduction to vol. 8 of G. Francesco Malipiero, ed., *Tutte le opere di Claudio Monteverdi* (Bologna, 1929). 2. *History in Documents*, 185.

Chapter 32   1. Letter of Leopold Mozart of 14 April 1770 as given in *Letters of Mozart*, I, 187.

Chapter 33   1. Michael Talbot, *Vivaldi* (New York, Oxford, Singapore, and Sidney, 1993), 42. 2. Correspondence of Charles de Brosses, translated in H.C. Robbins Landon, *Vivaldi: Voice of the Baroque* (London, 1993), 30. 3. Talbot, *Vivaldi*, 40.

Chapter 34   1. Translated from the preface of Georg Muffat's *Armonico tributo* (Salzburg, 1682). 2. In Froberger's original manuscripts the gigue usually, but not always, precedes the sarabande. Publishers of his music, however, invariably grouped them in the sequence allemande, courante, sarabande, and gigue. It was these posthumous publications that firmly established this as the "standard" order for the dance suite. 3. *The Philosophical Works of Descartes Rendered into English*, by Elizabeth S. Haldane and G.R.T. Ross, 2 vols. (Cambridge, 1973), I, 372, 377. 4. *History in Documents*, 218. 5. Kerala J. Snyder, *Dieterich Buxtehude: Organist in Lübeck* (New York, 1987), 57. 6. Snyder, *Dieterich Buxtehude*, 57–58.

Chapter 35   1. James Anthony, *French Baroque Music from Beaujoyeulx to Rameau* (Portland 1997), 66. 2. Evrard Titon du Tillet, *Second Supplément du Parnasse françois* (Paris, 1755), 791–92. 3. *Dictionnaire universel françois et latin*, 6 vols. (Paris, 1743), I, 1670.

Chapter 36   1. Most fixed-pitched instruments, such as harpsichord and organ, did not use equal temperament in this period, but one kind or another of "mean-tone" temperament which began by adjusting the fifth on C (or perhaps G or F) and proceeding by fifths from there. Thus the keys around C were generally well in tune, but those very far away from them around the circle of fifths, such as F♯, were unpleasantly out of tune. Whether the lute in seventeenth-century France was tuned in mean-tone temperament or equal temperament is not certain. 2. Davitt Moroney, "Prélude non mésuré," *NG*, 20:294. 3. Translated from the French as given in Margery Halford, ed., *L'Art de toucher le clavecin* (Port Washington, NY, 1974), 49.

Musical Interlude 5   1. Handel's letter to Mattheson, cited in Joel Lester, "Recognition of Major and Minor in Germany Music: 1680–1730," *Journal of Music Theory*, 22 (1978): 91–92. 2. Translated from *Traité de l'harmonie* (1722), preface, no page.

Chapter 37   1. An account reported by Sir John Hawkins and reproduced in Michael Burden, *Purcell Remembered* (Portland, OR, 1995), 71–72.

Chapter 38   1. Translated from Johann Mattheson, *Das neu-eröffnete Orchestre* (Hamburg, 1713), 211. 2. H.C. Robins Landon, *Handel and his World* (London, 1984), 88. 3. Charles Burney, *An Account of the Musical Performances in Westminster-Abbey* (New York and London, 1775; rpt. 1979), 27.

Chapter 39   1. *The New Bach Reader*, ed. Hans T. David and Arthur Mendel, rev. Christoph Wolff (New York, 1998), 92–93.

Chapter 40   1. Earlier, when Bach was at Mühlhausen in 1708, the town council sponsored the publication of his Cantata *Gott ist mein König* (BWV 71), but only because the work was in honor of the town council. This was Bach's sole vocal work to be published during his lifetime. 2. *The New Bach Reader*, 399.

PART V

Chapter 41   1. Benjamin Franklin, *Writings*, ed. Albert Henry Smyth, 10 vols. (New York, 1907), VII, 207. 2. Hedwig and E. H. Mueller von Asow, eds., *The Collected Correspondence and Papers of Christoph Willibald Gluck* (London, 1962), 22-24. A slightly different translation is given by Bruce Brown, "Gluck," *NG*, 10:48. 3. Patricia Howard, *C.W. von Gluck: Orfeo* (Cambridge, 1981), 107.

Chapter 42   1. As translated from the German by Robert Gutman, *Mozart: A Social Biography* (New York, 1999), 188. 2. Remark of Charles Burney quoted in Roland Würtz and Eugene K. Wolf, "Mannheim," *NG*, 15:772. Leopold Mozart's assessment is contained in a letter written from Mannheim in July 1763.

Chapter 43   1. Matthew Head, "'If the Pretty Little Hand Won't Stretch': Music for the Fair Sex in Eighteenth-Century Germany," *JAMS*, 52 (1999): 218. 2. Carl Philipp Emanuel Bach, *Essay on the True Art of Playing Keyboard Instruments*, trans. and ed. William J. Mitchell (New York, 1949), 15–16. 3. *Dr. Burney's Musical Tours in Europe*, ed. Percy A. Scholes, 2 vols. (London, 1959), II, 219. 4. Translated from the German given in Arthur Loesser, *Men, Women and Pianos: A Social History* (New York, 1954), 60–61. 5. Robert Marshall, *Mozart Speaks* (New York, 1991), 322. 6. Charles Burney as quoted in Daniel Heartz, *Music in European Capitals: The Galant Style, 1720–1780* (New York, 2003), 907. 7. Charles Burney as quoted in James Parakilas, *Piano Roles* (New Haven and London, 1999), 39.

Chapter 44   1. Some scholars have rightly questioned the use of the term *classical music*, believing it to be an overly simple label for a complex stylistic development. There is more than a kernel of truth to this view. Nonetheless, like all chronological labels, the expressions *Classical period* and *classical music* are useful terms that help us to identify and focus upon common musical traits. 2. *Mémoires ou Essais sur la musique*, 3 vols. (Paris, 1797), III, 356.

Chapter 45   1. Craig Wright, *Listening to Music* (Belmont, CA, 2004), 174; a slightly different translation is given in James Webster, "Haydn," *NG*, 11:176. 2. Webster, "Haydn," *NG*, 11:192. 3. A.C. Dies, *Biographische Nachrichten* translated in Vernon Gotwalls, *Joseph Haydn, Eighteenth-Century Gentleman and Genius* (Madison, 1963), 111. 4. A paraphrase of G.A. Griesinger's *Biographische Notizen*, as given in Gotwalls, *Joseph Haydn*, 20.

Chapter 46   1. A.C. Dies, *Biographische Nachrichten*, translated in Gotwalls, *Joseph Haydn*, 119. 2. Dies, *Biographische Nachrichten*, 130. 3. H.C. Robbins Landon, *The Symphonies of Joseph Haydn* (London, 1955), 509. 4. Dies, *Biographische Nachrichten*, translated in Gotwalls, *Joseph Haydn*, 123–24. 5. James Webster, "Haydn," *NG*, 11:189.

Chapter 47   1. Cliff Eisen and Stanley Sadie, "Mozart," *NG*, 17:276. 2. In fact, Mozart composed nearly sixty symphonies. The first complete edition of them, however, done in the nineteenth century, counted only forty-one. It omitted nearly two dozen early symphonies but counted three that were not by him. Nonetheless, the nineteenth-century numbering for Mozart symphonies remains with us today. 3. Letter of 26 May 1781, *Letters of Mozart*, III, 1095. 4. Letter of 14 February 1785, *Letters of Mozart*, III, 1321. 5. Letter of 13 February 1782, *Letters of Mozart*, III, 1187. 6. Translated from Cramer's *Magazin der Musik*, Hamburg, 9 May 1783. A similar rendering can be found in Otto Erich Deutsch, *Mozart: A Documentary Biography* (Stanford, CA, 1965), 215.

Chapter 48   1. These words were attributed to Mozart by an early biographer in connection with the first performance of his opera *Die Entführung aus dem Serail*; see Neal Zaslaw with William Cowdery, *The Compleat Mozart: A Guide to the Musical Works of Wolfgang Amadeus Mozart* (New York, 1990), 55.

Chapter 49   1. *Thayer's Life of Beethoven*, ed. Elliot Forbes (Princeton, 1970), 105. 2. *Thayer's Life of Beethoven*, 115. 3. *Thayer's Life of Beethoven*, 368. 4. *Thayer's Life of Beethoven*, 329. 5. *Thayer's Life of Beethoven*, 207. 6. Carl Czerny, "Recollections from My Life," *Musical Quarterly* 42 (1956): 306–307. 7. *Selected Letters of Beethoven*, trans. Emily Anderson, ed. Alan Tyson (New York, 1967), 31–36. 8. *Selected Letters of Beethoven*, 38.

Chapter 50   1. Charles Burney, *A General History of Music* (1776), ed. Frank Mercer 2 vols. (New York, 1935), I, 21. 2. Maynard Solomon, *Beethoven*, 2nd ed. (New York, 1998), 151–53. 3. Carl Czerny, *On the Proper Performance of All Beethoven's Works for the Piano*, ed. Paul Badura-Skoda (Vienna, 1970), 13. 4. *Thayer's Life of Beethoven*, ed. Elliot Forbes (Princeton, 1970), 375. 5. *Thayer's Life of Beethoven*, 232. 6. Solomon, *Beethoven*, 210–11.

Chapter 51   1. Auguste de La Garde-Chambonas, *Anecdotal Recollections of the Congress of Vienna* (London, 1902), 68. 2. *Louis Spohr's Autobiography* (London, 1865), 186. 3. *Thayer's Life of Beethoven*, ed. Elliot Forbes (Princeton, 1970), 909. 4. Georg Kinsky and Hans Halm, *Das Werk Beethovens: Thematisch-bibliographisches Verzeichnis seiner sämtlichen vollendeten Kompositionen* (Munich, 1955), 393. 5. *Thayer's Life of Beethoven*, 1057.

BIBLIOGRAPHY

What follows is a brief, preliminary bibliography. Far more comprehensive bibliographies are included in the Student Workbook and Instructor's Manual for *Music in Western Civilization*, and are also available on the Cengage Learning website (where they are updated). These bibliographies cite only works in the English language. Each of the books and articles contains either its own bibliography or copious footnotes that suggest still more useful sources for research. For help in the challenging task of writing about the ephemeral art of music, see the essay "Writing a Research Paper on a Musical Topic" by Sterling Murray that is included in the Workbook.

❀ DICTIONARIES AND ENCYCLOPEDIAS

By far the most useful tool for research in music—both for scholars and students—is **The New Grove Dictionary of Music and Musicians,** 2nd edition (London: Macmillan, 2001). It is available both in a 29-volume printed edition and online (www.grovemusic.com). Many colleges and universities subscribe to the online version, making it accessible to students at many locations on campus and at home. The online version is continually updated, as contemporary scholarship requires. In addition, the online version includes articles from the more specialized *The New Grove Dictionary of Opera* and *The New Grove Dictionary of Jazz*. Almost every subject dealing with classical and popular, Western and non-Western music, can be found in *The New Grove Dictionary*. Each entry is written by a world-renowned scholar and is followed by its own detailed bibliography. For major composers, a complete list of compositions is given, along with the date of publication or first performance, as well as references to scholarly editions in which a specific piece may be found. Other, much smaller but nonetheless useful, reference tools include:

Baker's Biographical Dictionary of Musicians. New York: Schirmer Books, 2001.

The Harvard Biographical Dictionary of Music. Cambridge, MA: Harvard University Press, 1996.

The Harvard Dictionary of Music, 4th ed., ed. Don Randel. Cambridge, MA: Harvard University Press, 2003.

The Norton/Grove Concise Encyclopedia of Music, ed. Stanley Sadie and Alison Lathan. New York and London: Norton, 1988.

The Norton/Grove Dictionary of Women Composers, ed. Julie Anne Sadie and Rhian Samuel. London and New York: MacMillan and Norton, 1994.

The Oxford Companion to Music, ed. Alison Lathan. Oxford: Oxford University Press, 2002.

❀ PRIMARY-SOURCE DOCUMENTS FOR WESTERN MUSIC

Music in the Western World: A History in Documents, ed. Piero Weiss and Richard Taruskin. New York: Schirmer Books, 1984.

Opera: A History in Documents, ed. Piero Weiss. Oxford: Oxford University Press, 2002.

Readings in the History of Musical Performance, ed. Carol MacClintock. Bloomington, IN: Indiana University Press, 1979.

Source Readings in Music History, ed. Oliver Strunk; rev. edition ed. Leo Treitler. New York and London: Norton, 1998.

❀ HISTORICAL SURVEYS OF WESTERN MUSIC

Part IV: Baroque Music

Buelow, George J. *A History of Baroque Music*. Bloomington, IN: Indiana University Press, 2004.

Hill, John Walter. *Baroque Music: Music in Western Europe, 1580–1750*. New York: Norton, 2005.

Palisca, Claude V. *Baroque Music,* 3rd ed. Englewood Cliffs, NJ: Prentice Hall, 1991.

Schulenberg, David. *Music of the Baroque*. Oxford: Oxford University Press, 2001.

Part V: The Enlightenment and the Classical Era

Downs, Philip G. *Classical Music: The Era of Mozart, Haydn, and Beethoven*. New York: Norton, 1992.

Heartz, Daniel. *Haydn, Mozart and the Viennese School: 1740–1780*. New York and London: Norton, 1995.

———. *Music in European Capitals: The Galant Style, 1720–1780*. New York and London: Norton, 2003.

Rushton, Julian. *Classical Music: A Concise History from Gluck to Beethoven*. London: Thames and Hudson, 1986.

❀ MUSIC JOURNALS

There are hundreds of journals (periodicals containing scholarly articles) dealing with various aspects of the history and performance of Western classical music. Some of these journals regularly publish an index to the articles found in previous issues, but most do not. There are, however, three useful indexes to journals that encompass English as well as foreign-language journals: *Music Index, International Index to Music Periodicals*, and *RILM* (acronym for *Répertoire international de littérature musicale*). All three are available online, usually through a university or college computer network, for a quick search of specific topics. Thus, to find out more about Mozart's *Don Giovanni* or Copland's *Appalachian Spring*, for example, simply go to one of these sites and type in the title in the appropriate search box. *RILM*, perhaps the most useful of the three, often provides helpful abstracts that allow the reader to determine if the article in question will be of use. For dissertations about musical topics, *Dissertations and Theses—Full Text* has not merely abstracts but, as the title states, entire dissertations and theses online (those written after 1997). Finally, more than forty of the most important music journals now also have back issues online through a link called JSTOR (*Journal Storage: The Scholarly Journal Archive*). Most university and college libraries subscribe to this online service.

ONLINE SEARCH ENGINES FOR ARTICLES, DISSERTATIONS, AND THESES ABOUT MUSIC

Music Index (Warren, MI: Harmony Park Press) http://www.hppmusicindex.com

International Index to Music Periodicals (Alexandria, VA: Chadwyck-Healey Inc.) http://iimpft.chadwyck.com/home

RILM (*Répertoire international de littérature musicale*; New York: International Musicological Society) http://www.rilm.org

Dissertations and Theses—Full Texts (Cambridge: ProQuest Company) *http://proquest.umi.com*

JSTOR (*Journal Storage: The Scholarly Journal Archive*; New York: JSTOR) http://www.jstor.org

IMPORTANT ENGLISH LANGUAGE MUSIC JOURNALS

Journal (earlier *Proceedings*) *of the Royal Musical Association* (British, 1874–)
Musical Quarterly (American, 1915–)
Music and Letters (British, 1920–)
Journal (earlier *Bulletin*) *of the American Musicological Society* (American, 1948–)
Ethnomusicology (American, 1953–)
Journal of Music Theory (American, 1957–)
Perspectives of New Music (American, 1963–)
Early Music (British, 1973–)
19-Century Music (American, 1977–)
Music Theory Spectrum (American, 1979–)
Early Music History (British, 1981–)
Journal of Musicology (American, 1981–)
Popular Music (British, 1981–)
American Music (American, 1983–)

CREDITS

GLOSSARY

a cappella: singing without instrumental accompaniment

Abendmusik: an hour-long concert of sacred music with arias and recitatives—something akin to a sacred opera or oratorio; a single religious theme unfolded in music over the course of five late-afternoon performances on the Sundays immediately before and during Advent in the city of Lübeck, Germany

Académie royale de musique: in effect, a French national opera company directly licensed and indirectly financed by the king; it performed in the center of Paris at the Palais Royal

academy: a learned society, sometimes devoted to presenting concerts; in Germany in the eighteenth century the term often referred to a public concert

acciaccatura: a technique of crunching dissonant chords used by Domenico Scarlatti

accompanied recitative: a recitative that features a full orchestral accompaniment; it appears occasionally in the sacred vocal music of Bach, but was used more extensively in the operas of Gluck and later composers.

Aeolian: the first of the four new modes added to the canon of eight medieval church modes by Heinrich Glarean in 1547; first official recognition of the minor mode

aggregate: in twelve-tone composition, a contiguous statement of the twelve notes with none repeated except in an immediate or repetitive context

agréments: French word for ornaments, or embellishments

air de cour: the French term for a simple, strophic song for a single voice or a small group of soloists

Alberti bass: an animation of simple triads brought about by playing the notes successively and in a pattern; a distinctive component of the style of keyboard composer Domenico Alberti (c1710–1746)

allemande: French for the "German" dance and usually the first dance in a Baroque suite; a stately dance in $\frac{4}{4}$ meter at a moderate tempo with upbeat and gracefully interweaving lines that create an improvisatory-like style

alternatim technique: a technique in which the verses of a chant are assigned to alternating performing forces, such as an organ and a choir

Ambrosian chant: a body of chant created by Ambrose (340?–397 C.E.) for the church of Milan in northern Italy

Amen cadence: a final phrase setting the word "Amen"; more specifically, a pla-gal cadence that English composers in particular employed to set "Amen" giving a piece an emphatic conclusion

antecedent phrase: the opening, incomplete-sounding phrase of a melody; often followed by a consequent phrase that brings closure to the melody

anthem: a sacred vocal composition, much like a motet but sung in English, in honor of the Lord or invoking the Lord to preserve and protect the English king or queen

antiphon: in antiphonal singing the short chant sung before and after a psalm and its doxology

antiphonal singing: a method of musical performance in which a divided choir alternately sings back and forth

Aquitanian polyphony: a repertory of about sixty-five pieces of two-voice organum surviving today from various monasteries in Aquitaine in southwestern France

arcicembalo: a sixteenth-century harpsichord constructed in Ferrara, Italy, that had two keyboards, each with three rows of keys

aria: an elaborate, lyrical song for solo voice more florid, more expansive, and more melodious than a recitative or arioso; an aria invariably sets a short poem made up of one or more stanzas

arioso style: an expressive manner of singing somewhere between a recitative and a full-blown aria

Ars antiqua: the music of the thirteenth century characterized by a uniform pace and clear ternary units (as contrasted with the *Ars nova* of the early fourteenth century)

Ars nova: musical *avant garde* of the early fourteenth century characterized by duple as well as triple relationships and a wide variety of note values (as contrasted with the *Ars antiqua* of the thirteenth century)

Ars subtilior: (more subtle art) a style of music exhibited by composers working in Avignon and other parts of southern France and northern Italy during the late fourteenth century; marked by the most subtle, sometimes extreme, rhythmic relationships

Artusi-Monteverdi Controversy: the conflict between Claudio Monteverdi, who composed in a new style inspired by a text-driven approach to musical composition, and Giovanni Maria Artusi, a churchman and conservative music theorist who advocated the older style of music that followed traditional rules of harmony and counterpoint, and who characterized Monteverdi's music as harsh and offensive to the ear

atonal music: twentieth-century harmony lacking consistent tonal center; atonal music normally has no large-scale functional harmonic progressions, uses tones of the full chromatic scale as though structurally equivalent, and emphasizes dissonant chords of any size and intervallic make-up

atonality: see atonal music

aulos: an ancient Greek wind instrument played in pairs that produced a high, clear, penetrating sound

authentic mode: in the eight church modes the authentic is the first of each of the four pairs of modes; each authentic mode has a corresponding lower mode (plagal), but both modes of the pair end on the same final pitch

BACH motive: a motive consisting of the tones B♭ A C B♮ (the musical letters in Bach's name, according to German usage); found in compositions by J.S. Bach himself and many later composers

Bach Revival: a movement originating in Germany in the early nineteenth century by which Bach's entire compositional oeuvre was published and performed

Bach-Abel concerts: a series of public concerts begun in London in 1764 by J.C. Bach (son of J.S.) and another German musician, Carl Abel; the concerts featured the most recent works of Bach and Abel as well as other fashionable composers; continuing for nearly twenty years, they became a model for the public concert series in London and on the Continent

bagatelle: a short instrumental composition

ballad: (1) a narrative poem or its musical setting; (2) a traditional, usually strophic, song that tells a lengthy story; in popular music, a love song in a slow tempo

ballad opera: a type of popular eighteenth-century English musical theater using re-texted ballads (or other popular songs) and spoken dialogue rather than recitative

ballade: one of the three French *formes fixes* that originated in the Middle Ages; a song always with the form AAB setting a poem with from one to three stanzas, or strophes; employs a lyrical melody accompanied by one or two voices or instruments

ballata: a dance song with a choral refrain; one of the three *formes fixes* of secular music in trecento Italy

ballet: a theatrical genre made from regulated dancing and mime, accompanied by orchestra

ballet de cour: (court ballet) a type of elaborate ballet with songs and choruses danced at the French royal court from the late sixteenth to the late seventeenth century in which members of the court appeared alongside professional dancers

ballet variations: passages in a ballet featuring soloistic dancing

Baroque: the term used generally to describe the art, architecture, and music of the period 1600–1750

baryton: a *viola da gamba*-like instrument with six strings

bas instruments: (soft instruments) one of the two classifications of instruments in the fifteenth century; constituted no set group but could include recorder, vielle, lute, harp, psaltery, portative organ, and harpsichord, individually or in combination

basse danse: the principal aristocratic dance of court and city during the early Renaissance; a slow and stately dance in which the dancers' feet glided close to the ground

basso continuo: a bass line that provided a never-ending foundation, or "continuous bass," for the melody above; also a small ensemble of usually two instruments that played this support

basso ostinato: a bass line that insistently repeats, note for note

bebop: a style of jazz originating in the 1940s for small improvising ensembles, often in fast tempos

Bebung: German term for the vibrating sound produced by the clavichord technique of holding and "wiggling" a key up and down

Belle époque: (beautiful era) name often given to the years straddling the turn of the twentieth century in France

big band: the dominant medium of jazz during the 1930s and 1940s; big bands typically numbered about fifteen players, divided into a rhythm section (usually piano, bass, guitar, and drums) and choirs of saxophones (doubling on clarinets), trumpets, and trombones

binary form: a structure consisting of two complementary parts, the first moving to a closely related key and the second beginning in that new key but soon returning to the tonic

blue note: a lowered scale degree (usually the third and seventh) in the major mode in blues and other jazz styles

blues: originally an improvised strophic folk song containing a succession of three-line stanzas, each sung to a twelve-measure phrase and using a standard recurrent harmonic progression; the blues form is also applicable to instrumental jazz

blues chorus: a principal subsection of a jazz work in blues form, usually twelve-measures in duration

bolero: Spanish dance in triple meter

boogie woogie: a style of piano blues with a driving ostinato accompaniment

bop: see **bebop**

branle (bransle): a fifteenth- and sixteenth-century group dance

break: in jazz, a sudden and momentary pause during which a player introduces an improvised solo

breve: one of the three basic note values and shapes recognized by Franco of Cologne around 1280 in his classification of musical durations

bridge: see transition

brindisi: a drinking song, often found in nineteenth-century Italian opera

Broadway musical: see musical

broken consort: a mixed ensemble of different types of instruments

burden: the refrain with which an English carol begins and which is repeated after each stanza

Burgundian cadence: (octave-leap cadence) when three voices are present, the contratenor often jumps an octave at a cadence to avoid parallel fifths and dissonances and to fill in the texture of the final chord

Buxheim Organ Book: one of the largest sources of Renaissance organ music; written about 1470, it contains 256 mostly anonymous compositions notated in tablature for organ, almost all of which are arrangements of sacred and secular vocal music

BWV (Bach Werke Verzeichnis): Bach Work List; an identifying system for the works of Johann Sebastian Bach, which functions much like the "K" numbers used for Mozart's works

Byzantine chant: the special dialect of chant developed by the Byzantine Church; it was eventually notated and a body of music theory emerged to explain it

cabaletta: the fast, virtuosic concluding part of an aria or duet, often found in nineteenth-century Italian opera

cabaret: a popular entertainment including songs, skits, and dancing

caccia: a piece involving a musical canon in the upper two voices supported by a slower moving tenor; one of the three *formes fixes* of secular music in trecento Italy

cadenza: a technically demanding, rhapsodic, improvisatory passage for a soloist near the end of a movement

call and response: a style of African-American song alternating phrases between two individuals, or between an individual leader and a group

canon: imitation of a complete subject at a fixed interval and time delay; in a canon (round) the following voice(s) must duplicate exactly the pitches and rhythms of the first, as for example in "Row, row, row your boat"

canonical hours (liturgical offices): a set of eight periods of worship occurring throughout the day and observed in monasteries and convents; first prescribed in the Rule of St. Benedict (c530 C.E.)

canso: the name for a song in southern medieval France, in langue d'oc (occitan)

cantata: the primary genre of vocal chamber music in the Baroque era; it was "something sung" as opposed to a sonata, which was "sounded" on an instrument; in its mature state it consisted of several movements, including one or more arias and recitatives; cantatas can be on secular subjects, but those of J.S. Bach are primarily sacred in content

cantate française: virtually identical to the late seventeenth-century Italian chamber cantata except that it set a French rather than an Italian text

canticle: a particularly lyrical and memorable passage of scripture usually drawn from the New Testament of the Bible

cantiga: a medieval Spanish or Portuguese monophonic song; hundreds were created on subjects of love, epic heroism, and everyday life

cantor: the practitioner who performs music, as distinguished from the *musicus*; in a medieval monastery or nunnery the person specially trained to lead the music of the community who sat with one of the two groups and led the singing

cantrix in a convent, the main female singer and, in effect, the director of the choir

cantus: the highest vocal part in an early polyphonic composition, what would later come to be called the superius and finally the soprano

cantus firmus: a well-established, previously existing melody, be it a sacred chant or a secular song, that usually sounds in long notes and provides a structural framework for a polyphonic composition

cantus firmus Mass: a cyclic Mass in which the five movements of the Ordinary are unified by means of a single cantus firmus

canzona: a freely composed instrumental piece, usually for organ or instrumental ensemble, which imitated the lively rhythms and lightly imitative style of the Parisian chanson

cappella: (1) a building consecrated for religious worship; (2) an organized group of highly trained musicians who sang at the services in such a chapel

cappella pontificia sistina: the pope's private vocal ensemble as it came to be called in the early seventeenth century and that sang in the Sistine Chapel

carnival song: a short, homophonic piece associated with carnival season, the text of which usually deals with everyday life on the streets

carol: a strophic song for one to three voices setting a religious text, usually associated with Christmas

carole: one of two main types of dances of the Middle Ages; a song and dance that often made use of the musical form called strophe plus refrain, in which a series of stanzas would each end with the same refrain; singers and dancers grouped in a circle and a soloist sang each successive strophe of text, while everyone else joined in for the refrain

castrato: an adult male singer who had been castrated as a boy to keep his voice from changing so that it would remain in the soprano or alto register

cauda (pl., caudae): in the vocabulary of the medieval musical theorist, a long melisma on a single syllable; used in a conductus to set off key words

cavatina: in eighteenth- and nineteenth-century Italian opera, an entrance aria; in German opera a simple aria in a slow or moderate tempo

Cecilianism: movement in Catholic Church music in Germany in the nineteenth century that favored the reintroduction of a pure style based on sixteenth-century principles

celesta: a small keyboard instrument on which tones are sounded by hammers striking metal bars

chamber cantata: a cantata performed before a select audience in a private residence; intimate vocal chamber music, principally of the Baroque era

chance music: twentieth-century music in which compositional decisions are made by chance procedures

chanson: the French word for song, monophonic or polyphonic

chansonnier: a book of songs, as created by musicians in the Middle Ages and Renaissance; a collected anthology of chansons

chant: monophonic religious music that is sung in a house of worship

character piece: a short instrumental work (especially for piano or orchestra) that establishes a particular mood

Charleston: a popular dance of the 1920s, fast in tempo with a distinctive asymmetrical rhythm

chekker: original name for the clavichord in England

choir: the eastern end of a cathedral or large church; contained the high altar and was the area in which most music was made; an ensemble of singers

choir festival: special occasion for the performance of choral and orchestral music; especially prominent in Germany and England during the nineteenth and twentieth centuries

choir school: a school that took boys at about the age of six, gave them an education with a strong emphasis on music, especially singing, and prepared them for a lifetime of service within the church

choirbook format: a layout common for writing religious music from the late Middle Ages onward in which the soprano voice was on the upper left, the alto or tenor on bottom left, alto or tenor in upper right, and the bass on the bottom right; contrasted with written music today where all the parts are superimposed on one another

chorale: a monophonic spiritual melody or religious folksong of the Lutheran church, what today is called by many Christian denominations a "hymn"

chorale cantata: a genre of sacred vocal music that employs the text and tune of a pre-existing Lutheran chorale in all or several of its movements

chorale fantasia: a lengthy composition for organ that takes a chorale tune as a point of departure but increasingly gives free rein to the composer's imagination

chorale prelude: an ornamental setting of a pre-existing chorale tune intended to be played on the organ before the singing of the chorale by the full congregation

Choralis Constantinus: a collection of nearly three hundred fifty motet-like compositions of Heinrich Isaac (c1450–1518) setting polyphonically all the Proper chants of the Catholic Mass; the first systematic attempt to provide polyphony for the entire church year since the twelfth century

chord inversion: a revolutionary principal codified by Jean-Philippe Rameau in his *Treatise on Harmony* holding that a triad may have different pitches other than the root in the bass but without changing the identity of the triad

choreographer: in ballet, the creator of the dance steps

chorus: a group of singers performing together; in jazz, a basic phrase in blues

(usually spanning twelve measures), or a refrain in a popular song

chromatic genus: a tetrachord employed by the ancient Greeks consisting of two semi-tones and a minor third

chronos: in ancient Greek musical notation the basic unit of time—a short value

church modes: the eight melodic patterns into which medieval theorists categorized the chants of the church; the four principal ones are Dorian, Phrygian, Lydian, and Mixolydian

ciaconna (chaconne): originally a separate and distinct bass melody, but during the seventeenth century the term came to mean almost any repeating bass pattern of short duration

cimbalom: a Hungarian dulcimer

circle of fifths: an arrangement of the tonic pitches of the twelve major and minor keys by ascending or descending perfect fifths, C-G-D-A etc., for example, which, because of the enharmonic equivalency of F♯ and G♭, ultimately come full circle back to C

clarino register: the very high register of the trumpet; playing in this register was a special technique of Baroque trumpeters that was exploited by Baroque composers

clausula (pl., clausulae): section, phrase, or "musical clause" in a medieval composition

clavecin: French word for harpsichord; the favorite chamber keyboard instrument in the late seventeenth and early eighteenth centuries

clavichord: a keyboard instrument that makes sound when a player depresses a key and thereby pushes a small metal tangent in the shape of a "T" upward to strike a string; the sound produced is very quiet, the softest of any musical instrument

closed ending: the term used in the Middle Ages for what we today call a second ending

coda: the musical section appended to a piece to add extra weight to the end to give it a feeling of conclusion

Codex Calixtinus: manuscript that survives today at the cathedral at Santiago de Compostela, Spain, written around 1150 and once believed to be the work of Pope Calixtus II; contains a service for St. James, which includes twenty polyphonic pieces; important in the history of Western music because it is the first manuscript to ascribe composers' names to particular pieces

colla parte: a technique in which all the instrumental parts double the vocal lines

collegium musicum: an association of musicians in eighteenth-century Germany, consisting usually of university students, who came together voluntarily to play the latest music in a public setting such as a large café or beer hall

color: the melodic unit that serves as a structural backbone in an isorhythmic composition

coloratura: florid figuration assigned to the soprano voice in an opera; also the high female voice capable of singing such a florid part

colossal Baroque: name for the style of large-scale sacred music employing multiple choirs of voices and instruments and sung in largest churches in Rome, Venice, Vienna, and Salzburg

combinatoriality: the capacity of two forms of a twelve-tone row to create multidimensional aggregates

combo: a small jazz ensemble

comic opera: a simple, direct type of musical theater that made use of comic characters, dealt with everyday social issues, and emphasized values more in step with those of the middle class

comping: the playing of accompanimental chords by a pianist or other instrumentalist in jazz

complementary hexachords: two collections of notes, each having six tones, which together contain all tones of the chromatic scale

complete works edition: a musical edition containing the complete oeuvre of a composer

compound melody: a melody made from two or more simultaneous stepwise strands whose tones are touched alternately

conceptual art: a loosely defined movement in art of the 1960s and 1970s in which the artist calls attention to ideas by which the art work is created rather than to traditional artistic objects

concert overture: an orchestral piece in one movement, usually programmatic in content, and intended for concert purposes

Concert spirituel: one of the first and foremost public concert series founded in Paris in 1725; originally formed to give a public hearing to religious music sung in Latin, its repertory soon came to emphasize instrumental symphonies and concertos as well

concert symphony: a three- or four-movement instrumental work projecting the unified sounds of an orchestra; has its origins in the Enlightenment

concertante: a special orchestral style; a concerto-like approach to the use of the orchestra in which individual instruments regularly emerge from the orchestral texture to function as soloists

concerted madrigal: a madrigal in the concertato style with strong contrasts in textures and timbres involving voices and instruments

concerted motet: a motet in the concertato style with strong contrasts in textures and timbres involving voices and instruments

concertino: the small group of solo performers in a concerto grosso

concerto: a purely instrumental piece for ensemble in which one or more soloists both complement and compete with a full orchestra

concerto delle donne: (ensemble of ladies) a group of female singers employed by the duke of Ferrara at the end of the sixteenth century; they constituted the first professional ensemble of women employed by a court

concerto grosso: a concerto in which a larger body of performers, namely the full orchestra (the ripieno, or tutti), contrasts with a smaller group of soloists (the concertino)

concerto-sonata form: a form, originating in the concerto of the Classical period, in which first the orchestra and then the soloist present the primary thematic material; much like sonata form but with two expositions

concrete music: see musique concrète

conductus: an extra-liturgical piece written for one, two, three, or occasionally four voices with texts that are metrical Latin poems arranged in successive stanzas; although not part of the canonical liturgy, most were serious and moralistic in tone; often used to accompany the movement of the clergy from one place to another in and around the church

confraternity: a Christian society of laymen emphasizing religious devotion and charity; in Florence performing laude was an essential part of their fraternal life

Congress of Vienna the meeting called by Emperor Francis I, King of Austria—after Napoleon Bonaparte abdicated his throne and fled France—inviting all the leaders of Europe to meet to redraw the boundaries of their continent and reestablish principles of legitimate rule

consequent phrase: the second phrase of a two-part melodic unit that brings a melody to a point of repose and closure

consort: an ensemble of instruments all of one family

consort song: one of two forms of the solo art song that flourished in England around 1600; the voice is accompanied by a group of independent instruments, usually a consort of viols

contenance angloise: the "English manner" of composition that fifteenth-century Continental musicians admired and adopted, though the exact nature of this style is not known

contrafactum (pl., contrafacta): the transformation of a piece of music from a secular piece to a sacred one, or (less often) from a sacred to a secular one

contralto: a low alto (a low female voice)

contratenor altus the upper of the two contratenor voices (the other being the bass); the medieval equivalent of our alto voice

contratenor bassus: the lower of the two contratenor voices (the other being the alto); the medieval equivalent of our bass voice

conversation books: notebooks used (by Beethoven and others with a hearing impairment) to communicate; one hundred forty of Beethoven's conversation books survive today

cool jazz: a style of jazz of the 1950s characterized by subdued playing and moderate tempos

Coptic chant: the music of the Christian Church of Egypt, which still exists today, passed along for nearly 2000 years entirely by oral tradition

cori spezzati: music for two, three, or four choirs placed in different parts of a building

cornett: a wooden instrument with fingerholes that is played with a mouthpiece and sounds in the soprano range with a tone something like a soft trumpet

Council of Trent: (1545–1563) a congress of bishops and cardinals held at the small town of Trento in the Italian Alps; the institutionalization of the spirit of the Counter-Reformation; its decision regarding music insisted that music must never interfere with the comprehension of the sacred word

counterpoint: from the Latin punctus contra punctum (one note moving against another note); the harmonious opposition of two or more independent musical lines

counterpoint, dissonant: see dissonant counterpoint

Counter-Reformation: the movement that fostered reform in the Roman Church in response to the challenge of the Protestant Reformation

countersubject: in a fugue, a unit of thematically distinctive material that serves as a counterpoint to the subject

countertenor: a male performer who sings in the alto or soprano range in falsetto voice

couplet: a term used in the rondo form of the seventeenth and eighteenth centuries to indicate an intermediate section (episode) distinctly different from the refrain

courante: a lively dance in triple meter characterized by intentional metrical ambiguity created by means of hemiola; one of the four dances typically making up a Baroque dance suite

Credo: a profession of faith formulated as the result of the Council of Nicaea in 325; one of the five parts of the Ordinary of the Mass

crook: a small piece of pipe that could be inserted in a horn if the player needed to change key; it altered the length of tubing within the instrument and consequently its pitch

crumhorn: a capped double-reed wooden instrument with a curving shape; has the range of a tenth and makes a sound like a kazoo

cultural bolshevism: a catch phrase used by Nazi ideologues to condemn art that was considered decadent on account of its association with foreign, Jewish, or Communist influences

cyclic Mass: a Mass in which all of the movements are linked together by a common musical theme; the first was Machaut's *Mass of Our Lady* composed in the mid fourteenth century

cyclicism: the recurrence of melodic ideas (often transformed) throughout a multimovement or multisectional composition

da camera: (of the chamber) a seventeenth-century designation for music that was not intended primarily for the church

da capo **aria:** an aria in two sections with an obligatory return to and repeat of the first (hence ABA); the reprise was not written out but signaled by the inscription "da capo" meaning "take it from the top"

da chiesa: (of the church) a seventeenth-century designation for music that was intended primarily for the church

dance suite: an ordered set of dances for solo instrument or ensemble, all written in the same key and intended to be performed in a single sitting

development: in sonata form, the middle-most section in which the themes of the exposition are varied or developed in some fashion; it is often the most confrontational and unstable portion of the movement

diabolus in musica: (devil in music) the dissonant, or disagreeable tritone such as F-B

diatonic genus: the basic genus within the ancient Greek musical system; reflects the primary tetrachord spanning the intervals S-T-T

Dies irae: (*Day of Wrath*) an anonymous thirteenth-century sequence; today the most famous of all medieval sequences, one which serves as the sequence of the requiem Mass

discant: a style of music in which the voices move at roughly the same rate and are written in clearly defined modal rhythms (as compared to organum purum)

diseme: in ancient Greek musical notation a long value of time—formed by two chronoi

dissonant counterpoint: term coined by Charles Seeger to refer to counterpoint in which the traditional roles of consonance and dissonance are reversed

dithyramb: in ancient Greece, a wild choral song, mingled with shouts, that honored Dionysus; a term applied today to any poem with these characteristics

divertimento: originally simply a musical diversion, it came to imply a lighter style of music and a five-movement format: fast/minuet and trio/slow/minuet and trio/fast; the term was used interchangeably with serenade

divertissement: (1) a lavishly choreographed diversionary interlude with occasional singing set within French *ballet de cour;* (2) an "entertainment" in an opera or ballet, only loosely connected to its surrounding scenes

Doctrine of Affections: a theory of the Baroque era that held that different musical moods could and should be used to influence the emotions, or affections, of the listeners

dot: following a note, a dot adds fifty percent to the value of the note; this concept entered music history in the early fourteenth century

double escapement action: a piano action in which a hammer falls back only halfway after striking a string, allowing the hammer to restrike more quickly

double leading-tone cadence a cadence with two leading tones in the penultimate chord, one pulling upward to the primary tone of the final chord and the other upward to the fifth degree

double verse structure: a distinctive feature of the sequence; each musical phrase is sung twice to accommodate a pair of verses

doxology: a standard formula of praise to the Holy Trinity

drum set: a collection of percussion instruments in a jazz ensemble that can be wielded by a single player

duplum: second voice in two- three- or four-voice organa

electronic music: works whose sounds are directly realized by a composer using electronic equipment

emancipation of dissonance: term used by Arnold Schoenberg to refer to a phenomenon in modern music by which dissonant chords and intervals are used as though equivalent to consonant ones

empfindsamer Stil: term applied to the hyper-expressivity that affected northern European, and particularly German, arts generally in the second half of the eighteenth century

emulation technique: see parody technique

English cross (false) relation: the simultaneous or adjacent appearance in different voices of two conflicting notes with the same letter name

English discant: a general term for the technique in fifteenth-century English music, both written and improvised, of using parallel 6/3 chords and root position triads in a homorhythmic style

English Madrigal School, The: the name given to the composers who fashioned the great outpouring of English secular music vocal music, mostly madrigals, in London between 1588 and 1627

enharmonic genus: a tetrachord found in ancient Greek music consisting of a major third and two quarter-tones; used for music demanding more subtle variations of pitch than that of the diatonic or chromatic genera

Enlightenment: a philosophical, scientific, and political movement that dominated eighteenth-century thought

ensemble finale: an energetic finish to an operatic act that is sung by a vocal ensemble rather than a soloist

envoi: one or more lines of verse added to the end of a chanson to suggest a leave taking

epic theater: a theatric style, associated with the plays of Bertolt Brecht, that dispels normal theatric illusion and "alienates" the audience from the narrative

episode: a passage in a musical work occurring between other passages that have more central thematic importance (as in a rondo form); in a fugue, a section full of modulation and free counterpoint that is based on motives derived from the subject

equal temperament: a division of the octave into twelve equal half-steps, each with the ratio of approximately 18:17; first advocated by some musicians in the early sixteenth century

estampie: one of two main dance types of the Middle Ages; originally a dance-song in which the dancers also sang a text, usually a poem about love; however, during the thirteenth and fourteenth centuries it evolved into a purely instrumental piece

étude: a study; a work intended to build a player's technique and often also having artistic value

Evensong: the final service of the day in the Anglican religion, an amalgam of Vespers and Compline

exposition: in sonata form the first main section in which the primary thematic material of the movement is presented or exposed; of a fugue, an opening section in which each voice presents the subject in turn

expressionism: a movement in twentieth-century literature and art in which symbolic means are used to explore irrational states of mind and grotesque actions

extended techniques: playing and singing in unusual ways in order to expand the sounds available in a musical work

faburden: a style of English medieval choral music that arose when singers improvised around a given chant placed in the middle voice; it is important because English composers began to incorporate this improvisatory style into their more formal written work

falsobordone: an improvisatory technique used by church singers that originated in Spain and Italy around 1480; at first three voices chanted along with the psalm tone making simple chant sound more splendid; by the seventeenth century, psalm tone and improvisation were abandoned and it became a newly composed piece for four or five voices but with the same simple, chordal style

fantasia: an imaginative composition the exact nature of which depends on the period of origin; in earlier eras these were usually contrapuntal works; later, the term suggested an improvisatory piece in free form, or sometimes pieces incorporating preexisting themes

fauxbourdon: the Continental style related to the English faburden; in fauxbourdon singers of sacred music improvised at pitches a fourth and a sixth below a given plainsong

fête galante: a popular social occasion among the French aristocracy of the eighteenth century

figured bass: a numerical shorthand placed with the bass line that tells the player which unwritten notes to fill in above the written bass note

fill: in jazz, a brief figure added between phrases performed by the principal soloist or singer

fin'amors: the theme of ideal love, an important value in chivalric society, as expressed in the poetry of the troubadours

flat trumpet: a slide trumpet, but one for which the sliding tube extended backward over the player's left shoulder, rather than extending forward from the right; had the capacity to play in minor keys more easily

formalism: in general, emphasis on strict formal principles or patterns in music; more specifically, a pejorative term used in the Soviet Union for music that seemed abstract or difficult, not in tune with the taste of the masses or with Soviet artistic ideology

formes fixes: the three fixed forms—ballade, rondeau, virelai—in which nearly all French secular art songs of the fourteenth and early fifteenth centuries were written

foxtrot: a social dance in $\frac{4}{4}$ time, popular in America in the 1920s

free jazz: a type of jazz of the 1950s and 1960s characterized by the removal or reinterpretation of key, normal harmonic progressions, and familiar jazz forms

French horn: the English term for the instrument that in other languages is simply called a horn; introduced into English ensembles only after 1700

French overture: a distinctive type of instrumental prelude created by the composer Jean-Baptiste Lully; came to be understood as an overture in two sections, the first slow in duple meter with dotted note values, the second fast in triple meter and with light imitation

frottola (pl., frottole): a catch-all word used to describe a polyphonic setting of a wide variety of strophic Italian poetry; the frottola flourished between 1470 and 1530 but had its origins in the improvisatory, solo singing that arose in Italy during the 1400s

fugue: a contrapuntal composition for two, three, four, or five voices, which begins with a presentation of a subject in imitation in each voice (exposition), continues with modulating passages of free counterpoint (episodes) and further appearances of the subject, and ends with a strong affirmation of the tonic key

fuguing tune: a hymn, often composed by American musicians of the eighteenth century, having fugal passages

functional harmony: a theory of harmonic syntax that defines the role of a chord

as a point of departure or arrival (a tonic), a secondary point of arrival or moment of harmonic tension (a dominant), or a prefix to a dominant

fusion: a style of popular music that mixes elements of jazz and rock

galant style: French term used by music historians (rather than "Enlightenment style") to describe eighteenth-century music that is graceful, light in texture, and generally symmetrical in melodic structure

galliard: a fast leaping dance in triple meter especially popular during the Renaissance

Gallican chant: the Christian music of early-medieval Gaul; it later mixed with chant coming from Rome and that fusion formed the basis of what we call Gregorian chant

gate: in electronic music, a device allowing for shifts in amplitude in an electronic signal; in the music of John Adams a point of modulation from one collection of tones to another

Gebrauchsmusik: (music for use) a term used in the 1920s by Paul Hindemith to designate his compositions for amateurs or for everyday settings; also used by Kurt Weill for music of artistic value that was accessible to a general audience

German flute: what is today called the flute (the transverse flute)

gigue: a fast dance in $\frac{6}{8}$ or $\frac{12}{8}$ with a constant eighth-note pulse that produces a galloping sound; the gigue is sometimes lightly imitative and in the Baroque era was often used to conclude a suite

Gloria: a hymn of praise originating in early Christian times; one of the five parts of the Ordinary of the Mass

Golden Section: the division of a line into two parts such that the ratio of lengths of the smaller to the larger division equals the larger to the whole

Gothic architecture: the style of architecture that emerged in Paris and surrounding territories in the twelfth century; a lighter style than its Romanesque predecessor, it was characterized by greater height, greater light, and an almost obsessive application of repeating geometrical patterns

Gradual: the first of the two melismatic, responsorial chants of the Proper of the Mass that are sung between the *Gloria* and the *Credo*; consists of two parts: a respond and a psalm verse

grand opera: a style of opera originating around 1830 in France characterized by lavish use of chorus and ballet and elaborate spectacle

grand piano: a term that first appeared in England toward the end of the eighteenth century that denoted a large piano with sturdy legs and strings running roughly in the same direction as the keys

graphic notation: in twentieth-century compositions, musical notation that includes unusual graphic designs

Greater Perfect System: the framework of the Greek two-octave scale formed by four tetrachords and the proslambanomenos

Gregorian chant (plainsong): a vast body of monophonic religious music setting Latin texts and intended for use in the Roman Catholic Church; the music sung daily at the eight canonical hours of prayer and at Mass

ground bass: the English term for *basso ostinato*

Guidonian hand: ascribed to Guido of Arezzo that involves a system of using the left hand to inscribe mentally all the notes of the Guidonian scale and thus provide a portable mnemonic aid for the musical staff and the notes set upon it

Gypsy scale: a scale used by Gypsy musicians of the nineteenth and twentieth centuries containing two augmented seconds (such as C D E♭ F♯ G A♭ B C)

hand-crossing: a technique in keyboard playing in which the left hand must cross over the right to create an exciting three-level texture (left hand, right hand, and left over)

hard hexachord: in the Guidonian system, the hexachord—six-note pattern of TTSTT—set on G

Harlem Renaissance: a literary and artistic movement of the 1920s in Harlem (an African-American district in New York City)

harmonics: overtones, or frequencies, that are components of a fundamental tone

Harmonie: German name for an eighteenth-century independent wind band; called thus because winds played mostly harmony and not melody in the symphony of the day

Harmoniemusik: music written for an eighteenth-century *Harmonie*, or independent wind band

harpsichord: a string keyboard instrument that first appeared in the West in the fifteenth century; it utilized a key-jack mechanism to pluck the taut wire strings; during the Baroque era it was the principal keyboard instrument for realizing the basso continuo, but it lost favor as the piano grew in popularity during the second half of the eighteenth century

hautboys: another name for the shawm; the term was in use in England and France in the sixteenth century, and in England was eventually transformed into "oboe"

hauts instruments: (loud instruments) one of the two classifications of instruments in the fifteenth century; included trumpets, sackbuts, shawms, bagpipes, drums, and tambourine

head arrangement: a jazz arrangement rehearsed and memorized by musicians, but not written down

heckelphone: a double-reed woodwind instrument in the bass range sounding as notated

Heiligenstadt Testament: Beethoven's will that he prepared while staying in Heiligenstadt, Austria, in 1802; ostensibly addressed to his two brothers, it is actually an expression of his innermost feelings for all posterity

hexachord: a collection of six pitches

Hoboken (Hob.) number: number by which Josef Haydn's individual works may be identified following the catalogue prepared by the Dutch musicologist Anthony Hoboken

hocket: a contrapuntal technique and a musical genre; it occurs when the sounds of two voices are staggered by the careful placement of rests, thereby creating a highly syncopated piece

Hofkapelle: the group of singers responsible for the religious music at the Hapsburg court of Emperor Maximilian I; they were the center of religious and musical life at the court

horn fifths: a characteristic musical figure assigned to the French horns in which the instruments slide back and forth through sixths, fifths, and thirds, sometimes ornamenting along the way

hot jazz: an intense and exciting style of jazz

hymn: a relatively short chant with a small number of phrases, often four, and a rather narrow vocal range; hymns are invariably strophic, the usual hymn having three or four stanzas

idée fixe: (obsession): term used by Hector Berlioz to describe a recurrent melody in his *Symphonie fantastique*; the *idée fixe* melody symbolizes the beloved in the work's program

imitation: duplication of the notes and rhythms in one voice by a following voice; from the mid fifteenth century onward it became an oft used technique to enliven polyphonic music and sacred polyphonic music in particular

impresario: a manager, as of a ballet or opera company

impressionism: a realistic style of French painting of the late nineteenth century using everyday subjects (especially sea- and landscapes) and emphasizing the effects of sunlight upon colors; used in music to designate the style of Claude Debussy and others composing evocative music partially freed from strict beat and normative harmonic progressions

improvisation: playing or singing without reference to an existing musical composition

indeterminacy: see chance music

indeterminacy of composition: term associated with the composer John Cage by which compositional decisions are largely determined by chance routines; see also chance music and indeterminacy of performance

indeterminacy of performance: term associated with the composer John Cage by which music results from spontaneous decisions made by players, not strictly dictated by a composer; see also chance music

intabulation: a piece of music notated in tablature and specifically for certain solo instruments such as lute or keyboard; an intabulation implies that a preexisting polyphonic vocal piece has been arranged for a single instrument

intermezzo: a musical diversion between the acts of an opera or a play

introduction: a passage at the beginning of a composition or movement that prepares for and is often slower in tempo than the music to come; in nineteenth-century opera, a musical number (usually called an *introduzione*) at the beginning of the first act that is multisectional and composite in medium

Introit: an introductory chant for the entrance of the celebrating clergy; the first item of the Proper of the Mass

inversion: (1) in traditional harmony, the placement of a bass tone into an upper voice; a melody is inverted if its contour is replaced by its mirror image; (2) a tone row in a twelve-tone composition (or set of pitches in freely atonal music) is inverted if each interval separating the notes is replaced by the octave complement—sometimes said to be a "symmetric" inversion

invertible counterpoint: counterpoint carefully written so that the vertical position of two or more voices can be switched without violating the rules of counterpoint or creating undue dissonance

Ionian: added to the canon of eight medieval church modes by Glarean in

1547; first official recognition of the major mode

isorhythm: in isorhythm (same rhythm) a rhythmic pattern is repeated again and again in a line, usually in the tenor voice; a technique introduced by composers in the early fourteenth century

jam session: in jazz, an informal making of music by improvisation

jazz: a collective term for various types of twentieth-century popular music originating among African-American musicians and often involving improvisation; see also swing, hot jazz, free jazz, cool jazz

jazz break: see break

jazz combo: a small jazz ensemble

jazz dance bands: bands of moderate to large size and flexible makeup, freely incorporating jazz idioms, that played for dancing in the period from about 1915 to 1925

jazz standard: see standard

jubilus: the melisma on the final syllable of the word Alleluia; called this because at that moment the full choir and community celebrates with jubilation the redemptive life of Christ

jungle style: a big band style, associated especially with Duke Ellington in the 1920s and 30s, evoking African or primitive musical effects

just tuning: a system in which, in addition to the ratios required by Pythagorean tuning, the major and minor thirds were also tuned according to strict ratios (5:4 and 6:5)

Kapellmeister: chief of music at court; the German equivalent of *maestro di cappella* (chapel master) in Italy

keyboard tablature: a combination of note symbols (for the fast-moving upper part) and pitch-letter names (for the lower parts)

kithara: the largest of all ancient Greek string instruments (an especially large lyre) usually fitted with seven strings and a resonator of wood

Köchel (K) number: an identifying number assigned to each of the works of Mozart, in roughly chronological order, by German botanist and mineralogist Ludwig von Köchel (1800–1877)

kuchka: (handful) the sobriquet given in 1867 to a group of Russian composers living in St. Petersburg: Mily Balakirev (the mentor of the group), Nicolai Rimsky-Korsakov, César Cui, Alexander Borodin, and Modest Mussorgsky; the group is sometimes called "The Five"

Kyrie: an ancient Greek text and the only portion of the traditional Mass not sung in Latin; in this the first section of the Ordinary of the Mass the congregation petitions the Lord for mercy in threefold exclamations

La Guerre des Bouffons: (The War of the Buffoons) a paper war over the relative merits of Italian and French musical style; it raged, on and off, for several years in Paris during the 1750s and centered on the question of what sort of opera was appropriate for the French stage

lament bass: a descending tetrachordal *basso ostinato* employed during the Baroque era as a musical signifier of grief

Landini cadence: the name for a cadential gesture used frequently by Francesco Landini in which he ornamented a cadence by adding a lower neighbor-tone to the upper voice as it moves up to the octave

langue d'oc (occitan): the vernacular language of southern France in the high Middle Ages; the language of the troubadours and trobairitz

langue d'oïl: the vernacular language of northern France in the high Middle Ages; the language of the trouvères

lauda (pl., laude): Italian for a song of praise; a simple, popular sacred song written, not in church Latin but in the local dialect of Italian; from its beginning in the thirteenth century, the lauda had been sung by members of a confraternity

Le nuove musiche: (*The New Music*, 1602) published by Giulio Caccini; an anthology of solo madrigals and strophic solo songs gathered over time, rather than all new music as was implied; the preface contains invaluable information on vocal performance practices of the early Baroque era

leitmotive: a musical motive, normally occurring in the orchestral part of an opera, which symbolizes a character or dramatic entity; associated primarily with the operas of Richard Wagner, and also used by later composers

libretto: the text of an opera or an oratorio written in poetic verse

Lied (pl., Lieder): (song) a German art song or popular song

ligature: in early notation a group of two, three, or four individual notes

lira da braccio: a Renaissance fiddle; a bowed five-string instrument tuned in fifths and played on the shoulder

Lisztomania: Heinrich Heine's term for the emotional effect that Liszt had on his audiences

liturgical drama: a religious play with music intended to be performed as an adjunct to the liturgy, sometimes before Mass

liturgical offices: see canonical hours

liturgy: the collection of prayers, chants, readings, and ritual acts by which the theology of the church, or any organized religion, is practiced

long: one of the three basic note values and shapes recognized by Franco of Cologne around 1280 in his classification of musical durations

lute: a pear-shaped instrument with six sets of strings called courses, as well as frets created with thin strips of leather wrapped around the fingerboard at measured intervals, and a distinctive peg box that turns back at a right angle to the fingerboard; during the sixteenth century the most popular of all musical instruments

lute ayre: one of two forms of the solo art song that flourished in England around 1600; the soloist is accompanied by a lute and possibly a bass instrument such as the *viola da gamba*; a strophic piece that depended on the solo singer to employ the expressive nuances of the voice to make each stanza sound distinctive

lute tablature: a special type of notation for lute music that directs the fingers to stop strings at specific frets so as to produce sounds

lyre: in ancient Greece a medium-sized instrument usually fitted with seven strings of sheep gut and a resonator of turtle shell; plucked with a metal or bone plectrum and used most often to accompany a solo singer

lyricist: the writer of the words of a popular song, especially the songs in a musical

madrigal: (fourteenth century) originally a poem in the vernacular to which music was added for greater emotional effect; having the form AAB, it was one of the three *formes fixes* of secular music in trecento Italy; (sixteenth century) like the frottola, a catch-all term used to describe settings of Italian verse; sixteenth-century madrigals were through composed rather than strophic and employed a variety of textures and compositional techniques

madrigalism: the term for a musical cliché in which the music tries to sound out the meaning of the text, such as a drooping melody that signals a sigh or a dissonance to intensify a "harsh" word

magister cappellae: musician who is leader of the chapel

Mannheim crescendo: a gradual increase from very soft to very loud with a repeating figure over a pedal point; a specialty of the highly disciplined orchestra at the court of Mannheim

Mannheim rocket: a triadic theme that bursts forth as a rising arpeggio; another specialty of the highly disciplined orchestra at the court of Mannheim

masque: an elaborate courtly entertainment using music, dance, and drama to portray an allegorical story that shed a favorable light on the royal family

Mass: the central and most important religious service each day in the traditional liturgy of the Roman Catholic Church

Matins: the night office of the canonical hours, required much singing, and on high feasts such as Christmas or Easter, might go on for four hours

mazurka: a triple-time Polish dance

megamusical: a type of musical appearing in the 1980s with large cast and lavish spectacle

melisma: a lengthy vocal phrase setting a single syllable of text

melismatic chant: chants in which there are many notes per syllable of text; Matins, Vespers, and the Mass have the most melismatic chants

mélodie: (melody or song) a French art song of the nineteenth century

melodrama: a musical genre in which spoken text is accompanied by, or alternates with, instrumental music

mensural notation: symbol specific notation developed in the late thirteenth century; the direct ancestor of the system of notation used today (in contrast to modal notation, a contextual notation system used prior to the late thirteenth century)

mensuration canon: a canon in which two voices perform the same music at different rates of speed, the corresponding notes of which grow progressively distant from one another

metamorphoses: changes in form; used by Richard Strauss as the title of his final orchestral tone poem (1945)

metric modulation: a term associated with the composer Elliott Carter designating a proportional change of tempo by which a small division of a beat is regrouped into a new beat so that a new tempo results

Micrologus: (*Little Essay*) music theory treatise written c1030 by Guido of Arezzo setting forth all that a practicing church musician needed to know to sing the liturgy

micropolyphony: a term associated with the composer György Ligeti designating a texture in which a large number of lines merge into a sound mass

mime: the art of portraying a character or narrative solely by bodily movements and facial gestures

minim: a new short note value recognized by the fourteenth-century theorists of the *Ars nova*; a subdivision of the semibreve

minimalism: a musical style originating in the United States in the 1960s in which works are created by repetition and gradual change enacted upon a minimum of basic materials

Minnesang: (a song of love in old high German) a song created by a Minnesinger

Minnesinger: in the high Middle Ages the name for a German poet-musician writing love songs

minstrel show: a theatric entertainment originating in the United States in the middle of the nineteenth century, containing skits, songs, and dancing, which parodies the language and manners of African Americans

minuet: originally a triple-meter dance that was often added toward the end of the Baroque dance suite; in the Classical period it was invariably written in rounded binary form and coupled with a matching rounded binary movement called a trio

minuet and trio: a pair of movements with each usually constructed in rounded binary form; the trio was often scored for fewer instruments, sometimes only three (thus the name); often served as the third movement of a symphony or piece of chamber music

modal notation: a new type of notation that came into music gradually around 1150–1170 and that allowed composers to specify rhythmic duration as well as pitch; in modal notation the context determines the rhythm as opposed to the modern system of mensural notation in which each sign (note) indicates a specific duration

mode: (*modus*) the division of the long into two or three breves

modernism: in general, a style that departs from traditional norms of musical materials and aesthetic principles in the name of contemporaneity and progress; the term is often encountered in musical criticism of the twentieth century, especially for music arising in its early years and in the decades following World War II

monochord: a ancient device with a single string stretched over a wooden block and anchored at each end; distances were carefully measured on the string to correspond to specific pitches

monody: the overarching term for solo madrigals, solo arias, and solo recitatives written during the early Baroque era

Morning Prayer: the first service of the day in the Anglican religion, an amalgam of Matins and Lauds

motet: (thirteenth century) originally a discant clausula to which sacred words were added; in a motet each of the upper voices declaims its own poetic text that comments on the significance of the single Latin word being sung by the tenor; (later) the term generally used to connote a sacred choral composition, either accompanied by instruments or sung *a cappella*

motet-chanson: (fifteenth century) a hybrid of a motet and a chanson; a genre in which a vernacular text in an upper voice is sung simultaneously with a Latin chant in the tenor

motetus: the second voice (immediately above the tenor) in the thirteenth-century motet

movable type: individual small pieces of metal type cut with the letters of the alphabet or musical symbols that can be arranged to form words or music; once a sheet using the type has been printed the pieces of type can then be "moved"—rearranged to create a completely different page

Mozarabic chant: the old Christian church music as sung by Christians living in Spain under Moslem rule; survives today in more than twenty manuscripts but is nearly impossible to transcribe and perform

multiple cantus firmus Mass: when two or more cantus firmi sound simultaneously or successively in a Mass

multiple stops: on a violin (or other bowed string instruments) playing two or more notes simultaneously as chords

multiple-impression printing: a process for printing musical notation in which the lines of the staff are first printed horizontally across the sheet, then the sheet is pressed a second time to place the notes on the staff, finally a third pressing adds the text, title, composer's name, and any written instructions

murky bass: German name for a rumbling octave bass, created by repeating a bass note in alternating octaves, that became a favorite technique of both Italian and German keyboard composers of the eighteenth century

muses: in ancient Greek mythology, the nine goddesses who attended Apollo and presided over the arts and sciences; root of our word "music"

music drama: a term associated with the operas of Richard Wagner, who rejected the genre term "opera" for his mature works; Wagner preferred the word "drama"—sometimes "music drama"—for his operas to stress their heightened literary value; but in his essay "On the Name 'Music Drama'" (1872) Wagner also rejected this term as misleading

music of the future: a slogan derived from the writings of Richard Wagner that points to a utopian state in which the various arts coalesce into an integrated or "total" work of art

music of the spheres: part of the ancient Greek world-view of music, which held that when the stars and planets rotated in balanced proportions they made heavenly music

Musica enchiriadis (Music Handbook): a music theory treatise that dates from the 890s and is ascribed to Abbot Hoger; it describes a type of polyphonic singing called organum and aimed to teach church singers how to improvise polyphonic music

musica ficta: accidentals not found on the Guidonian scale but that had to be added by medieval performers because, being theoretically "off the scale," they had to be imagined

musica humana: music of the human body—one of the three harmonies Boethius posited as part of his cosmology of music

musica instrumentalis: earthly vocal and instrumental music—one of the three harmonies Boethius posited as part of his cosmology of music

musica mundana: music of the spheres—one of the three harmonies Boethius posited as part of his cosmology of music; the belief that all the universe resonates with music as sounding number

musica reservata: text-sensitive music reserved for a small circle of connoisseurs

musica secreta: (*musica reservata*) progressive chamber music reserved for a small, elite audience; used to describe the performances by the *concerto delle donne* before the ducal family in Ferrara

musical: a form of popular musical theater of the twentieth century, normally with spoken dialogue alternating with songs, dances, ensembles, and choruses; synonymous with musical comedy, musical play, and Broadway musical

musical play: see musical

musicologist: a scholar of music

musicus: as defined by Boethius, the musicologist who studies and understands music; as distinguished from the *cantor,* who is a practitioner

musique concrète: (concrete music) electronic music (q.v.) made from recordings of natural or man-made sounds

mystic chord: a collection of six tones used in the later music of Alexander Scriabin; an example of the mystic

chord, placed into a compact scalewise order, is B C D E F♯ G♯

nationalism: in general, the love for or allegiance to a region of birth and its people, culture, and language; in music, nationalism is often expressed by the quotation of folk songs and dances or the use of folk stories

natural hexachord: in the Guidonian system, the hexachord—six-note pattern of TTSTT —set on C

naturalism: a movement in literature of the late nineteenth century that depicts society in an objective and truthful manner

nave: the western end of a cathedral or large church; the public part of the church, which functioned as town hall and civic auditorium as well as a space for religious processions and votive prayers

neoclassical architecture: term for the architecture of the eighteenth century that copied classical Roman qualities of balance, harmonious proportions, and an absence of ornate decoration

neoclassicism: a critic's term designating a dominant musical style of the 1920s through 1940s, especially associated with the music of Igor Stravinsky of that time; characteristics of neoclassical music include parody-like references to earlier music (especially works of Baroque and Classical periods), motoric rhythms, changing meters, a cool and detached tone, modernistic harmony, and an international tone rather than regional allegiances

neumatic chant: chants in which there are three, four, or five notes for each syllable of text

neume: in medieval musical notation, a sign used to delineate single pitches or groups of pitches; originally, around 900 C.E., neumes were just laid out on the parchment above text as a reminder of how it should be sung

New German School: a group of musicians gathering around Franz Liszt in Weimar and supporting the artistic outlook of Liszt and Richard Wagner

new music advisor: a position existing since the 1970s with many American symphony orchestras; the new music advisor typically composes new works for the orchestra and recommends other contemporary compositions

New Orleans style of jazz: a jazz style emerging in New Orleans in the early twentieth century characterized by small bands, an energetic ("hot") style of playing, and group improvisation

Nimrod variation: ninth variation in Edward Elgar's *Enigma* Variations for

orchestra; a musical portrait of Elgar's publisher, August Jaeger

nocturne: a type of piano character piece appearing in the nineteenth century distinguished by a dreamy mood, a lyric melody in the right hand, and widely-spaced, arpeggiated chords in the left hand

nota: (Latin for note) a symbol on a line or space representing a single, precise pitch

notes inégales: in which a succession of equal notes moving rapidly up or down the scale are played somewhat unequally, such as "long-short, long-short"

Notre Dame School: the name given by historians to the composers Leoninus, Perotinus, and their colleagues who created a huge musical repertory of more than a thousand pieces during the period 1160–1260 at and around Notre Dame of Paris

number symbolism: a system prevalent during the Middle Ages and Renaissance in which meaning in music was conveyed by the use of numbers representing religious themes and concepts; a composition might have certain structural proportions such as 6:4:2:3 in Dufay's motet that mirror the proportions of the cathedral of Florence

obbligato: indication that a composer has written a specific part for an instrument and intends it to be played as written

obbligato recitative: recitative in which the full orchestra is necessary to the desired effect (also known as accompanied recitative)

oblique motion: motion occurring when one voice repeats or sustains a pitch while another moves away or toward it; used in medieval organum as a way to avoid dissonant tritones

oboe d'amore: an oboe-like instrument in A, slightly lower in range than the oboe; used by J.S. Bach and revived in works by Gustav Mahler and Richard Strauss

occitan: see langue d'oc

occursus: a running together, Guido of Arezzo's term for cadence

octatonic scale: a symmetric scale alternating half and whole steps

ode: a multi-movement hymn of praise to a person or ideal usually lasting about twenty minutes and containing an instrumental introduction, choruses, duets, and solo arias, but no recitative because there is no story

Odhecaton: the first book of polyphonic music printed from movable type; although published in Venice, most of the nearly one-hundred compositions in it were the works of the great northern masters of counterpoint

open ending: the term used in the Middle Ages for what we today call a first ending

opera: a dramatic work, or play, set to music; in opera the lines of the actors and actresses are sung, not spoken, and music, poetry, drama, scenic design, and dance combine to produce a powerful art form

opera buffa: the name for Italian comic opera but which, unlike most other forms of comic opera, uses rapid-fire recitative rather than spoken dialogue

opéra comique: similar to Italian *opera buffa,* has characters from the everyday world, singing in a fresh, natural style, and the dialogue is generally spoken or sometimes delivered in recitative; the principals sing either simple airs or popular melodies

opera seria: serious, not comic, opera; the term is used to designate the heroic, fully sung Italian opera that dominated the stage at the courts of Europe during the eighteenth century

operetta: a genre of light or comic opera with spoken dialogue and traditional operatic numbers originating in the mid nineteenth century

ophicleide: an early nineteenth-century bass brass instrument, forerunner of the tuba

opus dei: "work of the lord"; the services of the canonical hours as referred to in the Rule of St. Benedict

oratorio: a genre of religious music developed in the seventeenth century to satisfy the desire for dramatic music during Lent; a musical setting of a dramatic text in Latin or Italian or, later, other languages that usually elaborates upon an event in the Old Testament; uses the essential processes of opera but without the lavish sets, costumes, or acting

oratory: a prayer hall set aside just for praying, preaching, and devotional singing

Orchésographie: lengthy treatise on dance published by Thoinot Arbeau in 1589; it details all the popular dances of the day with their steps, tells what is in fashion and what is not, and provides unexpected information about performance practices of the day

Ordinary of the Mass: chants of the Mass with unvarying texts that can be sung almost every day of the year; *Kyrie, Gloria, Credo, Sanctus,* and *Agnus dei*

ordre: the term used by François Couperin to designate a group of pieces loosely associated by feeling and key; similar to

what other composers of the Baroque era would call a dance suite

organ Mass: a Mass in which an organ alternates with, or entirely replaces, the choir

organ verset: an independent organ section in an *alternatim* organ Mass; a short piece that replaces a liturgical item otherwise sung by the choir

organum (pl., organa): a type of polyphonic religious music of the Middle Ages; the term came to be used generally to connote all early polyphony of the church

organum purum: florid two-voice organum of medieval Paris continuing the tradition of earlier Aquitanian polyphony in sustained-tone style

ostinato: see *basso ostinato*

overdotting: practice in which a dotted note is made longer than written, while its complementary short note(s) is made shorter

paean: in ancient Greece, a hymn that celebrated the deeds of primary gods such as Zeus or Apollo; today any poetic hymn of praise

pan-consonance: music in which almost every note is a member of a triad or a triadic inversion and not a dissonance

pan-isorhythm: a technique whereby isorhythm is applied to all voices, not just the tenor in an isorhythmic piece

parallel organum: organum in which all voices move in lockstep, up or down, with the intervals between voices remaining the same

paraphrase Mass: a Mass in which the movements are united by a single paraphrased chant

paraphrase motet: a motet that contains a paraphrased chant throughout

paraphrase technique: when a composer takes a preexisting plainsong and embellishes it somewhat, imparting to it a rhythmic profile; the elaborated chant then serves as the basic melodic material for a polyphonic composition

Parisian chanson: a newer (after 1500) style of French chanson in which the rhythm of the text begins to animate the rhythm of the music; almost every note has its own syllable and the duration of that note is often determined by the length or stress of the syllable; subject matter was also more "down to earth" and might include lusty lovers or drinking scenes

parlando-rubato rhythm: term used by Béla Bartók to describe the flexible rhythm of most ancient Hungarian peasant songs

parody technique (emulation technique): when one composer emulates another

by borrowing entire polyphonic sections of an earlier work

part book: a volume that contains the music of one voice part and only one voice part

partita: term used by J.S. Bach as a synonym for suite

partitioning: in twelve-tone music, the distribution of the notes of a tone row into several strands in a texture

partsong: a strophic song with English text intended to be sung by three or four voices in a predominantly homophonic musical style

passacaglia: (1) a musical form involving continuous variations upon a *basso ostinato,* originating in the Baroque period and virtually synonymous with the term chaconne; (2) originally a separate and distinct bass melody but during the seventeenth century it came to mean almost any repeating bass pattern of short duration

passion: a large-scale musical depiction of Christ's crucifixion as recorded in the Gospels; an oratorio on the subject of the passion

pastoral aria: a slow aria with several distinctive characteristics: parallel thirds that glide mainly in step-wise motion, a lilting rhythm in compound meter, and a harmony that changes slowly and employs many subdominant chords

patter-song: the rapid delivery of text on repeated notes

pavane: a slow gliding dance in duple meter performed by couples holding hands; replaced the fifteenth-century *basse danse* as the primary slow dance of the court

pedal point: on the organ, a sustained or continually repeated pitch, usually placed in the bass and sounding while the harmonies change around it

Penitential Psalms: the seven of the one hundred fifty psalms of the Psalter that are especially remorseful in tone and sung in the rites of the Catholic Church surrounding death and burial

pentatonic scale: a scale with five tones per octave; specifically, a scale having the form C D E G A (or a transposition or reordering of these tones); "pentatonic music" makes use of pentatonic scales

pes: (Latin for foot) the English name for a bottom voice that continually repeats throughout a polyphonic composition

phasing: a term associated with composer Steve Reich; a phase piece is one that begins with two sources of sound giving forth an identical ostinato; one sound source gradually pulls ahead, creating a constantly-changing rhythmic interaction with the other source

pianoforte: original name for the piano because, unlike the harpsichord, its mechanism allowed the player to control the force of a blow to the string and thus could play piano or forte

Picardy third: a shift from minor to major in the final chord of a piece

plagal cadence: a IV-I chordal movement with the bass in root position falling down by the interval of a fourth or rising up by a fifth

plagal mode in the eight church modes the plagal is the second of each of the four pairs of modes; plagal means "derived from" and each plagal mode is a fourth below its authentic counterpart; the Dorian mode, for example, has its plagal counterpart in the Hypodorian mode

plainsong: see Gregorian chant

player piano: a piano provided with a mechanical device that "plays" the instrument according to musical instructions entered on a perforated paper roll

point of imitation: a distinctive motive that is sung or played in turn by each voice or instrumental line

pointillism: an artistic style of the late nineteenth century in which dots of color merge into recognizable images in the eye of the viewer; a similar phenomenon occurs in music by modern composers including Anton Webern and Olivier Messiaen in which notes seem isolated and detached from larger context

polychord: a chord made by juxtaposing two familiar harmonies

polymeter: two or more meters sounding simultaneously

polyrhythm: the simultaneous appearance in a musical work of two or more rhythmic patterns or principles of rhythmic organization

polytonality: the simultaneous appearance in a musical work of two or more keys

popular art music: a term coined by Béla Bartók to describe songs composed by nineteenth-century composers, of low artistic value, that had been accepted by the populace as folk songs

portative organ: a small movable instrument that sounded at courtly entertainments, usually to accompany singers rather than dancers

positive organ: a large stationary instrument that began to appear in large numbers in churches in the West shortly after 1300; considered one of the technological wonders of its day, it was usually attached high on the wall in the nave of the church and was the only instrument sanctioned for use in the church

preghiera: a prayer scene, often found in nineteenth-century Italian opera

prelude: a preliminary piece, one that comes immediately before and introduces the main musical event

prepared piano: a piano whose sound is modified by the introduction of mutes and other objects between strings

prima donna: leading lady

prima pratica: a traditional style for church music that is in contrast to the freer writing found in some madrigals of the late sixteenth century; the musical embodiment of the restrained spirit of the Counter-Reformation

program music: instrumental music that explicitly embodies extra-musical content

programmatic symphony: a multimovement symphony that is explicitly programmatic

prolation: (*prolatio*) the division of the semibreve into two or three minims

Proper of the Mass: chants of the Mass whose texts change each day to suit the religious theme, or to honor a particular saint on just that one day

proportions: time signatures often written as fractions that modify the normal value of notes

proslambanomenos: term used by the ancient Greeks to indicate the lowest sounding pitch in their Greater Perfect System

psalm tone: eight simple recitation formulas (simple repeating patterns) to which psalms were chanted

psalmody: act or process of singing the psalms (of the Psalter); done each week during the services of the canonical hours

Psalter: the book of one hundred fifty psalms found in the Old Testament

punctum (pl., puncta): a pair of musical phrases (couplet) usually associated with medieval instrumental music

Pythagorean tuning: a process in which the octaves, fifths, and fourths are tuned in perfect 2:1, 3:2, and 4:3 ratios

quadrivium: the four scientific disciplines of the seven liberal arts—arithmetic, geometry, astronomy, and music— that used number and quantitative reasoning to arrive at the truth

quadruplum: fourth voice in four-voice organa

quattrocento: Italian for what we refer to as "the 1400s"

quodlibet: a genre of music created when several secular tunes are brought together and sound together or in immediate succession

rag see ragtime

ragtime: a style of American popular music, especially found in piano character pieces (called "rags"), in which a syncopated melody is joined to a rhythmically-regular accompaniment

rank: each group of similar sounding pipes in an organ

realism: in Russian music of the nineteenth century a style portraying people objectively and truthfully, often using a melodic style that is close to speech

recapitulation: in sonata form, the return of the first theme and the tonic key following the development; although essentially a revisiting of previous material it is usually by no means an exact repeat

recital: a concert given by a single performer or a small number of musicians

récitatif ordinaire: a style of recitative, developed by French composer Jean-Baptiste Lully, noteworthy for its length, vocal range, and generally dramatic quality

recitation tone: a constantly repeating pitch followed by a mediation or a termination; the recitation tone is the heart of the psalm tone

recitative: a musically heightened speech, often used in an opera, oratorio, or cantata to report dramatic action and advance the plot

reform opera: first created in the 1760s by Christoph Willibald Gluck and Ranieri Calzabigi in an attempt to combine the best features of the Italian and French operatic traditions, to yoke Italian lyricism to the French concern for intense dramatic expression

Reformation: the religious revolution that began as a movement to reform Catholicism and ended with the establishment of Protestantism

release: a contrasting phrase in a popular song refrain

requiem Mass: the burial Mass of the Roman Catholic Church

respond: the opening chant in responsorial singing; usually sung by the full choir, it is followed by a verse sung by a soloist, and is repeated by the full choir

responsorial singing: when the full choir prefaces and responds to the psalm verse, which is sung by a soloist (choral respond, solo verse, choral respond)

retransition: in sonata form, the point near the end of the development where tonal stability returns, often in the form of a dominant pedal point, in preparation for the return of the first theme (in the tonic key) and the beginning of the recapitulation

retrograde: backward in motion, as in twelve-tone music where a tone row is deployed with its tones in reverse order

reverberation time: the time it takes a sound to die out

rhapsody: a type of character piece of the nineteenth century, usually for piano, having no established form or mood

rhythm and blues: a style of American popular songs appearing in the 1940s that use the traditional blues form; forerunner of rock

rhythm section: in jazz, an accompanimental group of instruments

rhythmic imitation: process in which each voice in turn sings the same rhythmic motive, but to melodic motives that differ slightly in pitch

rhythmic modes: simple patterns of repeating rhythms employed in the polyphony created in Paris during the twelfth and thirteenth centuries; modal notation evolved into a system of six rhythmic modes

ricercar: (sixteenth century) an instrumental piece, usually for lute or keyboard, similar in style to the imitative motet; (seventeenth century) Frescobaldi perfected a tightly organized, monothematic ricercar that influenced the later fugal writing of J.S. Bach

rigaudon: a Baroque dance in duple meter

ripieno: the larger ensemble (full orchestra) in a concerto grosso

ripresa: a refrain

Risorgimento: (resurgence) the movement toward Italian political and social unification that began in 1814 and culminated in 1861 when much of Italy was brought together as a single nation under King Victor Emmanuel II

ritornello: a return or refrain

ritornello form: a carefully worked out structure for a concerto grosso, which employs regular reappearances of the ritornello

Robertsbridge Codex: the earliest surviving collection of keyboard music; preserves various pieces typically heard at the French royal court in the mid fourteenth century

rock 'n' roll (or rock): a type of popular song, gaining prominence in America in the 1950s, accompanied typically by amplified guitars, drums, and a few other instruments; early rock songs often had the form of a blues, elements of country music, and sexually-suggestive lyrics

rococo: term used to describe the decorative arts and the music of mid eighteenth-century France, with all their lightness, grace and highly ornate surfaces

Roman chant: the dialect of chant sung in the early churches of Rome; the principal repertory from which Gregorian chant would later emerge

romance: in nineteenth-century French music, a simple strophic song

romantic opera: a genre term used by Carl Maria von Weber for certain of his operas and by Richard Wagner for his early operas; the term suggests that the texts stressed mysterious or supernatural elements, as in the contemporary literary genre of the "romance"

Romantic period: a basic period in the history of Western music extending from the early nineteenth to the early twentieth century; although the music of this time is too diverse to admit meaningful generalizations about its style, there is a recurring impulse toward intense expressivity, which often drives the music to free forms expressed through innovative materials

romanticism: the general style of music of the Romantic period

rondeau: (fourteenth and fifteenth centuries) one of the three French *formes fixes* that originated as a dance-song with the troubadours and trouvères; its musical and textual form is ABaAabAB; (seventeenth and eighteenth centuries) a composition based on the alternation of a main theme (refrain) with subsidiary sections called *couplets* to allow musical diversity

rondellus: a distinctly English musical technique in which two or three voices engage in voice exchange, or more correctly, phrase exchange

rondo: one of the main musical forms of the Classical period; a Classical rondo sets a refrain (A) against contrasting material (B, C, or D) to create a pattern such as ABACA, ABACABA, or even ABACADA; it usually projects a playful, exuberant mood, and is often used as the last movement of a sonata or symphony, to bid a happy farewell to the audience

Rossini crescendo: a characteristic feature in operas by Gioachino Rossini in which a long crescendo is accompanied by ever shorter phrases, a thickening of orchestration, and quicker harmonic motions

rota: the English name for a canon that endlessly circles back to the beginning

rotulus: an oblong sheet of paper or parchment on which chansons were inscribed; the sheet music of the late Middle Ages and the Renaissance

Royal Academy of Music: George Frideric Handel's London opera company started in 1719; a publicly held stock company, its principal investor being the king

Russian Revolution: an uprising in the major cities of Russia in 1917 during which Tsar Nicholas II abdicated and power was seized by the Bolshevik political faction

sackbut: a slide trumpet common in the fifteenth and sixteenth centuries; precursor of the modern trombone

sarabande: a slow, stately dance in $\frac{3}{4}$ with a strong accent on the second beat; one of four dances typically found within a Baroque dance suite

Sarum chant: England's special dialect of Gregorian chant; called that from the old Latin name of the cathedral town of Salisbury; melodies and texts were somewhat different from the chant sung on the Continent

scat singing: in jazz, singing on nonsense syllables

scena: a passage of a nineteenth-century opera given largely in recitative and often leading to an aria or duet

scenario: the story outline of a ballet

scene: a passage in an opera or ballet calling to the stage a particular selection of characters

scherzo: (Italian for joke) an exuberant triple-meter dance that frequently replaced the more stately minute as the third movement in symphonies and chamber works of the Classical period; was favored first by Haydn (in his Opus 33 quartets) and then especially by Beethoven in his symphonies

scholasticism: the mode of thinking that rose to prominence at the University of Paris in the thirteenth century; it managed information by constructing chains of hierarchical categories and relationships

Schubertiad: a social gathering organized within the circle of Franz Schubert at which his music was performed

scordatura: tuning a string instrument to something other than standard tuning

seconda pratica: Claudio Monteverdi's term for the new text-driven approach to musical composition that he practiced; it allowed for "deviations" from conventional counterpoint if these moments were inspired by an especially expressive text

semibreve: one of the three basic note shapes recognized by Franco of Cologne around 1280 in his classification of musical durations

semi-opera: a spoken play in which the more exotic, amorous, or even supernatural moments in the story were sung or danced

sequence: a Gregorian chant, sung on high feasts during the Proper of the Mass immediately after the Alleluia, in which successive verses were paired into double verses; the most famous sequence today is the *Dies irae*

serenade: a piece of outdoor music for a small ensemble usually in at least five movements; the term was used interchangeably with divertimento

serialism: a compositional method in which the choice and ordering of elements is governed by a precompositional arrangement or system; see also total serialism

seven liberal arts: a framework of seven intellectual disciplines set forth by Martianus Capella (c435 C.E.) composed of the trivium and the quadrivium

shanty: a sailor's work song

shawm: a double-reed instrument with a loud penetrating tone, used to provide dance music during the Middle Ages and Renaissance; the ancestor of the modern oboe

sideman: in jazz, a section player

Silver Age: (in Russian art) common designation for an artistic period in Russia during the reign of Tsar Nicholas II (1894–1917); a time of changing tastes

simple recitative: a basic form of recitative in operas of the eighteenth and nineteenth centuries: narrative in text, speech-like in melody, and accompanied solely by keyboard or a minimal number of instruments; a recitative accompanied only by a basso continuo

sincopa: the medieval term for syncopation, a temporary shift of the downbeat

sinfonia: (Italian for symphony) a three-section or three-movement instrumental work that might preface an opera or stand alone as an independent concert symphony

single-impression printing: utilizes individual pieces of movable type that are both the note and a small vertical section of the staff; required only one pressing and was thus much more economical than multiple-impression printing

Singspiel: (sung play) a genre of German opera appearing in the eighteenth and nineteenth centuries using a folkish or comic spoken play with musical numbers inserted

Six, The: a critic's sobriquet given in 1920 to a group of six French neoclassical composers: Darius Milhaud, Arthur Honegger, Germaine Tailleferre, Georges Auric, Francis Poulenc, and Louis Durey

skolion: a song setting an aphoristic poem; the primary musical entertainment at an ancient Greek symposium

socialist realism: an officially-approved doctrine guiding the arts in Soviet Russia that promoted a style geared to the understanding of the masses

soft hexachord: in the Guidonian system, the hexachord—six-note pattern of TTSTT—set on F

soggetto cavato: *soggetto cavato dale vocali*—a cantus firmus extracted from the vowels of a name

solfege: the system of singing different pitches to the syllables "do (ut), re, mi, fa, sol, la, ti (si), do (ut)"

solo concerto: a concerto composed for only one solo instrument

solo sonata: a sonata played by a single melody instrument such as a violin, flute or oboe usually accompanied, in the Baroque era, by a basso continuo

sonata: originally "something sounded" on an instrument as opposed to something sung (a "cantata"); later a multi-movement work for solo instrument or ensemble

sonata form: the most important formal innovation of the Classical period, used by composers most often when writing a fast first movement of a sonata, quartet, or symphony; an expansion of rounded binary form, it consists of an exposition, development, and recapitulation, with optional introduction and coda

sonata-rondo form: a design often found in the finales of symphonies and concertos of the eighteenth and nineteenth centuries that merges elements of sonata and rondo forms

sonatina: a name sometimes used for the easiest and shortest sonatas

song "release": see release

song collection: a group of art songs having a loose connection, such as that coming from a single poet or literary theme

song cycle: a group of songs intended by the composer to be performed as a unit, having definite musical and textual interconnections

Song of Songs: (also called the Song of King Solomon) a particularly lyrical book in the Old Testament of the Bible portions of which have often been set to music over the centuries

song plugger: in the American popular song industry of the early twentieth century, a musician who demonstrated new works for a publisher

sound mass: a basic element in a modern composition made from a conglomerate of tones, lines, and rhythms

Spanish guitar: see *vihuela*

spiccato: designation requiring performers to play in a detached fashion, but not quite as short as *staccato*

spiritual: an American religious song

Sprechgesang: (speech song) a term coined by Arnold Schoenberg to describe the recitational part of his melodrama *Pierrot lunaire* (1912); in *Sprechgesang*, rhythms are notated exactly and pitches are only approximated; a synonym is *Sprechmelodie* (speech melody); the reciter herself is called the *Sprechstimme* (speaking voice); the style was later used in the operas of Alban Berg

square piano: a small box-shape piano with strings running at right angles to the keys, which could be set upon a table or simple stand

standard: in jazz, a popular song that is frequently arranged or used as the basis for improvisation; also called a "jazz standard"

stile antico: the name given to the conservative music emanating from the papal chapel in the seventeenth century

stile concertato: Italian for concerted style; a term broadly used to identify Baroque music marked by grand scale and strong contrast, either between voices and instruments, between separate instrumental ensembles, between separate choral groups, or even between soloist and choir

stile concitato: an agitated style particularly suited to warlike music; Claudio Monteverdi used this term for a new style of music he created that was more direct and insistent than previous martial music

stile rappresentativo: (dramatic or theater style) a type of vocal expression somewhere between song and declaimed speech

stochastic music: a term brought to music from probability theory by the composer Iannis Xenakis to designate works in which individual sonic events are not controlled by the composer, who focuses instead on shaping only their aggregate appearance and behavior

stop: a small wooden knob on an organ that activates a rank of pipes when pulled out

stop time: in jazz, a temporarily simplified rhythm in the accompaniment, which allows for a soloist briefly to improvise

stretta: the climactic section of a number in a nineteenth-century opera, often in a fast tempo; the masculine form *stretto* usually alludes to a passage in a fugue in which a subject is imitated at a shorter than normal time span

stride: a style of ragtime piano playing and composing in which the pianist's left hand moves regularly from chord tones in a low register to harmonies in the middle register

strophe plus refrain: a common musical form in which the strophe, or stanza, is sung by a soloist while all the singers join in with the burden, or refrain

strophic form: a song form in which the music composed for the initial stanza of text is repeated for each additional stanza

strophic variation aria: an aria in which the same melodic and harmonic plan appears, with slight variation, in each successive strophe

Sturm und Drang: (German for "Storm and Stress") as a musical term it refers to a small but significant group of works written around 1770 that are marked by agitated, impassioned writing, such as Mozart's Symphony No. 25 (K. 183) of 1773

style brisé: a modern term for a type of discontinuous texture in which chords are broken apart and notes enter one by one; such a style is inherent in lute music because the sounds of the lute are delicate and quickly evaporate

subject: in a fugue, the theme

substitute clausula: one clausula written in discant style intended to replace another

suite: a musical work that consists of a succession of short pieces, especially dances; also used for a concert work made from excerpts from an opera, ballet, or film score

surrealism: twentieth-century literary and artistic movement that confounds superficial reality or logic in order to evoke unconscious states of mind

sustained-tone organum: organum in which the bottom voice holds a note while the faster-moving top voice embellishes it in a florid fashion

swing: in jazz, a rhythm that drives forward in a triplet pattern; also a style of jazz of the 1930s and 1940s often involving big bands that play in an impulsive and dynamic mood

syllabic chant: chants in which there is usually only one note and only one note for each syllable of text

symmetric inversion: see inversion

symphonic poem: a one-movement programmatic orchestral work; roughly synonymous with tone poem

symphonie concertante: a concerto-like composition of the Classical period with two or more soloists

symposium: in ancient Greece, a tightly organized social gathering of adult male citizens for conversation and entertainment

syncopation: a temporary metric irregularity or dislocation by which beats or divisions of beats do not conform to their normal placement within the meter

syncope: the Renaissance term for a suspension

tablature: directs a performer's fingers to a specific spot on an instrument

tactus: the term used to indicate the beat by music theorists of the Renaissance

Tafelmusik: German name for chamber music, both vocal and instrumental, for the dinner table

talea: a rhythmic pattern, or unit appearing in an isorhythmic composition

tape music: a style of electronic music associated with Vladimir Ussachevsky and Otto Luening in which compositions are recorded and subsequently distorted (especially by reverberating feedback)

temperament: the tuning of intervals in something slightly more or less than strict mathematical ratios

tenor: one of the standard four voice parts; in early medieval polyphony the bottom most voice, often a preexisting chant, upon which the composition is built; called that because in these early works it holds or draws out the notes

Tenorlied: a polyphonic Geman song in which a preexisting tune is placed in the tenor and two or three other voices enhance it with lightly imitative polyphony

tetrachord: a succession of four pitches

text painting (word painting): the use of striking chord shifts, musical repetition, controlled dissonance, and abrupt textural changes to highlight the meaning of the text; a very popular technique with sixteenth-century madrigal composers

theorbo: a large lute-like instrument with a full octave of additional bass strings descending in a diatonic pattern

third stream: a term coined by the composer Gunther Schuller to describe a musical style merging jazz and classical elements

threnody: a musical lament

through composed: containing new music for every stanza of text, as opposed to strophic form in which the music is repeated for each successive stanza

tibia: Roman name for the aulos

time: (*tempus*) the division of the breve into two or three semibreves

Tin Pan Alley: the art and business of the American popular song of the early twentieth century

tintinnabuli style: (bells style) a term coined by the composer Arvo Pärt for a polyphony in which a melodic line is joined to a "bells" line limited to the three tones of the tonic triad

toccata: an instrumental piece, for keyboard or other instruments, requiring the performer to touch the instrument with great technical dexterity; designed to show off the creative spirit of the composer as well as the technical skill of the performer

tombeau: an instrumental piece commemorating someone's death

tonal answer: a following voice that imitates the subject at the interval of a fifth above or fourth below and changes the subject so as to keep the music in the home tonality

tone cluster: a dissonant chord made from sounding all of the tones within a boundary interval

tone poem: a one-movement programmatic work, usually for orchestra, and roughly synonymous with symphonic poem

tone-color melody (*Klangfarbenmelodie*): a term coined by Arnold Schoenberg to designate a melody-like line made from changing tone colors

tonos (pl., tonoi): ancient Greek term for a scale

total serialism: a compositional method in which the choice of most of the principal elements of a composition (including pitches, rhythms, and dynamics) is governed precompositionally by an integrated system or arrangement

total work of art (*Gesamtkunstwerk*): a term used by Richard Wagner to designate a goal for art in which its various branches are merged into a integrated and dramatic whole

tragédie lyrique: the term used to designate French opera in the late seventeenth and eighteenth centuries, which was a fusion of classical French tragedy with traditional French ballet (*ballet de cour*)

transformation of themes: a technique of thematic unity throughout a multi-sectional work by which one or a few initial themes recur, albeit changed in character

transition (bridge): in sonata form the passage of modulation between the tonic and the new key

treble: the highest of the three voices for which much late-medieval English polyphony was written; evolved in general musical terminology to mean the top part as well as the top clef (G clef), the highest clef in music

trecento: short for *mille trecento,* or the century of the 1300s, in Italian

trio: a composition for three solo instruments; also, a contrasting section of a work originally played by a trio of instruments; in minuets, band marches, and rags, the term refers to a contrasting section or episode, with no implications for medium

trio sonata: comprised a line for two treble instruments (usually two violins) and basso continuo

triplum: third voice in a piece of three- or four-voice organum of the Middle Ages

triseme: a triple unit long value of time in ancient Greek musical notation—formed by three chronoi

trivium: the three verbal disciplines of the seven liberal arts—grammar, logic, and rhetoric—which deal with language, logic, and oratory

trobairitz: a female troubadour (poet-musician)

trope: an addition of music or text, or both, to a preexisting chant; they more fully explain the theology inherent in the chants to which they are added

troubadour: a poet-musician of the courtly art of vernacular sung poetry that developed in the Middle Ages in southern France

trouser role: an opera role designed to be sung by a woman dressed as a man

trouvère: a poet-musician of the courtly art of vernacular sung poetry that developed in northern France during the late twelfth and thirteenth centuries

tuba: Roman name for the trumpet; a long, straight instrument with a cylindrical bore and a bell at the end, which originated with the Etruscans

Turkish music: the noise of Turkish military percussion instruments, which were introduced into Western European music in the eighteenth century during the Turkish Wars; some pianos of the day were equipped with special devices to effect the sounds of "Turkish" music, such as bass drum, cymbals, and the like

twelve-tone composition: a composition in which the twelve tones of the chromatic scale are systematically recirculated; the term usually refers to works using Arnold Schoenberg's "twelve-tone method," formulated in 1923, in which the recirculation of tones is joined to a serialized principle of order

unmeasured prelude: an opening piece without specific indications for rhythmic duration or metrical organization

variation technique: a procedure in which successive statements of a theme are changed or presented in altered musical surroundings

variations: a work, movement of a work, or a form in which an initial theme is subject to a series of modifications or paraphrases; see also ballet variations

vaudeville show: a popular theatric entertainment in America made from acts including dances, songs, and skits

verbal score: a musical composition represented not by conventional musical notation but by verbal instructions to the performers

verismo: (realism) a style of Italian opera appearing in the 1890s in short works in which characters from lower social strata are driven by the passions to violent acts

verse and refrain: a form for popular songs in which each stanza (sometimes only a single stanza) is divided into an introductory passage (the verse) followed by a more tuneful refrain

Vespers: the late-afternoon service, and most important of the eight canonical hours for the history of music; not only were psalms and a hymn sung but also the Magnificat

vida: a brief biographical sketch of a troubadour or trouvère; appears along with a small portrait of the artist in some French chansonniers

vielle: a large five-string fiddle capable of playing the entire Guidonian scale; often provided dance music during the thirteenth and fourteenth centuries

Viennese School: historians' term for composers Haydn, Mozart, Beethoven, and Schubert who capped their careers in Vienna and knew one another personally, however indirectly

vihuela (Spanish guitar): a plucked string instrument with a waisted body, and a long pole-neck that serves as a fingerboard; the direct ancestor of the modern classical guitar

Vingt-quatre violons du roi: twenty-four instruments of the violin family that formed the string core of the French court orchestra under Louis XIV (six violins, twelve violas, and six *basse de violons*)

viol: a six-string instrument fretted and tuned like the lute and *vihuela,* but bowed and not plucked; it came in three sizes—treble, tenor, and bass—and was played with the instrument resting on the lap or legs

viola da gamba: Italian name for the bass viol, so called because it was held between each leg (*gamba* in Italian)

violino: (little viol) original name for the violin

violino piccolo: a small violin usually tuned a minor third higher than the normal violin

virelai: one of the three French *formes fixes* of the Middle Ages yet more playful than a serious ballade; originated with the troubadours and trouvères as a monophonic dance that involved choral singing; the form is AbbaA

virginal: a diminutive harpsichord possessing a single keyboard with the strings placed at right angles to the keys

vox organalis: (organal voice) one of the two voice parts in an early organum; it is a newly created line added to the preexisting chant

vox principalis: (principal voice) one of the two voice parts in an early organum; it is a preexisting chant that served as a foundation for another newly created line

Wagner tuba: nickname for a tenor-range tuba used by Richard Wagner in his *Der Ring des Nibelungen*

walking bass: a bass line, especially in jazz, with a predominantly stepwise motion and steady rhythm (for example, entirely quarter or eighth notes)

waltz: a triple-time dance for couples that rose to great popularity in the nineteenth century

whole-tone scale: a scale with six notes per octave separated entirely by whole tones

Winchester Troper: a troper—chant manuscript mainly preserving additions to the liturgy called tropes—dating from c1000 C.E. from a Benedictine Monastery at Winchester, England; shows that the singers had a repertory of about 150 two-voice organa, but the troper was a memory aid and is not a prescriptive document that allows singers today to perform the music with confidence

Wolf's Glen Scene: the finale to Act 2 of Carl Maria von Weber's *Der Freischütz,* its most striking and most popular scene

WoO numbers: (*Werk ohne Opuszahl,* or work without opus number) a number given in a catalog of a composer's works designating those pieces lacking a traditional opus number; first used in the 1955 catalog of Beethoven's works compiled by Georg Kinsky and Hans Halm

word painting: see text painting

xylophone: a percussion instrument in which wooden bars are sounded with a mallet

INDEX